The New Deal in Georgia

AN ADMINISTRATIVE HISTORY

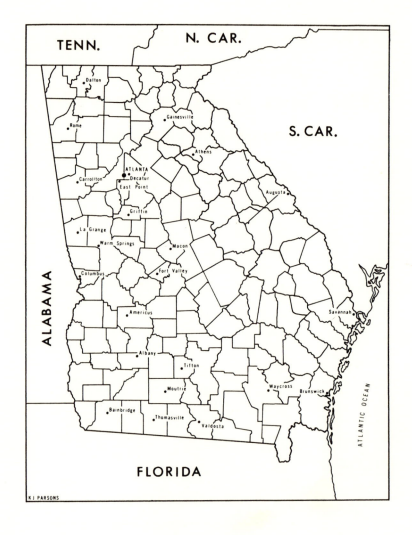

Georgia, 1935

The New Deal in Georgia

AN ADMINISTRATIVE HISTORY

Michael S. Holmes

Contributions in American History, Number 36

GREENWOOD PRESS

Westport, Connecticut ● London, England

LIBRARY
University of Texas
At San Antonio

Library of Congress Cataloging in Publication Data

Holmes, Michael S
   The New Deal in Georgia.

   (Contributions in American history, no. 36)
   Includes bibliographical references.
   1. Economic assistance, Domestic—Georgia.
2. United States—Economic policy—1933-1945.
3. United States—Executive agencies—History.
4. Federal government—United States. I. Title.
HC107.G43P634   338.9758   74-289
ISBN 0-8371-7375-2

Library of Congress Catalog Card Number: 74-289
ISBN: 0-8371-7375-2
First published in 1975

Greenwood Press, a division of Williamhouse-Regency Inc.
51 Riverside Avenue, Westport, Connecticut 06880

Manufactured in the United States of America

For Reva,
Helpmate and Heartmate

Contents

Tables

Acknowledgments

The intellectual debts of scholars are always many and frequently un-
recognized. I owe an interest in the South to the writings of C. Vann
Woodward and others, and to the charm and personal encouragement
of Frank E. Vandiver; a concern for the New Deal to David Shannon;
and a commitment to the value of grass-roots case studies in understanding broader national questions to those contemporaries and predecessors of similar persuasion. In a more general way, I must attribute
a love of history and a concept of the professional historian to my
colleagues and mentors at the University of Wisconsin at Madison.

Financial aid while at Wisconsin was extended to me through the
Department of History and a separate Ford Foundation summer fellowship. For this aid and much more I have Professor E. David Cronon to
thank. A scholar's way may be greatly eased by the cooperation and
active interest of the professional staff at the various archives and
libraries which he uses. Ms. Ellen Burke, Ms. Ruth Davis, and Mr. John
Peters provided such aid at the Wisconsin State Historical Society.
Mr. Robert Kvasnicka was of inestimable value to me at the National
Archives, while Ms. Carroll Hart and Ms. Ruth Corey guided me on
unfamiliar paths through Georgia. In the final preparation of the manuscript I gratefully thank Ms. Harietta Barker, Ms. Lois Wagner, and
Ms. Susan Gursky for long hours at the typewriter, and Professor John
D. Buenker for a thoroughly critical reading. Finally, to verbalize appreciation to my wife, Reva, in this short space would be to slight her
constant and heroic efforts. I shall, therefore, make no such attempt,
but simply dedicate this book to her.

The New Deal in Georgia

AN ADMINISTRATIVE HISTORY

Introduction

In 1933 a vortex appeared in the nation's capital, a vortex which drew to its center much of the country's power. Under the New Deal the federal government concerned itself with areas which hitherto had been the province of the states or had been left to the private sector. This required the vast expansion of federal apparatus and, concomitantly, an increase in its personnel. The vital personality of President Roosevelt and the bold promise of his administration attracted other illustrious men to his side and focused national attention upon Washington, D.C.

The history which those men carved is all that remains now, but Americans of the 1930s in the nation's cities and on its farms also saw the New Deal operate in the states. Families might gather around their radios and listen to the president's soothing chats or read in their newspapers of such famous agency heads as Harold Ickes, Harry Hopkins, Henry Wallace, and Hugh Johnson, but from day to day the New Deal they came in contact with, rejoiced in, or criticized was the New Deal as it existed in the states. The "average American's" opinion was formed in relation to the federal agencies operating in the states, and rightly so; for to a great extent it was the effectiveness of these arms of the government that determined success or failure for New Deal programs.

One might reasonably ask why students have so little information concerning that crucial phase of the New Deal. In the first place, historians, no less than others, have been attracted to the Washington scene. The pulsating vibrancy of the capital's tempo and the fascinating brilliance of the administration's greater lights have captivated them and often blinded their sense of perspective. Yet this alone does not suffice to explain the myopia, for many scholars of the New Deal have suggested that the story is not complete without an understanding of the vast pyramid of federal agencies in the states atop which those in the capital sat.

Unfortunately, although many have called this need to the scholarly community's attention, relatively few have responded by delving into state history and records. One reason for this lack of research has been the fear of being labeled a student with parochial concerns. Persons who served at the lower levels of government will most likely be little noted, if their names appear in a monograph, and most certainly not remembered in comparison to their famous bosses. Such concern with the New Deal at the state and local levels can also lead to a myopia of its own—a disregard for the tremendous changes sweeping the nation through an overemphasis on the trivialities of relative Lilliputians.

Perhaps more important than either of these considerations, however, is the extreme difficulty in achieving even the most basic understanding of the vast complexity of the major agencies in the states. If the material relating to events at the national level is immense, that concerning the states is gargantuan. Of course, the problem might be pared down were one to examine a single agency, or a single state, but even then, the task still would remain formidable. In fact, it is only through the advent of recent research techniques that such an endeavor is practical.

There is, furthermore, a curious paradoxical corollary to the problem of manuscript material. While the amount of information collected from national offices of the various agencies (excluding the Public Works Administration) is tremendous, that preserved from many state offices of the agencies is negligible. In the case of Georgia, for example, the only way to discover what happened in the state offices is to examine correspondence between the state and federal offices, or to personally interview those who were employed by the agencies at the state or local levels. This, obviously, leaves some questions that perhaps may never be answered, and practically insures that any history of the agencies in the states will be more or less an "in house" study.

The final difficulty of local studies is that, before one can evaluate the work of the various agencies in the states, he must know how these agencies operated at that level. Even those historians who have discussed the administration of a particular agency have concentrated very little on its organization at the state level and on the interworkings of the agency both with state and local governments and with the people of the states. Any discussion of the New Deal's effect in the states must be preceded by a rather lengthy, and often unexciting, description of the complex, usually confusing, administrative and operational structure of each agency involved.

The practical result of all these problems has been an unwillingness on the part of "New Deal historians" to consider in depth the operation of the agencies in the states. This unwillingness appears most graphically in studies that purport to discuss the New Deal in a state. What has emerged from such attempts generally is an examination not of the state's effect upon the New Deal, which would require overcoming the aforementioned obstacles, but rather of the New Deal's effect upon the state—usually on a political level. Such studies allow their authors to circumvent those problems and to concentrate instead on more traditional themes and sources. This is not to say the studies are valueless. The New Deal was a potent twentieth century force for political change in the states, but these treatises relate only part of the story. In fact, they are not really concerned with the agencies at all, but rather with the states themselves.

This book seeks to do just the opposite, that is, to illuminate the workings of the major New Deal agencies as affected by conditions in Georgia without falling too deeply into the traps which others have suggested are set, but which have not been confronted thus far. It is hoped, for example, that the reader, if not always the author, will retain his perspective of the overall impact of the New Deal while following the tortuous paths of the Works Progress Administration's Service Division. The work will endeavor to explain the operations of the agencies to the extent that they can be understood, but not to belabor their histories to the point that they become trivial. Finally, the author will concentrate on state politics, economics, and social conditions only insofar as they bear upon the effectiveness of the agencies. If all these aims are accomplished, the desired result will be the emergence of certain patterns inherent in each of the agencies which may apply to all agencies and ultimately to all states. The reader will then know, not only what happened to the New Deal once it left Washington, but also why it happened.

To this end the study will examine the administrative history of eight New Deal agencies: the Federal Emergency Relief Administration (FERA), the Civil Works Administration (CWA), the Works Progress Administration (WPA), the Public Works Administration (PWA), the National Recovery Administration (NRA), the Agricultural Adjustment Administration (AAA), the Resettlement Administration (RA), and the Farm Security Administration (FSA). These agencies represented the traditional tripartite aims of the New Deal, "Relief, Recovery, and Reform," and they exemplified the major variants in administrative structure.

While some details of the organizational histories presented will not relate directly to their effectiveness, they are necessary for a complete understanding of the agencies' operations. Conversely, some programs will receive a great deal of attention even though they were considered "minor" at the time. In their operations are revealed the elements which often spelled success or failure for the entire agency. Topics such as the WPA's Service Division are scrutinized much more closely than the Work Division, for example, even though the work programs were much more important in terms of money spent and persons employed. The operations of the Work Division were fairly straightforward and its projects of limited scope. In the Service Division one can begin to see the pervasiveness of the New Deal; that it permeated almost every area of human endeavor or need.

The success or failure of some agencies such as the NRA already are well established, yet they may yield new perspectives when viewed at the state level. Here one can see the dynamics of an agency completely unsuited to an agricultural state, and the terrible frustration of an administrator caught between a national agency which would not bend its rules and a populace which could not accept those rules as they were.

Each agency can be observed as a micro-history in the administration of the New Deal. Each had its own special problems generated by specific conditions. Yet when considered together, certain consistent types of problems, sources, and often solutions—or nonsolutions—emerge. Given the laws under which each agency operated, laws that applied to the nation as a whole, the success or failure of the agencies was determined by three conditions: 1) the willingness or unwillingness of national offices to allow state administrators to mold the programs to local needs; 2) the quality of state and local administrators, the structure of state administration, and the division of power between state and national offices; and 3) the local political, economic, and social conditions with which state and local officials had to contend.

Most of the laws were national in application, although some had more impact on certain geographical areas. Ostensibly, farmers throughout the country were affected by the provisions of the AAA, but for all practical purposes rules covering cotton production applied only to the South and parts of the Southwest. Beyond these de facto variances, some regulations allowed considerable leeway to national administrators in the area of implementation. Where a national official was willing to pass this discretionary power on to his federal subalterns in the states, there was a much greater chance of an agency's success, particularly in dealing with a state's peculiar variety of American social, economic, and political themes. Administrators in all agencies found it easier to work within a state's political and social climate when more decision-making power was in their hands. If this condition existed, projects could always be expedited with much more efficiency. Complaints from without and within the agency could be handled internally, and mistakes could be rectified with much greater ease and less chance of friction. This flexibility existed in the experience of Georgia's FERA and WPA.

At the other end of this spectrum was the NRA. Here the power of enforcement was essentially the power of persuasion. It should have been of paramount importance to give the state administrator free reign to modify code restrictions in the face of unusual local conditions. Only by doing so could the agency hope to gain the compliance of state businesses operating under a law which really did not apply to their economic circumstances. The state NRA administrator was given some leeway, but certainly not enough, and ultimately questions of special consideration were decided in Washington. This practice served to undermine his stature in the state and subsequently ruined what slim chances he might have had to gain compliance when appeals of undoubtedly selfish motivation came to him.

If the FERA and NRA represented the polar conditions, the AAA lay somewhere in-between. Secretary of Agriculture Henry A. Wallace was willing to allow state administrators a great deal of discretion in some crop programs, but not in others. Where he drew the line depended upon the state's importance as a producer of various crops. In Georgia he proved most uncompromising when state administrators

asked for increased allotments of cotton, but not so in the cases of
wheat or corn.

Another factor determining an agency's success involved a set of
conditions concerning the structure and management of state and
local offices. In general, agencies that were decentralized, with much
of the power resting in the state offices, appeared to be the most successful. Furthermore, agencies that depended least upon cooperation
with the state government or its departments found it easiest to promote their programs. Both of these prerequisites demanded that the
state office of an agency be headed by a strong administrator—one who
could wield the power bestowed upon him by Washington and resist
attempts by state government to turn the agency to its own uses,
whether political or economic.

The best administrators possessed strength of will and, at the same
time, were as apolitical as possible. They had to be completely honest,
but thoroughly committed to their agency and its work. The more
power an administrator held, the greater was the need for these attri-
butes. Forces from above and below were often quick to recognize
where decision-making prerogatives lay, and, once this occurred, tremendous pressure was brought to bear upon the administrator from
all sides.

The division of power between state and national offices was crucial.
Giving a state official partial power in any area proved confusing to
local citizens who often did not understand that beyond a certain point
their local administrator's hands might be tied. Furthermore, it did little
good in many cases to give officials restricted options. These options
might not be sufficient to deal with certain situations. Yet national
officials, not realizing this, might fix blame for the failure of a program
upon the administrator, rationalizing this position because that administrator had "options."

What was true of the state administrator applied all the way down
the line to the agency's lowliest official. The quality of the entire staff
could, and sometimes did, make or break an agency, depending upon
the amount of difficulty it encountered from the state and local governments and the populace. Conditions, of course, varied from state to
state and from agency to agency. Nevertheless, the ability of the state
administrator to assemble a competent staff certainly was a factor in
determining the agency's success.

One overall condition affected all these elements: the permanence of the agency's structure. In instances where there was not much reorganization during an agency's existence, its progress proved to be greater and more constant than in cases where changes continually disrupted operations. Even when programs took the most tortuous twists and turns, a stable organizational structure could minimize confusion. Such was certainly the case with the AAA which operated under no less than five separate, yet often overlapping, pieces of legislation from 1933 through 1938. On the other hand, an agency such as the WPA, which was fairly stable otherwise, found many of its troubles arising when structural changes were ordered.

The final circumstances determining the progress of New Deal agencies were the local conditions with which administrators had to contend. Georgia is the largest state in land area east of the Mississippi River. Its population from 1930 to 1940 hovered around 3 million. About a third of Georgia's citizens resided in her cities, of which only Atlanta could be called large (ca. 300,000), while over half of the people lived in "unincorporated rural territory." Thus the state's population was small for its size and rather scattered. These demographic conditions would make it difficult to administer effectively any statewide agency.

Of Georgia's 159 counties, fewer than 60 had any urban population. Each New Deal agency that was structured to operate on a county level had to establish, therefore, a large number of county offices. Offices, furthermore, needed minimum staffing, including a certain percentage of positions requiring "professional" skills. Every agency would demand not only a large, cumbersome, dispersed administrative structure, but also qualified personnel. The conditions inherent in Georgia made all agencies hard to operate.

Beyond this general situation were internal problems caused by political, economic, and social conditions, the first being the most obvious. The presence of so many counties meant there would be a like number of county political organizations. In some states, county governments held a minimal amount of power; this was not the case in Georgia, however. Included in the state's constitution was a device known as the county unit system. By this plan, the lower house of the general assembly was to contain 205 members elected on a county basis and apportioned as follows: the eight most populous counties, three each; the next 30, two each; and the remaining 121, one each.

This gave disproportionate power to the small rural counties. At the time of the New Deal, for example, Echols, Dawson, and Charlton counties with a combined population of about 13,000 had as many representatives as did Fulton County (Atlanta) with its 300,000 residents.

The importance of such a plan took on more significance with respect to statewide elections. In Georgia, with its typically southern one-party politics, victory in the Democratic primary was tantamount to election. Under the 1917 Neill law a candidate in such a race need only receive a county plurality to obtain a number of "electoral" votes equal to twice its representation in the lower house. A majority of these electoral votes was necessary to secure the party's nomination for governor or United States senator (a plurality for all other offices).

Many of the small rural counties in Georgia were controlled by "ruling families," so that, if a candidate could obtain the support of a fairly limited number of people, he could command enough votes to win. Of course, this also meant that these people assumed relatively great political importance, and they often reinforced this importance by demanding from those who courted their favor the right of dispensing local patronage. In any case, as each New Deal agency entered Georgia, it found that political conditions there demanded careful treatment of an unusually large number of people, simply because political power at the county level was so great and there were so many counties.

Some agency operations called for state support in the form of enabling legislation, requests for funds, or cooperation of state personnel. Here the attitude of the state's ruling faction and its leadership was crucial. Sometimes absolute intransigence on the part of a governor resulted in his being defeated for re-election. That did not generally happen for at least a few years after 1933, however, when the first and most important steps were being taken by the agencies, so that permanent damage still could be done. Even ousting a recalcitrant governor did not insure state cooperation when opponents of the New Deal remained in state departments and could not be easily weeded out by the new administrations.

Georgia's situation was consistent with the worst possible political conditions. Those plans which called for the most state support were least effective until 1936, for they were resisted venomously by Governor Eugene Talmadge. It was because of Talmadge, for example, that

Harry Hopkins "federalized" the FERA, and it was his faction's opposition which prevented Georgia from participating in the social security program until after the election of Eurith D. Rivers as governor in 1936.

Of course, this situation could be, and was, reversed in some instances. Rivers' allies could not make a clean sweep of the state legislature or do a thorough job of housecleaning in the state departments, but neither could Talmadge inculcate all of his public servants with the same hatred of the New Deal which possessed him. Those offices, such as that of the Highway Department, which were packed with "Talmadge men" proved to be especially uncooperative. In other departments, however, such as Health and Public Welfare, where more "professional personnel" were employed, relations with federal agencies were much more harmonious.

Political influence also acted outside these more formal contacts. Constituents brought pressure to bear upon state and federal solons in seeking certain programs for their districts. These men, in turn, prodded the state or federal executive branches which either acted as a buffer or demanded compliance from their subordinates. In a one-party state such as Georgia, party loyalty was severely tested when the first Democratic president since Woodrow Wilson confronted a very popular, but antagonistic, Democratic governor. In this particularly confusing atmosphere, citizens might work against their own best economic interests for political reasons, or vice versa. Such was often the case in counties where local leaders were willing to sacrifice the recovery of their domains because they feared that the tremendous influx of federal money needed to stimulate this recovery would undermine their power, secured in the past by the granting of political-economic favors.

In that there was distress, economic conditions were the same throughout the nation. There were, however, major differences in the nature and extent of this distress among various sectors of the economy and areas of the country. Some regions suffered more or less than others, and for different reasons. The agricultural problems of the South were more endemic than the industrial failures of the North. Southern industry, in fact, recovered much faster than either southern agriculture or northern industry. One of the New Deal's problems in dealing with the South was that it never really took into account these differences when devising its solutions. The major agricultural programs did not begin to actually attack the causes of agricultural distress in Georgia until the establishment of the Farm Security Administration. The NRA was created to aid economic recovery in highly industrialized areas of the nation. When applied to an overwhelmingly rural South, it simply did not work.

In terms of recovery the South, with its chronic economic ill health, had furthest to go. At the same time, most New Deal agencies evidenced a distinct tendency to be inapplicable to southern problems, at least not without major modifications. These two circumstances made it very difficult for administrators to achieve any sort of success.

In social terms, too, the South presented especially knotty problems. New Deal programs consistently challenged southern notions of caste and class and at times, according to southerners, threatened to overturn the entire political-social-economic structure. The New Deal attacked the problems of racism, agricultural thralldom, and the poor, and in doing so threatened the political-social-economic aristocracy.

None of the New Deal's laws was specifically racially discriminatory and social reformers in the federal administration intended that this should remain so in practice. White southerners were frantic, correctly assuming that federal regulations would destroy racial barriers. They refused to accept equal wage scales for blacks and whites or nondiscriminatory usage of public facilities. This was not merely a question of a racially liberal federal agency versus a conservative populace. Many federal administrators in the South, particularly at the local level, were southerners themselves and shared these racist attitudes. These people did not complain openly, as did those outside the agencies. They simply discriminated against blacks in the course of carrying out their duties, which was more insidious than outright racism and thus difficult to remedy.

Many southerners were willing to sacrifice advantages offered by the New Deal in order to preserve the racial status quo. Those in political power threatened to cancel entire programs unless racial customs were left undisturbed. At the other end of the spectrum were those social reformers in the New Deal who insisted that nondiscrimination not be abandoned whatever the result. Often the state administrators found themselves caught in the middle of this situation. Many agreed with nondiscrimination, and when the national office demanded compliance, they were happy to do so. These people, however, also were committed to their programs, and when no specific rules existed, they tended to rationalize an acceptance of racism. More than one officer claimed that he wanted to go as far as possible in helping the blacks as long as it did not result in the local government's rejection of the entire program. In the end, they reasoned, it was better to help some of the people rather than none of the people, if that were to be the choice.

In the South racial problems presented the most difficult social condition administrators had to deal with. Class attitudes, however, ran a close second. Southern class attitudes were tied not only to economic but to political circumstances. As in the North those with economic power also held political power, but here the expression of this power was much more overt and traditional. An accepted southern ruling class existed, particularly at the county level. So closely tied together were the economic, political, and social aspects of this structure that when certain agencies challenged local leaders' political power with federal money, they also attacked the social status of the ruling class. The southern aristocracy thus had a double reason to hate the New Deal. They resented it for trying to uplift those lower down on the social scale for status reasons and for undermining their primary base of political power. They intensely disliked the bright, young social workers and the flood of other federal officials who, they claimed, had descended uninvited upon the South. These new people had little or no regard for an aristocrat's position and certainly did not treat him with the respect and deference due his station.

Perhaps more important than this, however, was the effect these federal officials had upon the lower classes, especially the blacks. Although it was not so readily apparent during the New Deal period, the presence of outside government officials helped to break the stranglehold which southern leaders had upon the people. The New Deal did indeed invade the South in this respect, for it taught southerners that there were alternate routes of power that circumvented the traditional rulers. In doing this, it helped pave the way for later revolts against the "establishment," particularly by black people.

Since the evidence used to measure the effect of a state upon New Deal agencies was derived from a study of Georgia, the results are necessarily peculiar to that state. Racism as a factor in determining the effectiveness of an agency, for instance, was certainly more crucial in the South than elsewhere. Nevertheless, the hypothesis is that by asking the same general questions within a certain framework in every state one can discover certain common elements which influenced each agency's progress. By this method one may compare one agency to another despite differences which existed among them. Simultaneously, the difficulty in measuring the effect of the entire New Deal in one state vis-a-vis any other also can be overcome.

Of course, the validity of this method can only be proven by examining other states. As this is done, scholars will undoubtedly discover many peculiar, yet important circumstances which resulted from different local factors combined in various ways. Assuming that such a study were done for each state, the final picture would surely be complex. American society is complex itself, however, and this anticipated result must not deter historians. Furthermore, the task should be easier now. Scholars no longer will have to discover how each agency was organized and operated, and they can avoid many of the cul-de-sacs of manuscript research by concentrating on the specific areas herein suggested. They will not have to approach a study of the New Deal in a state by digesting all of the information available. They will have specific questions to ask, and they can discard information which clearly does not relate to the answers.

By adopting this procedure, two problems can be overcome. It will obviously be easier to study the New Deal in each state, and when other states are dealt with (assuming this method is indeed the correct one), a certain comparability will emerge. If this is done with some consistency, scholars may at last understand what befell the New Deal once it left Washington and why it happened that way.

1

A Massive Dose of FERA

The crash and depression descended upon the nation so quickly that neither the state or federal governments nor the various private charities were able to formulate the type of plans which such widespread distress seemed to demand. To be sure, depressions had struck before, but never with such force affecting so many different classes of citizens. Heretofore, relief had been thought of as something for the chronically poor, the aged, and the infirm. Relief statutes in most states were based on English poor laws of the "ruthless early seventeenth century" and were administered by people sharing a corrupted puritan ethic which presumed that those who failed to provide for themselves and their families were morally deficient.[1]

American tradition also held that relief was the responsibility of the states and their political subdivisions, and such was the case in Georgia where it was commonly recognized that "the 'Poor Fund' is a very poor fund, indeed." Under an 1880 law, counties could spend only one-fourth of the state's levy for the poor to alleviate poverty. In 1930, the state tax was four mills, so that counties could spend only one mill. Most counties, moreover, did not have an organization to disburse their money By 1932, only eleven counties had local county welfare associations, although a few of the larger counties had turned their funds over to existing social agencies to administer.[2]

Even with these financial and administrative handicaps, the state managed to increase its poor relief each year from 1927 to 1932 (except during 1931). Unfortunately, this rise in the total funds spent yearly was accompanied (except in 1931) by a decrease in the average amount each family received.[3] Some of the larger cities supplemented this rather meager aid with devices of their own. A number of communities paid their employees in scrip to ease the currency situation, and in Atlanta this fiat money was given to unemployed persons who worked in a "self-help" program. Some cities set up free employment bureaus to make sure that all available jobs were filled. In Atlanta, Augusta, Macon, Savannah, and elsewhere, the Better Business Commission helped by scanning local newspapers in search of job opportunities. In Augusta a group of civic clubs maintained an employment bureau in 1930-1931, and Atlanta's Mayor I. N. Ragsdale asked citizens who could not find jobs "to repair, remodel, and improve their homes and rental property."[4]

Many people, especially blacks, had migrated to the cities during the late 1920s, and some municipalities attempted to induce these newcomers to move back to the rural areas. Reverend D. D. Crawford, General Secretary of the General Missionary Baptist Convention of Georgia, made a plea that "the great mass of negroes now idle in the cities of the South be sent to agricultural sections, from which many of them came." He noted that such an experiment in Hancock County begun in 1932 proved the efficacy of the movement.[5]

Some cities encouraged this back-to-the-farm plan, but only in Columbus was it developed to any great extent. Atlanta's new mayor, James Key, and its Chamber of Commerce also endorsed a similar plan, under which the city would be able to save about $10,000 a year in relief expenditures. Atlanta residents responded favorably to the program, and over 1,600 "former farmers, heads of unemployed, charity-supported families" registered with the chamber. The local relief committee and the county board of commissioners opposed the effort and withheld their support, however, so that the chamber had to abandon its work.[6]

Rural areas were never as active as the larger cities, and they failed to develop many "ad hoc" programs. Most of them depended entirely upon private charities to supplement their small relief appropriations. Unfortunately, local charities were also in poor financial condition and did not have the organization necessary to undertake such a task. By 1932, Georgia had only seven family welfare societies, seven Red Cross chapters, fourteen Salvation Army units, four Travelers' Aid societies, and eleven county welfare associations.[7]

These organizations, notably the Red Cross which covered the most territory, were often handicapped by local attitudes toward relief, especially in rural areas. Housewives seeking cheap domestic labor opposed it. According to one possibly apocryphal account, a distraught woman asked her maid, "Oh, Manda, why didn't you come for the wash?" Manda replied, "Who, me, Miss Jane? Why, didn't you know I done quit washin' when I got on de Cross?"[8]

Planters complained that during the picking season "people in Red-Cross lines won't work," but since they were responsible for the feeding and clothing of their croppers, they encouraged application to the Red Cross after the harvesting season. One landowner said, "The more tenants get from the Red Cross, the less they'll have to have from the landlord," but he would not allow his tenants to stand in line for Red Cross supplies during the picking season.[9]

A small number of local nonrelief organizations in the larger cities also came to the aid of the distressed citizens as conditions worsened. In Atlanta one clergyman organized the "Cooperative Exchange Club" where residents could exchange work for goods "through issuing exchange checks." The club received the approval of Governor Talmadge and the Atlanta Retail Merchants Association, and thirty firms agreed to cooperate. The Atlanta Elks' Club established an emergency kitchen where it "administered food, clothing and hope to needy humanity" during the winter of 1932-1933. Kendall Weisiger, vice president of the state's Bell Telephone Company, in cooperation with the Community Chest sought to "rally different organizations to the relief effort." He published a pamphlet, "Feeding Your Family," which gave instructions for providing nutritious, low-cost meals. The pamphlet soon became "a handbook for social workers and more or less a gospel for all Atlanta folk."[10]

The state and local governments and private agencies, however, had proved to be ineffective in fighting the depression by 1932. In that year President Hoover, still basically unwilling for the federal government to interfere in what he considered to be the states' prerogatives, reluctantly created the Reconstruction Finance Corporation (RFC). The RFC was capitalized at $500 million which it could loan to private financial institutions, railroads, and government-owned corporations. On July 21, 1932, Hoover signed the Emergency Relief and Construction Act, further expanding the RFC's activities to include loans to states for relief activities. The RFC was given another $300 million for which governors could apply as loans to be repaid at 3 percent interest per year. Under the new act, the RFC also could finance self-liquidating public works undertaken by states or their political subdivisions.[11]

Georgia was in great need and Governor Richard B. Russell, Jr., immediately asked for emergency relief funds. Since, however, there was no existing state organization for their distribution, it was not until October that any money was forthcoming. Russell would only make applications for counties giving him a pledge of some sort of local revenue, and he insisted that the state Department of Public Welfare make sure that the county had set up an agency to disburse the funds. The Department of Public Welfare was to publish a "rather comprehensive manual of instruction for organizing unemployment relief," and although it had only four workers which it could assign to the task, it was able to do "a good job of it" by using volunteers.[12]

Since the counties had very little revenue with which they might expect to repay the RFC loans, the governor arranged for them to borrow on state highway certificates. The county commissioners, or committees appointed by them, made applications to the governor and handled the funds when they arrived. The first loan awarded was for $15,000 to Hall County. By the end of Russell's administration, the RFC had loaned $471,084.22 to nine counties, with Fulton County receiving three separate loans of about $105,000 each.[13]

In January 1933 Eugene Talmadge became governor of Georgia, and Russell took a seat in the United States Senate. Although the new governor generally disliked the federal government's intervention, he had opposed the "small efforts" of President Hoover and had "spoken very highly of the Welfare Department during his campaign," indicating that "with his inauguration some more definite action for undertaking relief work on a state-wide basis may be expected." Upon taking office, Talmadge proved true to his word. He immediately established the Georgia Relief Administration (GRA) and required each county receiving loans to set up a special committee (often made up of county officials) to administer the money.[14]

The GRA promptly issued a bulletin instructing counties of their duties. Loans still would be repayable at 3 percent interest per year, but the money would be automatically deducted "from future federal aid road funds due to Georgia beginning in 1935." The counties were ordered to select their committees, and the GRA advised them that they might employ "a welfare worker or investigator, a supervisor of work relief, a bookkeeper, and a paymaster." Finally, the GRA urged the committees to spend at least 75 percent of the funds left after administrative costs for work relief.[15]

To head the GRA, Governor Talmadge selected an old university classmate, Herman P. De La Perriere. A federal investigator in Georgia at the time reported that De La Perriere knew "nothing about relief and has no certain idea of a plan." Miss Gay Bolling Shepperson, director of the Department of Public Welfare, suggested to De La Perriere that the department continue its cooperation with the GRA in the supervision of field work for the RFC. She offered to send three of her employees to the GRA at first and to add more as she was able. This plan was acceptable to the governor, and Miss Shepperson herself became De La Perriere's assistant.[16]

The federal investigator took the opportunity afforded by this reorganization to meet with the director and his assistant in order to straighten out the new administration. De La Perriere had planned to separate his organization into two divisions: social service or direct relief and work relief. The federal adviser warned him that work relief should not be divorced from social service work. If this were done, it would invite "political influence." He also noted that supporting data accompanying loan applications had been poorly gathered. In fact, "there has been no real examination of the accounts of the four counties previously receiving funds." The adviser was concerned particularly about Chatham County, which he suspected of having a "considerable surplus on hand." Miss Shepperson told him, "Chatham takes the attitude that this is a loan to them which they may spend as they please, especially in view of the fact that Governor Russell required them to pledge their road certificates with him for the repayment of what was advanced to him."[17]

The federal observer reported that things were not going well. De La Perriere had "a desk in the Governor's outer office where he says most of his time goes to consulting individuals who seek patronage." The observer was worried because it seemed as if "the Governor will seek to distribute RFC aid pretty generally throughout his rural counties without special collateral [sic], which many of them could not find." The agent rather naively observed that it might be well "to lead the Governor's point of view in the direction of careful relief administration."[18]

After a month conditions were no better. De La Perriere had hired John Peterson, the governor's stepson, as his assistant field visitor. Peterson had no welfare training, and the Department of Public Welfare was upset about his appointment. By this time thirty-nine counties had applied for aid, but only twenty were able to give the requisite preliminary survey of their needs. The surveys were being made by the Department of Public Welfare's field staff of three workers, and at least three more were needed immediately to speed up the work. This lack of a trained staff caused delays and misunderstanding which often resulted in the misuse of RFC funds.

Talmadge did not help the situation, either. He was content to by-pass the committees and to deal through the more politically oriented county commissioners. The federal agent in the state met with the governor to tell him "that the Washington office would insist upon a trained field staff for supervision as a condition of further applications" and to urge him to enlist the assistance of Gay Shepperson in finding trained workers. By this time, however, the federal official was convinced that, although the governor readily agreed, he would do nothing without pressure from the RFC.[19]

The agent was correct in his assumptions, and conditions did not improve. By mid-March he reported "insufficient supervision and too much direct relief" in all counties except Fulton. Some counties did not "pick workers according to need," and others did not even investigate relief cases. Local officials simply "don't know what's going on," mainly because of the "unintelligent plans for relief." The agent again approached the governor about securing trained workers who would act through the Department of Public Welfare. Talmadge agreed, but it was doubtful that the official really believed him by this time.[20]

The months of April and May showed little improvement. The GRA's office was one room into which twelve persons were jammed along with the "constant stream of individuals from the general public . . . filing in and out." There was constant commotion and crowding. The Department of Public Welfare was across the capitol square in a "dilapidated residence," and the separation caused communication difficulties which impeded operations. Work supervisors across the state were "men with little or no experience," although Miss Shepperson had been able to begin training the relief supervisors. Most committees still did not know what was going on, and in some cases dissension had begun to grow within them. Conditions became so bad in the Augusta relief committee that Talmadge was forced to abolish it and appoint another.[21]

From January through June 1933, Georgia received $1,268,075 from the RFC. From the 22,683 families aided in January 1933, the GRA had been able to expand its program to help 85,700 heads of families by May. On January 10, 1933, loans were being made in only eight counties, but by May 11, 1933, the program was active in 108 counties. The June application to the RFC asked for $567,922 for 119 counties with applications from nine other counties pending.

The advances seemed greater than they actually were. Funds had been available as early as July 1932, but it was not until January 1933 that the state established the GRA and really began to take advantage of the loans. The amount requested during the first quarter of 1933 thus was much more than the state previously had received, but it was still "comparatively small and did not meet existing need." Furthermore, most white workers never received more than 90 cents a day for RFC work, and blacks often got only 40 cents a day, the average wage being about 50 cents a day for 10 hours' work.

De La Perriere felt that administrative conditions were improving, but in fact they were not. Although the GRA now was able to pour money into more counties, the proper administration of these funds was still not insured. The state, which had proven itself unable to provide relief from its own revenues, was also unable to administer funds from the federal government in an effective, nonpolitical manner.[22]

The New Deal's relief program, stretching from the Federal Emergency Relief Administration (FERA) through the Federal Works Administration, represented one of the most sustained and broadest efforts of the entire period. The FERA, Civil Works Administration (CWA), and Works Progress Administration (WPA) in Washington and in Georgia possessed a continuum of leadership, under which changing purposes, organization, and tactics operated with varying success. From minimal federal control and rather modest beginnings, the relief program burgeoned into one of complete federal suzerainty, one which permeated all facets of American life. In a larger sense the growth of these organizations indicated the overall failure of the New Deal to wrest America from the clutches of depression; for had recovery been forthcoming, relief would have shriveled and expired, as indeed it did after 1939. But this should not preclude a search for victory and defeat within the federal relief program itself.

Relief efforts to 1933 generally had proved unsuccessful. Local and

state agencies had broken under the strain of the depression, and the
Reconstruction Finance Corporation's relief funds would be exhausted
by May 1933. To fill this gap Congress passed the Federal Emergency
Relief Act on May 8 and 9. The act established the FERA, financed
by recently provided RFC appropriations. As head of the FERA,
Roosevelt appointed Harry Hopkins, formerly of the American Red
Cross and New York's Temporary Emergency Relief Administration.

The FERA made two types of grants to the states. Half of the money
was disbursed as grants-in-aid matching every $3.00 which a state spent
on relief with $1.00 from federal funds. The other half was released as
discretionary grants where states had no money for relief. Funds would
be sent to any state whose governor applied, subject to the approval of
the national administrator. All other control over the types and amounts
of relief spending and the organization of state relief agencies was left
to the states. The law allowed the national administrator to assume
control of the state administrations in certain instances, but in general
the federal government expected the states to supply adequate supervision for the program. These provisions gave more power to the state
administration of the FERA than to any of the other early New Deal
agencies.

The Georgia Relief Administration board membership was politically
appointed, and its state director, Herman De La Perriere, was the
archetype of the rotund, southern politician who had absolutely no
knowledge or ability in the fields of either relief or administration.
There were few professional social workers or administrators at either
the state or county levels. As plans for the FERA in Georgia proceeded,
it became apparent that this new program would demand much more
experience and efficiency than the GRA was capable of. Therefore,
Gay Shepperson, director of the state's Department of Welfare, suggested to Hopkins that her agency be placed in charge by Talmadge.[23]

Gay Shepperson was an amazing person. She was born on August
14, 1887, in Virginia, and by the time she came to Georgia in 1928 to
join the Department of Welfare, she had amassed an impressive record
of welfare work. She taught school from 1910 to 1917 in Virginia before
entering the War Department for a year. In 1918, she affiliated with the
Associated Charities and in 1920 began working for the American Red
Cross in New Orleans where she met Hopkins. From there she moved
to Virginia, then to New York, and finally to St. Louis in various welfare jobs. She was in St. Louis just before coming to Atlanta.

Miss Shepperson was a diminutive, slight woman with a "small, squeaky voice" that concealed a determined spirit and a strong will. Her stature belied her strength, for she was one of the very few female FERA administrators and the only woman whom Roosevelt selected to become a state WPA administrator in 1935. When she retired in 1939, she was the only state administrator to have served continuously since 1933. Furthermore, as a southerner in charge of the federal government's most expensive "give-away" programs, she possessed two very unusual qualities: She was completely honest and totally apolitical. For these reasons, and because she was a female, she became "the woman Gene Talmadge wasn't going to allow to be relief administrator in Georgia."[24]

Miss Shepperson told Hopkins that if the Department of Public Welfare were designated to administer the relief program, it would "considerably lessen the tension" in Georgia. Talmadge would never agree to it on her advice, she noted, but if Hopkins presented this idea to the governor as his own, "placing emphasis on the use of the Department rather than placing emphasis on me individually it would obviate any choice between me and Mr. De La Perriere." In this way it would not seem as if the federal administration was evicting Talmadge's man. Frank Neely of Rich's Department Store in Atlanta, a close friend of Talmadge, Miss Shepperson, and Hopkins, agreed with this plan and used his influence with Talmadge to obtain the governor's consent.[25]

In order not to alienate Talmadge, the governor was allowed to appoint a Georgia Relief Commission (GRC) to head the FERA in Georgia. Miss Shepperson was designated its executive secretary and placed in charge of compensation, selection, and direction of all personnel, both in the state administration of the funds as well as the county, subject to the approval of the commission and Hopkins. She also approved all expenditures and appropriations with the consent of a majority of the GRC. To further assuage Talmadge De La Perriere was named as "adviser" to the GRC, a post which he never assumed. Thus Miss Shepperson emerged as the effective head of the FERA in Georgia at Hopkins' behest and with Talmadge's consent.[26]

At first neither Talmadge nor De La Perriere recognized the change. That would have been far too obvious a victory for the administration. When the national office announced that the new Relief Administration would necessitate "the resignation of the entire personnel of the organization.... Mr. De La Perriere said that ... he had not resigned and had no intention of doing so." He also declared that no one else in the adminis-

tration had resigned either. Talmadge told the press that the only difference in the new organization was that relief now would be administered by a committee rather than by one person. He and De La Perriere
both denied that the change was being made because of "complaints
that some of the [RFC] loans made in the state were of a political
'flavor.'"[27]

Hopkins was able to have his way because he held the purse strings.
In writing to Atlanta banker Ronald Ransom, he made it clear that in
order to receive FERA funds, the GRC had to agree to his terms. Ransom apprised Talmadge of the situation, and the governor decided to
accede to Hopkins. In a press statement, Talmadge announced that Miss
Shepperson was to head the FERA as "supervisor of work projects," and
De La Perriere would remain as "coordinator."[28]

Two days later the Atlanta *Constitution* carried the story of the
FERA's housecleaning. All members of the former Georgia Relief Administration were to be released, and those who were qualified were to
be rehired as part of the GERA. Although not explicitly stated, this move
was taken by Miss Shepperson as approval to eliminate Talmadge's
political appointments. De La Perriere was allowed to stay as a sop to
the governor's ego, but his assistant, Arlie D. Tucker of Tennessee, and
Talmadge's stepson, John A. Peterson, were removed.[29]

By mid-June Talmadge had selected the five-man GRC. Three of his
choices had been approved by Hopkins, and two had not. As chairman
of the GRC, Talmadge chose Ronald Ransom. Miss Shepperson later
recalled that Ransom was a "decent person" and a "fine man." His
basic interest, however, was in having the state's funds deposited with
the Fulton National Bank, and he succeeded in having the FERA allotment placed there. He often attempted to act as a mediator when disputes between Miss Shepperson and Talmadge arose, but his final loyalty
was, by reason of personal interest, with the governor.[30]

Another member of the GRC was Mrs. Walter D. Lamar, known as
the "Dutchess of Georgia." She was a Talmadge backer and an influential figure in the women's clubs of the state. In selecting her for this
position, however, Talmadge made a mistake. Although she supported
him, placing her under Miss Shepperson tended to divide her loyalties,
so that when trouble arose between Talmadge and Miss Shepperson
she begged Hopkins "to stand by Gay Shepperson as director in charge
of this work." She spoke to Hopkins as the "only nonpolitical appointee

on the Georgia commission" and the "only woman representative," the second fact possibly being more important than the first.[31]

The third member accepted by Hopkins was A. Steve Nance, prominent Atlanta labor leader. Talmadge's choice of him was somewhat enigmatic. Nance was clearly the most "liberal" man on the GRC, but at the time he was associated with conservative trade unionism. Later he moved to the emerging Congress of Industrial Organizations, but in 1933 he probably was considered "safe" by the state administration.

Talmadge also selected John E. Whitley, La Grange businessman, and Judge John Rourke of Savannah to sit on the GRC, but these men were not immediately acceptable to Hopkins. Subsequently Hopkins approved Rourke's appointment, and Talmadge withdrew Whitley's name, replacing him with S. E. Vandiver of Lavonia. The governor had procrastinated in selecting the final member of the GRC, hoping to secure places for his sympathizers, but when Washington officials threatened to assume direct control of the GERA, he reneged and selected Vandiver.

On July 6, 1933, the GRC held its first meeting. Miss Shepperson was elected executive secretary, and her list of personnel was summarily approved. She had fired all former members of the relief organization, and she informed the GRC that henceforth she intended to use only trained welfare workers where possible.

For a while Miss Shepperson maintained amicable relations with the GRC. Ransom liked her, feeling that she was quite capable, and the other members did not stand in her way. Although the GRC had the power to make policy decisions, it never had any idea of how much aid a county needed or what the qualifications for relief should be. Hence most of her suggestions were accepted without question in the critical first few months when basic policies were set forth.

Once the GRC approved her office staff, Miss Shepperson set about to organize the rest of the state and county administration and to begin a massive survey to determine where relief funds should go. Alan Johnstone, southeastern field representative of the FERA, was present when the county organizations were set up. He reported to Washington that the previous administrative structure in Georgia had been unsatisfactory. Control of the local units had been in the hands of volunteer committees with little supervision or direction. Counties which formerly received funds had made no effort to control the relief case load, and until recently there had been no state commission to supervise the appointment of local personnel or to set their salaries. Such organization as did exist reached only 119 of the 159 counties in the state, and urgent requests for relief funds from 25 more counties remained to be investigated.[32]

Johnstone suggested to the GRC that the locally selected committees be advisory only. He wanted the GRC to pick the county administrators with the local committee having no veto over its choice. Furthermore, Johnstone asked that the GRC select and approve local auditors of units consisting of about ten counties.

The GRC rejected Johnstone's proposals and asked that the local committees choose the directors, work supervisors, and auditors. In explaining the commission's actions to Hopkins, Ransom said that, if the GRC selected county staffs, the local committees would surely realize that "they had very little authority in controlling relief operations in their local units." He claimed, furthermore, that the GRC could not "possibly undertake to reorganize the large number of local relief units which are now functioning in the State of Georgia," and in "nearly all instances" it would have to use "the services of those already in existence."[33]

Despite the GRC's wishes, Hopkins decided to back Johnstone and Miss Shepperson, and on July 27, 1933, Talmadge signed an agreement giving full powers to the GRC and making the local committees advisory and not administrative in nature.[34] Ransom, however, had assessed the probable reaction of county committees correctly. The members of the Augusta and Richmond County Relief Committee resigned even before a final decision was made. W. E. Mitchell, chairman of the Fulton County Special Relief Committee, informed Ransom that the decision represented "a wide departure from our previous practice." Under the circumstances he "had no desire to be part of any figurehead committee, nor yet to be responsible in any way for the acts of employees who are selected, appointed, paid and whose duties are set forth by other parties." Most counties, nevertheless, acquiesced in the decision, and in any case it was not rescinded.[35]

When the GRC provided for the organization of county relief agencies, it also discussed the procedure for the submission and supervision of work relief projects. These projects were to be "planned and approved by the county committee subject to the approval of the Georgia Relief Commission." Supervision of the projects would be provided by the political subdivisions unless more than 300 persons were on work relief, or the variety and number of projects required a work supervisor—essentially the process previously used by the GRA. Consequently there was no dissension when the new policy was announced.[36]

One of Miss Shepperson's decisions displeased both the GRC and Johnstone. Johnstone had told the GRC that county administrators did not necessarily have to be social workers, and that he felt the administrators should be men "unless there was a woman of unusual ability." It was impossible to tell whether this statement reflected some unspoken feeling about Miss Shepperson, but one comment was predicated on the other, since most social workers at the time were women. When Miss Shepperson ignored his advice and appointed women to all but one position, however, Johnstone stood behind her choices.[37]

Once the GERA's operation plans had been completed in Atlanta, Miss Shepperson called a series of public district conferences for county relief workers. At these meetings she, Alan Johnstone, and members of the GERA staff explained the program to local workers. When everyone understood the procedures, the state office began to distribute funds.

Miss Shepperson's rapid progress did not mean that everything was settled with Governor Talmadge. No sooner had the state office been set up than he attempted to exert influence over it. He insisted on signing all checks for relief funds, as well as those for the salaries and expenses of the state staff. On July 18, 1933, he refused to sign salary checks for several members of the state staff "on the ground that the people were not acceptable to him and the salaries were too high," even though they had been approved by the GRC. He also complained that these workers were neither southerners nor natives of Georgia. Johnstone reported that the matter was critical "because they [the workers in question] were above those of Messrs. John A. Peterson and S. H. Hollis who were placed on the payroll by the Governor or at his request." Neither De La Perriere, Peterson, Hollis, nor a stenographer put in the office by Talmadge had any duties, and Johnstone believed they should be dismissed. Ultimately Talmadge retreated, but he continued to harass Miss Shepperson about her employees. He still insisted on signing every check, and he demanded to know the name and address of every person on her staff.[38]

Talmadge did not confine his attacks to GERA personnel. He constantly had Miss Shepperson in his office to ask why she gave each county so much money. He also questioned the selection of relief clients and demanded to have copies of the relief rolls. The governor returned her budgets covered with his blue pencil marks, causing her to spend a great deal of time and energy rewriting them. Miss Shepperson later reminisced that it was not that Talmadge wanted the money to go elsewhere, but that he questioned this wasting of federal funds altogether. He told her that if she wanted to end the depression, she should "line them [the poor] up against the wall and give them castor oil." That would get them back to work.[39]

Talmadge wanted to control all expenditures in his state. In a political system that depended heavily upon the support of local politicians in very small counties, it was vital that all favors come from him. Now, suddenly there appeared an agency headed by a woman, no less, that was pouring more money into the counties than most of them had ever seen before. Talmadge was desperately afraid that his base of power would be undermined. What he did not realize was the extent to which Hopkins and Miss Shepperson would go to protect the program from his meddling. Had he supported the program and willingly lent his name to it instead of constantly attacking it, perhaps he would not have suffered the defeat handed to him in the 1936 senatorial contest by New Deal supporters in the state.

Ransom played the devil's advocate for Talmadge in the GRC, and he was relatively unchallenged by the other members. Nance was interested in making the relief administration enforce the labor provisions in the National Industrial Recovery Act. Johnstone noted that Nance was really "trying to serve the interests of three units," and he was confused in his approach to the relief problem. Rourke was "a typical small town politician" who existed by hanging on to Talmadge's coattails. Mrs. Lamar and Mr. Vandiver were well-meaning people, but easily influenced by Ransom. They did not fully understand what was going on, nor did they have the power to do anything about it, even if they had wanted to.[40]

Talmadge was not alone in his attack on the GERA. Local politicians stood to suffer greatly when the GERA took the distribution of relief out of their hands. Sometimes local political leaders asked help for constituents found suitable to serve the GERA, and Miss Shepperson could satisfy their requests while insuring an efficient organization. But on the whole the people in power emulated Talmadge and the GRC in their lack of sympathy or understanding. They felt that the federal government was giving too much free money to those who did not deserve it. To them poverty was still a sign of moral weakness. W. E. Mitchell, one of the FERA's strongest opponents, said of the unemployed, "I don't want to see them, don't let me see them. There will be casualties [?] of this movement and we must steel our hearts against them all as we did against wounds and death in the war."[41]

This type of opposition was based not only on a perverted puritan ethic, but also on a rural distrust of urban populations. Johnstone noted, for instance, that while Talmadge was vilifying "urbanites" for "chiseling," he was "insisting that farmers need help." Since most of the relief money eventually went to the cities, moreover, rural citizens were always wary of the FERA's intent.[42]

The GERA was more successful in stemming political opposition on the county level than in handling the governor. Johnstone reported in mid-September 1933 that the GERA had "succeeded in arresting the political control in most of the counties," and the relief committees had accepted the GERA with good grace. Johnstone concluded that northern Georgia was safe from Talmadge's influence. The governor had done his best to turn the people of Georgia against the program, and he had succeeded as long as the GERA's work was not fully publicized. When people began to understand the GERA's program, however, and especially as they received relief funds, Talmadge's attack was subverted. Johnstone had hoped for this reaction, but at first he did not believe it would occur. He suggested that if the governor kept up his interference and opposition, the FERA should "take the State of Georgia away from Talmadge on the question of relief."[43]

At the same time, the FERA was moving to increase Miss Shepperson's authority. On September 29, 1933, Johnstone exacted an agreement from Talmadge that Miss Shepperson's title was to be changed from Executive Secretary of the GRC to Georgia Emergency Relief Administrator, thus separating her in spirit from the GRC. She then was charged with the execution of the policies of both organizations. The agreement further stated that "the FERA may nominate and approve appointments to the membership and staff of the GRC, and such appointments shall as to membership be mutually agreeable to the FERA and the Governor of Georgia and as to the staff to the FERA and the GRC and that both shall be made on a nonpartisan basis of qualification only."[44]

The FERA also tried to make official a selection procedure that had existed in practice for some time. During the first six weeks following the establishment of the GERA, the state office had projected organizations in 143 counties. When the GRC met to consider Miss Shepperson's selections of county committees and personnel, they were able to complete action on only thirteen counties in five hours. The GRC then passed a resolution allowing Miss Shepperson to do the rest.

In October Johnstone proposed that this practice be made official. Miss Shepperson would appoint personnel to advisory committees and county offices and fix the budget for each, subject to the GRC's approval, if in session, and its subsequent confirmation, if not. Ransom strongly opposed Johnstone's suggestion, feeling that Talmadge would never agree. The arrangement would cause greater contact between Miss Shepperson and the governor, and Ransom had made every effort to keep them apart to avoid friction. The GRC did not follow Johnstone's advice and by a vote of three to two defeated his proposal. Subsequently the commission did agree to the establishment of a subcommision composed of Ransom, Nance, and Miss Shepperson to speed up the selection process, but in another attempt to restrict Miss Shepperson, it passed a resolution that she had to refer all complaints back to county administrators and advisory committees. Final adjudication over local matters thus remained in local hands.[45]

When Talmadge realized that the establishment of the GERA meant the end of his control over federal relief funds in the state, he moved to gain influence in its operations. While attacking the GERA and Miss Shepperson on all fronts, he created a fictitious contracting company through his henchmen to handle GERA construction projects in Atlanta. This attempt failed, so he turned his attention again to the GERA staff. There he found that Miss Shepperson had succeeded in appointing efficient, nonpolitical personnel.

Despite his September 29 agreement, Talmadge now planned to replace Miss Shepperson's hand-picked purchasing agents with men of his own choosing. In that way contracts could be let to those whom he owed a political favor. To hide this move, he first attacked the appointment of three GERA workers, one of whom was a welfare nurse, Miss Jane Van De Vrede. She had been approved by the subcommission of the GRC and by Judge Rourke, but when the governor objected, the commission refused to confirm her appointment. At a GRC meeting on

December 12, 1933, Rourke introduced a resolution to discharge
Miss Van De Vrede because she was not qualified for the work. Nance
and Mrs. Lamar stood firmly behind Miss Shepperson's choice, but
Vandiver and Rourke voted to release her. Ransom also voted "No"
to break the tie, and Talmadge's smoke screen was up.[46]

Miss Shepperson learned about Talmadge's alternate purchasing
agents when she presented the GRC with her list of twelve supervising
purchasing agents experienced in the army and in business. The commission vetoed the list and substituted Talmadge's choices, none of whom,
Johnstone and Miss Shepperson felt, was at all qualified. At this point
Talmadge waited. He evidently did not want to push the issue until he
could be sure of the FERA's reaction. Unfortunately, he had miscal-
culated.[47] Miss Van De Vrede not only was a splendid nurse, but also
had been one of those Red Cross workers with Hopkins in New Orleans.
When he received the news from Miss Shepperson, Hopkins was furious,
and when she informed him that she could not be responsible for the
FERA in Georgia if her purchasing agents were replaced, he moved to
assume control of the GERA.[48]

Although this proved to be the breaking point, it was not the only
problem confronting Miss Shepperson before the GERA was federalized
in January 1934. Talmadge had insisted that the relief agency be kept in
the capitol building even though its quarters were impossibly cramped.
At times the staff was forced to vacate its offices so that congressmen
could hold public hearings in them. Miss Shepperson begged the governor
to let her move the offices, but he refused, and the GRC sided with him.
Furthermore, when she had assumed her position, she found that De La
Perriere had taken all the office records pertaining to administrative
personnel in the counties and "placed them under lock and key in his
own personal office." By the end of 1933 she still had not recovered
them, and the governor refused to help her.[49]

Talmadge also put stumbling blocks in the way of state financial
participation. Neither the state, counties, nor municipalities could borrow
money in excess of 7 percent of the assessed tax values on property
within their boundaries, and by 1933 most political subdivisions had
reached this level. A law passed in 1880, moreover, limited a county's
authority to tax for support of the poor to 25 percent of the state levy,
which in 1933 stood at four mills. Using these laws as a weapon against
the FERA and the Public Works Administration, Talmadge refused to

let the state contribute to secure the matching funds offered under the 1933 Relief Act. The state's total contribution to the GERA, from its inception to its demise, was only $4.95, and this came during the first months of the GERA's operations.[50]

The counties had no option to provide matching funds under the FERA's rules, and some did not want the aid. In at least one case a county refused to accept FERA funds for its unemployed citizens. When the matter came before the GRC, it decided to let a neighboring county provide the necessary money, to be reimbursed by the GRC.

At the other extreme were the counties that attempted to place their entire relief burden upon the GERA. Most notable among these was Fulton, the greater part of which was within the Atlanta city limits. Although FERA inspectors agreed that the city was able to provide for about 25 percent of the relief load, the Atlanta Emergency Commission, under the direction of the ubiquitous W. E. Mitchell, dumped the whole relief load, including the city's pauper list, upon the GERA.

When Talmadge found that he could not control relief funds or personnel, his last-ditch effort was to refuse all federal money. He persuaded the GRC to send out a circular letter saying that relief would have to be cut during the winter of 1933-1934. Johnstone was worried about this move and called Aubrey Williams in Washington. Johnstone clearly had given up all hope of Talmadge's cooperation. He said, "Well, we have come to the parting of the ways in Georgia and can't get along with this bird." Williams assured Johnstone that the national office was working on a way to put federal money into a state without the governor's approval. Six days later Johnstone called Williams again to check on his progress. Williams noted that the governor had to "receipt for the money," but the law said that the word of the administrator was final, creating something of an impasse. Johnstone concluded, "We ought not to see a damn Governor do an injustice to a man or woman."

In the first few days of January 1934 both the financial and personnel issues came to a head, and Johnstone asked Williams to have Hopkins send a wire to Talmadge relieving him of FERA responsibilities. He noted: "Things are getting pretty tough. We have $800,000 in the bank, and I will ask the Old Buzzard to give me a check. If he refuses, I will report to you people and I will ask that Harry [Hopkins] ask for an amendment to this Act so we can send the money down here."[51]

On January 4, 1934, Hopkins designated Miss Shepperson as Relief

Administrator of Georgia and ousted the GRC. He also placed her in
sole control of the Civil Works Administration (CWA). Steve Nance told
the Atlanta *Constitution* that he was glad to be rid of a job that "brought
me nothing but abuse and grief." Talmadge said that he was "puzzled"
over the change. Hopkins had announced that the move was made in the
interest of economy and efficiency, but the state's newspapers speculated
that Talmadge's activities might have had something to do with it.[52]

When Talmadge saw that Hopkins meant to force him out, he became
more tractable. In a meeting with Johnstone the governor agreed to continue requesting such funds for the GERA and CWA as Miss Shepperson
should desire. Johnstone recommended, therefore, that Hopkins not
actually federalize the FERA of Georgia, and the relief administrator
agreed.[53]

Despite all of the problems which beset her from every side, Miss
Shepperson was able to launch an effective program. Her first consideration after a general housecleaning of the state office was to select her own
permanent staff, strictly on the basis of qualification. As her assistant
and head of engineering for the GERA, she picked Robert L. MacDougall,
a graduate of Georgia Tech and a licensed professor of engineering in
Georgia. He also provided the necessary presence of a man in Miss
Shepperson's office when construction projects involving large sums of
money were discussed. Miss Shepperson effectively used him to ward
off criticism from those who felt that a woman was not qualified to
make such decisions.

Her selections of Louisa DeB. FitzSimons and Jane Van De Vrede to
supervise social workers and nursing, respectively, continued her policy
of acquiring highly skilled professionals. These two women saw that
qualified social workers and registered nurses were put into positions where
they could best benefit the state.

Under the FERA, Georgia thus first experienced the marriage of the
practical and humanitarian aspects of relief. From Hopkins down through
the state FERA organizations, social workers were in control, and the
emphasis in the FERA's programs was placed upon the social work aspects of relief. In this respect it was much different from its successor,
the Works Progress Administration.

Regardless of its philosophical inclinations, the FERA was responsible for work and community service projects which required certain
pragmatic decisions. In addition the agency controlled the expenditure

of heretofore unheard-of sums of money. Each state administrator was required, therefore, to reach some point of balance between the two. For her part, Miss Shepperson achieved this goal through the services of men such as MacDougall and R. L. Lane, chief auditor and accountant.

To Lane fell the responsibility for the expenditure of all FERA funds. He presided over continuous hostilities between social workers, who spent large amounts of money rather freely, and local finance officers, who worried over each penny. Fortunately, he usually was successful, and with Miss Shepperson's help few serious controversies arose.

In following her policy of professionalism, Miss Shepperson assembled an extremely competent staff and avoided purely political appointments. She later stated that she was happy to do a favor for a senator or representative when possible, but only if the person being considered was qualified. Many of those she selected, especially for positions outside the state office, were taken from among her co-workers in the Department of Public Welfare. She knew these people and trusted their abilities. In areas about which she knew little, she was careful always to pick experts.

The ultimate verification of her sagacious choices came in their eventual promotion to higher positions. MacDougall replaced her as WPA Administrator in 1939 and then became director of the fifth region, and Miss FitzSimons moved to the Department of Public Welfare in 1937 as Director of Public Assistance.

As she assembled her staff, Miss Shepperson began to organize the state's program. The general relief program included two parts, direct relief and work relief, with much more money devoted to the latter. Apart from these two general areas, the FERA operated five special programs initiated at various times in its duration. The first of these special programs, the transient program, was set up in July 1933. It was followed that fall by the emergency education program. In July 1934 the Rural Rehabilitation Division was organized, and the college aid program came into being the following fall. The FERA also operated a drought relief program, in which Georgia participated to a minimal degree.

To operate these programs, Miss Shepperson and Johnstone set out to form an efficient county relief system. At a series of meetings in September 1933, they met with county relief officials and other interested persons to discuss what changes would be necessary for the effective management of the new relief program. By placing trained social workers in most counties and reducing the case load per worker, Miss Shepperson began to move away from the more archaic concepts of relief. Although she later stated that there was little time for actual case work during the FERA period, Miss Shepperson was able to direct the impetus of the state and county offices, making relief a rehabilitative process rather than a humiliating pauper's program.

Unfortunately, these actions placed the county administrator in a difficult position. Miss Shepperson's field supervisors were constantly discovering instances in which the ruling groups in the counties' political structures were applying great pressure upon county relief administrators. In many counties those higher up on the economic scale never could understand the philosophy that guided the actions of these social workers. In other instances influential members of county committees sought posts in the county GERA office for those to whom they owed favors. These same people also tried to increase their importance by interfering in the selection of relief candidates, thus making it appear that relief came from them rather than from the FERA.

Miss Shepperson was able to control these political forces only by retaining broad power over all decisions made at the county level. In many cases she found that the interests of the GERA in a county might best be served by appointing a relief administrator who was not a resident of the county. This tended to lessen the influence of the local advisory committee over the administrator, but it often irritated local leaders. Miss Shepperson advised her field staff to keep a close watch over the county offices, and numerous reports reached her desk concerning various difficulties.

In some counties, when local politicos found they could not have their way, they withheld aid from the county relief administrator. In one such county the field supervisor demanded cooperation from the mayor and county commissioners. With their backs against the wall, these officials excused their failure to provide office workers for the administrator by pleading that there was no one in the county who was qualified to do the work.

In Baker County the district supervisor found that the wife of the sheriff was employed as an interviewer. The local administrator believed that this woman was "not reporting fairly" but could not prove it. The administrator was certain that this investigator was intimidating the other investigator, but she could not prove that either. Often the attitudes of these local investigators were closer to those of the county

officials than to the relief administration. Some of them treated clients
in such a demeaning manner that they would not seek relief. In other
cases the investigators made the process of applying for relief too complicated and lengthy for clients to get on the county relief roll. Investigators had to ask unpleasant questions, and unsympathetic investigators
compounded clients' embarrassment by asking the questions a way that
discouraged the distressed from seeking relief at all.[54]

In some counties supervisors found that complaints from county
officials were justified. Often these complaints were made for political
reasons, but upon inquiry the supervisor found that the relief administrator was unqualified to hold her position. One such case occurred in
Ben Hill County. The supervisor reported that the local administrator
had "worked very hard" and had "kept the organization totally free of
politics," but she did not "know relief work." Some of the protests
concerning the administrator centered around her inclination to do all
of the work herself, thus making it difficult to progress swiftly.

In Butts County the supervisor found a situation of constant political
warfare between two "political factions of long standing." Butts was "a
very old county with many traditions, that have been and will continue
to be kept alive by the old families there." She found that "a person
must become affiliated with one or the other [of the factions] or he loses
general standing with the other until he switches over, which is not infrequent." The county relief administrator was caught in the no man's
land of this battleground, and the supervisor was hard pressed to find
a solution.[55]

There were some situations where supervisors found county administrators to be incompetent and removed them despite the protests of
the county officials who wanted to retain them. One such incident
occurred in Troup County. Here, as in a number of other counties, the
woman who had been administrator for the RFC program remained
under the FERA. When a field supervisor inspected the county office,
however, she found that the administrator had progressed no further
than the ninth grade in public school. The supervisor reported conditions
to be very poor in the county office. The administrator had little
grasp of the situation and of relief procedures. Furthermore, she was
uncooperative when suggestions were made to her. The supervisor
concluded that the only reason the office was not a complete shambles
was because the county administrator was fortunate in having a fairly
competent staff.

Miss Shepperson decided to replace this administrator as part of her statewide program to put trained social workers in these positions. When several citizens protested to Johnstone, Miss Shepperson set forth the facts of the situation. Although the citizens were not satisfied, Hopkins reaffirmed her course of action.[56]

In order to combat the influence of local politics, Miss Shepperson issued bulletins early in the program stating that no employee could be approved who was receiving a salary from some other source. She also ordered that no member of the immediate family of a local committee member or of other employees of a committee could be approved to work in the county GERA. In the early summer of 1934 pressure began to mount in the counties prior to the coming political campaigns. At this point Miss Shepperson found it necessary to amplify her position. She issued another bulletin stating that "whenever a person employed in an administrative office of the GERA has a member of his immediate family who holds public office or at any time runs for public office, this person will be requested to resign." She also broadened the definition of "immediate family" beyond that normally used by the civil service.[57]

County administrative irregularities were not the only problems the state office faced during the early period. When R. L. Lane became chief state finance officer, he undertook the reorganization of all county financial operations. He found a large number of unallowable expenditures to the counties. His audit of the counties' financial records also revealed instances of fraud and embezzlement. In one or two circumstances the GERA had to take the cases to court, although most were settled without resorting to such action. In a few situations Lane had to remove local administrators on charges of inefficiency.

In his reorganization program Lane was very careful to consider the prerogatives of the social workers and financial officers. There had been some friction in the division of responsibilities, but he handled the matter very tactfully to the general satisfaction of those involved. One of the FERA field representatives, commenting on Lane's work, declared that he "was one of the best of the chief auditors in the southeastern area."[58]

Despite obstacles which either were inherent in the program or were thrown in her way, Miss Shepperson managed to complete her organization with some dispatch. By the middle of September she had set up her state office and organized 114 county units. Those counties without a GERA office would be combined with counties already so served, or

were about to get one. Johnstone wrote on September 18, 1933, that
"in the counties north of Macon the personnel is professional and the
committees are cooperating." Johnstone was surprised at her swift
accomplishments and noted with some respect that the personnel was
of a "character better than I thought possible to secure." A month later
he submitted a report to the national office stating that "the crisis in
the relief administration in Georgia is passed."[59]

For the first time the federal government was providing a welfare
office in "every county." Many counties that had never seen a social
worker now had one permanently stationed within their borders. By
mid-September the Work Division was setting up projects in some
counties, and one of the most important programs, the malarial
drainage project, actually was under way. An agreement had been
reached with the state Department of Education to give teachers in
rural areas employment using relief funds, and the two agencies
set up programs for adult education and trade schools for people on
relief. The GERA office also had contacted county governments to
secure funds in cases where local cooperation was necessary for the
prosecution of certain projects.

The FERA's impact upon the lives of many Georgians was forceful
and immediate. Frank Neely told Miss Shepperson that during the
depths of the depression the center of Atlanta's retail business district,
"Five Points," was deserted. None of the stores was open; the entire city
was closed. In the first week of its operation, the GERA office on the
third floor of the state capitol continually was crowded with "samples
of the human material to be saved." The reliefers "sat slumped in the
waiting rooms, typical 'poor whites' defeated first by the old plantation
system and again by the transplantation system—the slump in the new
industry." They waited, "gray-faced, timid, patient" forming "painful
contrast to the social workers', bright fresh-colored college girls trooping
in at the end of the day's work like beings of a different breed of heralds,
as perhaps they are, of a new social order."[60]

Miss Shepperson and her staff constantly strove to increase the number of people to whom relief could be given. Georgia was second only to
the District of Columbia in the percentage increase (27 percent) in number of persons on relief rolls during August 1933. Only five states and
the District showed any rise at all that month. This trend continued to
the end of the year, although the rate of increase slowed somewhat during

the fall and winter. In a report to Hopkins at the end of the year, one field representative said, "Georgia has made one of the best records for improvement [since the first of the summer] of any of the southeastern states."[61]

Although the dole or direct relief was cheaper to administer, most FERA officials preferred work relief, both from physical and therapeutic points of view. With work relief, men could often use their skills to provide for their families, and the projects which they completed would be of real value to the community. Furthermore, they did not feel as if they were receiving charity. In this attitude they shared the traditional ideas of their "betters" about the value of work and the meaning of poverty.

Despite this, it was made clear as early as January 1933, when the first RFC work projects came to the state, that "Work Projects . . . are incidental to the reaching of our main objective in this work, namely— the relief of destitution." Approval of the projects themselves was based on "the type and necessity for the work contemplated, bearing in mind the provisions of the ACT that stipulates that Federal Funds are to be used only on work that WOULD NOT OTHERWISE BE DONE and THAT IT DOES NOT INVOLVE PRIVATE LOSS OR GAIN."[62]

Under the FERA these guidelines continued to operate. Work relief projects depended upon the supply of available labor with the skills necessary to complete the project. The acquisition of labor could not interfere with the needs of private enterprise in the area, and the projects had to be of a nature that ordinarily would not have been undertaken by the local government at that time.

For the GERA to provide work relief, county committees had to plan and approve projects within their boundaries, sending them to the GRC for final consideration. This was done in some cases, but in general the GERA entered the work relief program simply by taking control of projects that the GRA had begun with RFC funds. These proved of limited value and were soon superseded in importance by the federally sponsored projects provided for after August 1, 1933. On October 10, 1933, the FERA had completed negotiations with the necessary federal agencies and announced the institution of seven federal projects:

Malaria control
Rural sanitation
Control of rats as carriers of disease

Mosquito control
Control of rats as predatory animals
Tying in control surveys (coastal and geodetic)
Building census

These projects had barely begun when the entire FERA work program
was taken over by the Civil Works Administration (CWA). When the CWA
was abolished in the spring of 1934, the program returned to the FERA
until 1935, when the Works Progress Administration assumed the responsibility for it.[63]

Although the types of projects undertaken in the FERA and CWA
work programs varied greatly, the kinds of skills required on the different
projects did not. Most of the labor necessary could be unskilled, and
that which could not still usually required common construction-type
abilities. These programs were fairly straightforward, too. In terms of
relief, the work program provided the best laborers per project ratio.
Normally their worth was easily recognized, and their accomplishments were physically obvious. Finally, the program included the types
of projects that were needed in all parts of the state, particularly in rural
areas. For these three reasons many administrators felt the work program
was the most successful of the FERA's relief endeavors: The projects
were uniform and simple; they accommodated large numbers of unskilled
workers or workers with skills common in all parts of the state; and they
were generally appreciated.

The special FERA programs experienced diametrically opposite
conditions in almost every instance. They were purposely designed to
employ those ineligible for direct relief but with special training, each
project requiring a high percentage of this skilled labor. The projects were
more diverse and less universal, applicable mostly in urban areas. They
were more complex with greater differences both among and within them.
They often required a greater commitment and more cooperation from
state and local agencies, and, at the same time, their results were not as
tangible and thus less appreciated. All of this meant that they were harder
to administer and were considered of less overall value than the work
projects. It was here that most of the friction between the FERA and
the state and local governments, as well as the people, arose. Paradoxically, however, it was in these projects that much which was to prove
both innovative and enduring was begun. For both the negative and the

positive reasons a more detailed examination of some of these special programs is warranted.

The first program undertaken was in the field of education. In November 1933 Miss Shepperson received an initial FERA grant of $34,000, making Georgia the first state in the nation to acquire funds "for keeping the common schools open for a full year." The money was to be used to pay teachers' salaries and to purchase books. Miss Shepperson contacted Mauney D. Collins, state superintendent of education, in order to establish the educational aid program as well as illiteracy classes and vocational training.[64]

Collins and Miss Shepperson decided that the state Department of Education and local school authorities should administer the education program. All appointments for teaching positions were measured on the basis of work relief standards, but were made through the state's educational system. A state supervisor was appointed to decide what types of educational projects should be developed and where they should be located.

Financial difficulties of one sort or another constantly plagued the emergency education program. Counties found it difficult, for instance, to establish "need." Neither their records nor those of the state Department of Education were adequate. There was some indication, moreover, of manipulating teacher salary schedules to be eligible for more FERA money.

Rural schools were always in worse financial straits than their urban counterparts. The GERA decided at the inception of the program to handle rural and urban schools separately, but found this difficult. When it tried to set population limits for rural towns it found that often larger towns were "the centers of a very large consolidated rural district."[65]

Because of these and other problems, school conditions failed to respond sufficiently in relation to the amount of money poured into the state's education fund. The federal government spent $1.6 million in Georgia in 1934, and, although the FERA estimated the state's need to be about $1 million, the agency found that around 100 schools were closed at the beginning of 1935.

Upon investigation it was discovered that the state had collected about 88 percent of its school aid money, and the governor had turned 78 percent of this (or 86.6 percent of the actual revenue receipts for school aid) over to the schools. This left about $500,000 which he used to pay current state debts. The state school authorities had nothing to do with this chicanery and supported a state aid bill for $4.25 million for the next year, with a clause that the full amount should be paid to the schools.

This bill passed the lower house but died in the Senate when Talmadge threatened to veto it. Thus the legislative session ended without any appropriation. Under state law, however, the governor could levy a state tax and make appropriations without the consent of the legislature. This Talmadge intended to do. Hopkins sent Talmadge a telegram warning that the state would receive no funds for education unless the governor reconvened the legislature in special session to pass an adequate school appropriation bill.[66]

During the spring session of the state legislature, twenty-three bills providing for state aid to education were introduced, but none passed. At this point Hopkins decided to relieve the state Department of Education of its duty in distributing the FERA educational funds. Henceforth, county supervisors would have to submit financial statements to the GERA. These would be scrutinized carefully by Miss Shepperson to determine the extent of financial distress, and then the money could be turned over directly to the school system to be used only for teachers' salaries.

The GERA sent a circular letter to each school officer explaining the situation and limiting teachers' salaries to $15.00 a week, providing that this payment would be retroactive only to April 19. The Georgia congressional delegation appealed directly to Hopkins to alter his decision. They asked that salaries be made retroactive to February 1, but Hopkins refused, citing as his reason the failure of the fall session of the Georgia legislature to pass a funding bill.

Hopkins, moreover, forbade Miss Shepperson's use of her unexpended educational funds, and he withheld the state's May appropriation. He stated to the press that the blame for this decision lay "solely with Eugene Talmadge." Of the eighteen states receiving federal rural school funds, only Georgia had failed to cooperate. He said that as soon as the state was federalized, the May funds would be released, but because of the difficulties encountered between that time and the first of the year, he could not allow funds to be used to pay teachers' salaries before the federalization.[67]

Hopkins' move to federalize the state probably resulted as much from

local difficulties as from Talmadge's antics. One examiner found that
school districts around the state deliberately had underestimated their
probable tax collections in order to be eligible for more federal school
aid. Another report disclosed that many counties could have paid their
teachers during the spring of 1935, but did not do so.

On May 2, 1935, Hopkins gave Talmadge another opportunity to
receive federal school aid. At a press conference on that date he suggested that the governor hold a special legislative session to pass the
necessary funding bills. When Talmadge refused, Hopkins' decision
became final. Talmadge never made an effort in this direction, nor did
he ever make an official application for teacher relief for 1934-1935.

Hopkins' action put Georgia's schools in a precarious position. Many
had remained open after the first of the year only on assurances that
they would receive federal aid. When this was not forthcoming, a
number had to close. A special examiner reported that as a result less
than 20 percent could qualify for teacher salary support after April 19.
A delegation from these schools went to Hopkins to show him that the
rural schools had filed for federal aid several months before the federalization move. Hopkins, however, remained firm, not only because of
Talmadge, but also because of the reports he had received concerning
the counties' true ability to pay their teachers.[68]

The wrangling continued into the summer. Talmadge remained
adamant in his position. He wrote to Congressman Braswell Dean that
"there has never been any diversion of any of the school funds of
Georgia since I have been Governor." He said he had signed Collins'
application in February 1935, although he felt it was wrong, because
he "knew that the people of Georgia would pay their proportionate
part of tax money to the Federal Government, and the only way
Georgia could protect herself was to apply for it as the other States
of the Union were applying and receiving." He told Dean that the whole
business was a maneuver by Washington to force the states to raise
their taxes. At the time the educational program was taken over by the
Works Progress Administration, Georgia's teachers still had not received federal support for their salaries. It fell to this new agency to
untangle the fiscal problem and to smooth the ragged edges of irritated
state officials.[69]

Although finances presented the major problem of the emergency
education program, there were others. Some friction existed between
the GERA office and the state Department of Education regarding

the selection of personnel. The education department insisted that all teachers be certified, while the GERA was more concerned with putting destitute people to work. GERA education workers felt that business and trade people were needed to teach specialties. These persons, however, usually were not certified teachers, and the department would not allow them to work in the program. GERA officials felt that the department was hoarding the prerogative of selection by keeping its files on teachers closed to GERA education workers. When the FERA partially restricted the department's authority by taking away its right to pick supervisors, state Superintendent Collins bitterly complained that his offices were being "flagrantly mistreated."[70]

Besides the rural school program, the GERA emergency education program encompassed five other projects, each of which was rather far-reaching in concept, but inadequate in implementation. Classes to eliminate illiteracy were unpopular with both students and teachers, and, when finally established, they tended to be in the urban areas which least needed them. Emergency relief nursery schools for preschool children of destitute families promised much, but were able to accomplish little before 1935 because of insufficient funding. No money at all was appropriated specifically for vocational rehabilitation, and it depended solely on the generosity of the state relief administrator for its existence. Unfortunately Miss Shepperson already was spreading her funds very thin, and the rehabilitation program was not high on her list of priorities. The vocational training program, however, did receive some money and, as a result, fared much better as did a general adult education project which was open to all adults, regardless of their relief or employment status. Finally, a training program for nursery school teachers and teachers on relief met with some success, but was eventually hampered by Miss Shepperson herself, who insisted that all applicants have at least a high school diploma and be under sixty years of age.[71]

The FERA also sponsored a unique program for unemployed teachers who volunteered to serve in workers' education. The only black workers' school in the South was established in the summer of 1934 at Atlanta University. The six-week school enrolled thirty-nine black teachers from twelve southern states and the District of Columbia. At class sessions these teachers were introduced to the labor movement through courses in Current Affairs, Workers' Education Technique, Economic Status of the Negro, Labor through the Ages, Organized Labor, and Labor and the Government. Once graduated, the teachers came under the control of the FERA's Workers' Education Division, and they were expected to use their knowledge to educate industrial laborers in a manner that would make them aware of the implications surrounding their circumstances and lead them down the path toward unionism. R. K. White, director of workers' education in Georgia, also used the graduates to teach literacy classes among the "mill people." The program made solid if slow gains under White's dedicated, but uneven, leadership. Considering the section of the country, an observer noted that "very few persons could have done more than he in this short time." White constantly was forced to cope with men who understood little of the program, and he had to move very slowly in the face of an active "red baiting" campaign present in Georgia.

One other school program of note was begun by the FERA, though not directly under the emergency education program. Beginning in 1934 the federal government made grants available through the state FERAs to enable college students to remain in school. It was from this program that the National Youth Administration emanated in June 1935.[72]

Another of the special endeavors of the GERA was the transient program. As in all of its other efforts, the GERA imparted the social worker's attitude to the treatment of these wandering, homeless people in a way never before attempted. The transient problem was particularly acute in Georgia where droves of migrant workers traversed the state from Florida to South Carolina following the spring wave of the fruit and vegetable harvest. To these were added uncounted numbers who had been displaced by the depression and sought sanctuary from bitter northern winters in the "sunny South."

Unfortunately, these transients did not find succor in Georgia, and the problem increased rapidly as the depression wore on and as "higher types of people" joined the "down-and-outers" on the road. There were no adequate facilities for these people in the state. Towns were "defensive" and did little to aid those who passed through. Those agencies which did try to help provided only overnight care, and such relief as they offered was "inadequate and administered almost entirely on a mass basis without any regard for individual needs or background of the client."[73]

On July 11, 1933, the FERA made provisions for a Transient Division

and asked all states to make a survey of "needs and facilities" for
transients. Then, on July 26, 1933, the FERA issued a memorandum
describing how the program was to be set up. It was at this point that
the GERA established its own Transient Division.[74]

On August 21, 1933, Miss Shepperson appointed Major J. Arthur
Fynn, division officer of the Salvation Army, as head of the program in
Georgia. He served at this post until his death on August 15, 1935, when
his place was taken by F. F. Athearn. By the beginning of October Fynn
and his staff had submitted plans for the establishment of transient
bureaus in Atlanta, Savannah, Macon, Augusta, and Columbus. The
centers were under the direction of executive secretaries who were part
of the county relief administration. Under their control were trained
social workers who actually ran the centers.

Because the program was supported entirely by federal funds, Fynn
was authorized to select the best personnel available regardless of their
state of residence. Even so, he had difficulty in manning his centers. His
first move was to scour the state. But Georgia had "no public hotels"
or other such agencies from which to draw his staff. He thus was forced
to rely temporarily on the Young Men's (and Women's) Christian Association, the Salvation Army, and the Seaman's Institute for aid in
filling his positions. Where possible, Fynn made agreements with these
agencies that the GERA would reimburse them on a per capita basis
for the use of their personnel.

These people staffed the division's offices and were responsible for
registration and classification of transients. Fynn assigned trained case-
workers to handle family groups, women, the aged, youths, and the
handicapped. He also provided work supervisors for the men and for
infirmaries at the centers.

Where there was no center, Fynn placed agents in each local relief
office. The offices served as referral centers where overnight care or
incidental relief could be given to transients preliminary to their transfer
to the nearest center. Finally he established a Family Department in
each bureau to treat families as units. He wanted to isolate families
from the congregate units so that they would not be separated, the
ultimate goal being to return individuals and intact family groups to their
home communities.

October 1933 was the first month of actual operation. The agency
grew rapidly, and on November 1 enough buildings had been secured

at the transient centers for the other 154 counties to begin referral work. Immediately, the number of people moving into the centers increased. The FERA then quadrupled Georgia's allotment and allowed the Civil Works Administration to aid in "building, repairing, and renovating necessary facilities" for sheltering transients. This latter aid enabled FERA officials to move the transient program out of private facilities quickly.[75]

The flood of transients did not slacken appreciably in 1934, and the FERA had to expand the program, again relying on private facilities. The cost of operating the program remained high, so Washington constantly complained to Miss Shepperson. By the end of 1934 conditions had not eased, and the problem was exacerbated that year when Florida passed a law prohibiting migrants from entering the state. In rural areas near the Florida border, towns and highways "were overwhelmed with the number of families, boys and girls who were stranded in this section." There were four camps in the vicinity, and these quickly filled to capacity. Miss Shepperson reported to Aubrey Williams in December 1934 that Georgia was experiencing an increase of 2,500 transients a day. The state was getting "all the backwash from Florida," and they "are all stacked up here and they aren't passing on."[76]

Fynn attempted to ease the situation by placing notices in all of Georgia's bureaus telling transients not to go to Florida. The division made it mandatory for all male transients to be employed on work projects, hoping thus to force the transients out of the state. This effort accomplished little, however, and at the time the division was phased out there were still a great number of transients under its care in Georgia.

The Georgia Transient Division felt constant financial pressure. During each month of 1934 the division exhausted its budget before the next allotment arrived, requiring Miss Shepperson to seek additional funds. To reduce this deficit she reluctantly cut personnel costs by about 10 percent in most areas and by as much as 20 percent in others. The reduction was especially damaging since fewer personnel were being asked to care for more transients each month. The situation was particularly acute in Atlanta, through which most of the transients passed on their way to Florida. The long lines of transients in that city and their frequent abuse of food and shelter "tickets" created a hostile feeling which centered in city hall. As a result the city gave little assistance to the bureau. On the other hand, in places such as Savannah and Augusta where pressures were not so great, the relationship between the division and the city governments was more amicable.

Considering the number of reactions to transients before the initiation of the program, there were few complaints from clients or citizens. From December 1933 to May 1935 there were 368 complaints. During that time 104,427 people had been cared for in Georgia. Major Fynn, for one, felt that this was an impressive record.

Although the transient program was never more than a stopgap measure, it exemplified the rather substantive changes made by the GERA in assuming responsibility for relief. Under Miss Shepperson and Major Fynn, those who wandered on the state's roads were treated, not as criminals or moral degenerates, but as human symptoms of a disease which wracked the entire nation. The GERA always tried to do more for these people than simply give them food, clothing, and shelter and send them packing soon afterward. The division attempted, for instance, to preserve family units and to help these people regain some sort of dignity through useful work projects. In most cases the division provided for a small weekly allowance that the transients could spend as they wished. The money tended to restore their self-respect, and it pleased local merchants with whom the transients inevitably would spend their allowance. During their stay at one of the centers, the clients might learn a skill or be exposed to some rudiments of education. The bureau in Atlanta, for example, started a library for transients, and even though many of the local staff members were opposed to the project, it expanded rapidly and enjoyed moderate success.

Finally, the division sought to solve the transient problem completely. Its goal was to see all transients returned to their former homes in such a manner that they would not need to leave again. It was impossible to evaluate the success of the division in these terms, but the important factor was that it attempted to find a solution where its predecessors merely had tried to avoid a problem.

The FERA also provided for medical aid to those on relief, although not specifically until September 10, 1933. The GERA's program included some service by doctors and dentists, but the emphasis of its work was placed upon nursing projects. In November 1933 the state Department of Public Health was "forced to discontinue the services of the four child hygiene nurses who had been rendering itinerant service." No such service was available again until the GERA began early in February 1934 to initiate the first nursing project, providing for 40 nurses who were to serve 120 rural counties where there was no other help. The program also called for the hiring of four nursing supervisors, and this number was increased to six in June 1934, when the child health program was expanded under the leadership of Miss Jane Van De Vrede.[77]

From 1933 to 1935 these nurses, under the aegis of the Department of Health, visited "prospective mothers, babies, young children, and tuberculosis patients" and conducted classes for about 4,000 midwives who, at the time, were delivering about 42 percent of all babies born in the state. They "assisted in the control of communicable diseases through immunization clinics; located some 600 crippled children; and helped make a survey of maternal deaths and the distribution of cancer." They also organized clinics in almost every county.[78]

In the fall of 1934 the GERA received another federal grant to set up a rural health service in cooperation with the state Department of Public Health. This money was used to restore thirteen public health units that had been discontinued during the depression. These two programs eventually provided some sort of nursing service for every county in the state.

To supplement its nursing services, the GERA established tuberculosis diagnostic X-ray clinics and sanitary engineering projects. All the programs were aided by the GERA work projects in sanitation and malarial control. In his yearly report for 1933-1934, Dr. Thomas F. Abercrombie, Director of Public Health, thanked the GERA profusely for its aid. It was evident to him that, without the GERA, Georgia's citizens would have continued to suffer the ravages of disease for a long time. Furthermore, even if the Department of Public Health had managed to get some state funds, it would never have been able to act as quickly and as effectively as it did in cooperation with the GERA. Miss Shepperson shared Abercrombie's feelings, concluding that these health programs reached more people in the state than any of the GERA's other projects.[79]

The GERA also sought to aid the sick by subsidizing medical and dental expenses. A certain amount of resistance came from doctors and dentists to this program, and many counties were not given sufficient funds to provide medical aid to those on relief. Abercrombie complained that "physicians in many sections were not being paid for their services," and such payment as they did receive was often "long delayed." Atlanta dentists added their voices to the general opposition when the GERA made an agreement with the Atlanta Dental College for the use of its facilities in treating relief patients and the policy soon was discontinued.[80]

Besides their obvious value to the state, the nursing projects were among the few that provided work relief for women. The sewing program was the only other program that employed more than a negligible number of women. Although the sewing program did not flourish until after the establishment of the WPA, the GERA was able to make some advances. Its first step was to establish sewing classes for women on relief, paying them relief wages for the hours they spent learning to sew. The garments they produced were used by their families, or, when the material had been supplied by the Red Cross, the clothes went to the families of men on work relief. In some of the larger towns the GERA developed "Utility Projects." In these instances men on work relief went into business and residential areas of a city to collect used clothing, furniture, and other household or business equipment. The women were employed mending the clothing and repairing furniture. These articles also were distributed to destitute families.

Under the CWA the program expanded somewhat, but by January 1934 "less than one-third of the women who should be working on relief projects are working although they have projects approved for about one-half of the women who should be working." In May 1934 Jane Van De Vrede reported that "some excellent beginnings" had been made before the CWA was abolished, but with the decline in funds she anticipated that only 900 of the 14,500 women heads of families could be employed that month.

It was difficult for Miss Van De Vrede to find the kind of work which would be acceptable to the GERA and at the same time be within the capabilities of the women, many of whom had responsibilities at home. She concluded that it would be better to keep these women on direct relief and "teach them the fullest use of their own resources to make the most of a minimum budget." At the same time, the GERA could attempt to stimulate state action in passing old age, mother's, and widow's pensions and provisions for unemployment insurance that would help "the unattached woman in trades and business."[81]

The FERA's principal rural relief program was undertaken by the Rural Rehabilitation Division (discussed separately), but the agency also sponsored other, less ambitious projects in rural areas. There the GERA encouraged canning plants and garden projects. Begun in 1933 the garden program continued to the demise of the FERA. In each county there was a garden supervisor who often worked closely with the Agricultural Extension Service staff of that county. There was also a garden project section in the state office under Fred Welchel, state supervisor for gardens. Each year the projects ran from the spring to the fall. During the winter, garden-project personnel were switched to other rural projects. At the end of the 1934 program Miss Shepperson noted that "the social value of the project was teaching hundreds to work for themselves and pointed the way to ultimate rehabilitation for others and also provided a focal point of interest for entire families, who previously had known nothing but despair and insecurity."[82]

To preserve vegetables not immediately used the GERA began a food-preservation program in 1934, developed in close coordination with the garden program and Rural Rehabilitation Division and under the direction of GERA home economists. Pressure cookers were introduced for the first time into many rural homes where they were significantly misnomered, "precious cookers," and poor rural farm wives were able to display proudly row upon row of polished glass jars around their small cabins. The successful food preserver was the envy of all her neighbors. The preserving of vegetables and the gardens which produced them also introduced many rural families to new foods, and, under the guise of providing subsistence to destitute people, these programs opened the way for home economists to educate rural farm women in the advantages of a properly balanced diet.[83]

A canning program was also developed to handle the large amount of livestock being imported into the state in 1934. When a crippling drought struck the plains states in the spring and summer of that year, the federal government moved quickly to alleviate cattle raisers' distress. Under the FERA's Surplus Relief Corporation, cattle from these farms were purchased and sent to states with adequate pasturage to be fattened and then slaughtered in local abattoirs. L. H. Marlatt, agricultural extension agent in animal husbandry, was chosen to head the GERA's canning operations. He first traveled to Texas to inspect the canning plants already working. When he returned, he began selecting locations for the canning plants. The first was opened on

September 17, 1934, at Augusta, and by mid-November all plants had become operative.

Since most of the engineers and laborers had never worked in a canning plant, it was necessary for Marlatt to provide some sort of training. He had a GERA architect draw plans of the first building upon its completion. This blueprint was used by engineers in constructing the other plants. Marlatt felt that this training and experience provided additional value to the canned meat which was given to relief families during the winter.

At the end of the program the GERA distributed to the counties the equipment it had purchased for the plants. It was used by county agents, home demonstration agents, and vocational agriculture teachers in their live-at-home program. Thus the canning of meat served many purposes. It provided food for the destitute, and it gave work to those on relief rolls and trained them in a skill. The program helped to ease the distress of midwestern farmers, and subsequently the equipment went to the counties to be used by the Extension Service.[84]

In addition to the products raised and processed in the home food preservation program and the meat canning program, the GERA provided one other channel for the distribution of food. Of all the relief programs, none was more appreciated than the Surplus Relief Corporation (SRC). Its goods were used to supplement the wages of those on work relief and the grants to those on direct relief. Perhaps it was because the SRC's donation was in the form of food that the agency was so popular.

The program commenced in November 1933. Foodstuffs were consigned in carload lots to centrally located cities and then distributed to the various county relief administrations. Under the WPA the program was expanded so that the SRC supplied food, not only to relief families, but also to such special projects as the school lunch program.

Unfortunately, the products sent to the state were not always those that were needed. A 1935 University of Georgia report showed that out of seven indigenous products studied only two were produced in enough quantity to meet the state's needs (potatoes and pork). Both of these were pre-supplied by the SRC. Of the five products not produced in sufficient quantity only two were provided by the SRC. It undoubtedly was true that much of the potatoes and pork produced in the state was either withheld from the market or was too expensive for destitute families. In these cases SRC allotments helped, but it seemed wasteful to import products that the state already produced in more than sufficient quantity.[85]

The use of the carload-lot system also worked to the disadvantage of many reliefers. Foodstuffs often had to sit in cars or on docks for many days when bottlenecks occurred, so the SRC could provide only non-perishable items. Two of the seven products surveyed in 1935 which destitute farmers could not receive were milk and eggs, both perishable. Still the program remained quite popular and continued through 1940.

There were a few programs of a white-collar nature that operated outside of the work program, but they initially were of little importance. The GERA's recreation department, for example, sponsored an orchestra in Atlanta late in 1934. Amateur musicians were taken from nine community centers in the city and given free instruction. The GERA also sponsored community night sings, bands, vaudeville, and other such recreational projects around the state. These programs, however, tended to be more complex and less easy to implement. They provided for only a few employees in relation to the number of administrators necessary for supervision, and they produced less physical evidence of their accomplishments than the work projects, making it particularly hard to find sponsors for them. It was not until the WPA began its "service" programs, therefore, that these endeavors bore any real fruit.

NOTES

1. Josephine Chapin Brown, *Public Relief, 1929-1939* (New York: Henry Holt and Company, 1940), p. 43.

2. Arthur F. Raper, *Preface to Peasantry* (Chapel Hill: University of North Carolina Press, 1936), p. 254. State of Georgia, *Report of the Department of Public Welfare* (1932-35), pp. 4-5. "A History of the Georgia Civil Works Administration, 1933-1934," unpublished manuscript, Miss Gay B. Shepperson Manuscripts, pp. 8-9.

3. "The CWA in Georgia," pp. 8-9.

4. Franklin M. Garrett, *Atlanta and Environs: A Chronicle of Its People and Events* (New York: Lewis Historical Publishing Co., Inc., 1954), II, 895. Atlanta *Constitution,* July 14, 1932. Edward Aaron Gaston, "A History of the Negro Wage Earner in Georgia, 1890-1940" (unpublished Ph.D. dissertation, Department of History, Emory University, 1957), p. 370.

5. Atlanta *Constitution,* May 7, 1933.

6. Paul K. Conkin, *Tomorrow a New World: The New Deal Community Program* (Ithaca: Cornell University Press, 1959), p. 30. Russell Lord and Paul H. Johnstone, *A Place on Earth* (Washington: United States Department of Agriculture, Bureau of Agricultural Economics, 1942), pp. 12-13. Atlanta *Constitution,* May 20 and June 18, 1933.

7. "The CWA in Georgia," pp. 8-9.

8. Raper, *Preface,* pp. 256-7.

9. *Ibid.* "The Black Belt Farmers in 1933," unpublished manuscript, Arthur F. Raper MSS, AFR 2-B, 1931-33.

10. Atlanta *Constitution,* March 5 and April 17, 1933. "Community Team Work," *The Survey,* LXVIII, 10 (August 15, 1932).

11. 47 Stat. 709. Arthur E. Burns and Edward A. Williams, *A Survey of Relief and Security Programs* (Washington: WPA, 1938), p. 18.

12. Edith Abbott, *Public Assistance* (New York: Russell and Russell, 1966), II, 607. Thad Holt to Mr. Croxton, October 13, 1932, National Archives, Record Group 69, WPA, FERA, Old Subject Files, box 59 (Herein after cited as NARG 69).

13. "Total [RFC] Disbursements during Russell's Administration," Georgia State Archives, Record Group 24, Child and Family Service (Department of Public Welfare), General Administration, Division of Institutions (central files), WPA, General Correspondence, carton 38. "The CWA in Georgia," p. 13.

14. Holt to Croxton, October 13, 1932, NARG 69, FERA, Old Subject Files, box 59. Roy E. Fossett, "The Impact of the New Deal on Georgia Politics, 1933-1941" (unpublished Ph.D. dissertation, Department of Political Science, University of Florida, 1960), pp. 81, 107. "The CWA in Georgia," pp. 13-15. Atlanta *Constitution,* July 21, 1932, and July 13, 1933. *Report of the Department of Public Welfare* (1932-35), p. 81.

15. *Report of the Department of Public Welfare* 1932-35), p. 31, Georgia Relief Administration, Bulletin No. 1, January 1933, Georgia State Archives, RG 24, WPA, Gen. Corres., carton 38.

16. Interview with Miss Gay B. Shepperson, September 8, 1968. Sarah M. Lemmon, "The Public Career of Eugene Talmadge, 1926-1936" (unpublished Ph.D. dissertation, Department of History, University of North Carolina, 1952), p. 147. Atlanta *Constitution,* April 17, 1933. Savannah *Morning News,* April 17, 1933. Gay Shepperson to Herman De La Perriere, February 24, 1933 (memo), Georgia State Archives, RG 24, WPA, Gen. Corres., carton 38. Report of Robert W. Kelso, January 12, 1933, NARG 69, FERA, Old Subject File, box 59.

17. Report of R. Kelso, January 12, 1933, NARG 69, FERA, Old Subject File, box 59.

18. Report of R. Kelso, January 29, 1933, NARG 69, FERA, Old Subject File, box 59.

19. Report of R. Kelso, February 25, 1933, NARG 69, FERA, Old Subject File, box 59.

20. Report of R. Kelso, March 15, 1933, NARG 69, FERA, Old Subject File, box 59.

21. Reports of R. Kelso, April 20 and 28, and May 6, 1933, NARG 69, FERA, Old Subject File, box 59.

22. *Report of the Department of Public Welfare* (1932-35), p. 81. "Summary (Governor's) of Funds," March 9, 1933, Georgia State Archives, RG 24, WPA, Gen. Corres., carton 38. Atlanta *Constitution,* April 12 and May 11, 1933. Herman De La Perriere to Harry Hopkins, June 1, 1933 (telegram), NARG 69, FERA, State Files (1933-36), box 64. Also see "Black Belt Farmers in 1933," the annual narrative report of J. Cooper Morcock, Jr., 1933, NARG 33, Federal Extension Service, microfilm reel 63.

23. Interview with Gay Shepperson.

24. Aubrey Williams, "The New Deal, A Dead Battery," Williams MSS, Franklin D. Roosevelt Library, Hyde Park, box 44, p. 41. "Market Not Gay's Sole Interest," *The Literary Digest* (June 29, 1935), Gay Shepperson MSS, Random Clippings. "Miss Shepperson, W. A. Smith Hold Enviable Service Records," Richmond *Times Dispatch,* April 29, 1938.

25. Shepperson to Hopkins, June 5, 1933, NARG 69, FERA, State Files, box 64.

26. Memo to Talmadge, n.d. NARG 69, FERA, State Files, box 64.

27. Atlanta *Constitution,* June 11, 1933.

28. *Ibid.,* June 21, 1933. Hopkins to Ransom, June 15, 1933, NARG 69, FERA, State Files, box 64.

29. Atlanta *Constitution,* June 23, 1933. The term "GERA" stands for the Georgia Emergency Relief Administration, the official title of the FERA in Georgia. When Hopkins began to federalize the agency in the state in January 1934, its name was changed to the FERA of Georgia. The term GERA, however, will be used throughout in referring to the state agency.

30. Interview with Gay B. Shepperson.

31. Mrs. Walter D. Lamar to Hopkins, July 26, 1933 (telegram), NARG 69, FERA, State Files, box 64.

32. Report of Alan Johnstone, July 19, 1933, NARG 69, FERA, State Files, No. 406, box 66.

33. Minutes of the GRC, July 18, 19, and 20, 1933, NARG 69, FERA, State Files, No. 460, box 70. Ransom to Hopkins, July 20, 1933, NARG 69, FERA, State Files, box 64.

34. Johnstone and Talmadge, July 27, 1933 (memo), NARG 69, FERA, State Files, box 64.

35. Atlanta *Constitution,* July 20, 1933. W. E. Mitchell to Ransom, August 11, 1933, NARG 69, FERA, State Files, box 64.

36. Minutes of the GRC, July 18, 19, and 20, 1933, NARG 69, FERA, State Files, No. 460, box 70.

37. *Ibid.,* July 18, 19, and 20, and August 3 and 4, 1933.

38. Report of Alan Johnstone, July 19, 1933, NARG 69, FERA, State Files, No. 406, box 66. Johnstone to Hopkins, September 18, 1933, NARG 69, FERA, State Files, No. 406, box 66.

39. Interview with Gay B. Shepperson.

40. Johnstone to Hopkins, September 18, 1933, NARG 69, FERA, State Files, No. 406, box 66. Report of Alan Johnstone, October 19, 1933, NARG 69, FERA, State Files, No. 406, box 66. Interview with Gay B. Shepperson.

41. Johnstone to Hopkins, September 18, 1933, NARG 69, FERA, State Files, No. 406, box 66.

42. *Ibid.*

43. *Ibid.*

44. Johnstone and Talmadge, September 30, 1933 (memo), NARG 69, FERA, State Files, box 64.

45. Report of Alan Johnstone, October 19, 1933, NARG 69, FERA, State Files, No. 406, box 66.

46. Johnstone to Williams, December 12, 1933 (telephone conversation), NARG 69, FERA, State Files, No. 406, box 66. Talmadge to Hopkins, January 1, 1934, NARG 69, FERA, State Files, box 64. Johnstone to Hopkins, January 19, 1934 (memo), NARG 69, FERA, State Files, box 64. Minutes of the GRC, December 18 and 19, 1933, NARG 69, FERA, State Files, No. 460, box 70.

47. Ransom tried to keep Talmadge at bay while he worked on Miss Shepperson. Every night he sent her telegrams asking if Miss Van De Vrede had been fired yet. Although Ransom sided with Talmadge he did not want to have a showdown, so he tried to keep matters up in the air. (Interview with Gay B. Shepperson.)

48. Johnstone to Hopkins, January 19, 1934 (memo), NARG 69, FERA, State Files, box 64. Shepperson to Hopkins, January 2, 1934 (telegram), NARG 69, State Files, box 64. Interview with Gay B. Shepperson.

49. Watson to Corrington Gill, December 12, 1933 (report), NARG

69, FERA, State Files, box 64. Watson to Gill, December 13, 1933 (memo), NARG 69, FERA, State Files, box 64.

50. *Report of the Department of Public Welfare* (1932-1935), pp. 4-5. Atlanta *Constitution,* November 26, 1935.

51. Johnstone to Williams, December 21 and 27, 1933, and January 6, 1934 (telephone conversations), NARG 69, FERA, State Files, No. 406, box 66.

52. Hopkins to Shepperson and Hopkins to Ransom January 4, 1934, NARG 69, CWA, Administrative Correspondence (State), box 10. Hopkins to Talmadge, January 4, 1934, NARG 69, FERA, State Files, Box 64. Atlanta *Constitution,* January 6, 7, and 9, 1934. *The New York Times,* January 7, 1934.

53. Johnstone to Hopkins, January 19, 1934 (memo), NARG 69, FERA, State Files, box 64.

54. Report of Frances Steele, February 20, 1934, and report of Elizabeth A. Brown, January 2, 1934, NARG 69, CWA, Georgia, Administrative Correspondence, microfilm reel 44 C.

55. Reports of Nan Northam, December 29, 1933, and February 15 and 16, 1934, and unsigned field visit-report, February 20, 1934, NARG 69, CWA, microfilm reel 44 C.

56. Shepperson to Hopkins, February 27 and March 31, 1934, NARG 69, CWA, Admin. Corres. (State), box 10.

57. Shepperson to Robert T. Lansdale, July 21, 1934, NARG 69, FERA, State Files, box 64.

58. Watson to Gill, December 13, 1933 (report) (memo), NARG 69, FERA, State Files, box 64.

59. Johnstone to Hopkins, September 18, 1933, NARG 69, FERA, State Files, No. 406, box 66. Report of Alan Johnstone, October 19, 1933, NARG 69, FERA, State Files, No. 406, box 66.

60. "The CWA in Georgia," p. 19. Interview with Gay Shepperson. *The New York Times,* January 6, 1935.

61. FERA, "Monthly Report" (October 1933), p. 4 (August 1933), p. 3 (September 1933), p. 6. Watson to Gill, December 13, 1933 (report), NARG 69, FERA, State Files, box 64.

62. GERA, Bulletin, No. 4, January 1933, Georgia State Archives, RG 24, WPA, Gen. Corres., carton 38.

63. The work programs will be discussed at greater length in Chapter 2.

64. Atlanta *Constitution,* October 1, 1933. FERA, "Monthly Report" (November 1933), p. 19.

65. Alderman to Congressman Carl Vinson, March 14, 1935, NARG 69, FERA, Emergency Education Program, State Series (1933-35), box 5.

66. Klinefelter to Hopkins, April 3, 1935 (memo), NARG 69, FERA, Emergency Education Program, State Series, No. 430, box 59. Atlanta *Constitution,* April 11, 1935.

67. Letter to Congressman Dean, July 15, 1935, NARG 69, FERA, Emergency Education Program, State Series (1933-35), box 5. Atlanta *Constitution,* May 3, 1935.

68. Lent D. Upson to Alderman, May 8, 1935 (memo), NARG 69, FERA, Emergency Education Program, State Series (1933-35), box 5. Letter to Congressman Dean, July 15, 1935, NARG 69, FERA, Emergency Education Program, State Series (1933-35), box 5. Louis M. Stevens to J. Otis Garber, May 7, 1935, NARG 69, FERA, Emergency Education Program, State Series (1933-35), box 5.

69. Talmadge to Congressman Dean, August 12, 1935, NARG 69, FERA, Emergency Education Program, State Series, No. 434, box 59.

70. Klinefelter to H. A. Woodward, February 13, 1935, NARG 69, FERA, Emergency Education Program, State Series (1933-35), box 5. Woodward to Klinefelter, March 12, 1935, NARG 69, FERA, Emergency Education Program, State Series (1933-35), box 5. Collins to Alderman, August 28, 1935 (telegram), NARG 69, FERA, State Series, No. 430, box 59.

71. Punke, Harold H. "Literacy, Relief, and Adult Education in Georgia," *School and Society,* XLII (October 12, 1935), 517. Barrett to Alderman, December 12, 1934, NARG 69, FERA, Emergency Education Program, State Series (1933-35), box 5. Martha I. McAlpine to Dr. Grace Langdon, October 22, 1934, NARG 69, FERA, Emergency Education Program, State Series (1933-35), box 5. WPA of Georgia, Education Division, "Nursery Schools," 1937, p. 3.

72. Interview with Gay Shepperson. Barrett to Alderman, June 21, 1935, NARG 69, FERA, Emergency Education Program, State Series (1933-35), box 5. Barrett to Alderman, September 7, 1934 (telegram), NARG 69, FERA, Emergency Education Program, State Series (1933-35), box 5. Atlanta *Constitution,* June 4 and September 7, 1934. Ernestine L. Friedmann, "Report on Teachers Taining in Workers' Education, Summer of 1934," No. 5293, p. 4. NARG 69, FERA, Emergency Education Program. R. K. White to Hilda Smith, April 20, 1935, NARG 69, FERA, Emergency Education Program, State Series, No. 433, box 59. Ernestine Friedmann to Shepperson, May 15, 1935, NARG 69, FERA, Emergency Education Program, State Series, No. 433, box 59.

73. "Report of First Year's Activities of the Transient Program in Georgia, September, 1933, to July, 1934," NARG 69, FERA, Transient Division Files, Activities Summary (1933-34), box 30.

74. *Ibid.*

75. Shepperson to Hopkins, November 2, 1933, NARG 69, FERA, State Files, No. 420, box 66.

76. Shepperson to Hopkins, January 23, 1934 (telegram), NARG 69, FERA, State Files, No. 420, box 66. Inez F. Oliveros, "The NYA in Georgia," NARG 119, NYA. Atlanta *Constitution,* December 18, 1934. Shepperson to Aubrey Williams, December 19, 1934 (telephone conversation), NARG 69, FERA, State Files, box 64.

77. Georgia Department of Public Health, *Report* (1933-34), p. 144.

78. *Ibid.,* p. 134. Thomas F. Abercrombie, *History of Public Health in Georgia, 1733-1950.* (Atlanta: State Department of Public Health, n.d.), p. 135.

79. Roy E. Fossett, "The Impact of the New Deal on Georgia Politics, 1933-1941" (unpublished Ph.D. dissertation, Department of Political Science, University of Florida, 1960), p. 225. Interview with Gay Shepperson. Department of Public Health, *Report* (1933-34), p. 4.

80. Memo from Gertrude Sturges, April 17, 1934, NARG 69, FERA, State Files, No. 440, box 68. Johnstone to Dr. John T. Hanks, February 21, 1935, NARG 69, FERA, State Files, No. 440, box 68. Department of Public Health, *Report* (1933-34), p. 138.

81. Atlanta *Constitution,* January 13, 1934. Van De Vrede to MacDougall, January 16, 1934 (?) (memo), NARG 69, CWA, microfilm reel 44 C. Van De Vrede to Woodward, May 3, 1934, NARG 69, FERA, State Files, No. 453.1, box 68.

82. Atlanta *Constitution,* October 27 and 30, 1934.

83. Interview with Arthur F. Raper, September 13, 1968.

84. Annual Narrative Report of L. H. Marlatt, Extension agent in Animal husbandry, project 8-D, 1934, NARG 33, Federal Extension Service, microfilm reel 63. Atlanta *Constitution,* August 24, September 18, and November 12, 1934.

85. "Products Needed and Produced," 1935, NARG 33, Correspondence, box 476. U.S. Congress, Senate, Document No. 56, 74th Cong., 1st Sess., 1935, p. 585. See Appendix, Tables 1-7.

2

The Winter of Discontent – The CWA, 1933-1934

In the fall of 1933 national relief leaders realized the FERA's programs were not injecting funds into the country fast enough. Conditions were improving, but Harry Hopkins viewed the prospect of a hard winter with consternation. In response to this situation the Civil Works Administration (CWA) was born on November 9, 1933. The agency was to employ 4 million people, half of whom were to be transferred directly from state relief rolls. The other half were to be selected from among those not on relief, but who had registered with the United States Employment Service.

Unlike the FERA, the CWA was a purely federal organization. Hopkins selected state administrators without the advice of governors, although in most cases the state FERA administrator and his staff were simply given the responsibility for administering the CWA. This was the case in Georgia, where Hopkins designated Miss Gay Shepperson as Civil Works Administrator. He also advised Ronald Ransom that the GRC and the local relief offices would operate the CWA for Georgia. The state CWA's administrative structure corresponded with that of the FERA except that a few new positions, such as State Purchasing Agent and State Safety Director, were created.[1]

Once Miss Shepperson had assembled her state staff, planning at the county level could begin. The GRC notified all county relief organizations that they could accept no further applications for direct relief except in emergency cases. Each county FERA office was closed to be supplanted by a CWA organization, which in most cases remained the same. Each county was to have an administrator, an aide, relief workers, and clerical helpers, just as in the FERA. In addition, bonded assistant disbursing officers, bookkeepers, and safety supervisors were placed in the county offices. The CWA field service acted as the social service organ and supervised these county offices.

The work projects were superintended by a work project supervisor or engineer, aided later by sixty-two district engineers who presided over areas encompassing three or four counties. The county administrators and committees generally remained the same, although they had to be reapproved by the state office. The administrators were all social workers with varying degrees of training, and all but one were women.

Once the county offices were organized, the CWA began active program planning. Local committees suggested projects to the state office, although in most cases FERA projects already under way were simply transferred to the CWA with some changes in organization. The federal government agreed to pay all of the labor costs and half of the material investment. New projects had to be submitted first to the Public Works Administration (PWA), which required greater financial participation by the political subdivision. If the PWA rejected the project, the county committees then could turn to the CWA. Another restriction placed upon planning was that projects had to be of short-term duration. Since the CWA was only a temporary agency, designed to provide winter support, preference was given to projects which could be completed by February 15, 1934, and which involved "a minimum of materials." The CWA warned county committees that it had no plans for continuing the program after February. It was this condition which led to "leaf raking" projects and engendered some of the most severe criticisms of the CWA.[2]

The new projects were placed under extreme restrictions as to size, duration, and cost. The CWA refused to allow projects involving the construction of new buildings, and even if it had, few could have been built under the existing regulations. Thus most of the work done was of a renovating or repairing nature on existing facilities. Although it was of great benefit, there was little in the way of physical improvement clearly visible to the public. The CWA suffered because of this.

In the switch from the FERA to the CWA, methods of employee selection and remuneration also changed. Hopkins had stipulated that half of those employed were to be transferred directly from the FERA's work projects. The other half were to come from the "self-sustaining unemployed," those who had managed to keep off the relief rolls thus far, but who would be in dire need during the winter. Since most of the money for the CWA came from the PWA, wage rates were established according to PWA standards. In the South unskilled laborers were to receive 40 cents an hour and skilled laborers $1.00 an hour or the prevailing wage, whichever was greater. To satisfy rural conditions, counties were allowed to have projects requiring skilled labor when there was none present, but all skilled workers had to be employed for skilled work.

The job of selecting those not on relief to fill CWA positions was given to local managers of the National Reemployment Service (NRS). They were to give preference to veterans of World War I. As soon as the projects were approved, the county administrator was to ask the reemployment office for the requisite number of men. The administrator could continue to apply for workers until the county quota was reached or the project supervisor reported that all jobs had been filled.

There were numerous instances of CWA administrators vetoing the labor selected by the NRS, and other cases of their making specific appointments from the registration rolls. The state CWA office, therefore, warned that neither the administrator nor the project supervisor could interfere in any way with the selection of workers. Since many administrators were members of the reemployment committees, Miss Shepperson advised them to "withdraw from the meeting" when selections for the CWA list were being discussed. After a client had been selected for work on a project, he was "in regular employment," and the relief office was to have nothing further to do with him.[3]

In Georgia the regulations governing relations with the NRS were superfluous. The CWA allotted the state 62,500 relief jobs, of which half were to come from relief rolls. The only problem was that there were 76,597 people on the relief rolls already, and these people had to be cared for first. This situation led to the elimination of eleven counties from the first county job allotments, because they had not secured any projects under the FERA's work program and thus did not have anyone to transfer to the CWA. Eventually the state office cut the quotas for other counties so that by January 1934 most of these eleven counties had a small allotment, but in at least two cases counties received no allotment for relief labor and had to wait to begin a program using NRS replacement labor.

There was trouble everywhere: more people needed work than there were jobs for them to fill. In LaGrange, policemen had to be stationed at the CWA office because of threats from men who could not get jobs. Troup County's allotment was 576, but there were over 1,000 men who needed work. More than 1,800 persons who registered for reemployment in Carnesville were unable to get jobs, and they threatened to "riot and burn trucks and sack the CWA office." By the end of 1933 Lincoln McConnell, head of the NRS in Georgia, noted that 89,597 Georgians had been given work by the CWA, but there were still 176,000 unemployed people on the registration lists.[4]

As pressure grew, state officials petitioned the national office for aid. Ronald Ransom suggested to Hopkins that all intake at relief offices be closed and those on relief be referred to the NRS. This would insure at least some distribution of jobs to the "self-sustaining unemployed." Ransom later visited Hopkins and reiterated his plea, whereupon the relief administrator told him to employ some self-sustaining men.[5]

The national office subsequently increased the state's quota to 76,000, but this still did not provide enough jobs for the nonrelief unemployed. Later the quota was raised to a maximum of 88,949, and a provision was made that certain increases be used to acquire skilled workers "of the class most needed in that particular county." The immediate aim of this order was to promote rapid completion of projects under way, but it also meant that some of the nonrelief unemployed would get jobs. In addition the CWA stipulated that replacements should be made from the NRS and that after December 1, 1933, all labor had to come from the NRS. This latter provision was not followed.

Local trade unions were among those filing the greatest number of complaints concerning the job situation. Their members generally were the ones who had managed to stay off relief longest and were thus last in line for CWA work. The CWA attempted to placate this unrest by securing some of its subsequent labor "through recognized union locals."[6]

Businesses around the state complained of unfair practices in the awarding of contracts for project materials, so Miss Shepperson ordered that "all contracts for supplies and services should be awarded upon competitive sealed bids except in such emergencies where the health or life of persons would be endangered or where it is clearly shown that the government would suffer loss or delay," unless the contract amount was under $300. There were those who argued that this would cause further delays in starting projects, but Special Disbursing Officer C. A. Wood informed Miss Shepperson that the emergency method would "rarely save more than three or four days."[7]

Another complaint regarding bids came from those who had signed the National Recovery Administration code agreements. They charged that the CWA was awarding bids to companies that offered to provide materials at a price below that set by the code authority. Under the CWA's provisions the agency was required to accept the lowest bid regardless of the circumstances, but all bidders had to certify that they were complying with their industry's code. This did little to satisfy companies which felt that those ignoring the code would not hesitate to swear falsely that they were complying.

Various state offices often complained of a definite lack of cooperation on the part of the state CWA office. Commissioner of Agriculture George C. Adams went so far as to assert that Miss Shepperson "would approve no request from a State House official." Any request for the use of CWA or FERA labor would be refused if it came "directly or indirectly from an office of the Georgia State Government." Adams claimed that Miss Shepperson refused even to see him.[8]

Although Adams' comments were unrealistic, it was true that there was often a communication breakdown between the CWA and the state. The CWA, for instance, was asked to build a juvenile detention home in Bibb County. The state previously had considered undertaking the project itself, but had decided against it. When it was proposed as a PWA project, the state refused to apply for funds. Then the matter was brought to the attention of the CWA, and without consulting the state Department of Public Welfare, the office that would be in charge of the home, the agency accepted the project. Needless to say, the department was upset. It had spent considerable time reviewing the proposal and had gathered a great deal of information relative to it. The department claimed that the CWA had made no such study and thus was not in a proper position to pass judgment. The department noted that it always had given "one-day's service on projects that were satisfactory." There should, therefore, have been no objection on that account. If the project was not satisfactory, the "time spent in making it satisfactory is time well spent."[9]

If the state charged the CWA with lack of cooperation, the CWA could return this claim. During its tenure the CWA spent $14.1 million in the state. To this local political subdivisions contributed $1.3

million. The state, however, gave only $57.60, less than any other state
in the nation except for Tennessee, which contributed nothing at all.
The only way Georgia aided the CWA was through her officials. Some
state officers were employed by the CWA in an advisory capacity and
on certain occasions as supervisors of specialized projects. When they
supported the agency, they "cooperated very splendidly and materially
aided the continuance of the program."[10]

Considering the political situation in Georgia at the time, friction
between the state and the CWA was predictable. There were, however,
circumstances of lack of communication and cooperation within the
CWA administrative structure itself. In some instances the state office
expected too much from the local administrators. Many of the very
complicated sets of instructions distributed to the counties were
absolutely unintelligible to administrators who were poorly educated.
Often the county offices were not advised immediately of changes in
procedure and thus did not understand why so much of their paperwork was returned to them for corrections or revision. Added to this
lack of coordination and communication was the huge mass of forms
and plethora of instructions that deluged the county administrator to
the extent that she could not see the program for the paper.

When the county administrator was stymied, she became ineffective,
and local politicans, who felt they knew how to get things done, lost
respect for her ability and authority and often withdrew their support.
Thus the administrator was placed in a precarious position. A lack of
proper communication made her seem ineffective and brought her the
animosity of local residents who complained to Hopkins or Roosevelt.
When the state CWA office investigated these charges, it often repri-
manded the local administrator without considering its own contribution
to the situation.

Sometimes the criticisms of county residents were not the result of
inadequate state-county CWA communications, but stemmed from
mistakes made in the summer of 1933, when the FERA was organized
so quickly that officials were willing to accept unqualified people as
administrators, case workers, and office staff. These people, besides
being untrained, were poorly organized and supervised. Under the CWA,
programs grew even more and local personnel proved unable to cope
with their constant changes and increasing complexity.

Even some qualified county administrators, especially those who were natives, buckled under intense political pressure. Interference in the selection process was one of the most serious abuses reported by Miss Shepperson's field supervisors. In Martinez, Georgia, the clerk of the court was alleged to have "passed on all applications and if found of political value, the applicants were placed on Civil Works jobs." Lincoln McConnell reported "numerous cases throughout the state of enthusiastic project supervisors appointing people to the CWA jobs with little or no regard for either the local Civil Works Administrator or the local National Reemployment Office."

In Clayton County just the opposite circumstances appeared to exist. Here the "CWA administrator and the relief administrator seem to think that these agencies were created for their own benefit to give them the undisputed right to hand out favors to their friends and relatives and to the henchmen of 'Boss' of a certain political faction that happens to be, at this time, 'in the saddle.'"[11]

Another difficulty which field supervisors noted was that county staffs were often insufficient to handle large relief rolls. In Appling County, for example, the "aide" was forced to carry over 100 cases. Frequently, where personnel was limited, a particularly heavy burden fell upon the county administrator, who was forced to assume a substantially greater load than anyone else. This gave her less time to devote to the supervision of those in her office who were often untrained and desperately needed personal control.[12]

The state office's problems did not end when a supervisor discovered incompetent personnel, for often it was impossible to find qualified replacements within the county. Situations such as these led Miss Shepperson to hire county administrators and staffs from the outside. This served a twofold purpose in allowing them to build an efficient relief machine and in lessening the chance of their succumbing to political pressure.

The success of local administrations depended upon other conditions, too. Relief offices might be "inadequate, crowded, and cold," and sometimes there was no separate office space in the county or city buildings for the CWA. Supervisors reported that county staffs frequently occupied jury and courtrooms, and that when a trial was in progress, all office work had to be suspended.[13]

The same pressures and problems affecting the county administrations extended throughout the operation of the CWA, most significantly to the workers and the projects themselves. It was predictable that there would be trouble in the transfer of so many people from the FERA to the CWA. Both the state and county offices worked diligently to make the transition as smooth as possible, and it was to their credit that relatively little trouble arose. Outside influence was always present when there were jobs to be handed out, and it was not always personal in nature. Citizens of Statesboro in Bulloch County, for instance, put extreme pressure upon the city engineer to pad his estimates for CWA labor so that the city could use the extra money to pay its part of material costs on the projects.[14]

Other complaints arose over the projects themselves. Some were shifted from the PWA when the CWA was formed, radically changing the nature of their implementation. Cities occasionally discontinued their support of such projects and in doing so lost what money they already had contributed. The situation was particularly critical in the bigger cities of the state where larger projects were planned involving a greater contribution from municipal governments. Here the relief load was especially heavy, and the cities demanded "a reasonable return" for the money they spent. The CWA was hard pressed to develop suitable projects under these circumstances, so cities became hesitant to contribute any more money.

All of these difficulties triggered a steady stream of complaints to Washington and Atlanta. Initially the investigation office of the PWA handled these complaints, but after February 20, 1934, Miss Shepperson was required to do it herself. She informed her division heads of their new responsibilities and cautioned them to be particularly conscious of complaints coming from "Senators and Congressmen the White House and Mr. Hopkins' office." Investigators usually found allegations to be unfounded. Often the dissatisfaction arose from those who had not received jobs and felt that they were more qualified for relief than the workers selected in their place. Veterans, for example, always claimed that it was their country's duty to provide for them first.[15]

In some instances complaints were made that could not be proven, most often in regard to political or personal interference in the selection process. In these cases investigators had to deal with advisory committeemen or others who were also county officials, and, even where this was not true, the investigator might expect to find a certain bias when local patricians sat in judgment over a depressed class of people.

Unfortunately, some complaints were lodged that were not considered properly. The state office's initial response to critical letters was to refer them to the very people accused of the infraction. There were also many occasions where complainants received no reply at all. Miss Shepperson later noted that these problems occurred by accident and not by design. She informed her mail-room staff to be on the lookout for such letters and to refer them to her as they arrived. There was always a flood of mail, however, and some complaints were either lost or referred to the wrong division.[16]

As of March 1, 1934, of 6,829 complaints sent the CWA, 3,801 already had been investigated. In addition there were 1,013 second complaints indicating perhaps that only about one-seventh of all those filed were initially settled improperly. The record was fairly impressive, considering the rapidity with which the program was implemented and the temporary nature of its existence.[17]

Local work projects were the responsibility of local governments. The county commissioners and county engineers drew up plans for proposed projects and submitted them to the state office. The local government agreed to pay for half of the materials, and the project had to be "socially useful." When these conditions were met, the county or city submitted the proposals to one of the six district engineers who examined them and sent them on to the state office with his recommendations. It was at the state office that final decisions were made on all local projects.

These projects represented a small but important part of the total program. Those such as street, school, and governmental building repairs could never have been undertaken at the time if the CWA had not provided the labor and half the materials. Road and street repairs usually consisted of grading, ditching, and topsoiling county roads, clearing right-of-way, constructing culverts, and repairing bridges. The state government did not favor these projects because of their impermanence and because it felt this work was the proper concern of the "road commissioners." The CWA responded that they employed a large number of men with little material that was not obtained from local governments. There was less opposition to the roadwork in cities and towns where the program consisted of paving streets and sidewalks. These improvements were more permanent in nature and did not involve any encroachment on the state's prerogatives. Unfortunately, municipal street projects were harder to arrange because local communities were unable to "furnish their share of the material."[18]

Projects concerning work on schools, playgrounds, and parks were very popular in the cities, although the latter two areas were subject to the "leaf raking" stigma. Projects which involved schools were the most popular of all. In addition to improving conditions for local school children, they put considerable pressure upon the state government to play a greater role in raising standards within recently remodeled buildings. The great popularity of the school-repair projects led the state CWA Works Division to place more emphasis on them than on any others.

Most of the work on school buildings was concentrated in the northern part of the state. In the southern counties, drainage projects and water works took priority. Many cities had fallen far behind the needs of their residents in providing these facilities, and because of the relation of these two types of projects to the health of the communities, they took precedence over the school improvements. The need was greater in the low, level southern part of the state which tended to accumulate large amounts of stagnant water. The topography of south Georgia also presented more of a problem in relation to the removal of waste products. It was there that the federal drainage programs were undertaken, and the local projects dovetailed nicely with them, increasing their usefulness beyond the contribution of an individual municipality.

If the local work projects played a relatively small part in the CWA, the service projects were even less successful. Most of these fell under the jurisdiction of the Division of Women's Work which controlled:

> Sewing projects
> Home demonstration projects
> Canning plants
> Hot lunch program
> Nursing projects
> Dental assistance
> Maternity and infancy programs
> Nursery schools
> Library projects
> Clerical service
> Historical research
> Community service projects
> Music projects
> Light work projects

None of these projects came to be well developed under the CWA. In the first place, most were planned very quickly and under severe restrictions as to cost and duration. The temporary nature of the CWA limited their scope. The agency was designed primarily to disburse a lot of money in a short time, and the service projects suffered because they were unable to fulfill that role. In 1935, when the WPA arose and assumed the responsibility for all FERA programs, many of the service projects which barely had begun under the CWA were expanded and given new life. Even though the CWA service projects failed in 1933-1934, they provided the basis upon which the WPA was able to build a successful program.

Of far greater importance to Georgians that winter were the federal projects. These were drawn up by various federal departments in cooperation with the CWA. The CWA then allocated money to each state to finance them under the general supervision of the state CWA office. The actual work came under the command of federal supervisors who acted much as the project supervisors in the local programs. The state office handled all other matters and acted as a liaison between the project supervisors and various cooperating state departments and federal agencies in the state.

At first the CWA set aside a quota of 20,000 employees for federal projects in Georgia. At the time there were 67,000 people on the relief rolls, 55,000 of whom were slated for work on nonfederal projects. This left an "overage" of 12,000 people, so that the federal allocation actually created 8,000 new jobs. Because the federal projects were of greater value than the local projects, Miss Shepperson decided to transfer workers from the latter to the former to insure satisfactory progress.

Although projects were broken down by county, a master plan was drawn up in the state office. This caused some initial delays, but the lost time was more than recouped in the understanding resulting from clear instructions to the counties and project supervisors. Insofar as possible, the state office tried to use only labor from the county in which each project was situated, and all but ten persons employed were residents of the state.

On December 1, 1933, the first project was sent to the counties, and by January 1, 1934, 487 approved projects covering 19 federal subjects had been distributed. Before February 15 the total had risen to 1,003 approved projects covering 37 subjects.

The 16 statistical projects comprised the greatest number of different undertakings of a single type, from surveys of cotton statistics to retail

price reporting. The Department of Agriculture sponsored two programs
in phoney peach disease and sweet potato weevil eradication, and there
were two research programs, one in archaeological excavations and the
other an historic American buildings survey. Eight projects were initiated
to improve government properties, and work was done in Georgia's
national forests and parks. Improvements were made at fish hatcheries,
at the buildings and grounds of the Veterans Administration's property
in the state, and at four army posts. The two engineering projects were
concerned with a coast and geodetic survey and photo mapping under
the geological survey. One reemployment office was maintained as was
one transient camp in Fulton County. The most important federal
projects, however, were the health projects undertaken in cooperation
with the Treasury Department and the Department of Agriculture.
These programs dealt with rodent control in connection with typhus
fever, typhus fever control, pest mosquito control, malarial control, and
rural sanitation.[19]

The Bureau of Entomology of the Department of Agriculture and
the Treasury Department's Public Health Service joined with the state
Department of Public Health under Dr. Thomas F. Abercrombie and
the Georgia CWA to rid the state of malaria. Although the mortality
rate from this disease had declined since 1860, in 1930 it was still one
of the seven major causes of death in the state. Georgia had begun
operations in malaria control as early as 1923, but the depression had
severely curtailed its ability to continue. The FERA initiated projects
in 120 counties which were now bolstered by CWA labor, and plans
were laid to undertake similar projects in the other 39 counties. The
agency concentrated primarily upon drainage projects, and its accomplishments were noteworthy.[20]

Although Abercrombie was generous in his praise of the CWA, he
noted that its restrictions had caused some problems not present in
1933. The "lack of provision for the matching of local material contributions with CWA material contributions . . . led local governments
to conserve such few funds as they had for donation on those types of
building construction projects which would receive CWA materials to
match local material contributions." This caused a drop in the quality
of malarial projects "where materials were necessary for proper engineering design." Areas which needed the most work invariably could
provide the least amount of labor. The result was that certain com-

promises had to be made with "planned malaria control principles,"
and the projects which were undertaken were "far more secondary in
value than uncared for projects in other areas."[21]

The Public Health Service, the state Department of Public Health,
and the CWA also cooperated in the rural sanitation projects, the major
purpose of which was to construct sanitary privies in rural areas. A
study of rural sanitary conditions showed that 10 percent of all black
farm families and over 2 percent of all white farm families had no
facilities of any kind. The Farm Housing Survey published in 1934
revealed much the same conditions in relation to screening for blacks,
although its samples were very small. Even where screens and privies
did exist, they were often useless and sometimes hazardous.[22]

The CWA experienced problems in initiating the sanitation program because of regulations which prohibited the use of its labor on
private property. Still the agency managed to construct 8,470 privies,
and, after the program was taken over by the FERA in April 1934,
a new ruling liberalized these restrictions, although a decline in
available funds partially negated its effect.[23]

Even where sanitary work was undertaken, its value was often
limited. It did no good to put screens on sharecropper shacks with wide
cracks in the walls and floors. Furthermore, many of the poorer people
who received screens did not own their own homes and thus had no
incentive to maintain the improvements. Many of the screening jobs
were not properly reinforced, and since it was much easier for a child
to kick open a door than to use his hands, these screens did not last
long. The most serious impediment to the success of sanitation projects,
however, was the recipients' lack of health education. They simply
did not understand the proper use or the importance of these improvements, and as a result screens were abused and privies ignored. Those in
other CWA programs, particularly the nursing services, tried to correct
this problem, but their work was not well coordinated with that of
the sanitation program, so there was no assurance that those who received
these facilities would be trained in their care and use.

On February 2, 1934, ten federal projects were terminated or, if
incomplete, transferred to state and local programs. The rest of the
federal programs were continued through April, when they were all to
be completed or discontinued. The federal projects had "filled a gap that
existed in the state program by employing an unusually large percent of

skilled employees that the lack of a state quota prevented placing on
state and local projects." The large numbers of workers who left the
program during its course for outside work gave some indication of the
quality of personnel on CWA projects. The populace greatly appreciated
the federal work programs, and, when it was announced that they were
being terminated, the state office was flooded with appeals that
certain projects not be left unfinished.

A contemporary observer noted that these people were not so concerned "with the amount of money spent as with the accomplishment
and local benefits." Unlike the local projects, these federal programs
provided a good deal of permanent improvement, which he ascribed
to the "generally high type of supervision furnished by the Federal
government and the earnest and conscientious attitude of the workers."
Whatever the validity of the reasons, the result was apparent. The federal
projects had left more concrete signs of their existence than the local
projects, and it was perhaps because of this lasting corporeal evidence
that they were deemed the more successful of the two programs.[24]

At the same time that federal projects were being curtailed, the rest
of the CWA moved toward liquidation. Beginning on February 16,
1934, Miss Shepperson started to "taper off at ten percent a week,"
making the first cuts in the rural areas. She anticipated that with the
coming of spring, rural workers would be able to find jobs on farms,
while specific provisions would have to be made for their urban
counterparts.[25]

Although Miss Shepperson was determined to make the closing of
projects and reduction of workers as painless as possible, there was still
dissatisfaction. She did not intend to leave any project incomplete
which could be finished by May 1, but the large number of complaints
arriving at the CWA's state and federal offices just after its demise indicated that many people were unhappy. Some letters reported that
projects begun under the CWA were useless now because they were
only half finished. In other cases cities had made large purchases of
materials which were standing in rotting piles. Many letters dealt
with the care given to displaced workers. Most of these indicated that
there were no provisions for those taken off CWA projects, although
later many were rehired under the FERA's new emergency work
program.[26]

While Georgians criticized the quality and type of some local projects,

their opposition was relatively mild compared with that in other parts
of the nation. It was in relation to labor policies that the Georgia CWA
evoked the most violent attacks. Since all unemployables became the
responsibility of local governments when the CWA was formed, that
agency had to deal only with workers.

The CWA's labor regulations for wages and hours were those of the
PWA, so there was a general 30 hours per week or 130 hours per calendar
month limit on working time and a three-zone wage scale. The southern
scale, of which Georgia was a part, paid 40 cents an hour for unskilled
and $1.00 an hour for skilled labor, the lowest in the nation. These hours
and rates held for all except clerical workers and professionals and those
on CWA roadwork. The former were paid a somewhat higher wage than
the skilled rate ($12.00 a week) and could work up to 39 hours a week.
The latter were paid at a rate of 30 cents an hour in accordance with
section 204c of the National Industrial Recovery Act.

Hopkins never wanted to use the PWA wage scale for the CWA, and
southerners heartily agreed with him. Many Georgians felt it was too
high, causing undue pressure upon prevailing wage scales in the state and
luring workers away from private enterprise. The CWA, therefore, provided
that workers might be dropped from the relief rolls if they were offered
jobs in National Recovery Administration code businesses.

The greatest furor, however, was created by the farm community. The
Georgia Relief Commission ruled that CWA laborers should be "laid
off . . . if needed for agriculture" and did not have to be given their jobs
back after seasonal employment such as cotton chopping or picking.
Miss Shepperson notified her county administrators not to put the names
of farm laborers on the relief rolls after early December 1933. Only
those whose names were already on the rolls were to remain, and "farm
day laborers, sharecroppers, or renters who have made nothing beyond
their indebtedness for the year and are penniless and without any means
of support" could be added.

The farmers seemed satisfied during the early winter, but many still
warned that the cotton reduction program was going to force farm
laborers out of agriculture. Miss Shepperson herself estimated that 25,000
of the 75,000 to 80,000 people on relief in the spring would be there
because of the government's farm program. When she announced forthcoming labor reductions in February 1934, her office was flooded with
rural letters asking for the continuation of CWA projects. Petitioners

claimed that the CWA was the only source of income left to them after the reduction program.

Some observers felt that landlords were "unloading white and negro tenants, who they used to care for during the winter, onto relief rolls," a practice reminiscent of the Red Cross experience in giving rural relief. One commentator warned, "When the whole thing is over there will be terrible labor problems. You can't expect a man getting from 30 to 40 cents an hour to go back to farm labor at a dollar a day and less."[27]

In the weeks before the planting season, Georgia farmers came to realize the truth of this prophecy. When laborers proved reluctant to return to the farm, several local administrators and committees forced them. Occasionally, county committees voted to give no work relief during the cotton-picking season, because farmers were unable to persuade workers to pick cotton at 40 to 50 cents per 100 pounds when they could get CWA work at 30 cents an hour. In one county the administrator gave "almost no relief in February and March," since on March 1, landlords customarily made their yearly contracts with tenants. The administrator's plan was to "starve" laborers into taking farmwork. In essence the state office approved of "encouraging" these people to return to the farms, but this method "carried it too far."

Farmers complained about their loss of labor, but government officials viewed conditions differently. Reemployment Director Lincoln McConnell explained, "There is no occasion for alarm that the CWA program will disturb farm operations in Georgia. There is cause for grave concern, however, in that approximately 200,000 destitute unemployed may not share directly in the benefits of the program for no better reason than that they had somehow managed to stay off relief rolls." McConnell asserted that there was no labor shortage on the farms. He had sent out "hundreds of letters with stamped, self-addressed postcards enclosed, offering to supply labor to any farmer or employer who had been a victim of this situation." He received not a single reply.[28]

There were those who agreed that farmers would suffer from the CWA's wage scale, but saw the situation as a blessing in disguise. One observer noted that farm labor got $3.00 a week or less, while common labor received $9.00 a week on CWA projects. Farmers could never compete with this wage scale and would have to plant less. Ultimately this was good, he reasoned, because Georgia and the other southern states were "just about through as cotton producing states." The CWA wage scale merely would hasten the shift from cotton to more profitable crops.

This commentator saw another advantage to the CWA. He explained, "For 65 years the South has been the sweatshop of the nation," because southerners "were afraid of the Negro." In "keeping him [the Negro] down . . . we dragged ourselves down too." Of course, this was precisely what many large landowners wanted to do. It was the only way of making a profit in a severely depressed market. By discarding racial wage differentials, the CWA would help to eliminate this situation.[29]

Workers as well as employers had complaints about labor policies. Local trade unions wrote to Miss Shepperson and to Hopkins that heretofore their men had been able to stay off the relief rolls. When the CWA program was announced, union members registered with the NRS. Those already on relief, however, received work first. This practice was especially unfair, the unions claimed. Many of those who previously had registered as skilled laborers, but really were not, now got the jobs that union members should have had.

Veterans charged that nonveterans on the relief rolls were given jobs first, despite the government's long-standing policies to the contrary. Some workers complained that they were displaced from state or municipal jobs that were taken over by the CWA. When such cases came to the attention of the state office, however, adjustments were made.[30]

Most CWA workers were happy with the program. There were some instances where local supervisors treated workers unfairly, but these were infrequent. Even when the CWA cut the minimum wage in the southern zone from 40 cents to 30 cents an hour, there was little dissatisfaction. Miss Lorena A. Hickok, a special investigator for Hopkins, reported that the general feeling seemed to be, "It's a whole lot better than being laid off." Workers found that after the wage cut they still were getting more than they ever had received. What they lost in wages was often made up for by the distribution of surplus commodities.

White-collar workers were particularly happy with the CWA. Many had "reached the end of their resources," and the CWA provided more white-collar jobs than there had been under the earlier FERA program. Miss Hickok noted that the plight of the white-collar worker in Atlanta was "pitiable." These people had made a decent salary and generally counted themselves among the upper classes. It was harder for them to ask for relief work than it was for the blue-collar laborer who always had been near the bottom of the economic ladder. All Georgians, whether they agreed with the wage scale, clamored for more jobs, but the cry was particularly prevalent in Atlanta. It was there that Miss Hickok encountered the greatest lack of realization that the program was only temporary.[31]

When the people of the state received more money, retailers were happier, and the situation was no different when the paymaster was the federal government. Merchants responded to the CWA with avid support as their sales increased. The only entrepreneurial complaints about the CWA arose where relief workers were paid wages that exceeded NRA code levels. These instances were restricted mainly to lumber, fertilizer, and sugar refining.[32]

The federal government's insistence upon standard wage rates for all races provided ammunition for the CWA's opponents. Southern critics of the New Deal never missed an opportunity to attack Roosevelt when any agency appeared to destroy racial customs. Local officials frequently attempted to circumvent or ignore provisions that tended to equalize the races. Failing in this tactic, they raised age-old Confederate banners in defense of southern womanhood. Henry A. Hunt, black principal of the Fort Valley Normal and Industrial School and later special adviser for the Farm Credit Administration, felt that in regard to CWA wage scales these people had been successful. He claimed that whites working on roads and school buildings were getting 90 cents a day while blacks received only 40 cents. Even where such blatant discrimination did not exist, blacks seemed to get less. Few blacks could qualify as skilled laborers, so the great majority of them always were paid the minimum wage.[33]

When Governor Talmadge attacked the CWA, Hopkins sent Miss Hickok to Savannah to evaluate the situation there. Her investigations revealed an intense dissatisfaction based primarily on ignorance, racism, and politics. She noted five specific areas of dissension concerning the city's CWA program. First, and perhaps foremost, was the racial antagonism that surrounded the CWA. Blacks were getting $12.00 a week, twice as much as common labor had been paid previously. Blacks, who had been quick to apply for relief under the FERA, now held CWA jobs, whereas whites, who had "held on as long as possible," were jobless. Savannah residents also were suspicious of the CWA, because they believed it to be drawing blacks into the city from the surrounding countryside. Major William Artley, the local Civil Works Administrator, denied the charge, but the fear persisted.

The third problem Miss Hickok mentioned arose from initially inadequate case investigations which resulted in "many people being on the CWA who did not need relief." During the first weeks of the FERA, there were "no trained investigators to speak of." Politics had played a great part in the selection of workers, and political prestige had influenced the choice of staff. Miss Hickok noted that the city office was "full of Junior League members." Although the mayor was now "yelling for investigations" by city detectives, "in the beginning he fought against trained investigators." All of this had resulted in the placement of unskilled or semi-skilled workers in jobs which called for skilled labor. With the quota filled, well qualified union men could not be hired.

Miss Hickok could have begun a reinvestigation of relief families, but that would have been especially difficult in regard to the blacks. Many of them did not know how old they were, who their parents were, or what their past employment experience had been. Families often were broken; frequently fatherless. A great deal of movement within the black ghetto areas made it difficult to locate families.

The fourth problem which Miss Hickok discovered involved local employers and nearby farmers who claimed there was a labor shortage. Miss Hickok's probe re-enforced Lincoln McConnell's statement that such allegations were unfounded. Finally Miss Hickok noted the influence of politics upon the CWA. A man told her, "Before Hopkins kicked out the Governor and his committee, it was well known here that you didn't have a ghost of a show to get relief or anything else without the approval of judge Rouke [*sic*], the Savannah member of the committee." The entire city was "alive with politics," and those who depended upon political favors were reluctant to support a program that was a bone of contention between the mayor and his following and Major Artley and the county commissioners.[34]

Miss Hickok's report on Savannah was the only remaining document of its scope; however, other reports and letters regarding isolated subjects indicated that the conditions she found in Savannah were widespread. She and others who were able to achieve an overview of the state agreed that the CWA was not going to be of much help. In the first place, it was only temporary, notwithstanding the optimism of local newspapers and the desires of those the agency employed. Second, and far more important, the CWA really did not get at the root of Georgia's troubles. While residents were complaining about labor shortages, perspicacious observers saw a "huge labor surplus" caused by the gradual decline of the one-crop cotton system and the failure of industry to develop quickly enough to absorb those leaving agriculture.

The people of the state were "overwhelmingly ignorant and backward, and they have terrible health and social problems" which could not be solved by such stopgap measures as the CWA. To cope with Georgia's problems, local officials and those higher up on the economic scale would have to mobilize to help the poor. The state's infant industries, in competition with established northern firms, claimed they were forced to economize by maintaining rock-bottom wages, which they propagandized to whites as holding the color line. Farmers struggling with the cotton and tenancy systems established by their predecessors were in the same position, and all of their problems were exacerbated by the depression.

In turn the traditional social attitudes often created to mask pecuniary motives grew to trap these people in their own hypocritical catch phrases. By the 1930s even those who need not have feared the black's competition responded passionately to the demagogic appeals of the Talmadges all over the South. These feelings even penetrated the upper echelons of the relief agencies. Miss Van De Vrede, head of Women's Work, told Miss Hickok that her greatest problem was with the "southern gentle women, last survivors of the old aristocracy, and Negresses." Miss Van De Vrede wanted to establish a program wherein the former would instruct the latter in domestic service. "The only trouble," she lamented, "is that the Negresses won't go in for it. They don't want to learn how to be servants."[35]

Miss Shepperson, one of the most "liberal" New Deal officials in Georgia, simply noted that she went as far as possible in helping blacks. When aiding them meant the withdrawal of local support and subsequently the complete cancellation of projects, she backed down. Perhaps one could not have asked for more, but ironically the very programs designed to help all people often were used to perpetuate further injustices upon the black race.

Backed fully by Harry Hopkins, Miss Shepperson ultimately had little trouble with local opponents, but when her adversaries consisted of the governor and her own advisory committee, she had to appeal to her boss for help. Opposition from Talmadge and the GRC grew to a climax during the early days of the CWA. The GRC was more of a nuisance than a threat as Talmadge's lackey, but it still caused Miss Shepperson a great deal of anxiety. She reported that "individual members sat in her office making decisions on important matters" in "continued session." She felt that the GRC was attempting to take over the control of the FERA and the CWA, and she asked Alan Johnstone to remind the commission of its advisory status.[36]

Of far greater importance to both Hopkins and Miss Shepperson than the GRC was Governor Talmadge himself. Talmadge had opposed both the FERA and the CWA work programs from the beginning, but had made no real disturbance until after the CWA came into being. Under the FERA, wages had been pegged at 30 cents an hour. Talmadge remarked in his newspaper, the *Statesman,* that, although work relief was a good thing, 30 cents an hour was too much to pay workers unless farm prices were first tripled.

When the CWA was established and the minimum wage raised to 40 cents an hour, Talmadge became more vitriolic in his attacks. On February 16, 1934, Hopkins ordered the minimum wage reduced to 30 cents an hour or the prevailing wage (whichever was higher), effective no later than March 2. Talmadge hailed this as a victory for the South, although the move was really just one of a series of provisions designed to curtail the program so that its liquidation would not be too great of a shock.

This wage-rate reduction followed a rather personal and highly publicized exchange of insults between Hopkins and Talmadge. On December 19, 1933, the governor had lashed out at the CWA, saying that wage scales were too high to permit business and the farmer to compete. Hopkins wired Ransom that the CWA stood ready to withdraw its program from Georgia if it really was in competition with private enterprise. He told reporters, "All that guy [Talmadge] is looking for is headlines. . . . He doesn't contribute a dime, but he's always yapping."[37]

Ransom replied that the governor "has at all times cooperated fully with the Georgia Relief Administration and the Georgia CWA and I greatly regret your undignified reference to him as a yapping guy." The people of Georgia, however, did not agree with Ransom. Telegrams from all over the state poured into Hopkins' office condemning the governor and pleading for continuation of the program. Some letters not only supported the CWA, but also praised Hopkins' stand against the man who seemed to hold Georgia in a political stranglehold. Undoubtedly, part of the support for Hopkins' action came from the governor's opponents who were not concerned with the labor situation, but many more made no mention of the political angle and indicated a genuine interest in the CWA.[38]

Talmadge's outburst had nothing to do with Hopkins' subsequent removal of the GRC and the placing of all relief activities directly under Miss Shepperson's control. The furor created over this public exchange of enmities, however, served as a smoke screen to hide Hopkins' real motives—a reaction to Talmadge's attempt to place his own purchasing agents in the agency. In any case the move to federalize the FERA in Georgia made the state's residents more aware of the temporary nature of the CWA.

Perhaps the greatest limitation of the CWA was that it lasted for such a short time. Many projects no sooner had gathered full steam than they were reduced, and employment peaked only two months after the program began. In phasing out the CWA, Miss Shepperson had to decide which of the local projects to complete. To speed up progress on the more favorable projects, she transferred workers from other areas, leaving some projects unfinished, and upsetting local residents.

Miss Shepperson handled the reduction well, so that there was relatively little trouble in the transition from the CWA to the FERA's emergency work program. The administration and nature of the projects changed very little, except that everything operated on a much smaller scale. The federal government could no longer share in the cost of materials, except where such purchases had been arranged under the CWA. Also all labor except for certain skilled workers had to come from relief rolls.[39]

Similar changes took place in administration. First, the field staff was reduced, and in December 1934 the entire structure was reorganized with smaller county office staffs. Alan Johnstone applauded this move to "reduce administrative expense and personnel," and noted "a splendid esprit de corps in the organization, which is manned in all its divisions by professional personnel of a higher order than is found in most relief administrations." The field service of the FERA was "organized on a functional basis . . . and professional personnel have perfect freedom of operation and authority in their fields without friction." Johnstone's observations were confirmed by a report from James H. Genung, an assistant to Aubrey Williams. He was "more than impressed with the enthusiastic and efficient Georgia Administration."

The Georgia program was retarded only by local and state officials who refused to cooperate. In the educational program, for example, all appointments were made "through the County and District School Boards." The state's educational administration was "political throughout" and thus presented serious problems for the FERA.[40]

Observers could offer no solution to these political intrusions other than the complete federalization of the FERA in Georgia. The political problem came to a head in the early months of 1935 when Georgia House Speaker Pro-Tem Ellis Arnall (later governor) introduced a resolution "assailing the federal government for allegedly depriving Georgians of administrative jobs in the state." He called on the Georgia congressional delegation "to put an end to this new era of carpetbag days." Senators Walter F. George and Richard B. Russell, Jr., took up Arnall's call, first in relation to outsiders in the administration of the Home Owners Loan Corporation (HOLC) in the state, and later to those in all federal agencies.

The legislature struck a committee to investigate relief in Georgia. In the meantime, Representatives Robert C. W. Ramspeck and Paul Brown introduced an amendment to the pending HOLC Bill providing that "no one can be appointed in any regional or state offices of the HOLC who is not a citizen of the state or region served by the office." Senators George and Russell supported the Brown Amendment when the bill reached the Senate in March.[41]

Curiously, Talmadge took no part in this action. He told Johnstone that he "had no patience with the 'carpetbag' charges; that he thought Miss Shepperson was administering relief as well as anybody could administer it." Talmadge believed that the whole idea of relief was wrong in principle and ought to be abolished in Georgia. He "hoped the committee would recommend a cessation of relief in Georgia," and to help matters along he would "hold up signing applications for relief in Georgia until they should report." Johnstone informed Hopkins that the governor's kind words for Miss Shepperson were nothing more than a cover-up for his own actions. He said, "The Governor finds himself embarrassed by reason of his opposition to the Recovery Program and wished to make an approach to the Administration." A more probable explanation was that Talmadge thought he had gained some allies in the state legislature who would do his dirty work for him. He had little to lose; if the delegation found nothing wrong with the recovery program and suggested that the state pass legislation in support of it, he could always veto such legislation. The state still had given no money to the relief programs and was not about to do so now.[42]

As soon as Arnall introduced his motion to the state house, the FERA began an investigation into his charges. It discovered that of the 3,998 administrative employees as of February 7, 1935, 3,894 or 97.4 percent were state residents at the time of their employment. Of the 104 non-residents, 52 or 1.3 percent of the total number were from the South, and an equal number were from other regions. Furthermore, the FERA indicated that of the 3,518 persons in the state administration as of October 1934, 3,301 or 98.83 percent were recruited from the relief rolls.[43]

For its part, the legislature's committee sent a delegation to Washington composed of Speaker Eurith D. Rivers; Roy V. Harris, House floor leader; William M. Lester, Senate Appropriations Committee chairman; Hermon Watson, House Education Committee chairman; W. Fred Scott, Senate floor leader; and L. A. Farrell, a reporter for the Atlanta *Constitution*. Once there, these men became convinced of the relief program's value and they returned to Atlanta supporting it. Alan Johnstone then drew up six enabling bills, and Rivers introduced one of them under his own name. It was at this point that Rivers and Arnall moved out of the Talmadge camp in support of Roosevelt. Rivers' bill called for state cooperation with the Public Works Administration on a "rental basis."[44] He also proposed an amendment to the state constitution allowing appropriations for "Pensions and Relief" and asked for the establishment of a Department of Welfare "to operate and control a [Social] Security program." Finally, Rivers proposed amendments to sections of the state's Poor Laws that would permit counties to raise revenue for the new Social Security program. Needless to say, Arnall's original resolution was never reported out of committee. Johnstone wrote to Hopkins that with the change in attitude in the state legislature these laws might pass, but they certainly would be vetoed by the governor.[45]

Predictably Talmadge did not cooperate, and Hopkins completed the federalization of the FERA, which he had begun in January 1934. On April 19, 1935, he formally assumed control of the FERA in Georgia and appointed Miss Shepperson as his lieutenant in the state. At a press conference on the same day, President Roosevelt assured Georgians that this move did not mean the end of all relief in Georgia. He asserted that he would not allow "the federal relief program for Georgia . . . [to] be curtailed by political controversies," and there would be no change in the state's relief program.[46]

Coming on the heels of an announcement by Hopkins that all direct relief would be halted after June 1, the federalization move caused much anxiety. Hopkins assured Georgians, however, that the change would not interfere with the work program. The suspension of direct relief was the result of the state legislature's failure to provide matching Social Security funds, and not the outcome of Hopkins' move to federalize the state FERA administration.[47]

Actually, Talmadge's attacks on the work program had subsided after November 1934. Under the FERA's new emergency work program the CWA wage scale was abolished, although the 30 cents an hour minimum was maintained. All those living in rural areas and towns of under 5,000 population were taken out of the work program and transferred to the Rural Rehabilitation Division to avoid further criticism from farmers. On November 19, 1934, Hopkins rescinded all wage provisions, relying entirely upon prevailing standards to set work relief wage rates. Talmadge applauded Hopkins' move and they resumed "cordial relations, at least in public." This rapprochement, however, was not destined to be long-lived. Talmadge never allowed the state to participate financially in any of the federal programs, and friction continued to build until Hopkins decided to federalize the state's programs completely in the summer of 1935.

Apparently this action infuriated the governor, and his attacks shifted from the New Deal agencies to the president himself. Talmadge's diatribes culminated in this alleged reference to Roosevelt's physical condition: "The greatest calamity in this country is that President Roosevelt can't walk around and hunt up people to talk to. He can only talk to those his secretaries and assistants allow to come and see him, and 99 percent of the crowd is the 'gimme' crowd. The next President who goes to the White House will be a man who knows what it is to work in the sun 14 hours a day. That man will be able to walk a 2 x 4 plank, too."[48]

Under the new work program Georgia's projects proceeded smoothly if slowly. Throughout its existence the FERA found most of its relief clients were concentrated in the five urban counties of the state where the percentage of the population receiving relief was two to three times as high as in rural counties. In rural areas relief was centered in the small towns, where the landlords controlled its distribution and tended to disburse it sparingly for fear they would lose their labor. Since the landowners preferred to have easily controllable blacks as tenants and wage hands, these small communities were besieged primarily by poor whites.[49]

In the large cities with a greater number of relief clients, there never was enough money for all requests, and the most serious troubles occurred there. In August 1934, for instance, reliefers held mass meetings in Atlanta protesting the distribution of funds. The National Emergency Council (NEC) director blamed the difficulties on a "lack of community contact on the part of the workers employed by the Administration," but these workers certainly were hampered by the tremendous demands made upon them.[50]

The tensions created in the cities occasionally resulted in fraudulent practices on the part of the clients and, in a few instances, on the part of administrators. Most prominent was the theft and forgery of relief checks. The practice became so critical in Atlanta that the administration finally asked merchants not to cash relief checks unless they knew the customer.[51]

Considering the large amount of money which the federal government spent in Georgia, surprisingly few irregularities were found in the relief offices. The most publicized event occurred in Fulton County where an office manager was found guilty of embezzling relief funds. The incident created much notice, because the county relief administrator was charged with having "muzzled employees" to squelch information which might have cleared the accused. She replied that she had issued a bulletin requesting all "criticism" to be made to her rather than to the press, but that she had not threatened employees with discharge. Miss Shepperson backed the administrator, noting that charges had been brought against the manager with much regret and certainly not without a thorough investigation.[52]

Even though Miss Shepperson would liked to have kept such investigations within the relief family, the Fulton grand jury undertook an examination of the county office. Its investigation exonerated the agency, and the subsequent charges against the office manager proved Miss Shepperson's sincerity in seeing that her office policed itself.[53]

Unfortunately, many citizens and even some relief officials never accepted the FERA. They responded negatively to the tremendous shock of so much money being poured into the state. Part of their opposition centered around a self-righteous view of relief. Anyone who needed relief was bound to be morally deficient, and if relief had to be given, it should be as little as possible. These indigent people, they felt, were receiving far too much.

Opponents realized that the cost of relief eventually would be taken out of their pockets through higher taxes. If anyone in the state did not know this, the governor was there to remind him. Citizens of the state who were not dependent upon relief thus became increasingly edgy about waste in the programs and ultimately came to favor an outright dole over work relief. It seemed that their pocketbooks were of more importance than the self-respect of those on relief. Finally, local residents distrusted social workers, especially when they were from outside the county. Although residents claimed that their dissatisfaction was due to an outsider's presence, it was likely that they were fearful of any official who spent an amount likely to exceed the entire annual county budget. This situation could have grave effects upon their control of the poor people of the county.[54]

In April 1935 Hopkins had announced that the entire relief set-up would be reorganized under new agencies created to handle the various expanding programs of the FERA. The FERA itself was abolished and its duties distributed to the Resettlement Administration, the National Youth Administration, and the Works Progress Administration (WPA). Direct relief was completely abandoned and given over to the states and their political subdivisions. The transition to the first two agencies was carried out more efficiently than the transition to the WPA.

Administratively, the WPA found few problems in Georgia, probably because the early federalization of the FERA had produced an organization similar to that provided for in the new agency. Also the state office took care to make a gradual reduction in FERA cases beginning in May 1935 in preparation for shifting the proper number and type of workers to the new program. Unfortunately, blacks, rural residents, and women—the same groups that had been cut first when the CWA was eliminated—again were the first to be removed from the lists. Nevertheless, Miss Shepperson was able to achieve a 16 percent reduction in the relief rolls by the end of July, compared to a 3.3 percent reduction for the rest of the country.[55]

Despite all her preparations, the official transfer of work projects from the FERA to the WPA did not take place on July 1, 1935, as planned. The date of transfer was moved to July 15, but it was not until the end of November that all workers had been removed from the FERA's rolls. To add to Miss Shepperson's troubles, the state's newspapers "tended to mislead the public"; however, she was able to secure additional funds for the FERA to keep most workers employed until they could be put on the new WPA projects. Miss Shepperson maintained the state FERA office with a drastically reduced staff, often transferring extra personnel to the WPA. This move won the approval of the state's citizenry, both as an economy measure and as a sign that the WPA was progressing.[56]

In September about 30,000 workers (or 60 percent of those on the rolls in May) remained on the FERA's rolls, and by the first of November there were only 1,000 people left untransferred, mainly school teachers and other female "nonmanuals." When the WPA provided projects for these women, the FERA of Georgia officially passed out of existence on November 11, 1935. At that point over 48,000 people out of a 50,000 person quota were working on WPA projects.[57]

The FERA's accomplishments meant different things to different people. One observer said that "screens and privies" were of greatest value, while another pointed to the transitory nature of these projects and picked the road projects as the most important. In 1934 Miss Shepperson told Lorena Hickok that the "$7,000,000 a month we've been spending in Georgia has been largely wasted, outside the cities, where an emergency *does* exist." She noted that the rural problems were endemic, and the FERA and CWA were not going to solve them with emergency programs. In this area thousands of people were without jobs, and some way had to be found to remove them from the limited labor market. If that were not done, "the situation where half-starved Whites and Blacks struggle in competition for less to eat than my dog gets at home, for the privilege of living in huts that are infinitely less comfortable than his kennel" would continue, as would the terrible lynchings and deep-seated racial prejudice. At the time Miss Shepperson suggested that the rural rehabilitation projects might be the answer, but these were bound to fail in an area which was wedded to cotton, where newly diversified farms would have to compete with established growing areas.[58]

Perhaps the greatest achievement of the FERA and the CWA was, after all, not in the projects done, but in the groundwork laid. Out of these two agencies came most of the administrative structure, procedure, and personnel for the WPA. Miss Shepperson was able to transfer most of her FERA personnel to the WPA, and some of the people who began working in the summer of 1933 remained until 1939. All of the WPA's projects were anticipated to some extent by those of the FERA. Miss Shepperson had been able to learn much about the limitations of various projects and about the abilities of the state's labor force. She had discovered the difficulties in finding projects for white-collar workers and for women, and under the WPA she increased her efforts to provide for these people who, like the black, heretofore had been the last hired and the first fired from CWA and FERA projects.

NOTES

1. Charles F. Searle, *Minister of Relief* (Syracuse: Syracuse University Press, 1963), p. 50. Atlanta *Constitution,* November 28, 1933. Hopkins to Ransom, November 13, 1933 (night letter), NARG 69, CWA, Administrative Correspondence (state), box 10.

2. "The CWA in Georgia" (unpublished MSS in possession of Gay B. Shepperson), p. 34. Atlanta *Constitution,* November 19, 1933. Minutes of the GRC, December 18 and 19, 1933, NARG 69, FERA, State Files, No. 460, box 70.

3. J. S. Stone to Congressman B. T. Castelow, February 3, 1934, NARG 69, CWA, Admin. Corres. (state), box 11. Ransom to Hopkins, November 21, 1933 (telegram), NARG 69, CWA, Admin. Corres. (state), box 10. Unsigned letter to Mrs. C. C. Hill, December 16, 1933, NARG 69, CWA, microfilm reel 50 C. Shepperson to all Civil Works Administrators, January 25, 1934, NARG 69, CWA, microfilm reel 44 C.

4. Arthur F. Raper, *Preface to Peasantry* (Chapel Hill: University of North Carolina Press, 1936), p. 257. Shepperson to J. A. Davis, n.d., NARG 69, CWA, microfilm reel 49 C. Shepperson to Bruce McClure, December 21, 1933, NARG 69, CWA, Admin. Corres. (state) box 11. "The CWA in Georgia," pp. 36, 41, 42. Senator Russell to Hopkins, December 1, 1933 (telegram), NARG 69, CWA, Admin. Corres. (state), box 10. Shepperson to McClure, March 5, 1934, NARG 69, CWA, Admin. Corres. (state), box 10. Arthur F. Raper, *Tenants of the Almighty* (New York: Macmillan Company, 1943), p. 194. Atlanta *Constitution,* December 21 and 30, 1933. Lorena Hickok to Hopkins, January 23, 1934 (report), Hopkins MSS, FDR Library, Selected documents.

5. Ransom to Hopkins, November 21, 1933 (notation on telegram), NARG 69, CWA, Admin. Corres. (state), box 10. About 50,000 self-sustaining men were eventually put on CWA projects.

6. Atlanta *Constitution,* November 19, 1933. "The CWA in Georgia," p. 41. McConnell to Woolford, November 29, 1933, NARG 69, CWA, Admin. Corres. (state), box 11.

7. C. Q. Woods to Shepperson, March 17, 1934, NARG 69, CWA, microfilm reel 44 C.

8. Central Sash and Door Co., Macon, Georgia, to Senator Walter George, February 17, 1934, NARG 69, CWA, Admin. Corres. (state), box 10. McClure to George, February 24, 1934, NARG 69, CWA, Admin. Corres. (state), box 10. Mitchell to Walker, May 15, 1934, NARG 44, NEC, Division of Field Operations, General Correspondence with State Directors (1934-35), box 174.

9. Thomas B. Mimms to Shepperson, January 2, 1934, NARG 69, CWA, microfilm reel 44 C.

10. WPA, *Analysis of Civil Works Program Statistics* (Washington: U. S. Government Printing Office, 1939), p. 230. "The CWA in Georgia," p. 64.

11. Report of Nan Northam, December 11, 1933, NARG 69, CWA, microfilm reel 44 C. Mrs. J. F. Goolsby to Hopkins, December 8, 1933, NARG 69, CWA, Admin. Corres. (state), box 11. Unsigned report, March 13, 1934, NARG 44, Periodical Reports (1934-38), box 400. Shepperson to Hopkins, January 20, 1934, NARG 69, CWA, Admin. Corres. (state), box 10. McConnell to Shepperson, December 30, 1933, NARG 69, CWA, microfilm reel 44 C. Wade G. Sanders to Senator Russell, n.d., NARG 69, CWA, Admin. Corres. (state), box 10.

12. Memo from Miss Frances Steele (?), February 2, 1934, NARG 69, CWA, microfilm reel 44 C.

13. Williams to Mr. Victor Davidson, March 13, NARG 69, CWA, Admin. Corres. (state), box 10. Memo from Miss Frances Steele (?), February 2, 1934, NARG 69, CWA, microfilm reel 44 C. Report of Leslie Robinson, December 11, 1933, NARG 69, CWA, microfilm reel 44 C.

14. Jasper Mayer to W. D. Thompson, January 9, 1934, NARG 69, CWA, Admin. Corres (state), box 11. C. E. Layton to Shepperson, January 20, 1934, NARG 69, CWA, microfilm reel 44 C.

15. Crawford to Carmody, n.d. (telegram), NARG 69, CWA, Admin. Corres. (state), box 10. Atlanta *Constitution,* March 9, 1934. Andrew Soule to Frank C. Walker, February 20, 1934, NARG 44, General Corres. with State Directors, box 174. Shepperson to all division heads,

n.d. (memo), NARG 69, CWA, microfilm reel 44 C.

16. "Complaints," NARG 69, CWA, Admin. Corres. (state), box 11. Interview with Gay Shepperson.

17. "List of Complaints," March 17, 1934, NARG 69, CWA, microfilm reel 44 C.

18. "The CWA in Georgia," pp. 53, 56.

19. *Ibid.*, pp. 56, 60, 96, 97. Georgia State Department of Public Health, *Report* (1933-34), p. 25. Federal CWA of Georgia, "Federal Projects Operating Under the Civil Works Administration for Georgia," April 30, 1934, NARG 69, CWA.

20. U. S. Department of Commerce, Bureau of the Census, *Vital Statistics* (1940), pp. 336-7. "The CWA in Georgia," p. 77. Department of Public Health, *Report* (1933-34), p. 36. From December 1, 1933, to March 31, 1934, the CWA drained 2,302 ponds of 61,328 acres and constructed 4,061,170 lineal feet of ditches and canals and 769 miles of ditches and canals.

21. Department of Public Health, *Report* (1933-34), p. 37.

22. Richard M. Sterner, *The Negro's Share* (New York: Harper and Brothers, 1943), pp. 172, 395.

23. "The CWA in Georgia," p. 77. Department of Public Health, *Report* (1933-34), pp. 25, 26, 35.

24. "The CWA in Georgia," pp. 97, 109, 118, 119. CWA, "Federal Projects in Georgia." Atlanta *Constitution,* February 16, 1934.

25. Atlanta *Constitution,* February 17, 1934.

26. Arthur Goldschmidt to Congressman Malcolm C. Tarver, March 6, 1934, NARG 69, CWA, Admin. Corres. (state), box 10 "Complaints," NARG 69, CWA, Admin. Corres. (state), boxes 10 and 11.

27. Minutes of the GRC, December 18 and 19, 1933, NARG 69, FERA, State Files, No. 460, box 70. Unsigned report, January 1934, NARG 69, CWA, microfilm reel 44 C. McClure to Russell, February 2, 1934, NARG 69, CWA, Admin. Corres. (state), box 10. Etta Blanchard Worsley, *Columbus on the Chattahoochee.* (Columbus: Columbus Office Supply Co., 1951), p. 475. H. G. Hastings to Warburton, January 1, 1934, NARG 33, Federal Extension Service, Corres., 1934, box 235. Unsigned petitions from Valdosta, n.d., NARG 69, CWA, Admin. Corres. (state), box 11. Shepperson to Mrs. Mabel R. Gunnels, December 8, 1933, NARG 69, CWA, microfilm reel 44 C.

28. Unisgned report, January 1934, NARG 69, CWA, microfilm reel 44 C. Hopkins and Shepperson, May 8, 1934 (telephone conversation), Hopkins MSS, selected documents. Report of Lorena Hickok, January 23, 1934, Hopkins MSS, selected documents. Report of Alvaretta Kenan,

August 17-19, 1933 (?), NARG 69, CWA, microfilm reel 44 C.
29. Report of Lorena Hickok, January 11, 1934, NARG 69, FERA, Old Subject Files, No. 278, box 10. Shepperson to McClure, December 21, 1933 (telegram), NARG 69, CWA, Admin. Corres. (state), box 11.
30. Brotherhood of Painters, Decorators, and Paperhangers of America, Local Union No. 30, Savannah, to Hopkins, January 13, 1934, NARG 69, CWA, Admin. Corres. (state), box 10. Shepperson to McClure, February 28, 1934, NARG 69, CWA, Admin. Corres. (state), box 11. Atlanta *Constitution,* December 23, 1933.
31. "Complaints," NARG 69, CWA, Admin. Corres. (state), box 10. Hickok to Hopkins, January 11, 1934, NARG 69, FERA, Old Subject Files, No. 278, box 10. Atlanta *Constitution,* January 9 and February 9, 1934. Hickok to Hopkins, January 23, 1934, NARG 69, FERA, Old Subject Files, No. 278, box 10.
32. Hickok to Hopkins, January 11, 1934, NARG 69, FERA, Old Subject Files, No. 278, box 10. Hickok to Hopkins, January 16, 1934, Hopkins MSS, selected documents.
33. Atlanta *Constitution,* November 25, 1933, Francis Allan Kifer, "The Negro Under the New Deal, 1933-1941" (unpublished Ph.D. dissertation, Department of History, University of Wisconsin, 1961), p. 216.
34. Atlanta *Constitution,* January 19, 1934. Report of Lorena Hickok, January 16, 1934, Hopkins MSS, selected documents.
35. Report of Lorena Hickok, January 23, 1934, Hopkins MSS, selected documents. Hickok to Hopkins, January 11, 1934, NARG 69, FERA, Old Subject Files, No. 278, box 10. Arthur Raper experienced similar problems with FERA employees on the county level.
36. Interview with Gay Shepperson. Watson to Gill, December 13, 1933 (report), NARG 69, FERA, State Files, box 64.
37. The *Statesman,* II, 42 (October 23, 1933). Atlanta *Constitution,* December 20 and 22, 1933, and January 18 and 19, 1934. Johnstone to Hopkins, January 19, 1934 (memo), NARG 69, FERA, State Files, box 64. "Georgia's CWA Centered Now in Single Head," unmarked clipping, "Random Clippings," Shepperson MSS.
38. Ransom to Hopkins, December 20, 1933 (telegram), NARG 69, CWA, Admin. Corres. (state), box 10. Atlanta *Constitution,* December 17 and 23, 1933. W. W. Driskell to Hopkins, December 20, 1933, NARG 69, CWA, Admin. Corres. (state), box 10. J. P. Walker to Hopkins, December 20, 1933 (telegram), NARG 69, CWA, Admin. Corres. (state), box 11.
39. Joseph Hyde Pratt to Shepperson, April 18, 1934, NARG 69, FERA, Old Subject Files, No. 278, box 10.

40. *Ibid.* Atlanta *Constitution,* December 15, 1934. Georgia Emergency Relief Administration, "Monthly Review of Relief Statistics," I, 2 (December 1934), 2. Atlanta *Journal,* December 14, 1934. Genung to Williams, March 20, 1935 (memo), NARG 69, FERA, State Files, box 64.

41. Atlanta *Georgian,* February 11, 1935. Atlanta *Constitution,* February 13, 18, and March 17, 1935.

42. Johnstone to Hopkins, March 6, 1935 (memo), NARG 69, FERA, State Files, No. 406.1, box 66. Atlanta *Georgian,* December 16, 1934.

43. "Analysis of Administrative Personnel as of February 7, 1935, and as of October, 1934, by Employment Status," NARG 69, FERA, State Files, box 64.

44. See Chapter 5 for methods of state support of projects.

45. Johnstone to Hopkins, March 6, 1935 (memo), NARG 69, FERA, State Files, No. 406.1, box 66. Johnstone to Hopkins, March 6, 1935 (report), Hopkins MSS, selected documents.

46. Hopkins to Shepperson, April 19, 1935, NARG 69, FERA, State Files, box 64. F. S. Bartlett, "Financial Procedure in the Federally Operated Relief Administrations in Six States," in FERA, "Monthly Report" (June 1936), 134. Atlanta *Constitution,* April 20, 1935.

47. Atlanta *Constitution,* April 20, 1935. Atlanta *Journal,* April 19, 1935.

48. FERA, Administrative Order No. 21. Sarah M. Lemmon, "The Public Career of Eugene Talmadge: 1926-1936" (unpublished Ph.D. dissertation, Department of History, University of North Carolina, 1952), pp. 87-8. Atlanta *Constitution,* November 24, 1934. Atlanta *Journal,* December 30, 1934. The *Statesman,* November 27, 1934. George Creel, "Wild Man from Sugar Creek, Georgia's Governor Gene Talmadge," *Colliers,* XCVI (December 21, 1935), 67.

49. Lemmon, "Eugene Talmadge," p. 216. FERA, "Monthly Report" (March, April, 1934). GERA, "Monthly Review of Relief Statistics," I, 2 (December 1935), 19. Leonard W. Dobb, "Poor Whites: A Frustrated Class," in John Dollard, *Caste and Class in a Southern Town.* (New Haven: Yale University Press, 1937), pp. 446, 455. Raper, *Preface,* p. 259.

50. Atlanta *Constitution,* February 5, 1934. Leggett to McClure, August 7, 1934 (from NEC director's report), NARG 44, Gen. Corres. with State Directors (1934-35), box 174. Unsigned report, August 1, 1934, NARG 44, Periodical Reports (1934-38), box 400.

51. Atlanta *Constitution,* February 4, 1934, and August 8 and 29 and September 9, 1935.

52. *Ibid.*, December 7 and 8, 1934.

53. *Ibid.*, February 10, 1934.

54. Interview with Gay Shepperson. Unsigned report, December 29, 1934, NARG 44, Digests, box 487. Mitchell to Richberg, November 11, 1934 (report), NARG 44, Gen. Corres. with State Directors (1934-35), box 174.

55. Atlanta *Constitution,* April 10, 1935. Unsigned report, July 2, 1935, NARG 44, Periodical Reports (1934-38), box 400. Edward Aaron Gaston, Jr., "A History of the Negro Wage Earner in Georgia, 1890-1940" (unpublished Ph.D. dissertation, Department of History, Emory University, 1957), p. 385. Unsigned report, July 23, 1935, NARG 44, Digests, box 488.

56. Unsigned report, July 2, 1935, NARG 44, Digests, box 488. Unsigned report, August 20, 1935, NARG 44, Digests, box 489. Unsigned report, July 3, 1935, NARG 44, Digests, box 489. Unsigned reports, August 13, 1935, NARG 69, FERA, New Subject Files, No. 070, box 116.

57. Unsigned report, September 24, 1935, NARG 69, FERA, New Subject Files, No. 070, box 116. Unsigned report, September 10, 1935, NARG 44, Digests, box 491. Unsigned report, September 16, 1935, NARG 44, Periodical Reports (1934-38), box 400. Unsigned report, September 24, 1935, NARG 44, Digests, box 492. Unsigned report, November 2, 1935, NARG 44, Digests, box 495. Atlanta *Constitution,* November 12, 1935. The federal government had allotted $57,141,528 to the GERA during its existence, of which $53,072,004 was spent. This represented 1.757 percent of the total FERA funds spent in a state with about 2.4 percent of the nation's population. Georgia's contribution to the GERA was only $4.95, and upon the abolishment of the FERA Hopkins named Georgia as one of six states (Georgia, Florida, Nebraska, North Dakota, and North and South Carolina) that had given no funds whatsoever.

58. Hickok to Hopkins, January 28, 1934, NARG 69, FERA, Old Subject File, No. 278, box 10. Interview with Gay Shepperson. Interview with Miss Hilda Smith, September 28, 1968. WPA, "Final Report," 1942, NARG 69, p. 5. See Appendix, Tables 8-10.

3
Hopkins Prescribes
a New Agency – The WPA,
1935-1942

In the summer of 1935, when it became evident that the depression was not to be short-lived, federal officials instituted a major reorganization of relief activities. The FERA was not structurally equipped to handle increasingly complex programs nor to promote long-range solutions to the depression. President Roosevelt therefore ordered the FERA to be phased out and its various programs to be reassembled under diverse independent agencies. The youth program of college aid was taken over by the National Youth Administration and was expanded to include aid to high school students. The direct relief program was dropped entirely, although it was partially reconstructed under the Social Security Administration in cooperation with the states. The FERA's farm programs were consolidated under the Resettlement Administration, and the massive new work program was handled by the Works Progress Administration (WPA).[1]

Unlike the FERA, the WPA was strictly a federal agency with the state governments neither requesting nor disbursing relief funds. State and local governments still participated in proposing, administering, and financing projects, but actual control and responsibility for the program rested with the WPA through its state offices. All state WPA officials and workers were now federal employees and were paid by checks issued by the federal Treasury.

The types of projects generally remained the same as those developed under the FERA's emergency work program, although the nonmanual programs were vastly expanded. Local offices still certified relief candidates, and local sponsors drew up plans for projects. These projects then were approved in the national offices and sent to the state administrator, who had the final choice of projects to initiate with the funds allocated. Under the WPA, however, the wage scales were altered. The "budgetary deficiency principle" which operated under the FERA was changed to a "security wage" plan under the WPA. Workers earned less than the local prevailing wage, in order to keep labor from deserting private industry.

Unlike the Public Works Administration (PWA), the WPA was required to hire at least 90 percent of its workers from the relief rolls. These laborers were certified only once, at the time of their registration (as compared to the FERA which had demanded frequent reinvestigations), and they were required to register with the National Reemployment Service, making themselves available for private employment.

In states such as Georgia, where there had been good FERA administrators, the FERA administrator automatically assumed command of the new agency. In the beginning there were three operating divisions in the state office. The first, made up of social workers, was the Intake and Certification Division (later the Employment Division). The other two divisions were Finance and Work Projects (Operations). Later the Women's Work Division, the Labor Management Division, the Office Management Division, and the Safety Division were added. These divisions were not static. Miss Shepperson continuously reorganized them to meet shifting needs. For example, the Women's Division underwent three changes before 1940. It was known during this time as the Women's Work Division, the Women's and Professional Division, the Professional and Service Division, and finally the Community Service Division. Furthermore, its duties changed as various programs were either added or removed.

To adminster the WPA, Miss Shepperson organized eight districts, each with its own director and staff corresponding in structure to that of the state office. The internal organization of these district offices changed with that of the state office, and from time to time the number of districts also fluctuated. Originally there was to be a state advisory board appointed by the governor to aid in the selection of projects. Controversy arose over its membership, however, and Miss Shepperson later noted that she was never forced to consult it.[2]

Miss Shepperson's state staff had proved so capable in administering the FERA, that she asked Hopkins to transfer it intact to the WPA.

Hopkins trusted her judgment and allowed her to make the switch. Miss Shepperson then began to fill out her administrative organization with people who also had worked with the FERA, particularly in the areas of social work, accounting, and engineering. Because of the abundant supply of qualified persons in the latter two fields, she was able to recruit only those licensed in the state. This was not true for social workers, however, or for those lower down on the administrative scale. Because of strong public opinion, Miss Shepperson tried to lure social workers, who were also native Georgians, back to the state, but there were so few that she met with little success. On the local level she used teachers and nurses as social workers with good results, and she secured "technically trained" personnel to work as local project supervisors. She was able to avoid the kind of "carpet-bagging" attacks she had incurred under the FERA.[3]

Although the state office was well organized and received praise from WPA officials (especially the Division of Intake and Certification which was regarded by one regional social worker as "the strongest field staff . . . in this area"), the district offices proved troublesome. District directors argued that they could not investigate project proposals because the state office withheld administrative and engineering staff. Furthermore, during the early months of the WPA a great deal of friction arose among the new WPA district offices and those of the FERA that still remained. The situation was exacerbated by the constant movement of personnel from the FERA to the WPA, particularly since the original selection of the FERA district staffs had been made under policies different from those governing the WPA. Miss Shepperson was criticized for hiring individuals who had been with the FERA in preference to those who were equally qualified and in need of relief. When these problems arose she acted quickly to stem the friction and confusion, and as the organization progressed she brought district offices up to full strength and defined more clearly policies regarding spheres of influence.[4]

Initial difficulties did not stop Miss Shepperson from pushing for an early start to the program. The public had responded positively to the WPA and expected its projects to commence that summer. Local governments moved swiftly to prepare project proposals, and Miss Shepperson rushed them to Washington. It was there that both federal and local projects piled up. Observing this logjam, local governments withheld further proposals until they could determine what sort of project the WPA was likely to approve. The national office also was late in sending the necessary forms and instructions to local offices, so that when approval finally came, the projects still could not begin. Finally there were delays involving appropriations and procurement of materials while policy decisions were being formulated in Washington. All this led to a growing impatience and dissatisfaction in the state.[5]

Miss Shepperson had striven to gather and submit as many projects as possible in late June and early July, and she was discouraged seeing that her work had been in vain. By August 5, 1935, although 1,045 projects had been submitted, funds for only 82 of them had been allotted. Additional delays occurred when vendors who still had not been paid for materials sold to the FERA the previous spring hesitated to deal with the new agency.[6]

Conflicts over the redistribution of FERA labor also slowed progress. Although the WPA controlled most of the work projects in the state, many relief clients could be put to work on projects developed by the PWA or by the various agricultural agencies. Each of the agencies using relief labor claimed that its needs were most important and should be taken care of first. The WPA, moreover, was late in instructing Miss Shepperson in the operation of the Labor Management Division, so that she had to reassign 2,290 FERA workers to 81 converted projects on her own.[7]

Local conditions added to her difficulties. The relief labor transfer coincided with the cotton-picking season in Georgia, so that she could not be sure exactly how many men could be moved. She had to make labor available for private industry, and she was hampered by a lack of skilled manual laborers (especially in rural counties), on the one hand, and by the absence of any approved nonmanual projects for professionals and white-collar workers on the other. Because of this, most of the early projects approved were in cities with large concentrations of relief labor. These bigger cities, however, experienced trouble in voting bonds to cover the sponsor's cost, in validating these bonds, and in offering them for sale.

In approving a project from the Washington list, Miss Shepperson had to consider a number of factors which severely limited her choices. Each project had to be capable of completion within the one-year time limit of the funds. For each project there had to be a sponsor willing to supply some of the materials and, in some instances, supervision. The proper number and type of workers had to be available and within easy access to the projects. Initially she solved these problems by merely transferring unfinished FERA projects to the WPA, but as the program expanded new projects required more intensive study.

Late in the summer of 1935 Miss Shepperson learned that all projects had to be submitted to Washington before September 15. She quickly informed local governments of this deadline, and they responded by increasing the number of applications sent to the state office. To facilitate the handling of this new surge, Miss Shepperson drafted districtwide applications "each covering a particular character of work." To her dismay, however, the national office ruled that this method was unacceptable, and all projects thus submitted had to be rewritten.[8]

In a report covering the first half of September, Miss Shepperson summed up conditions in the state. Despite serious obstacles she had managed to begin work on 350 projects employing 15,573 people. Public interest in state projects centered around the malarial control program, begun under the CWA, although school building and repair projects also were popular. Miss Shepperson reported that the general public was enthusiastic, and local governmental agencies sponsoring projects were cooperating splendidly. The transfer of workers was proceeding smoothly, although confusion and delay persisted on new projects. Only the nonmanual workers proved hard to place, since it was difficult to find suitable projects which local governments were willing to sponsor. No direct opposition to working conditions or to the new security wage system had arisen, but Miss Shepperson saw some clouds gathering within the ranks of organized labor.[9]

District reports covering the same period revealed that WPA wages were graduated in much the same way as those of the FERA and the CWA. Wage rates were determined according to prevailing wages, which varied by geographical location and population concentration. The minimum rate set for Georgia in May 1935 was $19 a month for unskilled rural labor, and the maximum rate was $75 a month for skilled urban labor. The minimum rate for Georgia and the other southern states was the lowest in the country, and the state's maximum rate stood tenth from the bottom. When compared to the cost of living, wages for unskilled labor in Atlanta and Mobile proved to be the worst in the nation. Notwithstanding popular conceptions, the cost of living in Atlanta was nine-tenths of a point above the national average in March

1935 and only 5 percent lower than the average for all southern cities. One survey showed that the unskilled rates in Atlanta provided 39.5 percent of the estimated monthly emergency standard of living, which in itself was below normal.[10]

The number of working hours was set at a maximum of 8 a day and 40 a week, but there was an upper monthly limit to earnings. The hours regulations worked a particular hardship on major construction projects which demanded skilled laborers. Since the skilled workers were paid higher wage rates, their working hours often had to be reduced below those of unskilled workers on the same project. As a result, construction either had to be delayed or work crews had to be shifted from project to project to maintain adequate progress.[11]

When the security wage was announced there had been some expressions of dissatisfaction, but these appeared to have subsided by the end of August. As the projects began, and more FERA workers were transferred to them, however, criticism again arose. Farmers and businessmen contended that the rates were too high, and labor claimed they were too low. Other agencies and small rural towns argued that there was not enough labor. Miss Shepperson had the prerogative to shift workers from one project to another and from one agency to another, and she spent a great deal of time doing so when such complaints came to her attention. Employers felt that WPA wages were higher than those of private enterprise, but it appeared that the major problem was that the WPA provided the job security that businesses and farm employment lacked.

Labor leader A. Steve Nance led the workers' protest against the security wage. He noted that while the security wage was higher than that paid by the FERA, the per capita income of WPA employees often was lower than the FERA's budgetary deficiency income which took the size of the worker's family into consideration. When Nance complained to Nels Anderson, WPA adviser on labor relations, Anderson replied that he was sorry, but there was nothing he could do. He told Nance that the security wage was never meant to supplant the prevailing wage, but was "a reasonable approximation of 'man year' earnings." The real problem, however, was that funds were limited, and the WPA meant to accomplish as much as possible with them.[12]

Labor's troubles were exacerbated by the slowness with which FERA workers were transferred to WPA projects. Miss Shepperson's task was to put nearly 50,000 people to work within a few months on projects which met WPA requirements. While sympathetic to the problems facing the Georgia administrator, Hopkins insisted on the achievement of this goal. Miss Shepperson met Hopkins' November deadline, but only by upsetting the distribution of projects around the state, initiating a number of very large projects in the big cities, and placing workers in positions with which they had little or no experience.

Hopkins recognized the pressures which he had placed upon Miss Shepperson and the friction likely to be created by the security wage. When a WPA strike broke out in New York City, he cautioned the state administrator not to "let the newspapers get you on this." If a strike threatened and people inquired about it, she was to "just tell them to pipe down." Hopkins was so touchy about the subject that when Miss Shepperson asked about the New York strike he replied, "There is no such thing as a strike." When she reported that Nance had visited her about the security wage, the WPA head was evasive and merely reminded her that she had the prerogative to raise the security wage by 10 percent.

Georgia managed to escape an immediate repercussion to the New York strike, but not for long. In October, organized labor in the state began to agitate for reduced hours at the same monthly rate to "conform to the union rates." Miss Shepperson agreed to reduce the hours in the seven most populous counties of the state. Her compromise was ineffective, however, for having won this concession labor demanded that there be "prevailing union wage scales for all types of labor engaged on government projects." Miss Shepperson was unwilling to be pushed further and flatly refused to comply.[13]

The situation was rapidly building to a crisis. The state's newspapers gave extensive coverage to the controversy, emphasizing the possibility of a strike. By calling labor's hand, the press forced officials to call a strike for October 15, but Miss Shepperson was able to persuade them to postpone it and negotiate, accepting in the meantime the security wage "under protest."[14]

This agreement gained Miss Shepperson another three weeks, but no understanding was reached. On November 5, 1935, Georgia Federation of Labor President Nance and J. A. Harper, head of the Georgia Federation of Trades, called a mass meeting in Atlanta. About 1,700 WPA workers attended and unanimously voted to strike on November 12. The speakers placed the entire blame for the situation on Miss Shepperson and promised to submit one more petition to the national WPA office before calling the strike.[15]

Accordingly, Nance telegraphed Washington of the meeting's decision.

He insisted upon a scale equal to prevailing wages and an hourly schedule of 120 hours a month for unskilled labor. Nance protested the transferral of skilled FERA workers to positions as unskilled workers in the WPA just so the state's quotas could be met. Since such a move meant the lowering of income "below budgets," Nance asked that these workers be kept on the FERA at deficiency wages until skilled positions could be found for them in the WPA. Finally he accused the WPA of being more interested in the projects than in the workers, a telling criticism.[16]

With the threatened strike only five days away, Miss Shepperson spoke to Hopkins about her course of action. She was especially worried because the leaders "haven't got it under control." Nance had a good command of union members, but only a small number of those involved were in his unions. Some blacks were involved, and Hopkins feared the possibility of race riots. Miss Shepperson complained that, although she was ultimately responsible for relief wages, organized labor had seen fit to deal only with the national office.

Hopkins needed to know what kind of community approval the strike could garner. A report filed the previous day indicated that Nance had little support in Atlanta even within the city's organized labor. Miss Shepperson agreed with this assessment of the situation and said, "I think the whole community down here is waiting for me to answer or for you to answer them on this. I think we have the sentiment in this town [Atlanta] absolutely with us." Hopkins replied that Miss Shepperson should not give in to Nance and should tell him "to go jump in the lake." He suggested that Nance was "just threatening you and bullying you. Let him take the responsibility of calling those fellows out."

Miss Shepperson agreed, but she still feared that Nance would go ahead, and the strike would get out of control. Hopkins reminded her that she had the option of raising security wages 10 percent, and this might stem the tide should Nance succeed. In any case, the final decision was hers.

During the next days the threat of a strike spread from Atlanta throughout the state. Miss Shepperson again met with labor leaders in a two-hour conference. J. A. Harper reported that "she talked very sympathetically, rehashed former discussions, but insisted that she could not pay the wage scale without cutting out some of the projects or getting more money from Washington." She did agree, however, to give the 10 percent wage increase to unskilled labor in Atlanta. Nance's other demands would have to be met in Washington even though Hopkins was playing "hands off."[18]

Finally Hopkins capitulated and agreed to change the wage schedule so that it would be uniform across the country. Miss Shepperson announced that skilled employees would be paid prevailing wages, and 10 percent of the others would receive the 10 percent increase. Labor, having won these concessions, demanded that all unskilled workers get the 10 percent increase, but state observers, seeing that the main force of labor attacks had shifted to the PWA (whose wages were now lower than the WPA), advised that the administration go no further.

The strike threat in the fall of 1935 netted labor some gains. The whole affair, moreover, indicated that the WPA might not be living up to its priorities. It seemed Miss Shepperson was correct in assuming that Nance was out for labor's interests, regardless of the effect it might have on the program. For a brief moment, however, Miss Shepperson and Hopkins revealed what appeared to be an overriding concern for the physical success of the WPA in terms of work completed instead of their stated goal of giving jobs to the destitute.

The threat of a major strike averted, the WPA proceeded with little difficulty. Ineffective communication between the state office and local governments caused some minor problems, but until the spring of 1936, when funds began to diminish, the program operated smoothly. The first allotment had been made to Georgia on July 23, 1935. During the late fall and early winter of 1935, project approvals increased substantially, but the limited amount of money and the labor restrictions in rural areas did not allow rapid growth in the number of projects actually initiated. The state office had to explain to local governments that the quotas of money and labor restricted the program. Once the governments understood the situation, however, their complaints subsided.[19]

By the winter of 1935-1936 enough white-collar projects had been approved so that all such workers previously enrolled with the FERA were working for the WPA. Hopkins assured Miss Shepperson that the national office would reduce neither funds nor labor quotas, so that "the integrity of your projects" could be maintained. He congratulated the Georgia administrator on her perseverance and patience in the face of so much adversity and told her that he understood what she had been through.[20]

Some problems arose within the agency, but none were unmanageable. There were isolated instances of WPA paychecks being forged (a practice encountered by the FERA), and the state office turned these cases over to the Department of Justice for investigation. At one point Savannah businessmen accused the WPA's purchasing agents of awarding most contracts to Atlanta companies, but both the Savannah *Evening Press* and the *Morning Press* disproved these charges by showing that 92.51 percent of the material purchased for projects in Savannah came from local businesses.[21]

The only potentially dangerous situations occurred when politics were involved. Local residents continually wrote their congressmen for more projects, and these solons put pressure on Hopkins and Miss Shepperson. Miss Shepperson tried to apportion projects equally among the counties on the basis of population, but it was predictable that some persons should remain unsatisfied. These conditions gradually tended to create a group of people who were disaffected and ultimately opposed the entire program.[22]

Allies of Eugene Talmadge needed no such excuses, and articles attacking the WPA and particularly Miss Shepperson appeared from time to time in newspapers which supported the governor. Although the state administrator had lived in Georgia for eight years, her adversaries regarded her as a Virginian unable to understand and deal with Georgians. Her friendship with Hopkins spawned other stories, one of which was that he had discovered her in a school for delinquent girls. The most scandalous statements emanated from the office of the director of the state Veterans' Service Bureau. Allen Henson, the director and close personal friend of the governor, later simply referred to her as a "crabbed old maid" in his biography of Talmadge, but at the time his attacks were much more vitriolic.[23]

Perhaps the most notorious example of political interference in the WPA was in the Alexander Howell case. Howell, former state school superintendent, secured a job with the WPA in the fall of 1935. He supervised a group of girls who were to compile and publish school records in the Georgia Archives. Howell and his brother, State Democratic Committee Chairman Hugh Howell, were avidly pro-Talmadge. Instead of carrying out the project assigned to him, Alexander Howell used his workers to wrap and mail issues of the *Georgia Women's World,* a stridently anti-New Deal periodical which eventually found its way to the seats of all delegates at Talmadge's 1936 "grass roots" Macon convention. When this chicanery was discovered, Alexander Howell was brought before the federal grand jury in Atlanta and indicted for misuse of WPA funds. His brother lamented, "This charge marked the beginning of a new deal 'reign of terror' in Georgia."[24]

Although Talmadge generally left most of the WPA baiting to his henchmen, he was not inactive. At one point he asked Attorney General Manning Jasper Yeomans about the possibility of filing a suit in the Supreme Court against a WPA appropriation to test its constitutionality. Yeomans replied that the state could not file such a suit, since it could not act on behalf of a citizen to protect him from a federal statute.[25]

Throughout the existence of the WPA, its opponents in the state took every advantage to snipe at it. When the agency released 130 persons in early February 1936, Allen Henson sought to enjoin the move since seven of the men removed were veterans. Evidently Talmadge persuaded one of the men, who was not a veteran but a good friend of the governor, to "round up some veterans who had been fired and go to Henson." Henson announced that he would use a recent decision of a Philadelphia court providing for preferential treatment of veterans on WPA projects to seek an injunction against the WPA in Georgia. An observer in the area noted that the American Legion probably did not agree with Henson, and, in fact, Henson's move simply may have been a ploy to gain that organization's support for the governor.[26]

Even those who liked the president often did not hesitate to attack the WPA, although their criticism was usually linked to some anticipation of personal gain. One distinguished Georgia lawyer and a Roosevelt supporter complained that Miss Shepperson's payroll was "literally loaded with Talmadge appointees." The lawyer warned, "When the battle begins," these people "are going to bite the hand that fed them by helping Talmadge carry Georgia against Roosevelt." In other instances, notably in Elbert County, citizens wanted a project, but no one had registered for relief. They asked the county relief administration to certify laborers, and when it would not, they flooded Congress, Hopkins, and the White House with complaints.

Miss Shepperson noted that every time there was an election accusations arose of people being put on relief who did not belong there. The worst of these cases occurred in Augusta during a mayoralty race. Tremendous demands were made upon the county relief administrator by both sides to certify certain voters. Miss Shepperson sent Robert MacDougall and Miss FitzSimons to investigate. They reported such a terrible situation that Miss Shepperson impounded all relief funds in the city. When the local politicians discovered what had happened, they besieged Miss FitzSimons and complained to the Georgia congressional delegation. One man threatened to make Miss Shepperson "pay for it."[27]

Another avenue used to attack the WPA, along with other New Deal agencies, was racism. A number of organizations demanded to know why blacks and whites were using the same drinking fountains in the Fulton County Relief Office. Members of the quasi-fascist "Silver Shirts" appeared in Miss Shepperson's office one day "so mad they were white" and could "hardly speak." They questioned her about the drinking fountain and wanted to know why black and white male workers were forced to go through the same hallway to get to separate restrooms in the relief office. They also had heard that black men and women were addressed as Miss, Mrs., and Mr. in the office and asked whether that were true. In reply Miss Shepperson told one of her staff members to escort these men to the state capitol and the county courthouse where there were no separate drinking fountains. The men did not return.[28]

Miss Shepperson was able to deal successfully with most of these potentially explosive racial attacks. Her general rule was to draw the line in helping blacks at the point where it might seriously jeopardize her program. Her rationale—that she did as much as possible under the circumstances—was typical of liberals whose loyalties might be divided (often unequally) between the administration and the cause of Negro betterment. Neither she nor Hopkins was ever able to please all parties in this respect, however, and both frequently were attacked for ignoring the southern racial problem.

Just three months after all FERA employees had been transferred to the WPA and most projects were under way, Miss Shepperson was forced to begin thinking about a reduction in labor and projects. At the end of February 1936 the state National Emergency Council (NEC) director reported that all WPA funds would be exhausted by May 1. Delays in PWA construction caused by winter weather conditions meant that only about 50 percent of its projects were in progress. The WPA could not expect its sister works agency to absorb labor reductions.[29]

By May the situation had become acute. Funds were very low and much of the labor that remained had to be used for emergency work when devastating tornadoes demolished Gainesville and Cordelle. Congress had not yet voted additional funds, but the Emergency Relief Appropriation (ERA) Bill was in Congress, and communities with applications pending closely watched its progress.

On June 22, 1936, the ERA of 1936 became law, and the WPA could proceed with renewed vigor. The national office reorganized the WPA's administrative structure, abolishing the Office Management Division and making its director the state office manager. Programs for training administrative employees and for developing adequate efficiency ratings never were undertaken.

During the next month Miss Shepperson rearranged the field organization of the WPA in Georgia by breaking down the districts into fourteen "areas." These areas had much less authority than the former districts and were headed by an engineer and an employment officer, each with equal authority. Unfortunately, this change created a situation where there was no single head, opening the way for disagreement, friction, and confusion. Miss Shepperson retained this organization for over two years, but it never was very successful.

Despite the administrative shake-up and the formulation of new policies, local programs remained unchanged, as did many of their previous problems. The inconveniences caused by short-term allotments continued after the summer of 1936. Planning projects and purchasing materials in the state required a good deal of time. Plans had to be detailed, and when construction was involved, blueprints had to be included. Purchasing was on a project basis and was subject to certain delays inherent in the advertising and awarding of bids. The state NEC director suggested that the WPA should allow "planning for projects for a longer period of time" and provide for the purchase of materials in larger quantities. The latter provision, besides enabling engineers to proceed with projects as soon as the state office approved them, would tend to lower the unit cost.[30]

Seasonal labor demands, particularly on the farm, periodically forced the curtailment of WPA projects, and white-collar projects were always difficult to initiate. Other agencies continued to ask for workers, and many people still believed that the high wages and security afforded WPA laborers were keeping them out of private enterprise. Government officials and businessmen, as usual, lined up on opposite sides of the

issue. The state NEC director felt that, if industry raised wages and
lowered working hours, "work relief could be reduced by 15 or 20
percent." Businessmen, on the other hand, opposed the security wage
which they felt was too high. Relief workers complained of delays in
the payroll.[31] Some dissatisfaction came from those seeking WPA jobs.
Sporadic letters reached the state office in which disaffected laborers
charged that there were people working for the WPA who did not
need relief. Investigations by the state office, however, generally disproved these allegations.[32]

In 1935 and 1936 there had been a constant turnover of relief labor
on the WPA, but by 1937 the labor force was more static. The WPA
had provided no real job training except in the sewing rooms and in the
white-collar program. Training in skilled crafts might have attracted
opposition from organized labor. Industry had been generally unable
to absorb large numbers of laborers, especially women and white-
collar workers, and in many cases employers preferred to hire nonrelief labor when jobs opened. Positions which were available went
primarily to young people, so that the number of older workers on the
WPA programs increased. By mid-1937 the WPA appeared to have
become a reservoir for the employment of men over forty-five years
of age and for women.[33]

By the fall of 1937 WPA employment was below the state's quota,
having declined about 20 percent from June to September. Therefore,
despite public preference for construction projects and the difficulty
in securing sponsors for nonmanual programs, the state office began
to emphasize white-collar projects. Miss Shepperson appointed a special
supervisor, hoping to mold the WPA's programs to the needs of those
who remained on the rolls. She also reduced the number of areas in
Georgia from fourteen to nine. The state NEC director forecast an
increase in the relief load during the winter of 1937-1938, but saw no
real need to step up the WPA's programs. The WPA seemed on its way
to becoming a minor agency, but this all was changed by the recession
of 1937-1938.[34]

The 1936 reorganization did not alter substantially the WPA's programs, nor the reaction to them. Although a poll of the Georgia Press
Association membership showed that about 92 percent of the state's
newspapers supported the New Deal programs, opposition continued,
especially on the political front. During the reorganization some mem-

bers of the state staff resigned, and Miss Shepperson had to seek replacements. Congressman Robert Ramspeck took the occasion of one such
resignation to write the federal administrator asking that only state
residents be hired to WPA posts in the future. He told Hopkins that
the "Administration and myself have been bitterly criticized about
this . . . [because] the heads of most of the departments were not
residents of the area served by the office." When the national office
replied that it had difficulty in filling technical positions with qualified
personnel, Ramspeck remarked that this was absurd. Both he and
Senator Russell had been attacked on this matter in their recent political
campaigns. If the WPA could find no suitable staff in the area, then
Ramspeck offered to suggest the names of qualified people. The national
office still maintained that it did try to hire local persons where possible,
and pointed out that of the 396 workers employed in the Atlanta area
office 368 were from the Atlanta area, 18 from elsewhere in Georgia,
and 10 from other states. Senator Russell also wrote to Hopkins complaining of the situation, and he received much the same answer.[35]

As a result of this friction, the Atlanta *Journal* speculated that "the
Georgia delegation in Congress would not be adverse to a change in the
setup of the WPA in this state." Talmadge's second term as governor
would be ending in 1936, and when the pro-administration candidate,
Eurith D. Rivers, was elected to succeed him, the newspapers predicted
that the majority of congressmen would "go to bat to change the . . .
setup as soon as practicable after the anti-Roosevelt organization of
Eugene Talmadge has been supplanted by Rivers."

Editorialist Tarleton Collier agreed with this theory. He saw the
"vague, but numerous attacks" on Miss Shepperson and the WPA as
"trial balloons" sent up by her opponents to see if "the state of Georgia
. . . [would] take a shot" at them. If the public responded favorably
to the idea, the congressional delegation would propose a change. Collier,
himself, did not support the plan. He noted that claims of the WPA in
Georgia being singled out for federalization were false. It was true that
Hopkins had taken over the FERA, but the WPA was a federal program
in all states. Furthermore, the epithets of carpetbagging hurled at Miss
Shepperson were not true. Not only had she resided in the state before
the New Deal, but she had served in the state's public welfare agency.
Collier concluded that the three things which bothered people most
about Miss Shepperson were that she was a woman, that she was honest,

and that she was inaccessible. Collier denied that she was inaccessible; her office was always filled with people who had come to see her. Miss Shepperson later agreed that many people (among them Senator Russell) disliked the idea of a woman administrator, especially one who controlled such a great amount of money. She felt that it was not that these people were interested in promoting graft for personal benefit as much as they resented a woman having "all that money and power," especially since she was the only woman administrator in the nation.[36]

Miss Shepperson and the WPA became involved in one other major political controversy that centered around the 1938 senatorial election. Roosevelt desired to oust Senator Walter George, but the president made the mistake of personally entering the lists. He took the occasion of a dedication ceremony in Georgia to launch a political attack on the senior senator, becoming so concerned with this that he "forgot to throw the switch." The president's speech signaled the formation of political lines in the state as all sides prepared for a bitter battle.

Speculation arose as to what sort of pressures the administration might apply to gain support for Lawrence Camp, Roosevelt's candidate. To complicate matters, Eugene Talmadge also entered the fray. If the administration had expected Miss Shepperson to lend a hand, it was to be sorely disappointed. Hopkins had chosen her to lead the relief work in the state because of her loyalty and honesty, and he and the president soon found that the latter quality transcended the former.

Of course, she could not control what took place at the local level completely, and she certainly would not attempt to prevent relief employees from supporting Camp. In fact the "WPA union organization" did endorse him. There were many complaints from the local units of officials trying to coerce relief workers, but these charges were not restricted to those who supported the president. Miss Shepperson scrupulously investigated all such allegations and found most of them to be unsubstantiated. In the one case where a WPA official had campaigned (not coerced) on a project, Miss Shepperson suspended him for thirty days. When Senator George won an easy victory, many pro-New Dealers blamed the state administrator and Governor Rivers for Camp's defeat. Talmadge, however, also had lost in his bid for the Senate. It was ironic that he had been beaten by Senator Russell in 1936 because he did not support Roosevelt, and he was defeated now because the president had attacked George.

The role of the agencies in the election was not as easily defined as the president's supporters claimed. Political commentators in Washington and Atlanta pointed out that the programs were not really very strong in Georgia. Miss Shepperson always had tried to avoid making political appointments, so that there were relatively few politically oriented officials in her agencies. Finally, as Atlanta *Constitution* reporter Ralph McGill noted, about 40 percent of the 53,000 people on WPA rolls were blacks who were not allowed to vote in the Democratic primary at all.[37]

Camp's defeat brought forth serious accusations if not actions. On December 15, 1938, Miss Shepperson's assistant administrator, Robert MacDougall, resigned to accept a position as technical director of the Atlanta Housing Authority. His move broke up a team which had existed since 1933, longer than in any other state. Coming as it did on the heels of the summer's senatorial campaign, observers viewed MacDougall's resignation as one of its results.

During the fall of 1938 Camp supporters had kept up a barrage of criticism against Miss Shepperson and MacDougall. They claimed that these relief officials were "able to throw blocks of WPA votes to George." They also accused the state office of "using the WPA enrollment to 'punish' Camp supporters." Miss Shepperson's relation to Hopkins made it impossible for him to remove her, they suggested, but he had offered her the regional directorship of the Social Security Administration in Birmingham to get her out of the state. With conditions so uncertain, they felt MacDougall resigned, so that if there were a shake-up in the WPA, he would not be involved.

Both Camp and MacDougall denied these allegations. Camp had not expected the aid of the WPA in his campaign and was certainly not trying to change its administration in the state. MacDougall denied that he was leaving a sinking ship. He told the press that he was accepting the new position because "he wanted to help build slum clearance projects" and for no other reason. Upon Miss Shepperson's retirement in November 1939, MacDougall returned to the state WPA and took her place. Perhaps this indicated that he had been tired of being second in command when he resigned, but it did not mean that he was returning to the ship now that it was stabilized.[38]

Those who felt that the WPA was beginning to atrophy in the summer and early fall of 1937 did not anticipate the severe recession which began late that fall. Both farmers and wage earners felt the impact of plummeting cotton prices and the cutback in New Deal programs. The WPA had room in its quota to absorb some of these people, but "successful" farmers were not eligible, and businessmen retained their laborers, working them as little as one shift in every two or three days. Since part-time workers could not be hired by the WPA, wage earners caught in this situation were ineligible for relief.

The relief rolls grew tremendously that winter, but since the crisis had occurred at the end of an appropriation period, the state office did not have enough funds or projects. As of April 1, 1938, for example, about 2,850 unemployed families had been certified in Fulton and DeKalb counties, an increase during the preceding four months of over 100 percent. The state office estimated that by the end of the month about 2,500 more persons would be certified if the daily rate continued at even one-half of the previous week's certifications.

This tremendous pressure was intensified by the passage of the Emergency Relief Appropriations Act approved on June 21, 1938. Although the new law provided more funds, it allowed the agency to give part-time work to farmers. This accelerated the rate of applications from August to November and put a great strain upon the local offices of the state Department of Public Welfare, which now was responsible for certification. The state office responded by increasing the budget for intake in the Department of Public Welfare and providing a special registrar in almost every county to assist in filling out new, abbreviated certification forms.[39]

The rush of applicants to the WPA brought forth complaints from farmers who could not afford to compete with the agency's higher wages. The WPA admitted that while it had not "been an important factor in the abandonment of farms," it probably had hastened the movement. Heretofore the WPA had drawn its workers from "a previously existing pool of labor," but it now found that many regular tenants, sharecroppers, and wage hands were not even attempting "to make farming arrangements." The state office, therefore, agreed to release all farm laborers during the 1938 harvesting season.[40]

The recession of 1937-1938 also promoted unrest within industrial labor's ranks. After the establishment of the Committee for Industrial Organization in 1935, unions began to make advances in Georgia (although the trade unions still were much stronger). The passage of the

Wagner Act the same year also gave labor new strength, and unions became more vociferous in expressing their dissatisfaction with the WPA. The unions complained that WPA projects hurt skilled labor in that they pre-empted construction which otherwise would have gone to private contractors. They claimed that the WPA fostered "legalized peonage." The Georgia Federation of Labor informed Hopkins that "county officials in Georgia have termed the WPA a 'racket' and boasted that they would take advantage of the reliefers by making them work at very low wages." On the other hand, some skilled workers complained that they could not get jobs with the WPA unless they joined a union.[41]

The Emergency Relief Appropriation Act of 1939 instituted new labor provisions, abolishing the prevailing wage concept, reducing the allowable work time to 130 hours a month, and providing that all workers employed continuously for a period of 18 months were to be dropped and could not reapply for work for 30 days. Labor reacted strongly to the 130-hour section, and some workers threatened to walk off their jobs. The unions, however, were not yet strong enough to carry out their plan. At most only 113 laborers walked out, and 55 of them returned. These failures forced labor officials to find other ways of imposing their will upon the WPA. For a time one such leader came very close to disrupting the Atlanta office completely.

Despite isolated instances of opposition, the state office reported that most groups were willing to accept the new conditions. The provisions did not change the farm situation, since WPA wages always had been considerably above farm wages. The new wage scale was lower than that of private industry in large cities, so complaints from businesses there were few, and those that did arise usually were linked to the employer's failure to request labor through the Georgia State Employment Service. Although sponsors had to increase their contributions under the 1939 act, they too accepted the measure fairly gracefully.[42]

In 1939 two events occurred which substantially changed the organization and purpose of the WPA. Since January 1937 the president had been trying to consolidate all relief agencies. He finally achieved this reorganization in July 1939 under the Federal Works Agency. The WPA, now titled the Works Projects Administration, became part of the new agency, and several administrative changes were made. Of greatest importance was the shift in emphasis from relief to works. The WPA promised more efficiency in the operation of projects concentrating upon "service rendered to the community," rather than upon the relief afforded workers. In February 1940 the Georgia administration responded by reorganizing its state and field setup. An administrative division was formed in the state office, and the original district structure was re-established. The state was divided into five districts, each headed by a district manager with four divisions under him: Employment, Operations, Finance, and Professional and Service. Although this solved the problems created by the area arrangement, it led to increased autonomy in the districts. The state office still made policy decisions, but the district managers did not have to carry them out. After 1940 the state office came to serve more and more in an advisory capacity to the districts. This system remained until a few months before the final liquidation of the WPA in Georgia. Then, for the short time left, the areas were re-established, and the divisions again came under the direct control of state division heads.[43]

The second major occurrence of 1939 was the outbreak of war in Europe. On a policy level this resulted in the gradual inclusion of defense projects in the WPA's program. The war also had a tremendous effect upon the labor market. WPA officials did not expect war industry to boom in Georgia, since the state's major products were non-essential cotton and tobacco, but they were soon proved to be mistaken. As the nation's need for cotton rose, farmers insisted that WPA workers be released to take jobs in agriculture. Defense industries began to move into the state, creating a great demand for workers. Local governments insisted that labor be available as an incentive for industry to locate in their counties, and they were perfectly willing to use the force of law to remove WPA workers from their projects.

Factories were needed, and contractors always had preferred black construction labor, so the district manager for Bibb County removed all blacks from the WPA's rolls, even though there was a large supply of white labor present in the county. The blacks complained, saying that they did not mind working for private businesses even though the hourly rate was some seven cents lower. They did oppose, however, the contractors' "double call" system of asking for twice as many men as they required. Blacks were forced to leave the WPA to be put into "bullpens," seatless, fenced in, shadeless areas, where they had to spend days waiting for jobs without their WPA pay.[44]

By the fall of 1939 it was clear to Miss Shepperson that there was really no longer any need for a social worker to head the program. She had been with the relief agencies for seven years and had been subjected to much pressure. In her regretful letter of resignation she simply noted, "I am too tired to continue carrying this responsibility." In mid-November Roosevelt accepted her resignation and appointed her former assistant, Robert L. MacDougall, to succeed her. He served until late 1940 when he, too, resigned and was replaced by a newcomer to the Georgia administration, Harry E. Harmon, Jr. Harmon held the post until January 1943, when he quit to take a job with the War Department. He was succeeded by an acting administrator, R. Marvin Porter, until the program was terminated that same year.[45]

To many people the WPA was synonymous with the New Deal. It was the largest of the work programs both in terms of the amount of money it spent and the number of different projects it undertook. Over half of the funds were used by the Division of Operations for construction projects, and a fourth went to the Service Division. Most of the remainder was used by the Divisions of Training and Reemployment.

The Operations Division ran the work projects through its field engineers who were responsible for their "planning and development." Before an application was submitted, an official of the division made a "field inspection" to determine "the availability of local materials, equipment, and the required classes of labor." If he found all of these necessities present, he met with the sponsor to draw up preliminary plans, always guided by the tenet providing for the maximum use of relief labor without loss of efficiency. When this had been completed, the sponsor submitted its "preliminary project application together with plans and specifications approved by registered architects or engineers."[46]

Often in rural areas such personnel were not available, and the division supplied qualified people to aid in the work. After approval at the district or area level, the application was passed on to the state office to be considered by the Engineering and Review Unit of the Operations Division. This unit drew up the operating plans and resubmitted them to the sponsor for final approval. Although the procedure was fairly complicated, it insured that project forms then submitted to the national office would be acceptable.

The state office's concern for a proposed project did not end with its approval by the national office. Before Miss Shepperson allowed any project to begin, the state director of the Operations Division had to receive a "plan-in-hand" inspection report (made after approval of the project application), a certification from the district or area director that the sponsor had complied with its duties and all regulations, a sponsor's agreement "certifying ownership" of the property and compliance with "all statutory provisions," and a copy of the "cost estimate" of the project. The state Planning and Control Section of the Division of Operations reviewed these documents, and, if they were in order, the state director allowed work to commence.[47]

The state office did not relinquish control or supervision of the projects once they were begun. Initially Miss Shepperson allowed sponsors to provide their own supervisors, but as the program matured the division provided an increasing number of these men. Supervisors picked by the sponsors tended to look to the sponsor for instructions and often lost sight of the WPA's priority of labor over product. The Operations Division also monitored the proportion of federal nonlabor costs and sponsor's contributions. For the first two years this responsibility lay in the district offices, and the state's nonlabor budget was distributed "at the discretion of the District Directors." When the state division found, however, that this practice "did not encourage advance planning for nonlabor needs," it assumed personal responsibility for the allotment of these funds. Further revision was necessary before this cumbersome process operated smoothly.[48]

Despite all the care which the state office took in trying to guarantee the efficient operation of the work program, there were still many problems. Regional investigators found that sponsors' interest and enthusiasm declined from the time they first submitted their applications to the actual inception of the project. Lengthy delays caused by the approval process occasionally created "active resentment."[49]

Careful planning sometimes went for naught. An investigator touring the state in 1936 reported that in Atlanta, Marietta, and Savannah, "The present difficulties observed in the efficient execution of the work can be traced to lack of plans; lack of organization of work; lack of progress schedules; delay in furnishing right-of-way; deficiency in engineering personnel; failure of material to arrive on time and uncertainties with regard to future allotment of funds." The last problem was inherent in the yearly allotment limit of the WPA, but all the others should have been prevented by careful scrutiny and stringent requirements of the Operations Division.[50]

Difficulties within local governments also impeded progress. Often sponsors could not raise the required funds to finance their share of the project costs, and the WPA was forced to withdraw. Sometimes politics or internal friction resulted in the delay or abandonment of projects, especially when political leaders attempted to use them to bolster personal support.

The problems which the state office faced were not confined to the projects themselves. Farmers claimed that the WPA usurped their labor supply and attacked the whole program through the projects in their vicinity. Private enterprise, especially the construction companies, constantly charged that the WPA was in direct competiton with them. They never accepted the agency's claim that its work would not have been undertaken by local governments without WPA help.

A survey taken in 1938 by a state appraisal committee in 148 counties reflected the public's favorable opinion of the WPA's construction program. Sponsors preferred the WPA to the FERA, because the former was more strictly a work program. An outright dole would have been cheaper, but sponsors felt that the extra cost was offset by the public improvements that they obtained. Sponsors indicated that the ability and efficiency of relief labor compared favorably with that found in private construction. The committee stated that "there has been no suggestion of misuse of money," and "sponsors commend highly the administrative officials." As an expression of their support of the WPA, sponsors were "almost unanimous in asking for a continuation of the programs."[51]

The sanitation and malarial control projects were among the most popular in the state. The sanitation program was a carry-over from the CWA and the FERA. Under the WPA (and the PWA) it was expanded to include a statewide community sanitation project for the construction of small sewage treatment plants and sewerage systems. Vying with sanitation for popularity were the school projects. The WPA constructed new buildings or made additions to 346 schools in Georgia and reconstructed or improved 544 schools. The black population of the state was particularly pleased with this program. Georgia's school system always had been poor, and black schools rarely received money to erect or maintain educational facilities. County governments still hesitated to sponsor black school projects under the WPA, but more progress came about under the agency than would have been possible otherwise. Paradoxically, that section of the country reputed to give blacks the

worst treatment was always the first to point out the things it did for
them. Thus the Atlanta *Constitution* was proud to claim that the first
black school in the nation built with WPA funds had been constructed
in Georgia. The entire project took just three weeks to complete,
giving some indication, perhaps, of the quality of the work.[52]

The WPA also built parks, playgrounds, athletic fields, swimming and
wading pools, utility plants, airports, and similar facilities. The largest
single undertaking, however, was the highway program. The WPA spent
42.1 percent of all its funds through June 1942 to build or improve
highways, roads, and streets; to build bridges and viaducts; and to construct culverts.[53]

The WPA construction programs always were hampered by an inability
to formulate long-range plans. If President Hoover lost the nation's
confidence by claiming that prosperity was just around the corner,
President Roosevelt and Congress indicated by programs, if not words,
that they felt the same way. Although the administration recognized
that the depression was not going to be overcome quickly and consequently reorganized the relief structure in the summer of 1935, the
resultant policies still reflected the attitude that relief was only
"temporary." The WPA never was more than an emergency agency, and
the administration took care to reiterate this fact every six months "to
each employee in the State."

All planning, funding, and administration revolved around the emergency image. Each year a new bill was presented to Congress providing
for the continuation of the WPA for another twelve months. Since
funds were available for only one year, project planning had to be considered in this light. Furthermore, the yearly laws often included administrative changes so that inevitably the months of "July and August of
each year [had] to be devoted largely to reorganization." It was to the
credit of Miss Shepperson and her staff that they were able to keep
the program moving in the face of such obstacles. As time passed she
was able to devise a schedule whereby projects could be completed in
yearly units, so that if the WPA were suddenly abolished, the work
would not be lost.

The state office bemoaned the restrictions placed upon it by national
decisions. It felt that many of the procedures corresponded to the needs
of the "industrial East," and not the agricultural South. Georgia was
limited by the nature of work which could be undertaken and the

makeup and skills of the relief population. The service program, for instance, was extremely difficult to run in the state, and federal orders restricting the use of nonrelief personnel hampered its operations.

After proposing a number of specific changes in its final report, the Georgia office made a particularly revealing suggestion: that the state administrators take part in major policy decisions regarding the operation of the WPA. This statement possibly represented what Miss Shepperson could not say directly to her friend Hopkins: Often her achievements came in spite of the national office, rather than because of it.[54]

NOTES

1. The WPA's name was changed to Work Projects Administration in the reorganization of July 1939, reflecting, in part, a shift in emphasis from relief to works.

2. Interview with Gay Shepperson. Atlanta *Constitution,* April 12 and 13, 1935.

3. Shepperson to Hopkins, June 24, 1935, NARG 69, WPA, State Series, No. 630, box 1119. WPA, "Final Report," NARG 69, WPA, p. 7.

4. Unsigned report, July 29, 1935, NARG 44, National Emergency Council (NEC), General Correspondence with State Directors (1934-35), box 174.

5. Report of Ralph Langley, August 7, 1935, NARG 69, Region III, No. 132.3, box 185. Shepperson to Miller, August 5, 1935, NARG 69, Region III, No. 132.3, box 185. Unsigned report, August 20, 1935, NARG 44, Digests, box 489.

6. Shepperson to Miller, August 5, 1935, NARG 69, Region III, No. 132.3, box 185. Unsigned report, August 27, 1935, NARG 44, Periodical Reports (1934-38), box 400.

7. Unsigned report, July 29, 1935, NARG 44, Corres., Directories, Repts., box 347. Shepperson to Miller, August 5, 1935, NARG 69, Region III, No. 132.3, box 185.

8. Shepperson to Hopkins, June 12, 1936, NARG 69, State Series, No. 651.101, box 1131. Unsigned report, September 10, 1935, NARG 44, Digests, box 491.

9. Atlanta *Constitution,* September 28, 1935. Edward Aaron Gaston, Jr., "A History of the Negro Wage Earner in Georgia, 1890-1940" (unpublished Ph.D. dissertation, Department of History, Emory University, 1957),

p. 386. Semi-monthly narrative report, September 1-15, 1935, NARG 69, State Series, No. 650, box 1128.

10. Margaret Loomis Stecker, *Intercity Differences in Cost of Living in March, 1935,* WPA, Research Monograph No. 12, Social Research Division (1937), pp. 162, 177. Arthur F. Raper and Ira DeA. Reid, *Sharecroppers All* (Chapel Hill: University of North Carolina Press, 1941), p. 165. Atlanta *Constitution,* May 23, 1935. Donald S. Howard, *The WPA and Federal Relief Policy* (New York: Russell Sage Foundation, 1943), pp. 160, 177, 178.

11. Interview with Gay Shepperson.

12. Unsigned report, August 27, 1935, NARG 44, Digests, box 490. Interview with Gay Shepperson. Shepperson to Lawrence Westbrook, October 2, 1935 (telegram), NARG 69, State Series, No. 610, box 1113. Westbrook to Shepperson, October 3, 1935 (telegram), NARG 69, State Series, No. 610, box 1113. Nels Anderson to A. Steve Nance, July 13, 1935, NARG 69, State Series, No. 641, box 1122. William Belcher to Roosevelt, May 29, 1935 (telegram), NARG 69, State Series, No. 641, box 1123.

13. Shepperson to Hopkins, October 27, 1935 (telegram), NARG 69, State Series, No. 610, box 1113. Hopkins and Shepperson, August 13, 1935 (telephone conversation), NARG 69, State Series, No. 610, box 1113. Unsigned report, October 8, 1935, NARG 44, Digests, box 493. Atlanta *Constitution,* October 11, 1935.

14. Unsigned report, October 12, 1935, NARG 44, Digests, box 493. Atlanta *Constitution,* October 15, 1935.

15. Brehon Somervoll to Chief Engineer and Administrative Assistant, November 6, 1935, NARG 69, State Series, No. 610, box 1113. Atlanta *Constitution,* November 5 and 6, 1935.

16. Congressman Robert Ramspeck to Jacob Baker, November 7, 1935 (telegram), NARG 69, State Series, No. 641, box 122. Nance to Baker, November 6, 1935 (telegram), NARG 69, State Series, No. 641, box 1123.

17. Brehon Somervoll to Chief Engineer, November 6, 1935, NARG 69, State Series, No. 610, box 1113. Shepperson and Hopkins, November 7, 1935 (telephone conversation), NARG 69, State Series, No. 610, box 1113. Atlanta *Constitution,* November 7, 1935.

18. Atlanta *Constitution,* November 7 and 9, 1935. J. A. Harper and George L. Googe to A. Steve Nance, October 15, 1935, NARG 69, State Series, No. 641, box 1122.

19. Atlanta *Constitution,* July 24, 1935. WPA, "Monthly Review of Relief Statistics," II, 1 (November 1935), 1. Unsigned report, October

26, 1935, NARG 44, Digests, box 495. Unsigned report, December 28, 1935, NARG 44, Digests, box 499. Bruce Hall to Morton Mildord, December 6, 1935, State Series, No. 610, box 1113.

20. Unsigned report, January 1, 1936, NARG 44, Digests, box 499. Hopkins to Shepperson, November 2, 1935, NARG 69, State Series, No. 610, box 1113.

21. Unsigned report, January 18, 1936, NARG 44, Digests, box 500. Westbrook to Oliver Griswold, May 1, 1936 (memo), NARG 69, State Series, No. 614, box 1117. Savannah *Evening Press,* April 27, 1936. Savannah *Morning Press,* April 27, 1936.

22. Interview with Gay Shepperson. Westbrook and Congressman Braswell Dean, January 22, 1936 (telephone conversation), NARG 69, State Series, No. 610, box 1113. Shepperson to Westbrook, February 2, 1936, NARG 69, State Series, No. 610, box 1113.

23. Glen S. Taylor to Thomas B. Rhodes, February 20, 1936, NARG 69, State Series, No. 610, box 1113. Allen L. Henson, *Red Galluses: A Story of Georgia Politics* (Boston: House of Edinboro Publishers, 1945), p. 115.

24. Walter Davenport, "Shouting Dies," *Colliers,* XCVII, 18 (May 2, 1936), 34. "Brothers Howell," *Time,* XXVII, 8 (February 24, 1936), 17.

25. Attorney General to Talmadge, October 11, 1935, Georgia State Archives, RG 1, Series 5, Executive Department Correspondence, Eugene Talmadge, 1935.

26. Glen Taylor to Thomas Rhodes, February 20, 1936, NARG 69, State Series, No. 610, box 1113. Atlanta *Journal,* February 18, 1936.

27. Interview with Gay Shepperson. Columbus *News Record,* August 17, 1935.

28. *Ibid.* Atlanta *Constitution,* August 8, 1935.

29. Atlanta *Journal,* February 16, 1936. Unsigned report, February 11, 1936, NARG 44, Periodical Reports (1934-38), box 400. Unsigned report, February 29, 1936, NARG 44, Digests, box 502.

30. Unsigned report, August 4, 1936, NARG 44, Periodical Reports (1934-38), box 400.

31. Unsigned report, October 10, 1936, NARG 44, Digests, box 509. Unsigned report, November 11, 1936, NARG 44, Digests, box 509. Atlanta *Constitution,* September 19, 1937. Unsigned report, July 15, 1937, NARG 44, Digests, box 511. Shepperson to Niles, May 29, 1937, NARG 69, State Series, No. 640, box 1120. Unsigned report, March 10, 1937, NARG 44, Digests, box 510. "General Information About the WPA Program," October 1937, NARG 69, State Series, No. 640, box 1121. Hal J. Wright to M. J. Miller, April 22 and 23, 1939 (report),

NARG 69, Region III, No. 132.3, box 185.

32. Unsigned report, March 10, 1937, NARG 44, Digests, box 510.
Unsigned report, June 15, 1937, NARG 44, Digests, box 511.

33. Unsigned report, June 15, 1937, NARG 44, Digests, box 511.
Unsigned report, July 21, 1936, NARG 44, Periodical Reports (1934-38),
box 400. Unsigned report, July 14, 1937, NARG 44, Periodical Reports
(1934-38), box 399. Unsigned reports, April 10 and August 16, 1937,
NARG 44, Digests, box 511.

34. Unsigned report, October 15, 1937, NARG 44, Digests, box 512.
Unsigned report, September 15, 1937, NARG 44, Digests, box 512.
Williams to Shepperson, October 27, 1937, NARG 69, State Series,
No. 610, box 1113.

35. Bruce Hall to David K. Niles, July 28, 1936, NARG 69, State
Series, No. 614, box 1117. Ramspeck to Hopkins, August 26, 1936
(telegram), NARG 69, State Series, No. 610, box 1113. Correspondence
between Ramspeck and Emerson Ross, August 28-December 10, 1936,
NARG 69, State Series, No. 610, box 1113. Russell to Hopkins, October
5, 1936 (telegram), NARG 69, State Series, No. 693, box 1151. M. J.
Miller to Aubrey Williams, November 10, 1936, NARG 69, State Series,
No. 693, box 1151. Marinel F. Whitlock to Hopkins, November 27,
1937 (telegram), NARG 69, State Series, No. 610, box 1113.

36. Atlanta *Journal,* December 14 and 16, 1936. Interview with
Gay Shepperson.

37. Robert S. Allen and Drew Pearson, "The Daily Washington
Merry-Go-Round," Atlanta *Journal,* August 3, 1938. Raymond Clapper,
"Blunders in Georgia," Atlanta *Journal,* August 31, 1938. *The New York
Times,* August 20, 1938. Atlanta *Constitution,* August 7 and 19, 1938.
Roy E. Fossett, "The Impact of the New Deal on Georgia Politics, 1933-
1941" (unpublished Ph.D. dissertation, Department of Political Science,
University of Florida, 1960), p. 304. Melton D. Inabinet to Hopkins,
September 13, 1938, NARG 69, State Series, No. 610, box 1113.

38. Atlanta *Georgian,* December 16, 1938. Fred M. Baker to Dallas
Dort, November 28, 1939, NARG 69, State Series, No. 630, box 1119.
"Complaints," 1938, NARG 69, State Series, No. 610, box 1113.
Atlanta *Constitution,* December 12 and 17, 1938. Atlanta *Journal,*
December 16 and 18, 1938.

39. "Interpretation of Figures Reported on WPA Form 166," NARG
69, State Series, No. 640, box 1121. C. A. Strickland to Emerson Ross,
April 2, 1938, NARG 69, State Series, No. 640, box 1121.

40. C. A. Strickland to David K. Niles, September 27, 1938, NARG
69, State Series, No. 642, box 1123. Macon *Telegraph,* September 7,

1938. "Brief Summary of the WPA," NARG 69, State Series, No. 610, box 1114.

41. Shepperson to Anderson, December 22, 1938, NARG 69, State Series, No. 640, box 1121. Hopkins to Senator Russell, July 22, 1938, NARG 69, State Series, No. 641, box 1124. Mrs. Grace Darnell to Harrington, February 20, 1939, NARG 69, State Series, No. 641, box 1125.

42. Shepperson to Corrington Gill, July 12, 1939 (telegram), NARG 69, State Series, No. 640, box 1121. Shepperson to Rauch, July 17, 1939 (telegram), NARG 69, State Series, No. 640, box 1121. Shepperson to Rauch, July 20, 1939, NARG 69, State Series, No. 641, box 1125. "Factual Information as to the Effect of the Schedule of Monthly Earnings Which Was Established by General Order No. 1 Issued August 15, 1939, as Required by Section 15(a) of the Emergency Relief Appropriations Act of 1939," NARG 69, State Series, No. 640, box 1122.

43. WPA, "Final Report," NARG 69, pp. 3, 5-6. "WPA Manual of Procedure," 1940 (?), NARG 69, State Series, No. 640, box 1121.

44. Shepperson to Howard O. Hunter, September 23, 1939, NARG 69, State Series, No. 640, box 1121. R. L. MacDougall to Rauch, May 2, 1940, NARG 69, State Series, No. 641, box 1125. W. J. Trent, Jr., to John Carmody, June 18, 1941 (memo), NARG 69, State Series, No. 641, box 1125. Macon *Telegraph,* June 6, 1941. H. E. Harmon, Jr., to M. J. Miller, July 1, 1941, NARG 69, State Series, No. 641, box 1125.

45. Fred M. Baker to Dallas Dort, November 28, 1939, NARG 69, State Series, No. 630, box 1119. Shepperson to Harrington, November 21, 1939, NARG 69, State Series, No. 630, box 1119. Shepperson to Harrington, , August 7, 1939, NARG 69, State Series, No. 630, box 1119. Harmon to George H. Fild, January 11, 1943 (telegram), NARG 69, State Series, No. 630, box 1119. Howard O. Hunter to Roosevelt, October 28, 1940, NARG 69, State Series, No. 630, box 1119. Franklin M. Garrett, *Atlanta and Environs: A Chronicle of Its People and Events.* (New York: Lewis Historical Publishing Company, Inc., 1954), II, 1004.

46. FWA, WPA, *Report on Progress of the WPA Program.* (Washington: U.S. Government Printing Office, 1942), pp. 73-75. WPA, "Final Report," III, 2.

47. WPA, "Final Report," III, 2.

48. *Ibid.*, pp. 1, 7.

49. Langley to Fellows, October 19, 1935 (report), NARG 69, Region III, No. 132.3, box 185.

50. Report of Lt. Col. Brehon Somervoll, March 12, 1936, NARG 69, Region III, No. 132.3, box 185.

51. *Public Welfare,* XIII, 3 (May 1938), 8. WPA, "Inventory: An

Appraisal of the Results of the Works Progress Administration"
(Washington: U.S. Government Printing Office, 1938), pp. 93, 95.

52. WPA, *Report on Progress of the WPA Program.* (Washington: U.S.
Government Printing Office, 1942), pp. 73-75, 83-84. Georgia, State
Department of Public Health, *Report* (1937), pp. 71, 74. Department of
Public Health, *Report* (1938), p. 123. Department of Public Health,
Report (1939), p. 58. Atlanta *Constitution,* September 28, 1935. Georgia,
State Department of Education, *Reports* (1934-36), p. 24.

53. WPA, *Report on Progress,* pp. 73-75, 83-84. Shepperson to
Roosevelt, November 23, 1935, NARG 69, State Series, No. 610, box 1113.

54. WPA, "Final Report," p. 1; III, 1; and X. See Appendix, Tables 11-14.

4

How the Medicine Works: The WPA Service Program

While every type of project carried out by the WPA, both manual and nonmanual, had been anticipated under the FERA and the CWA, the nonmanual program emerged in 1935 as the least developed. No solution had been found to the special problems of labor, administration, and sponsorship which it presented to the relief agencies, and thus it was passed on to the WPA in an unsatisfactory state. The haste with which the WPA was implemented left little time for additional planning. The construction programs were already running rather smoothly, but the women's and service programs were destined to remain disorganized and insufficient until the WPA put forth considerable efforts to remedy the situation.

Originally the WPA made no plans for a separate service or women's division. However, seeing the need for increased attention in this area, it created the position of Director of Women's Work in the Works Division. At first, Georgia's Director of Women's Work, Miss Jane Van De Vrede, handled only women's projects, but by the fall of 1935 she had obtained control of more nonmanual programs. Eventually the education, recreation, and research and records sections, which had reported directly to Miss Shepperson, also came under Miss Van De Vrede's command. Miss Shepperson raised Women's Work to divisional status equal to, and separate from, the Operations Division. As white-collar and professional projects became more important, the division's name was changed to Women's and Professional, and finally to Professional and Service, as the male-female distinctions in the programs were leveled. When the WPA girded itself for war, the Professional and Service Division became the Community Service Division, representing the changing emphasis in all programs to meet war needs.

The structure of the Service Division paralleled that of the Operations Division. Each program was under the control of a state supervisor, who had responsibility for the technical aspects of the projects. District supervisors were responsible to the state supervisor in technical matters and to the district director of the Service Division administratively. This separation of technical and administrative spheres of accountability caused the same difficulties that arose under the "area" structure of the Operations Division. With "careful planning and training," however, the effect of the flaw was minimized.[1]

As head of Women's Work, Miss Van De Vrede quickly discovered that conditions were not going to change very much from those existing under the FERA. Early in August 1935 she outlined the problems for which "no satisfactory answer has been found." Foremost were time and personnel. The national office placed top priority on construction projects, ostensibly because they could be initiated quickly and would use a large number of workers. Unmentioned, but undoubtedly equally important for political reasons, was that state and local governments preferred the construction projects which left more physical evidence of their accomplishments. Since by law only 5 (later 10) percent of the WPA's funds could be spent for administrative purposes, the Service Division absorbed the loss of personnel pre-empted for the Operations Division.[2]

Without an adequate staff the Service Division lacked sufficient supervision for its projects and found it extremely hard to make effective and continuous contact with prospective sponsors. Even with a full complement of personnel the Service Division would have had difficulty finding sponsors for its projects, but without enough staff it was especially hard to "convince public officials that furnishing materials for women's work is as important as furnishing construction materials, and that the labor of women offers an economic way to supply institutions and families with clothing, bedding, house furnishings and supplies, including canned and dried vegetables and fruits." Miss Shepperson believed that, had such staff been available, the Service Division would have been able "to convince public officials that this program is not extraneous to business recovery, especially the training and retraining of individuals, that the needy for whom they are responsible will receive greater benefits because of it, . . . and that such work might lead to a permanent work or welfare program for the county and cut down delinquency and vagrancy."[3]

The Service Division encountered other serious obstacles in finding sponsors. Unit costs for the projects were high. Many cities and towns had limited funds, and they preferred to spend what money they had on the construction projects. Local governments tended to operate on monthly budgets, moreover, which prevented them from "set[ting] aside large sums of money for material at any one time." Had local governments been able to lower material costs through bulk purchases, they might have been more willing to sponsor service projects.[4]

If and when sponsors were secured, there remained the problem of finding projects suitable to the abilities of local women. Early in the program Miss Van De Vrede remarked that there were few projects of a "public nature" that unskilled women could do. The CWA and the FERA had been confronted with this same problem and had found only one, the sewing rooms, that fit these circumstances. Paradoxically, however, the great diversity of types of skills which the women possessed made it difficult for the WPA to develop large scale projects utilizing any particular ability.[5]

Another group of women for which the WPA was hard pressed to find work included that 50 percent of female breadwinners on relief with children under sixteen years of age. Miss Van De Vrede suggested that "a mother's aid program on a subsistence or assistance basis, affording education in homemaking and housekeeping and the care and rearing of children" would serve the needs of these women, but there was no such provision in the WPA's programs.[6]

In rural Georgia administrators faced the choice of either transporting women to population centers or setting up a large number of small projects in outlying areas. For women who also were housekeepers and had small children the first solution was out of the question; the second greatly increased the cost per unit in projects which many prospective sponsors felt were too expensive already. As a result Miss Shepperson expended a great deal of effort in moving women and other nonmanual workers to WPA projects.

In June 1935 there were 9,509 women working on relief projects in Georgia, 6,217 of whom were employed in sewing rooms. Upon analyzing the relief load, Miss Van De Vrede anticipated being able to transfer 7,725 women to the WPA, leaving 11,679 families with a female bread-winner and children under sixteen years old for whom there was as yet no program. Miss Van De Vrede suggested that the FERA be allowed to carry these women on its rolls while training them and studying their work histories in hopes of developing suitable projects for them. She noted that it was impossible to use all of the employable women in Georgia on work projects, so the best course of action seemed to be to teach women in their homes. She was convinced that "the home training programs we have begun in Georgia will match any school building or sewer we have constructed."[7]

Miss Van De Vrede's pessimism regarding the WPA's ability to absorb female relief workers was well founded. Although the national office provided some money at the end of August 1935 for women's work, by mid-September only one women's project had been approved, and there was no one working on it. Despite her plans for the employment of women and white-collar workers exclusively in positions for which they had been trained, Miss Shepperson was soon forced into some dis-tasteful compromises. Confronted on one side by the national office, which wanted to liquidate the FERA quickly, and on the other by women and white-collar workers who were anxious to receive a secure position with the WPA, she began to place these people in jobs for which they had not been trained. Stenographers, for example, often found themselves laboring as seamstresses at reduced wages. By the end of 1935 a large number of complaints had piled up in the office of Repre-sentative Robert Ramspect, and he appealed to the national office for an explanation. Assistant WPA Administrator Jacob Baker replied that the positions were only temporary and that the WPA was doing all it could to set up suitable programs for skilled women and white-collar workers.[8]

The problem rested partly in the national office. Miss Shepperson told Hopkins that she had enough money to employ all former FERA workers but lacked the necessary nonmanual projects. Even when these were approved, the national office's priority of construction made it difficult for her to secure materials for nonmanual projects. The Women's Work report of November 23, 1935, claimed, "Washington has not yet signed our original requests [for materials] for October, to say nothing of subsequent requests for November and December."[9]

Still, conditions had improved by that November report. Miss Van De Vrede wrote that of 21,777 eligible women, 13,782 were working for the WPA, and 204 had jobs with other governmental agencies. The rest were awaiting placement or reassignment. By the middle of December, 1,117 projects for women had been approved, 382 of which were in operation, employing 16,223 women.[10]

The Service Division grew at a gradual but steady pace. A forced reduction in the state's labor quota in 1937 allowed it to release "inefficient" and "physically disabled" workers. The program was scaled down, promoting a "greater opportunity for individual attention and closer supervision," and better records were kept.

The Service Division consolidated related projects, such as book mending and library work, thus releasing additional supervisors for the training programs. Those projects employing only a few workers were closed during this period, and the division placed increasing emphasis on "the promotion of projects of low man-year costs."[11]

The state nonmanual project administration was elevated to the divisional level in 1937. The change insured that there always would be a cohesive group in the state office to protect the interests of the program and to assume a greater part of the WPA's funds and labor quota without disruption or confusion as the service projects took on greater importance in later years. The Service Division constantly worked to improve the program in Georgia. The problems within the state were numerous, and since there was very little specific direction from the national office, most of the success state leaders experienced was the direct result of the division's interests and efforts in the molding of the program to fit Georgia's peculiar needs.

By the late fall of 1938 Miss Van De Vrede had decided that the program's best chances for success lay in statewide projects, of which there were 25 at the time. In presenting her conclusions to the national office, the division director noted that most of these 25 projects could not operate on a county level. Of the 159 counties in the state, over 100 lacked towns with a population over 5,000. This factor alone suggested the impracticality, and even impossibility, of county-sponsored projects.

Miss Van De Vrede gave six reasons for instituting more statewide projects. In the first place the state legally was able to undertake more programs than the counties. Counties preferred to sponsor construction projects, and this tended to drive women and nonmanual workers to

larger centers of population where they could find employment. Miss
Van De Vrede suggested that it would be well to keep these people
in the counties, and this could be accomplished if the state sponsored
projects there. She felt that the small towns needed "community
service" more than the large cities. As examples of the type of efforts
she had in mind, she cited library and housekeeping aide projects. The
library projects were better sponsored by the state because "the sources
of service are not locally available in sufficient amount as yet." Both
preferably were statewide because "the service is technical and must be
safeguarded." Other projects, such as indexing, also lent themselves to
state sponsorship due to the need for uniformity.

Economy was the fourth reason Miss Van De Vrede gave for statewide
projects. The WPA could contact one sponsor, saving large amounts of
paperwork, and could make more mass purchases, reducing the unit price
of materials. The administration of statewide projects would be easier
since uniform standards of operation could be set and projects could be
"analyzed, compared, and coordinated" more effectively.

Finally, the supervision of these projects could be centralized, improving efficiency and simplifying distribution of the goods produced.
The counties simply could not supply qualified supervision for technical
projects. Since most of the WPA's "technical" projects came under the
Service Division, this factor was extremely important.[12]

Miss Van De Vrede's report gave evidence of the careful consideration
and planning of service programs in the state WPA office. It was the
devotion of such leaders as Miss Van De Vrede that allowed a program
which had begun in confusion and disarray to grow to such size and
sophistication. Of course, this was possible only in a situation where the
national office was willing to give free rein to state officials. Evidently
Hopkins realized that with so complex an agency he could not reasonably
expect to maintain strict control of all the programs in Washington.
Ultimately, his willingness to give state administrators wide decision-
making powers, combined with the most fortunate circumstance in
Georgia of having a superior state administrator with a competent staff,
resulted in one of the more successful efforts.

If the construction program was the largest in terms of work done and
money spent, the nonmanual program was the broadest and most innovative. Those who spoke of the New Deal as instigating "cradle to the
grave" socialism might have indeed been correct (though not necessarily

about the socialism) in respect to the efforts of the Service Division. In every area of human endeavor the average citizen of the 1930s might find the WPA involved, employing those with almost every conceivable skill and involving almost every area of human need.

Although each of the projects was important, their histories are too numerous to recount here, and there was enough similarity in their methods of operation and problems to make that unnecessary. Therefore only those which were the most important, which revealed patterns applicable to the others, and which the most is known about are discussed in detail. The rest are mentioned to indicate the scope of the Service Division's endeavors, but not studied in depth.[13]

The sewing program was the first and by far the largest of the WPA's activities for women in Georgia. Although other women's projects had been developed under the CWA and the FERA, only the sewing program had met with any sort of success by 1935. In rural areas it consisted of "many small sewing groups" of the "sewing circle" type. Sewing projects in urban areas employed more women, but there "the housing was generally poor and the equipment wholly inadequate for several years."[14]

The WPA sewing program was sponsored by the state Department of Public Welfare and cosponsored on the local level by the county commissioners and/or the city councils which were financially responsible for them. A state supervisor, assistant state supervisors, and a chief clerk comprised the state administrative staff, with one assistant being responsible for patterns and one for cutting. On the local level no such division of labor existed. There the unit supervisors had complete control of the projects aided by clerical and timekeeping assistants.

The early sewing projects had succeeded because they were suited to conditions in Georgia. They demanded little skill from women beyond that normally acquired in the home, and originally they used "no machines, little material, and no planning." As more money became available the state office purchased some machines, but funds were so limited that these were often secondhand and outdated. In keeping with the WPA's new concern for "work rather than the workers" most of the machinery went to the larger projects, and supervisors began operating in two shifts, reducing the number of hand sewers and increasing the output. The sponsors, who were given the completed articles of clothing, responded positively.[15]

Under the WPA the program grew swiftly until projects were operating in 135 counties employing 7,078 women or 79 percent of all women in the WPA. When the program became statewide, central control was achieved, and the Service Division was able to purchase better machinery and establish work standards. It also periodically reduced the number of projects so that by 1939 there were only 3,687 workers employed in 118 units. These steps, however, did not always result in improved conditions. A sample taken of garments produced in Georgia as late as 1941 still showed "very inferior" workmanship, though Miss Van De Vrede argued that this was due to her limited, qualified supervisory staff.[16]

The reorganization of the program into a statewide project served to abolish the "sewing circle" type of operation completely in favor of "work center" units. Local sponsors did not respond favorably to this shift, preferring to keep "the local unit intact." Once the program became statewide, many of the sponsors lost the privilege of distributing articles, that duty being taken over by the Surplus Relief Corporation.[17]

The sewing program was not without impediments and criticism. An early decision in the national office encumbering 40 percent of all project funds for materials meant that some $2 million would be withheld in Georgia. The Service Division's district directors and many sponsors complained of this order, claiming that they would never use this amount of money for materials. Field Representative Malcom J. Miller reported a general view that no more than $750,000 or 15 percent needed to be encumbered. The national office ultimately agreed to a 20 percent compromise which also satisfied the state.[18]

Other attacks upon the sewing program came from the counties. Whenever a project was closed or consolidated, the Service Division inevitably received complaints from those relieved of their jobs. Often these women alleged that workers less in need were retained while more destitute persons were dropped.

Complaints came from outside the program as well as from within. In September 1936, for example, the Georgia Women's Democratic Club (a rabid opponent of the New Deal) charged that women in WPA sewing rooms were "humiliated and embarrassed, subjected to disgraceful personal searches, and denied the benefits of a rehabilitation program expressly designed to aid them." Some letters accused the state office of allowing black and white women to work side-by-side, and others told of poorly lighted and unheated working rooms. The state office investigated these various charges and corrected them where possible. Most of the problems that could not be resolved had resulted from limited funds.[19]

Despite minor disputes with the national offices and scattered dissatisfaction in the state, the sewing program was of major value in providing work for women and clothing for the destitute. As the country began to prepare for war, the sewing program was geared to defense work. Although the women were not used in making uniforms, in some cases they did mend and sew "markers" on them. Limited as its contribution was, the sewing program lent its efforts to the war movement, its work benefiting the defense program rather than the destitute.

Another enterprise which the WPA took over from the FERA was the library program. The first library project began in December 1933 under the CWA. This agency had placed a number of trained librarians in "technical cataloging of book collections and other specialized work." Later the program was expanded to public high schools where clerical workers organized book collections. In 1935, however, 115 counties in Georgia lacked free libraries, and the WPA promised to "extend library service to the population of the state and improve existing service."[20]

Unlike the sewing projects, the library project came to the WPA as a statewide program, one of the first in the nation. The Georgia Library Commission sponsored it, and its secretary, Miss Beverly Wheatcroft, doubled as state supervisor of library projects. The commission established the state Library Planning Committee to advise the WPA on library work. County and city governments acted as cosponsors to individual projects and set up local library boards which were responsible for "securing funds and paying bills." The selection of Miss Wheatcroft as state supervisor (without federal pay) symbolized the harmonious relationship which existed between the Georgia Library Commission and the WPA throughout.[21]

To aid in administration, Miss Wheatcroft selected two assistants to be in charge of training and cataloging-classification service and a chief clerk who doubled as assistant state supervisor in charge of bookmobile projects. The local administration consisted of district supervisors at first, then a supervisor for every three work areas, one or two area library supervisors, and one or more library clerks in each work area. Individual project supervision rested with the sponsor, who provided a trained librarian for the job. Often this person was assisted by local WPA personnel.

The first library project opened in January 1936, and from 1935 to 1942, 31 of the state's 44 public libraries were assisted by the WPA.

Where no libraries existed the WPA set up "Demonstrational Libraries."
The total number of libraries in the state grew from 44 in 1935 to 210
in 1942. (A total of 145 were "WPA libraries" and three developed from
WPA library projects.) Some additional aid was given to high schools and
special city libraries.[22]

The primary task of the WPA was to maintain these libraries, but
the program reached much further than that. Among its accomplishments were the extension of opening hours, special services for children,
establishment of branch libraries, service to special groups such as
hospitals, gathering of pamphlet and iconographic collections, and
especially creation of the mobile book (bookmobile) service—a WPA
innovation. The library project was of particular value to rural areas
where no such services were available, and most of the WPA's effort
went into building rural libraries, although its services accounted for
"three-fifths of all public library circulation" in 1941. The culmination
of the rural library service began in 1940 with the creation of "countywide libraries."[23]

In towns which desired libraries, the WPA provided the technical
knowledge. The city supplied "adequate quarters, equipment and working
materials, and also the initial book collection plus at least $10.00 a month
for new books." The Library Commission's report for 1937 showed
that local communities had responded favorably to WPA offers. By July
of that year there were only 58 counties without libraries, and there
were 175 projects operating in the other 101 counties. The monthly
circulation of these libraries was about 120,000 books. The results of
the program were so gratifying that, when a reorganization in the state
office forced Miss Shepperson to reduce the number of supervisors to
four in July 1937, she agreed to provide special assistants for them in
cases where their territories proved too large.[24]

In rural areas where library construction was not feasible, the WPA
began by dispatching the supervisors for four days each week to distribute
75 books at a time, collecting the books lent the week before as they
went. As the program grew, this service was supplemented by the bookmobile and by special programs in existing libraries to serve those who
could not come to the central depository. There was some question
in Washington about the concentration of Georgia's library program in
rural sections, but when Miss Wheatcroft explained the value of
"smaller units spread over a wide area" over the preoccupation in other

states with a "more elaborately developed library program in a few
places in the state," her decision was accepted. The Washington office
really could do little else in the face of such widespread support from
official bodies and the general public. The program was such a success
that local authorities responded by maintaining all of the WPA libraries
after that agency withdrew its personnel. In fact, in September 1939,
when the WPA had to release some of its trained librarians because of
the 18-months rule, it could find no replacements—they were all employed elsewhere in the state.[25]

The library program represented a WPA venture of limited scope,
but great depth. It affected only libraries; however, it affected all
libraries. The WPA surveys and records program exemplified just the
opposite sort of endeavor, one of great breadth. The public records
program had begun with FERA indexing projects, but no similar effort
was undertaken by the WPA until late in 1936. In this hiatus Georgia's
records had grown more disorganized, and Miss Louisa DeB. FitzSimons
reported that "we can only pay for the case aides and supervisors out
of the residue of FERA money and the amount of clerical help which
the counties can provide is inadequate to keep such records as are of
any value to our administration or in the event of the permanent program." To make matters worse the number of nonmanual projects in
general was dropping. Miss FitzSimons noted that the projects coming
through were either "so involved that our persons cannot do them, or
else they seem to be supplementing the regular administrative functions
of public agencies, and therefore, cannot be approved on that account."[26]

In 1938 the WPA formed the first statewide program combining the
county real property indexing projects. Later the agency incorporated
the vital statistics records to form the county records indexing project.
The consolidation was called the public records program and included
such elements as deed and mortgage indexes, birth and death record
indexes, state record indexes, marriage records, superior court dockets
indexes, county police records indexes, city ordinance codification, and
numerical real property indexes. The statewide program was sponsored
by the state Planning Board with local agencies acting as cosponsors
and supplying a portion of the supervision. The technical direction for
the program rested with a state supervisor, assistant state supervisors, a
project technician, a chief clerk, and a secretary. The project technician
was responsible for the "operation and performance of units," and

the state supervisor handled "organization and promotion." The assistant supervisors operated at the same level as WPA district supervisors, but with more territory to cover, and there were district supervisors in areas with a large enough demand. As in other WPA programs which separated technical and administrative authority, this arrangement proved to be weak.

The WPA also initiated a great number of surveys which operated in much the same manner as the indexing program. The three largest of these were the public administration project, the socio-economic survey, and the historical records survey. The public administration program operated under the public (administrative) records project, and was later combined with the land use survey project under the defense records phase of the "clerical program." This project included the rural real property identification survey, the land use and zoning survey, the cartographic section, and the air-raid warden mapping project. All but the last of these were sponsored by the state Planning Board, the air-raid warden mapping project being sponsored by the University of Georgia at the request of the Citizens Defense Committee of Georgia.

The socio-economic surveys began in Atlanta and Savannah and were subsequently expanded to cover the entire state. The WPA also undertook a traffic and transportation survey, a truck and bus inventory, a mineral resources survey, a public utilities survey, a social security survey, a trends in population mobility survey, a dairy farms and cost of milk production survey, an Atlanta milk shed survey, a criminal court procedures survey, a crippled children's survey, a tax survey, an historic buildings survey, an archaeological survey, and a survey of the financial statistics of local governments. Later the WPA and the state Planning Board initiated resource studies of ports, commercial fisheries, parks, parkways, semipublic recreational areas and facilities, recreation and conservation areas (in seventeen East Georgia and three Northeast Florida counties), and forest planning.

Both the indexing and survey programs were difficult to publicize adequately in comparison with the construction program. This made relations with sponsors and the general public tenuous, so that troubles which often beset all of the WPA's endeavors were accentuated in the records program. For example, the early emphasis on workers rather than works resulted in the approval of some unsatisfactory projects, causing sponsors to become displeased or lackadaisical. On occasion, sponsors attempted to shift the workers on poor projects to other work not covered by the original agreement. The WPA could not allow this, and further friction often developed. The upshot of such incidents was that, once burned, sponsors hesitated to undertake additional projects.[27]

The memoirs of Robert Wauchope, a WPA archaeologist from 1938 to 1940, provide an interesting glimpse into the state and local operations of one type of research and survey project. Archaeological projects were divided into three parts: A statewide survey to "discover, identify, and investigate prehistoric sites to determine significance using mobile field groups" (the project with which Wauchope was connected); exploration at the Irene Mound near Savannah; and a dig at Ocumulgee National Monument at Macon.[28]

Miss Shepperson found the digs and their yields interesting. Her reminiscences of these digs were largely idyllic, but Mr. Wauchope told a different story in his day-to-day accounts of the operations. Wauchope's first and major complaint concerned the unfortunate marriage of two contrasting philosophies of operations, that of the archaeologist and the WPA. When the WPA's emphasis on workers prevailed over archaeology's interest in the work, archaeology suffered. Thus, Wauchope lamented, he had a lot of people without much ability. This condition was not critical in excavation where workers could be "held for longer periods," thus training them "to greater usefulness." When there was more time available, the supervisors could create the amount of work needed to justify the hiring of qualified personnel under the 90 percent rule.

Surveys presented a different problem. This work was mobile, offering none of the opportunities to train the "green help" that the digs presented. Wauchope complained that it was only with the greatest difficulty that he was able to transport his workers across county lines. His greatest problem was "the violence we knew our archaeological materials were being subjected to." He wrote, "When several hundred unskilled men, with sparse supervision, dug up artifacts, dropped them into boxes, passed unusual specimens around from hand to hand (and, I might add, from hand to pocket), tied them up and labeled the containers, packed them on trucks and unpacked them at headquarters, washed them, and reboxed them—all this in what was often a spirit of lighthearted irresponsibility and incomprehension—the chances are that proveniences were garbled, if not deliberately falsified."

Such conditions with respect to unskilled WPA laborers might have
been expected, but when Wauchope's chief foreman admitted to having
transferred shreds from one site to another in order to make yields more
impressive, the archaeologist despaired of any significant accomplishment.
He was on the horns of a dilemma—whether to employ no needy people
and do no work, or to employ "too many getting it done in a slovenly
way."

Wauchope complained that the system bred false values, for "big
efficient operations too often became the symbols of the successful
archaeological director." Furthermore, the amount of paperwork was
excessive, and the type of information which the WPA required was
ridiculous. Some of the questions asked on WPA forms were unanswer-
able, and Wauchope lamented, "Even if we made up the answers out of our
heads (and who didn't!), it was criminally time-consuming nonsense,
imposed on already harried archaeologists who urgently wanted to devote
more attention to the research itself."

These reports, for example, had to be submitted regularly: "Major
purchase requisition for sponsor, balance sheet, petty cash account,
report of sponsor expenditures other than payroll (this involved estimat-
ing, among other things, the university's room space in square feet devoted to the project and assigning it a rental value), laboratory time
sheets, field party's time sheets, laboratory cost analysis, field party cost
analysis, travel expense sheets for sponsor, WPA travel expense sheets,
mileage records for each vehicle, equipment inventories, equipment
transfer sheets (whenever we moved from one area to another we had to
report every pick and shovel taken along), accident reports, equipment
receiving reports, and monthly budget requests for WPA-furnished
supplies."

An academician and a trained archaeologist rather than an administrator, Wauchope did not see the need for such procedures. Men hired
to do a specific job which required a certain skill in order that other
men might work were often prevented from doing their tasks by the
bulk of administrative duties heaped upon them. The WPA provided
very little clerical assistance in any of its manual or nonmanual programs.
Wauchope recorded that many times he came to a dig in the morning
only to find the workers sitting around while the supervisor was off
somewhere "fill[ing] out a paper or attend[ing] a safety meeting."

As an example of the preposterous sorts of information required by the WPA, Wauchope reported that the average monthly cost of an "archaeological unit" was $.000048, "and the total average per unit for the entire project was written in ten-thousandths of a dollar." At one point Wauchope sarcastically noted in his diary, "We found to our great alarm that the average cost per unit for our project had risen to two ten-thousandths of a dollar!" The archaeologist had arrived at this figure honestly, but it was so absurd that "the local WPA headquarters begged me to doctor the statistics so that they would come out in a reasonable figure that they could enter in dollars and cents."

The same sort of finagling with other statistics clearly revealed the inanity of certain bureaucratic minds at work in Washington. Wauchope was especially conscientious about figures he knew he would have to report, but he soon discovered that "you cannot put down what actually happened, but instead what you think they are going to believe." As an example he cited a trip of 43 miles he made in an hour. When he submitted the account, it was returned with a note saying that he could not possibly have done that. If he did not use his automobile during the weekend, the account was again returned saying that he should indicate some mileage for that period. He always departed for a dig on the quarter hour, but when he entered this, the account was returned— "chances were that I would not leave on quarter hours and I must give the exact minute: 10:17, 11:36." The archaeologist exclaimed, "I scarcely recognized my travel when the girl in the WPA office finished doctoring it." As an added injustice, he was asked to "swear before a notary that the statement was correct."

Wauchope was plagued constantly by the state office and the Executive Committee of the Society for Georgia Archaeology to provide publicity for the newspapers. When he finally agreed to take some members of the committee on a field trip, "half the crowd decided they would not go any further" because of the rough terrain. When the tour was completed, one member was designated to write a report covering the project. Wauchope claimed that she never did so; however, twelve days later another committee member called him to complain about "the continued lack of publicity." When Wauchope did persuade a newspaperman to cover a project, it soon became apparent that the paper's interest was not exactly professional. After spending an entire day with an Associated Press feature writer, he received the following headline and was asked for "supporting data": "First Gunmen or

Gangsters in America were the Roving Hill or Mountain Indian Tribes
Who Preyed on the More Peaceful Indian Tribes Habitating Swamps."

The archaeologist was hard pressed to get enough qualified personnel,
and he had constant problems with his labor. Although many were
"deserving cases," there was always "the usual quota of alcoholics
and bums." One timekeeper had to be locked in his room every night
to "let him sleep off the previous night's binge," but inevitably he
slipped out the window and got drunk again. His "Principal 'engineer'
disappeared so often and for such long periods we finally asked that
he be transferred; he retaliated by bringing charges against us in
Atlanta, where the foreman and I had to appear at a formal hearing
to defend ourselves against accusations." One letter which Wauchope
received via President Roosevelt, the WPA, and the local office was
unusual enough to merit its reproduction verbatim:

Dear Mr. Franklin D-Rosey Bell

Dea Dea Mr. President of USA

I am Wrighting you in the name of our Dear Lord and Savior
Jesus christ a most noble Presedent I honor our Dear Lord and
Savior Jesus Christ for a great Roaler lik you—the WPA
tranfered me [name deleted] to Archaeological Survor that is a
digging up Ded Peple and I am a Precher And dont bleav in digging
up the ded hit is aginst my Righes Bleaf Wish you would help me
to git off from diging Up the dead your to greater Precedent tan to
make me Dig them up Aginst the Word of Jesus from you
Sinseare Friend [name deleted] to Franklin D. Rosey the Worlds
reatest Presedent. I worked with them 3 days before I new I was
digging them Up They told me we were hunting pots don't think
Hard of me for wrighting you I need your help the rist don cear
for me I will starve if you dont Help me to git off from digging
Up the Ded.

your Best Friend [name deleted]

Such a letter was typical, not only in the archaeological or service
projects, but also in the construction areas, and it reflected many things

besides the ignorance, superstitions, and illiteracy of its writer. It indicated that most people, including those employed by the WPA, really knew little about the whole series of programs with which they came into contact daily. These people were still a long way, not just from Washington, but from civilization. It was piteously easy for officials of federal, state, or local agencies to abuse them, and for each person who managed to scribble a note to the "President" on a rough, children's ruled tablet there were many more who were too illiterate to do even that much. On the other hand, such letters, especially in the numbers received in the state office and in Washington, revealed that the programs were at least reaching these people and making them understand that their landlords or the local political hierarchy were not the only benefactors to whom they could turn in their distress.

Wauchope's use of this letter perhaps showed the attitude of WPA officials towards those they helped. Such men as he were primarily interested in their professions. They were not social workers, and often many had little sympathy for those whom they supervised.

Wauchope's memoirs, although incomplete, are one of the few such published documents to remain from this period, but it appears from other fragmentary evidence that his circumstances were not unusual, especially in the Service Division with its high concentration of specialized personnel and technical projects. Similar situations existed throughout the WPA in varying degrees and limited the agency's ability to undertake effective projects and achieve personal rehabilitation. Most of the archaeologist's problems with local staff members were not necessarily the fault of these people, but of the Washington office, whose stringent regulations and lack of personnel often hampered state administrators in their work.[29]

The recreation program was not added to the Service Division until a later reorganization. Nevertheless, the Service, Recreation, and Education divisions of the WPA and the National Youth Administration (NYA) all worked together rather closely, the state director of WPA education serving as state NYA director until 1938. In 1936 the Education and Recreation divisions combined, and were subsequently absorbed by the Service Division. The work of the NYA became more clearly defined and separated.

The recreation program included numerous activities, all rather loosely linked as "leisure time" pursuits. The program consisted of playground

and sports supervision, arts and crafts, community drama, music, a
weekly radio program, community centers, and training institutes for
those involved in all types of projects. Originally Miss Shepperson appointed August Fischer, who had done this work under the FERA, as
recreation leader, but for some reason their relationship was strained.
When he wanted a pay raise in the spring of 1936, for example, he went
over her head to seek it.

National officials liked Fischer's work and wanted to keep him,
particularly since there seemed to be no qualified replacement. By the
fall of 1936, however, they were forced to admit "growing difficulties"
with him. Miss Shepperson sometimes doubted "his administrative
ability," and the "Atlanta people" were "bitterly opposed to him."
The national office still did not want to fire the state recreational leader,
both because the situation was not yet critical and because there was
no replacement for him. Fischer, therefore, remained.[30]

Some of Fischer's problems centered around the city of Atlanta.
Miss Shepperson insisted that the city's recreation projects be included
in the state program under Fischer's direction. Local recreation workers,
however, felt otherwise. A similar situation existed in Augusta where a
group of people had been "conducting a partial municipal program
there for a few years." The head of Augusta's program did not want
WPA assistance, and an investigator reported that "underneath the
situation we find City politics, involving the Catholic element in
Augusta." The group running the program feared that the WPA would
"interfere." The WPA finally ordered Miss Shepperson to allow a dual
program in these two cities and to make Fischer "accept the situation
for the best interest of Recreation in Georgia." This action seemed to
calm the antagonists, although Fischer's opponents continued to hold
their grudge against him.[31]

One other group, the articulate blacks, were dissatisfied with the
recreation program which, they said, did not reach them. WPA Investigator Harold D. Meyer talked with Fischer about this, and the recreation
head promised to do more. Meyer felt that this failure to provide
projects for blacks was due to the administration's being "politically
frightened about the race issue." Nevertheless, by July 1936, when Meyer
made this report, the program "had gained a great deal of strength."
The "general personnel is fair and the organization is good." The leaders
were "enthusiastic and earnest," and the program's "greatest accomplish-

ment next to the training of workers was the contacts made with the people of Georgia and the salesmanship of the Recreation program." Miss Van De Vrede echoed Meyer's impressions to Miss Shepperson later that summer, adding that the program's success was the result of local participation and "a great deal of work on the part of the District Supervisor of Women's and Professional Projects, who, for the most part, selected or recommended the project personnel."[32]

Unfortunately, the reorganization of 1937 had the same adverse effect upon recreation as upon all other WPA programs. In a report that year the state office noted that what was needed most in the next six months was "freedom from change or reorganization." Disruptions in the recreation section affected the most successful part of the program, the training projects, first.

The state office also complained about national office restrictions. When Washington criticized her actions, Assistant Recreation Director Marie Parker justified the choice of the training program's discussion topic, "Religious Viewpoint of Recreation," by arguing that it was picked because of local conditions. The assistant director tried to correlate her program in rural areas with the churches which had readily lent the WPA their facilities and had often sponsored recreation projects. Her decision was "an act of diplomacy since our program has had some criticism in the smaller areas, especially as to folk dancing and social recreation."

On the other hand, the national office often was willing to help the state program. When Fischer complained that he lacked "specialized people" in the training program, Washington sent two roving supervisors to supplement the training staff. The recreation program also experienced difficulties in rural areas where the staff was generally insufficient. Activities were often "led by local supervisors who, in many cases, are not up on rules of the games in which the various groups participated." The national office therefore allowed the state to consolidate NYA, Education Division, and Recreation Division personnel in these areas.[34]

The projects of the recreation program were always very popular. This was perhaps exceptional considering that the public generally responded less positively to programs which showed little in the way of physical accomplishments. It may have been that recreation projects offered an escape from the extreme pressures created by the depression, and people were thankful for this relief. The state leadership consistently reported good attendance at athletic contests, dramatic presentations, and other spectator events. In response to the success of the recreation program, some of the state's larger cities and counties began to undertake a greater part of its activities. By March 1937, two cities had assumed complete control of their programs, and by September seven cities and one county were moving in that direction. Private agencies also approached the Recreation Division wanting "to take advantage of special instruction in the crafts, drama, and music."[35]

As this trend continued, the Recreation Division was able to concentrate its efforts in rural areas. Interest centered in towns where local advisory councils were formed, demanding more facilities in community centers. The administration took this opportunity to set up a rural program which expanded outward from county seats. The division first developed "a good, all-around, wholesome program" and tried to develop a cadre of qualified specialists in the immediate areas. As more people became available, the local office sent them to smaller communities to initiate programs there, thus slowly penetrating isolated rural areas. The program proved so popular that often other agencies such as the Extension Service and the state Department of Health were willing to cooperate when activities could be modified to suit both the Recreation Division and the agency involved. The flexibility which the national office permitted the Recreation Division allowed it to mold its program to the needs of these agencies, and even more importantly, to the needs of individual communities. It was partly because of this freedom at the program-planning level that there was little or no friction and the division was accepted with such great enthusiasm.[36]

The Education Division, like the Recreation Division, existed for a time apart from the Service Division and, like all the other WPA programs, found its beginnings under the FERA and the CWA. Unfortunately, at the time of transfer from the FERA to the WPA, relations between Miss Shepperson and the sponsoring state agency, the state Department of Education, were strained. The rather stringent restrictions that the FERA had placed upon the administraton and operation of the program were continued by the WPA. There had also been political interference, both from within the department and from the governor's office. With the formation of the WPA as a strictly federal agency, the governor was for the most part taken out of the picture, but opposition continued from within the department, most notably in the persons of Mauney D. Collins, state superintendent of schools, and P. S. Barrett, the department's director of the emergency educational program. There was constant wrangling, both between the department and the state WPA office, and among warring factions within the department itself, using ammunition provided by unpopular WPA regulations governing the program.

Much of the trouble between the state office and the department arose as a result of the increased control exercised by the WPA. Both Barrett and Collins, for example, balked at Miss Shepperson's ruling that all teachers employed on the program had to be certified. Another problem concerned the diversion of "accumulated funds" by Miss Shepperson to be used in the nursery school projects. Both Barrett and Collins felt that the projects for illiterate adults were more important, although "too much vocational, nursery school, or adult work will bog the wheels." A large number of counties had received no funds at all because they had applied late, and both men believed the money should be used to correct this condition.[37]

Barrett complained, "Confidentially we find ourselves doing a number of things that we do not think are best for the program, but in order to get along with some of the 'higher ups,' [Miss Shepperson in particular] we agree and do the best we can." Barrett acceded to Miss Shepperson's wishes, but he was not pleased with the situation. When the WPA came into being he lamented, "Since Georgia has transferred from the FERA to the WPA, so much red tape has become involved that it is not likely that much more progress will be made. I have never been able to understand why it is necessary to transfer from one alphabetical agency to another about the time things get organized and operating satisfactorily."[38]

Collins also disapproved of the WPA. He noted that the new educational program was supposed to "follow plans adopted for previous years," but he maintained that "previous plans have not been followed insofar as the State of Georgia is concerned." Collins asked that the state be "un-federalized," since the department had always "cooperated with emergency forces." The state superintendent claimed, "Local school officials from all over the state have been critical. They will not give full support unless the Federal Educational Program is more closely aligned with the Georgia educational set up."

It appeared, however, that Collins's main concern was over his loss of power under the new administration. Now he "sponsored the Federal

Educational Program, but has not directed the work." Collins threatened
to withdraw as sponsor unless this changed. Sometime later Harold D.
Meyer, then regional director of the Division of Education and Recreation, noted that Collins wanted "absolute control of the program." The
state superintendent "is building a powerful political machine and needs
this program. He wants to develop the program the way he wants it."

Barrett, who disliked both the WPA and Collins, sought to embarrass
the latter when he wrote to the Washington office that the department
was "in no way consulted regarding the supervision or any other phase
of the program." He stated, "The State WPA officials are making such
appointments as they care to without either consulting this office or
even notifying us of the appointments after they have been made."
Collins put the entire blame for the situation upon Barrett. He told
Miss Shepperson that he "had no knowledge of Barrett's letter . . . and
he deplores it"—all this notwithstanding the fact that Collins also had
written Washington indicating almost these same sentiments. Evidently
seeing that he could not win, Collins had decided to make his peace
with the WPA, especially since a pro-Roosevelt man, Eurith D. Rivers,
appeared to be headed for the governor's mansion. He thus decided to
use Barrett as his scapegoat and evidently succeeded in doing so. From
that time on, Collins gave Miss Shepperson little trouble.[39]

The state WPA office constantly endeavored to improve education in
Georgia. The major problem was one of almost unbelievably poor schools
and standards, and, with the limited funds at its disposal, the state office
could never have realistically hoped to eradicate it. It nevertheless made
a valiant effort, trying to balance its program both among the various
educational projects and between large cities and rural areas.

The state office diligently sought the best possible staff in a state
which provided few qualified persons. The culmination of this objective
came in 1939 when Miss Shepperson appointed Emmet V. Whelchel as
educational director. Frank Bentley, regional supervisor of the Professional and Service Division, ranked Whelchel "second from the top
of the list of directors in this region." Not only was he a good administrator and socially minded, but he did not hesitate to see that minority
groups, specifically blacks, were treated well. He suggested, for example,
that blacks be taught black history "with emphasis on present day needs"—
a plea that black teachers had made in 1936.[40]

The problems of the Educational Division exemplified the difficulties inherent when responsibilities for a program were divided among the national office, the state office, and an agency of the state government. Restrictions placed upon the state administrator by the national office limited the program so that the division could not adjust to special conditions in the state. Political and personal ambitions and differing "philosophies" of education determined, to a large extent, the type of relationship the state office was to have with the sponsor. Finally, the condition of a professional program operated for relief purposes necessarily limited its effectiveness in much the same way as it had in the archaeological program.

Four WPA nonmanual programs were run from Washington rather than from the state WPA offices: the Federal Artists, Music, Writers', and Theater projects. The state administrators were asked to cooperate with the state heads of the federal programs, and often this involvement, which lacked the prerogatives of direct control, caused tension in the state WPA office. Residents of the state often did not understand the administrative separation of powers and criticized the state WPA for conditions which were beyond its power to affect.

The Federal Artists Project evolved from the Treasury Relief Art Project in 1937. It had been relatively unimportant in Georgia, employing only one person in the state up to that year. The Federal Music Project was also limited. At its height the project included only two orchestras, one in Atlanta and one in Augusta.

The Federal Writers' Project was much larger than either the music or art projects. The Washington office initiated the program throughout the nation with the announcement of the American Guide Series, one to be compiled for each state. Workers also were to write general WPA progress reports in order to relieve state WPA staffs of some paperwork. Miss Shepperson was hesitant about the project's possibilities, and she wrote to its director, Henry G. Alsberg, early in October 1935, "In Georgia there are almost no qualified professional people who would be capable of being employed on the work you have outlined." She pointed out that there were only about twenty people presently on relief rolls who might qualify, and she was not even sure that these people were still unemployed. She offered to divert some personnel from the educational program, but advised against appointing a state supervisor, suggesting that she might make Director of Public Relations William O. Key, acting supervisor.[41]

Alsberg agreed to Key's appointment, but insisted that he be made director of the project. Evidently this move created hostility between Key and Miss Shepperson that was to end in Key's release within three months. The trouble began as soon as he assumed his new position. He reported that Miss Shepperson told him "there were no funds to hire assistants to get the American Guide going in Georgia. She told me to proceed along to determine what relief-roll talent exists in the eight WPA districts in Georgia and then confer with her about getting permission to hire the assistants." Key did not believe that this was the proper course of action, but he agreed to follow Miss Shepperson's orders.[42]

By October 19, 1935, Key had acquired most of his administrative staff, and they were combing the relief rolls to find qualified personnel. He selected Mrs. Carolyn Dillard to be state District Supervisor and his assistant in Atlanta; then he placed supervisors in six of the eight districts. Key complained to Alsberg that his office space was inadequate and that the national Reemployment Bureau in Atlanta was pre-empting all of the qualified clients to work on the Service Division's health survey. Alsberg suggested that Key talk the matter over with Miss Shepperson.[43]

Evidently Key wrested some concessions from Miss Shepperson, for by the end of November, fifteen projects were under way "in every city over 10,000," and by the end of December the state staff was complete. Meanwhile, he again ran afoul of Miss Shepperson, who evidently wanted to have some control over those he hired. A field report to Alsberg claimed that Miss Shepperson wanted to make appointments "of the right political color," and one disaffected worker later charged that Key "was forced from the first to take on persons out of Atlanta who were on the patronage list of Senator Russell, the list [of six people] being given him by Erle Cocke [National Emergency Council director]." This informant noted that Mrs. Dillard, for example, was the wife of Russell's cousin and was selected for that reason.[44]

Key complained that he did not have enough funds for his growing program. He was also harassed by a group of blacks demanding that more of their race be employed. Key responded that he could not "place additional employees without almost outright dismissal of several white persons." He promised, however, to do what he could, and he began interviewing more black applicants.[45]

Despite Key's progress, Miss Shepperson was dissatisfied. On January

4, 1936, he abruptly fired one of his district supervisors, Miss Ann Jarrell, claiming that "she has done no work and her attitude has been almost openly insubordinate." Miss Shepperson called Key into her office to talk about the dismissal, but he apparently refused to reconsider. Meanwhile, reports had been coming to her of Key's constant state of intoxication in his office.

Key was upset over an appointee to his office staff, a Miss Lola Pergament, whom he said was masculine and dictatorial. She boasted that she was "the only one [in the office] who had never been on relief," and she "intrigued considerably among the social workers." Key and some of the other professional staff resented her and the social workers of the WPA who had administrative control over them.[46]

Miss Shepperson finally decided to remove Key and to rehire Miss Jarrell. She replaced him with Mrs. Dillard, a move that one of the office workers charged had been planned for some time. The employee claimed that Miss Shepperson knew of Key's drinking problem from the very beginning, but had been forced to use him as "the only man who could start a project of this magnitude." The state administrator had placed Mrs. Dillard in Key's office "to learn the ropes under him and be ready to take his place when the inevitable crash came."[47]

Key was very upset and went to Washington to protest. He returned claiming that he was to be made regional director. Alsberg assured Mrs. Dillard that she had his backing and that letters from the disaffected office worker "are not given much weight." Alsberg approved Mrs. Dillard's request to transfer this worker, but refused to allow a salary increase for Miss Pergament. Since a number of Miss Shepperson's immediate subordinates had approved of Key's work and Alsberg himself seemingly gave some credence to charges coming out of the Writers' Project office, it appeared that Key had become the victim of a personality clash with Miss Shepperson. The problem was exacerbated because Miss Shepperson desired control over the federal projects. She wanted all personnel, for example, to be approved through her office "before appointments are made within the State." She often complained that she knew nothing of what went on in the Writers' Project office, since she had no direct control over it and its work was specialized enough to be distinctly apart from the other nonmanual programs.[48]

Key's allegations were, to some extent, borne out when Mrs. Dillard had to confront the same problems that he had faced. By now the

American Guide projects were in full swing, but the workers were incompetent and "so much of the research has to be checked and supplemented that in many cases it is almost equivalent to a new job." She reported to Alsberg, "Though the districts are producing copy, I am increasingly aware that the burden of the work will fall on the State Office. When copy is returned to the districts for rewriting the delay is greater than we can stand." She also found it difficult to get qualified people to fill vacancies, and if the national office wanted her to continue to prepare WPA progress reports, she would have to take some of the staff away from the American Guide project.[49]

By June 1936 conditions had improved somewhat. The writing was "better than average, but still not acceptable as prefinal copywriting." Workers showed a "tendency to overwrite," and their products were "amateurish in continuity and organization" showing "little preplanning." Writers often were confused about their assignments. Some of the problems reflected the nature of the personnel on the project. A final report covering the Writers' Project in Georgia noted, "Newspapermen, professional writers, and persons who called themselves writers were frequently the most difficult and least profitable to use. They were often superficial, muddled, biased, or addicted to certain peculiarities of style."

The 90 percent relief rule forced the state office to hire great numbers of totally unqualified people in order to get enough suitable persons to run the program. The final report commented, "The requirements for workers were modest, yet during the entire period of 7 years there were perhaps not more than 20 workers whose work could be edited and used at first hand." This put a tremendous pressure upon district and state personnel who acted as writers as well as administrators.[50]

Prevalent traits in the state's population influenced the type of work turned out. There was an overwhelming emphasis on history in the American Guide pieces, and "contemporary scenes" were neglected almost entirely. The history section itself ended with Reconstruction. Observers found "obvious prejudice against Negroes and Jews" in the American Guide. One investigator suggested that anti-Negro prejudice be left in because it was representative of the state's attitude and not just of the writer.[51]

In 1937 Mrs. Dillard left the Writers' Project to become state Supervisor of Workers' Education, and in her place Miss Shepperson selected Samuel Y. Tupper, Jr., who had succeeded Mrs. Dillard to the position of assistant state director and supervisor of the fifth district. It was also in 1937 that Washington began to make cuts in the state Writers' Project staff.

The state staff worried about these employment quota cuts, but by 1938 Tupper found himself with more positions than personnel. When the national office set his quota at seventy persons, Tupper informed it that he had only sixty-five people "qualified in the state." In 1939 the federal government dropped the Writers' Project, and the WPA continued it as a statewide project called the Georgia Writers' Project or Program. The University of Georgia assumed sponsorship along with various cosponsors around the state who agreed to take financial responsibility in the form of "advanced orders for copies of the book in the amount of $1,000 or more." Tupper remained to head the program which was controlled, as before, from the district offices. By this time, however, the number of district offices had been reduced to three— Atlanta, Savannah, and Augusta. This tended to stabilize operations and to provide a means for absorbing successive quota cuts.[52]

Tupper lacked the "administrative control" that was necessary with a dearth of qualified personnel. By 1941 a WPA investigator was reporting that "the project seems to be unimaginative and/or blocked by a defeatist attitude in securing sponsorship." There was sufficient office space in Atlanta, but it was poorly used. The reporter stated, "Files are scattered; most of them are in a small passageway. . . . The entire office seems down at the heels, with old papers, boxes, and pamphlets lying around, outdated posters on the walls."[53]

Tupper operated out of the Atlanta office and seemed "to have insufficient knowledge of the Augusta and Savannah staffs and insufficient control of projects undertaken in those offices." Although a number of new projects had been instituted, the entire program still overemphasized historical research. The observer noted that with the exception of the "non-certified workers and possibly Mr. Thigpen [a member of the Atlanta staff] none of the staff is qualified for writing or constructive research work." Tupper claimed it was the fault of the Employment Division which insisted on sending him unqualified personnel, but others found it hard to believe that no better potential existed in a city as large as Atlanta.[54]

By the fall of 1941 the Writers' Project began to ease its way into the war effort. State WPA Administrator Harry Harmon first suggested this

emphasis on "defense work," and soon afterward such a move began to
take place. In July 1942 the Writers' Project came under the War Services
Project as a phase of the Educational and Cultural Program.

The Federal Writers' Project represented perhaps the epitome in
specialized work, limited work quotas and funds, and federal control. One
of the project's greatest achievements was in "learning to make effective
use of inadequately qualified people for highly technical work." Procedures were developed to circumvent a worker's lack of training. Often
district offices sent these people into the countryside with specific
questions to ask regarding the project at hand. In that way the workers
did not have to make substantive or subjective judgments. The results
of their work were better than might have been expected, for although there
was never much public awareness in the early stages, the publication of a
volume attracted a great deal of publicity. Surprisingly most of the
reviews were "highly favorable," and these works found particular approval in historical societies, libraries, schools, and colleges and especially
in areas mentioned in the guide where "considerable pride in local points
of interest has been aroused."[55]

The limited work quotas damaged all of the technical programs to
some degree. The 90 percent rule meant that a great number of unqualified people had to be hired before any administrative personnel could
be added, and the 18-months rule made it impossible to retain those
people whom the supervisors had been able to train. Funds were a problem in all programs, of course, not only because they were limited, but
also because they were uncertain and often fluctuated, making it
impossible to initiate long-range planning.

The close federal control exercised severed the Federal Writers' Project
from the rest of the state WPA administration. Because anything done
under the auspices of the WPA was taken by the public as a reflection
of Miss Shepperson's capabilities, she was greatly distressed about her
lack of control and the absence of communication which existed from
the outset. Perhaps her relationship with Key revealed some uncompli-
mentary stridency and even possibly some actions that were not exactly
aboveboard. Given her sense of frustration in having little authority over
the program, and at the same time ultimately being held responsible for
it, her rather sharp reaction was at least understandable. After all, her
two greatest concerns were honesty and efficiency, and both were beyond
her control under these circumstances.

The Federal Theater Project (FTP) did not open in Georgia until January 19, 1937, but drama activities existed earlier under the WPA's Recreation Division. Planning for a civic theater in Atlanta under the FTP had begun in October 1935, when John McGee, assistant to Federal Theater Project Director Hallie Flanagan, traveled to Georgia to sound out possibilities for such a program.

Miss Shepperson reacted to the FTP much as she had to the Writers' Project—with a good deal of skepticism. She wrote to the national office, "In the judgment of those who have talked with Mr. McGee and with the personnel who would be placed on such a project (the Atlanta civic theater) if set up, it would be very much of a gamble as to whether the project would be successful, since, frankly, the capabilities of the actors now on relief in Atlanta are such that only a very few would be likely to fit into the type of drama that should be given in such a theatre."[56]

McGee disagreed with Miss Shepperson. He wired Miss Flanagan, "This judgment based upon judgment largely of one woman [Miss Shepperson's] who is trained in social service, but not a theatre person. This is in violent disagreement with my judgment and that of theatre leaders in Atlanta." Actually Miss Shepperson did not oppose a dramatics program, only the establishment of a theater in Atlanta. In March 1936 she had told Miss Flanagan, "It is our desire to further our recreation program in the field of dramatics," but she lacked the technical supervision for such projects. She asked Miss Flanagan to put someone on the state recreational staff to supervise all dramatic activities and suggested that the state's dramatic projects "be carried on as a unit of the Federal Theater Project and paid from funds allocated to that project." Besides being concerned about adequate supervision for such a program, Miss Shepperson wanted to make sure that she did not have to use any of her own funds to finance it. She was having enough trouble satisfying demands for other types of projects to consider taking on additional responsibilities.[57]

Miss Shepperson got her adviser, and he worked out so well that the state office asked for an extension of the project for fiscal 1936-1937. The national office approved and provided for the employment of Eugene J. Bergmann as a nonrelief consultant to cover the entire state "instructing our supervisors and leaders in recreational drama."[58]

Meanwhile, the national office ignored Miss Shepperson's warnings concerning a permanent theater and by the end of 1936 had drawn up plans for such a project. In the fall of 1936 private citizens in Atlanta established the Atlanta Theatre Guild, and the organization approached the FTP offering to serve as sponsor for a project. The national office sent Josef Lentz to Atlanta, where he found fourteen "certifiable" stagehands "plus a small group of tent show personnel." The guild pressured the WPA to move ahead with the project, and a contract was signed by December 1936. The FTP was to establish a theater in Atlanta and take over much of the state's dramatic activities.[59]

Lentz reported that he had gathered twelve certified technicians and ten certified actors "of medium class." The FTP promised to supplement these people with a loan company from New York City. The national office also decided that since plans were going ahead, it would close the Birmingham theater project and transfer its personnel to Atlanta, making that city the "tour center" for the South. In retrospect, Lentz realized that plans had been pushed too quickly. There was insufficient professional staff in Atlanta, and the guild, though enthusiastic, did not possess a good enough organization to guarantee success. At the time, however, Lentz was impressed by the guild's rapid progress. He told Miss Flanagan, "Every factor is in our favor for splendid work on this project."[60]

The national office moved Herbert S. Price from Birmingham to Georgia, and the state office placed Bergmann as drama consultant in Atlanta. Price toured the state selecting sites for five other drama centers, which were to be closely tied to the Recreation Division. They were more experimental in nature than the Atlanta project, involving not only drama but other performing arts as well. The national office agreed to send five drama leaders from New York City to aid in these activities.[61]

While the Atlanta staff anxiously awaited the arrival of the New York company, it began rehearsals for *The Drunkard*, an old-fashioned tear-jerker which Lentz felt was easy enough for a nonprofessional company to do successfully. The director of the production, Albert Lovejoy, complained, however, that of 28 actors listed for the project, "actually 4 or 5 can, by any stretch of the imagination, be *called* actors."[62]

The play opened on January 19, 1937, and was well received by the city. The Atlanta project, bolstered by this success, proceeded rapidly during the winter and spring of 1937, its program culminating in the April world premiere of the controversial play *Altars of Steel*. It was evident, however, that this progress was not due to the work of the

Atlanta Theatre Guild which had failed to engender community support and to provide adequate personnel to staff the theater. Eventually the FTP terminated its contract with the guild.

Conditions within the project itself worsened during this period. Price proved to be "too young and inexperienced," and he was replaced by Mrs. Sara Thomas from the state WPA office while Lentz searched for a new director. There was also the usual bickering within the casts and a growing opposition in New York City to the transfer of actors to other parts of the country. During the summer of 1937 the Atlanta project was without a permanent director. Guest directors produced *Altars of Steel, One More Spring,* and *Faustus.* These plays were presented under "very trying circumstances," and FTP administrators began to see the difficulty in attempting to make their professional personnel conform to WPA regulations.[63]

The program outside of the Atlanta theater grew in 1937, but not without its own brand of troubles. Experimental Dramatic Workshops were established in four cities, but because of delays in readjusting the projects when outside people were brought in, the program had not developed as well as had been expected. The community drama project in Rome was faltering. Supervisors there had trouble in casting, and because of the unfavorable publicity given the project by the local anti-administration newspaper, the project failed to gain "initial response." A drama consultant present at the time attributed Rome's problems, not to a lack of interest, but to a "class" barrier which prevented the project from attracting certain people.[64]

The Marietta and Atlanta projects were doing much better, although some people in Atlanta complained that actors were being brought in from the outside. Bergmann had done a fine job in Atlanta and by May 1937 had established adult choruses, minstrel and stunt nights, playground theaters, puppet theaters, folk dances, rhythm bands, orchestras, and community theaters. With his experience, Bergmann was able to use the "strange mixture of talent" in a special type of program. During the summer of 1937 the Georgia FTP began its tours. Traveling troupes (mostly minstrel shows) traversed Georgia, Alabama, and North Carolina, bringing their shows to small towns and to Civilian Conservation Corps camps where they staged a popular play *Murder in the CCC Camp.*[65]

The Atlanta theater managed to survive the summer of 1937 without a permanent director, and with the appointment of John Cameron as supervisor that fall, conditions promised to improve. This, however, was not immediately the case. Mrs. Thomas, who had run the program during the late spring and summer, did not want to give up her "theatrical" role. Cameron was egotistical and quite temperamental, and when Mrs. Thomas attempted to interfere with the casting of a play, he "blew up." To make matters worse, Cameron discovered when he arrived that the theater was about $300 in the red, forcing him to curtail his production costs. Since Mrs. Thomas was responsible for the administration of the theater, he tended to blame her for the conditions which existed. Lentz finally stepped in and abolished the joint administrative responsibility, making Cameron director and Mrs. Thomas supervisor. This compromise failed, however, and, since Lentz felt that Cameron was "less imaginative than some of our worst directors," he decided to replace him with Albert Lovejoy.[66]

Lentz was "very impressed" with Lovejoy, who was "off to a good start and seems to be liked by everyone." Just to make sure that there would be no further conflicts with Mrs. Thomas, Lentz maintained the separation of duties and reduced her responsibilities considerably. Lovejoy really had not wanted to come to Atlanta in the first place, fearing that during his absence from New York City he would "lose precedence for directorial work there at some future date." Furthermore, he knew that he was being sent to Atlanta to "help straighten out a difficult situation," and this evidently displeased him.[67]

Lovejoy was more successful than Cameron. He ruled the actors with an iron hand and would brook no disobedience. He did not hesitate to fire intransigent actors. By the end of the year the Atlanta *Journal* reported that the theater had "been designated the most successful Federal Theater outside New York."[68]

Unfortunately, this condition was short-lived, for gradual deterioration began in 1938 that finally ended in the abandonment of the project the next year. It seemed as if an altercation with Mrs. Thomas was not to be avoided. Her continual "under-cutting" of Lovejoy's authority prompted Lentz to remove her.[69]

Mrs. Thomas, however, presented only one of many problems which arose in 1938. The FTP did not have complete control over its theater, and the "wrestling matches and Hill-Billy contests" which continually interrupted the play runs were "dragging prestige down." Furthermore, the overhead at the Atlanta Theater was very high, so the state office began negotiations to move into the Erlanger Theater which had gone into receivership that year. The move to better quarters resulted in more problems and constant delays forced the cancellation of the highly touted *One-Third of a Nation.* [70]

The national office had pushed for the production of this play in Atlanta because of its "natural tie-up with the local Federal Housing Administration." The FTP wanted the Housing Authority and the city government to sponsor the production, but found it difficult to persuade them that a play dealing with poverty and slums would be well received. As a final stumbling block, some of the play's scenes had to be rewritten because of a city ordinance prohibiting the appearance of whites and blacks together on the same stage. [71]

Difficulties in play selection came not only from within the state where sponsors were difficult to secure, but also from the FTP's Play Policy Board to which theater seasons had to be submitted for approval. Lovejoy claimed that this New York board made decisions without knowing either Atlanta audiences or the theater company. The Atlanta Post No. 1 of the American Legion, for example, offered to sponsor a production of *What Price Glory,* but Lovejoy was denied permission to do the play because it "glorified war." Miss Flanagan subsequently approved an alternate production of *Journey's End.*

The play was produced, but Lentz felt that the reviews were not good enough. He warned Lovejoy that the 1939 season "must prove . . . a financial success as well as a complete selling job to the Atlanta community, . . . [for] the Atlanta project will be . . . under the most serious fire in the South." Lovejoy was incensed by Lentz's letter. He suggested that the reviews were "almost enthusiastic" for "Atlanta critics," and if Lentz had taken the trouble to see the play while it was *"actually on,* he would find that newspaper criticism does not always reflect audience reaction, or the opinion of discriminating theatre-goers." This disagreement between Lentz and Lovejoy pointed to a problem common to many of the professional programs. Lovejoy, the director, was primarily concerned with producing an artistic success, while Lentz, the administrator, insisted upon a financial success as well. [72]

If administrative relations were strained, the same applied to the actors and technical staff. Lovejoy was constantly writing the National Service Bureau to send him additional actors and materials, neither of which were provided in sufficient amounts. One actor assigned to

Atlanta never arrived, and Lovejoy speculated, "Perhaps when the chill winter winds start blowing through the tattered cloaks of Broadway, it may be easier to find a man who will welcome a few months in Atlanta." When actors did arrive from New York, Lovejoy found that they were not compatible with local personnel. The director reported that many were "meddlesome, quarrelsome, and in some instances insubordinate." Some actors "made the mistake of antagonizing the Southern actors by trying to impress on them a New York superiority which manifested itself in open criticism of Southern actors and veiled (even direct) reference to the latter as 'amateurs.'"

The same held true for technical staff sent from the North. A northern stage manager coming to Atlanta "has the cards stacked against him," Lovejoy noted. If possible, he "should be a Gentile" and should be able to handle a large crew "with the capacity to adjust himself to the trying conditions."[74]

In the end, Lovejoy was unable to cope with all of his troubles. Lentz saw as early as December 1938 that the project was crumbling, and he suggested the possibility of terminating it and sending the staff to Jacksonville, Florida, or to New Orleans. He did not, however, want to close the Atlanta project without giving it one more chance to succeed, so he devised a long-range plan for consolidation which allowed for the inclusion of the Atlanta project should it prove its worth.[75]

Improvement was not forthcoming, and as many professionals returned to private employment during 1939 and funds diminished, Lovejoy admitted that liquidation seemed advisable. The project was written to run through June 10, 1939, but it closed "with one week's notice on May 15." All of the properties and some of the personnel went to Jacksonville, and the state WPA office assigned the remaining staff to other jobs.

Lentz wrote to Miss Van De Vrede that he felt "badly that this step was necessitated," but Lovejoy did not think that Lentz was so sorry after all. Initially he argued that "after six major producions in the Erlanger Theatre . . . it has been effectively demonstrated that if there ever was a public in Atlanta for Federal Theatre productions it was long ago alienated by short-sighted business policies and slip-shod amateurish productions." After some months had passed, however, he changed his mind. He then wrote, "The truth is that the former regional director found it convenient to offer several excuses for the closing of the project, although the *real* reason at least the *chief* reason, for his action, was that

if the Atlanta Federal Theatre had continued to function, his office
stood in danger of being transferred from New Orleans, where his residence was, to Atlanta, where he did not want to make his headquarters,
domestic or official."[77]

Whatever the reasons for closing the project, it was certainly not an
abject failure. The Atlanta FTP produced 36 plays giving 329 perform-
ances to about 100,000 people during its tenure. The administration
distributed 35,000 free passes, and of these 30,000 were given to those
who had "never seen a legitimate play." In 1937-1938 the living theater
traveled about 6,000 miles in its four-state area, covering more territory
than any other similar company. Finally, the Atlanta project served to
"reestablish Atlanta as a show town" attracting more traveling commercial companies. These accomplishments were well received by the public,
whose attitude toward the "escapist" possibilities it provided was similar
to that towards the recreational program.[78]

The operations of the Service Division in general, and of its various
projects in particular, seemed to demonstrate that when the federal
administration allowed the states to tailor activities to their own needs,
the resulting programs were the most successful. When such leniency
was not forthcoming, Miss Shepperson inevitably found herself confronted by irritated sponsors or state officials. The programs of the
Service Division also indicated how the state offices worked with the
state and local governments and what sort of problems were likely to
arise in those relationships. There were, of course, always those who
opposed the New Deal entirely, and they proved to be constant
obstacles. In other instances, however, the WPA was able to work
harmoniously with governments and sponsors as long as they were made
to feel like partners rather than servants and if the programs seemed to
help the people whom they represented. The Service Division exemplified
the continued polarity of interests and procedures between those who
were concerned with works and those who were concerned about workers.
It was axiomatic that as the programs became more specialized, the
likelihood of friction between professionals and social workers increased.

NOTES

1. WPA, "Final Report," III, 5.
2. *Ibid.* Van De Vrede to Key, August 3, 1935, NARG 69, State

Series, No. 660, box 1146. (When speaking in general terms the title "Service Division" is used throughout.)

3. WPA, "Final Report," III, 5 ff. Shepperson to M. J. Miller, August 5, 1935, NARG 69, Region III, No. 132.3, box 185.

4. Shepperson to Miller, August 5, 1935, NARG 69, Region III, No. 132.3, box 185. Van De Vrede to Key, August 3, 1935, NARG 69, State Series, No. 660, box 1146.

5. Van De Vrede to Key, August 3, 1935, NARG 69, State Series, No. 660, box 1146. "Women's Projects," September 12 and November 23, 1935, NARG 69, State Series, No. 660, box 1146.

6. "Women's Projects," September 12, 1935, NARG 69, State Series, No. 660, box 1146. Van De Vrede to Key, August 3, 1935, NARG 69, State Series, No. 660, box 1146.

7. "Women's Projects," September 12, 1935, NARG 69, State Series, No. 660, box 1146. Unsigned memo, March 21, 1935, NARG 69, State Series, No. 660, box 1146. Van De Vrede to Woodward, July 13, 1935, NARG 69, State Series, No. 660, box 1146.

8. "Women's Projects," September 12, 1935, NARG 69, State Series, No. 660, box 1146. Atlanta *Constitution,* November 21, 1935.

9. Hopkins and Shepperson, October 25, 1935 (telephone conversation), Hopkins MSS, selected documents. "Women's Projects," November 23, 1935, NARG 69, State Series, No. 660, box 1146.

10. "Women's Projects," November 23 and December 15, 1935, NARG 69, State Series, No. 660, box 1146.

11. Narrative reports, April-June 1937, NARG 69, Narrative Reports of Women's and Professional Projects, June 1937, Professional and Service Division, Narrative Reports, box 6.

12. Jane Van De Vrede, "Advantage of State-Wide Projects," October 29, 1938, NARG 69, State Series, No. 661, box 1147.

13. See Appendix, Table 15.

14. Atlanta *Constitution,* November 1, 1935. WPA, "Final Report," NARG 69.

15. WPA, "Final Report." Woodward to Senator Russell, September 25, 1936, NARG 69, State Series, No. 660, box 1146. Woodward to Shepperson, November 22, 1935, NARG 69, State Series, No. 660, box 1146.

16. WPA, "Final Report," Catherine E. Cleveland to Mrs. Florence Kerr, October 6, 1941 (memo), NARG 69, State Series, No. 651.321, box 1141.

17. WPA, "Final Report." Woodward to Shepperson, November 22, 1935, NARG 69, State Series, No. 660, box 1146.

18. M. J. Miller to Corrington Gill, December 2, 1935 (telegram), NARG 69, State Series, No. 660, box 1146. Correspondence between Van De Vrede and Woodward, October 30, 1935 to December 8, 1935, NARG 69, State Series, No. 660, box 1146.

19. Atlanta *Journal,* September 14, 1936.

20. WPA, "Final Report."

21. *Ibid.*

22. "Newsletter to Georgia Libraries," No. 2, February 1936, NARG 69, State Series, No. 661, box 1147. WPA, "Final Report."

23. WPA, "Final Report."

24. Excerpts from Georgia Library Commission, Secretary's Report, January 1, 1936, to June 30, 1937, NARG 69, State Series, No. 661, box 1147.

25. "Newsletter to Georgia Libraries," No. 2, February 1936, NARG 69, State Series, No. 661, box 1147. Miss Beverly Wheatcroft to Kerr, April 12, 1939, NARG 69, State Series, No. 651.318, box 1140. Wheatcroft to Edward A. Chapman, September 16, 1939, NARG 69, State Series, No. 651.318, box 1140.

26. FitzSimons to Miss Lucy Williams Brown, October 28, 1936, NARG 69, State Series, No. 651.37, box 1145. On December 31, 1935, only 7 out of 17 projects had been approved. One year later, 11 of 33, had been approved. (Report of projects submitted to the coordinating committee of the central statistical board, 1935, 1936, NARG 69, Professional and Service Projects, Review of Projects, California to Kansas [1935-37], box 431.)

27. WPA, "Final Report." Leo Day Woodworth to W. M. Lester, December 19, 1935, NARG 69, State Series, No. 651.37, box 1145. Bruce McClure to Shepperson, March 21, 1936, NARG 69, State Series, No. 651.35, box 1143.

28. Professional and Service progress report, May 15, 1939, NARG 69.

29. Robert Wauchope, "Archaeological Survey of Northern Georgia," *American Antiquity,* XXXI, 5, Pt. 2 (July 1966), vii-xv.

30. Jacob Baker to Shepperson, May 4, 1936, NARG 69, State Series, No. 651.36, box 1144. Harold D. Meyer to Miss Irma Ringe, October 28, 1936 (memo), NARG 69, State Series, No. 651.36, box 1144.

31. Meyer to Ringe, July 1936 (?) (memo), NARG 69, State Series, No. 651.36, box 1144. Fischer to Ringe, May 25, 1936, NARG 69, State Series, No. 651.36, box 1144. Meyer to Ringe, July 1936 (memo), NARG 69, State Series, No. 651.3666, box 1144.

32. Meyer to Ringe, July 1936 (memo), NARG 69, State Series, No. 651.36, box 1144. Van De Vrede to Shepperson, August 24, 1936

(memo), NARG 69, State Series, No. 651.36, box 1144. "Report of
Recreational Activities for June 1937," July 15, 1937, NARG 69, State
Series, No. 651.364, box 1145. By September 1939 one-third of the
employment in the state was black. (Ringe to Lindeman, September
27, 1939 [memo], NARG 69, State Series, No. 651.36, box 1145.)

33. "Report on Recreational Training Program," 1937, NARG 69,
State Series, No. 651.36, box 1144. Marie Parker to Miss Dorothy I.
Cline, May 25, 1937, NARG 69, State Series, No. 651.36, box 1144.
Report of Miss Lawler, June 1, 1938, NARG 69, State Series,
No. 651.36, box 1144.

34. Fischer to Ringe, February 25, 1938, NARG 69, State Series,
No. 651.36, box 1144. Bentley to Miller, September 20, 1938, NARG 69,
No. 651.364, box 1145. "Report for Recreational Activities, October
1938," December 8, 1939, NARG 69, State Series, No. 651.36, box 1145.

35. "Report for Recreational Activities, October 1938," December
8, 1938, NARG 69, State Series, No. 651.36, box 1145. "Monthly State
Recreation Report," April 30, 1936, NARG 69, State Series, No. 651.36,
box 1144. "Report of Recreational Activities for March 1937," NARG 69,
State Series, No. 651.36, box 1144. Fischer to Ringe, August 31, 1937,
NARG 69, State Series, No. 651.36, box 1144.

36. "Report for Recreational Activities, January 1939," NARG 69,
State Series, No. 651.36, box 1145. Van De Vrede to Robert B.
Bradford, April 27, 1939, NARG 69, State Series, No. 651.36, box 1145.
"Report for Recreational Activities, November 1938," NARG 69, State
Series, No. 651.36, box 1145.

37. P. S. Barrett to C. F. Klinefelter, October 9, 1934, NARG 69,
Emergency Education Program, State Series (1933-35), box 5.
Klinefelter to Barrett, October 12, 1934, NARG 69, Em. Ed. Prog., State
Series (1933-35), box 5. Barrett to Klinefelter, October 16, 1934,
NARG 69, Em. Ed. Prog., State Series (1933-35), box 5. M. D. Collins
to Dr. L. R. Alderman, October 20 (?), 1934 (telegram), NARG 69, Em.
Ed. Prog., State Series (1933-35), box 5. Barrett to Klinefelter,
November 2, 1934, NARG 69, Em. Ed. Prog., State Series (1933-35),
box 5. Barrett to Alderman, November 25, 1935, NARG 69, Em. Ed.
Prog., State Series, No. 430, box 59.

38. Barrett to Alderman, n.d., NARG 69, Em. Ed. Prog., State Series
(1933-35), box 5.

39. Collins to Alderman, October 6, 1936, NARG 69, Em. Ed. Prog.,
State Series (1936), box 58. Meyer to Dr. G. L. Maxwell, July 30, 1937,
NARG 69, Em. Ed. Prog., State Series, No. 430, box 99. Alderman to
Barrett, October 21, 1936, NARG 69, Em. Ed. Prog., State Series (1936),

box 58. Barrett to Alderman, October 16, 1936, NARG 69, Em. Ed. Prog., State Series (1936), box 58. Shepperson to Miller, November 2, 1936, NARG 69, Em. Ed. Prog., State Series (1936), box 58.

40. WPA, "Final Report." Bentley to Mrs. Blanche M. Ralston, April 3, 1939 (report), NARG 69, State Series, No. 651.341, box 1141. Frank S. Horne to Shepperson, June 22, 1936, NARG 69, Em. Ed. Prog., State Series (1936), box 58.

41. Shepperson to Alsberg, October 2, 1935, NARG 69, Federal Writers' Project (FWP), Admin. Corres.

42. William Key to Alsberg, October 15, 1935, NARG 69, FWP, Admin. Corres.

43. Key to Alsberg, October 19, 1935, NARG 69, FWP, Admin. Corres. Key to Alsberg, October 30, 1935 (telegram), NARG 69, FWP, Admin. Corres. Alsberg to Key, October 31, 1935 (telegram), NARG 69, FWP, Admin. Corres.

44. Key to Alsberg, November 30, 1935, NARG 69, FWP, Admin. Corres. George Raffalovich to Alsberg, February 22, 1936, NARG 69, FWP, Admin. Corres. There are a number of letters from Raffalovich in this file, all reflecting what a professional person "suffered" at the hands of social workers. Key to Alsberg, December 23, 1935, NARG 69, FWP, Admin. Corres. Darel McConkey to Alsberg, December 26, 1935 (report), NARG 69, FWP, Field Reports, box 58.

45. Note from Key (?), January 13, 1936, NARG 69, FWP, Admin. Corres. "Note," n.d., NARG 69, FWP, Admin. Corres., Georgia (1935-39), box 10.

46. Alsberg, to Shepperson, January 6, 1936, NARG 69, FWP, Admin. Corres. Shepperson to Alsberg, January 11, 1936, NARG 69, FWP, Admin. Corres. Raffalovich to Alsberg, February 22, 1936, NARG 69, FWP, Admin. Corres. Key to Alsberg, January 4, 1936, NARG 69, FWP, Admin. Corres.

47. Raffalovich to Alsberg, February 22, 1936, NARG 69, FWP, Admin. Corres. Key to Alsberg, January 4, 1936, NARG 69, FWP, Admin. Corres.

48. Dillard to Alsberg, February 24, 1936, NARG 69, FWP, Admin. Corres. Alsberg to Dillard, March 5, 1936, NARG 69, FWP, Admin. Corres. Jacob Baker to Shepperson, January 15, 1936 (telegram), NARG 69, FWP, Admin. Corres., Georgia (1935-39), box 10. Mrs. Kathryn Cordell to Alsberg, June 9, 1936 (report), NARG 69, FWP, Field Reports, box 58.

49. Dillard to Alsberg, February 27, 1936, NARG 69, FWP, Admin. Corres., Georgia (1935-39), box 10. Dillard to Alsberg, February 21,

1936, NARG 69, FWP, Admin. Corres., Georgia (1935-39), box 10. Key to Alsberg, January 16, 1936, NARG 69, FWP, Admin. Corres., Georgia (1935-39), box 10 (?).

50. WPA, "Final Report." "Mr. Beck's preliminary report of the Georgia State Guide Book," June 12, 1936, NARG 69, FWP, Editorial Corres., box 87.

51. "Mr. Beck's report," June 12, 1936, NARG 69, FWP, Editorial Corres., box 87.

52. Tupper to Alsberg, August 26, 1938, NARG 69, FWP, Admin. Corres. WPA, "Final Report."

53. WPA, "Final Report." Van De Frede to C. E. Triggs, n.d., NARG 69, State Series, No. 651.317, box 1139. Tupper to William R. McDaniel, September 5, 1941, NARG 69, State Series, No. 651.317, box 1139. Stella Bloch Hanau to Mr. Newsom, October 26, 1941, NARG 69, State Series, No. 651.317, box 1139.

54. Hanau to Newsom, October 26, 1941, NARG 69, State Series, No. 651.317, box 1139. Tupper to Newsom, February 3, 1942, NARG 69, State Series, No. 651.317, box 1139, WPA. "Final Report."

55. *Ibid.*

56. Shepperson to Jacob Baker, October 31, 1935, NARG 69, State Series, No. 651.312, box 1135.

57. John McGee to Hallie Flanagan, November 4, 1935 (telegram), NARG 69, State Series, No. 651.312, box 1135. Shepperson to Flanagan, March 26, 1936, NARG 69, State Series, No. 651.312, box 1135.

58. Gilbert H. Boggs to Flanagan, July 8, 1936, NARG 69, State Series, No. 651.312, box 1135. August Fischer to Robert Enger, October 10, 1936, NARG 69, State Series, No. 651.312, box 1135.

59. Josef Lentz to J. Howard Miller, May 18, 1939 (report), NARG 69, Federal Theatre Project (FTP), National Director's Letters to Regional Directors, Monthly State Reports to Regional Directors, Regions I-III, box 546. Lentz to Flanagan, December 3, 1936, NARG 69, State Series, No. 651.312, box 1135.

60. *Ibid.*

61. Albany *Herald,* January 11, 1937, Herbert S. Price to Miss Linda Donalson, December 19, 1936, NARG 69, State Series, No. 651.312, box 1135.

62. Lentz to Flanagan, December 3, 1936, NARG 69, State Series, No. 651.312, box 1135. Lentz to Flanagan, December 4, 1936, NARG 69, State Series, No. 651.312, box 1135. Albert Lovejoy to McGee, January 1, 1937, NARG 69, FTP, Atlanta, Georgia (1937-38), box 609.

63. Flanagan to Irma Ringe, March 15, 1937, NARG 69, State Series,

No. 651.312, box 1135. Lentz to Miller, May 18, 1939 (report), NARG 69, FTP, National Director's Letters, Regions I-III, box 546.
    64. Harold D. Mayer to Miller and Lindeman, March 1, 1937 (memo), NARG 69, State Series, No. 651.312, box 1135. Edward J. Hayes to Miss Charlotte Holt, March 20, 1937, NARG 69, State Series, No. 651.312, box 1135.
    65. Hayes to Holt, March 20, 1937, NARG 69, State Series, No. 651.312, box 1135. Monthly report of Eugene Bergmann, May 1937, NARG 69, FTP, Narrative Reports (1937), box 88. Report of Josef Lentz, May 15, 1939, NARG 69, Professional and Service Progress Reports, Narrative Reports, box 6. "Note," n.d., NARG 69, FTP, Atlanta, Georgia (1937-38), box 609.
    66. Lentz to Miller, May 18, 1939 (report), NARG 69, FTP, National Director's Letters, Regions I-III, box 546. Lentz to Miller, October 4, 1937 (report), NARG 69, FTP, National Director's Letters, Regions I-III, box 546. Lentz to McGree, October 7, 1937, NARG 69, FTP, National Director's Letters, Regions I-III, box 546. Lentz to Miller, November 20, 1937, NARG 69, FTP, National Director's Letters, Regions I-III, box 546.
    67. Lentz to McGee, December 3, 1937, NARG 69, FTP, National Director's Letters, Regions I-III, box 546. Lovejoy to Irwin A. Rubinstein, December 24, 1937, and January 1, 1938, NARG 69, FTP, Atlanta, Georgia (1937-38), box 609.
    68. Lovejoy to Rubinstein, February 2, 1938, NARG 69, FTP, Atlanta, Georgia (1937-38), box 609. Atlanta *Journal,* December 26, 1937.
    69. Lentz to Flanagan, December 1, 3, and 24, 1938, NARG 69, FTP, National Director's Letters, Regions I-III, box 546. Lentz to Miller, February 19, 1938, NARG 69, FTP, National Director's Letters, Regions I-III, box 546.
    70. Lentz to Miller, May 31, 1938, NARG 69, FTP, National Director's Letters, Regions I-III, box 546. Lentz to Miller, May 18, 1939 (report), NARG 69, FTP, National Director's Letters, Regions I-III, box 546.
    71. Lentz to Miller, May 18, 1939 (report), NARG 69, FTP, National Director's Letters, Regions I-III, box 546. Lovejoy to Flanagan, April 14, 1939 (monthly report), NARG 69, State Series, No. 651.312, box 1136. Miller to Emmet Lavery, March 27, 1939, NARG 69, FTP, National Office, Alabama-Illinois (1937-39), box 69.
    72. Lovejoy to Flanagan, November 29, 1938 (monthly report), NARG 69, FTP, National Office, Alabama-Illinois (1937-39), box 69. Lovejoy to Lavery, March 14, 1938, NARG 69, FTP, Atlanta, Georgia (1937-38), box 609. Lovejoy to Flanagan, January 29, 1939 (monthly report),

NARG 69, State Series, No. 1938, and January 29, 1939 (reports), NARG 69, FTP, National Director's Letters, Regions I-III, box 546.

73. Lovejoy to Flanagan, November 29, 1938 (report), NARG 69, FTP, National Director's Letters, Regions I-III, box 546. Lovejoy to Rubinstein, October 5 and 7, 1938, NARG 69, FTP, Atlanta, Georgia (1937-38), box 609.

74. Lovejoy to Rubinstein, October 1, 1938, NARG 69, FTP, Atlanta, Georgia (1937-38), box 609.

75. Lentz to Flanagan, December 10, 1938, NARG 69, FTP, National Director's Letters, Regions I-III, box 546. Lentz to Flanagan, February 14, 1939, NARG 69, State Series, No. 651.312, box 1136.

76. Lentz to Miller, May 18, 1939 (memo), NARG 69, FTP, National Director's Letters, Regions I-III, box 546. Lovejoy to All Project Workers, May 1, 1939, NARG 69, State Series, No. 651.312, box 1136. Lovejoy to Colonel F. C. Harrington, July 22, 1939, NARG 69, State Series, No. 651.312, box 1136.

77. Lentz to Miss Van De Vrede, May 1, 1939, NARG 69, State Series, No. 651.312, box 1136. Lovejoy to Harrington, July 22, 1939, NARG 69, State Series, No. 651.312, box 1136. Lovejoy to Flanagan, May 5, 1939, NARG 69, State Series, No. 651.312, box 1136.

78. Report of Josef Lentz, May 15, 1939, NARG 69, Professional and Service Progress Reports, Narrative Reports, box 6. Lentz to Miller, May 18, 1939 (report), NARG 69, FTP, National Director's Letters, Regions I-III, box 546. See also: Appendix, Tables 16 and 17.

5
Dr. Ickes Tries His Remedy

The final major action of the special session of the Seventy-third Congress was to pass the National Industrial Recovery Act (NIRA). The bill was signed by President Roosevelt on June 16, 1933, the day the Congress adjourned. Title II of the NIRA created the Public Works Administration (PWA), and the president selected Secretary of the Interior Harold L. Ickes to be its head. The act provided funds to pay 30 percent of the labor and material costs on major construction projects. If the project was self-liquidating, the federal government would lend the balance to the sponsoring political subdivision; if not, the subdivision had to supply the remaining 70 percent out of its own funds.[1]

Private contractors selected by competitive bidding were to do the work, subject to certain restrictions. Original orders called for labor to be paid a "just and reasonable wage," but a later ruling set up three zone scales. In the southern zone, which included Georgia, skilled labor received $1.00 an hour and unskilled labor, $.40. This was the lowest in the nation. No convict labor was to be employed, veterans were to be given job priority, and a certain portion of a project's labor force had to be taken from relief rolls. As far as possible, the contractor was to use materials produced by companies operating under National Recovery Administration codes, and bidding was not restricted to local businesses.[2]

The PWA did not establish actual state administrations as in the other relief or works agencies; each state had an engineer and an advisory board. It was the state advisory board's duty "(a) To stimulate the submission of projects, (b) to inform the public of the classes of projects eligible for the benefits of the act, (c) to elicit from applicants the supporting data . . . necessary for the consideration of the project, (d) to consider the project from the standpoint of local coordinated planning, social and economic desirability, provision of employment, diversification of employment, engineering soundness . . . [and] (e) promptly to submit to the Administrator with its recommendations all projects considered." This advisory board functioned until February 1934, when it was disbanded as part of Ickes's program to demobilize the PWA's field forces.[3]

Each state engineer was appointed by Ickes himself and was responsible only to him. The engineer served as the executive officer of the advisory board and supervised all office activities. It was his duty to examine applications to ascertain their completeness. Ickes chose J. Houstoun Johnston, former engineer for the Georgia Public Service Commission, to fill this post. It had been the policy of the administration to select a technical expert from outside of a state in order to avoid "local pressure," but Ickes made an exception in Johnston's case.

Prior to the board's first meeting, Ickes instructed Atlanta businessman Cator Woolford to act as the state's PWA director in order to initiate planning at the county level. Woolford was empowered to "name local committees in all communities of the state" which would assist in preparing relief labor lists so contractors could secure needed workers quickly. Current PWA policy required that at least 50 percent of those working on PWA projects be from the relief rolls. In the meantime Ickes told the advisory board to begin its work. He suggested that the board first consider applications for sewage disposal plants, then turn to municipal and county projects, and finally to state-sponsored projects. Since the board had not met when the first projects were approved in Washington, Georgia received no funds until September. The board sat from August 14 to August 18 to review some 75 to 100 projects. It sent those which it approved to Washington and on September 15, 1933, received its first funds.[4]

One of the primary factors inhibiting the program's growth in Georgia was the state's limited borrowing power. Since the depression had depleted most governmental treasuries, the only option open to cities, counties, and even to the state was to apply for the self-liquidating projects. The federal government would then cover the entire cost with either loans or grants. Neither the state government nor its political subdivisions, however, could borrow more than 7 percent of its "tax values." By 1933 most local governments had reached their constitutional limits. Furthermore, the state could not borrow beyond the current fiscal year, so that it was unable to follow the federal government's method of deficit financing. The state legislature attempted to alter this, but Talmadge would not agree.

There was never any consensus as to the extent the governor's actions impeded the PWA's progress in Georgia. In the 1934 gubernatorial campaign, one of Talmadge's opponents, Ed A. Gilliam, charged that the incumbent had deprived the state of $75 million in PWA funds. On the other hand, the Atlanta *Constitution* reported earlier that "despite the constitutional limitations on its borrowing powers, Georgia has obtained a larger total of PWA funds than any other southeastern state."[5]

In 1933 the state qualified for only 43 projects in 24 counties, but the pace quickened considerably once it found that it could obtain projects without borrowing. One provision of the financing rules allowed the federal government to pay the entire cost of a state project if the state were willing to "rest" the project upon its completion until the state's share was paid for. The Georgia legislature approved such a plan, and the governor did not object. The PWA was not entirely pleased with this arrangement, but agreed. The first project undertaken in this manner was a state prison in Tattnall County. A prison appealed to the federal government, because if the state failed to fulfill its part of the bargain, the federal government could always use the structure as a federal prison. Subsequently, other state projects were financed in this way.[6]

The counties were not so fortunate. They could not operate in this fashion, and many applied for no projects whatever until 1936 when the PWA agreed to cover 45 percent of the material and labor costs. Some counties were forced to abandon projects when they reached the limits of their borrowing power. This left unfinished projects and much dissatisfaction in the counties.

Neither Talmadge nor his ostensibly pro-New Deal successor, Eurith D. Rivers, ever promoted the necessary changes in the state's constitution to remove the borrowing restrictions. Then, in 1938, President Roosevelt prohibited the state from financing projects by leasing them from the federal government. Some of Rivers' friends claimed that this was the president's revenge for the governor's failure to marshal successfully the

state's political machine behind the senatorial candidacy of former
State Attorney General Lawrence S. Camp in his campaign against the
incumbent, Senator George.[7]

The PWA made slow but sure progress in 1933 and 1934, during
which time four projects were completed. There were, however, some
internal problems which inhibited the PWA's success. Foremost was the
slowness with which these projects were begun. The tremendous amount
of red tape Ickes used to bind his program caused serious delays in
getting contracts approved. The minimum time required was three months,
and the average time was eight to nine months. In January 1935 the
state NEC director reported that only 50 projects had been initiated
"aggregating less than seven million dollars, of which only about 2.5
million dollars had actually been spent."[8]

Once the projects had been approved there was little delay in prosecuting them; however, there was great dissatisfaction with the wage
scale. Private contractors were "using every subterfuge to avoid paying
wage rates—[because] the minimum established in many classes is
higher than present prevailing rate." The Whitley Construction Company
of La Grange was the worst offender. The owner, a close personal friend
of the governor, paid his common labor from 10 to 12.5 cents an hour.
When Whitley encountered severe criticism which resulted in a court
case, Talmadge put all highway construction under the state Highway
Department, thus removing the control over wage scales from the PWA.[9]

Although the PWA could boast little physical progress by the spring
of 1935, it was able to educate Georgians in its possibilities, so that when
a new program was inaugurated that summer, municipalities and counties
were ready to cooperate. The Emergency Relief Appropriation Act of
1935 (which created the WPA) provided for the extension of the PWA
until June 30, 1937, and afforded Ickes the chance to reorganize. He
increased the government's share of financing from 30 to 45 percent
of the project costs and encouraged more non-federal projects. The
new cost split attracted Georgia's attention and approval as "a fair and
equitable program," and many communities began to prepare project
proposals. The state's press cooperated fully in stimulating local interest,
and during the late spring and early summer the goal was set of having
at least one project in each county.[10]

As new proposals were completed, they were forwarded to Johnston
in Atlanta, who assumed full responsibility. NEC director Erle Cocke

was afraid that Johnston was too closely associated with the old program. The state engineer was "about 64," a technical engineer, and a
close stickler for regulations. Cocke feared he would find it "hard to
fully assimilate any liberalization under the new program." Johnston
had "probably [been] a little too delicate in pushing the cause of the
PWA in contradistinction to the programs of the WPA," because he
was dealing with a woman administrator of the WPA with an outstanding
record and did not want to step on her toes. Despite Cocke's reservations, Johnston remained in his position.[11]

Under the new program applications were to be accepted at the state
office until September 6, 1935. Johnston appealed to "cities, counties,
and school districts" to submit their plans quickly to meet the deadline.
The first nonfederal project was approved on July 7, but by August it
had become apparent that Georgia would not meet her allotment in time,
and the deadline was moved to September 16. On August 26, 1935, when
this decision was made, there were still over 70 applications outstanding.
The national office sent a "flying squadron" to Atlanta to help speed up
processing so that the quota might be reached.[12]

By September 7, a total of 290 projects had been presented from 121
counties. Various reasons were given for the slowness with which these
applications were arriving. One observer blamed the limitations on borrowing. Another noted that the PWA projects were larger and required more
participation by applicants than those undertaken by the WPA. In some
instances local governments had to hold bond elections to secure enough
funds to proceed.[13]

A problem arising in the summer of 1935 which plagued the administration until 1939 was the confusion caused by the formation of the
WPA. Both agencies were "works" programs, and many people felt that
the WPA required less of them in terms of contributions. The confusion
was not surprising, for Ickes and Hopkins themselves had a hard time
determining who should control which projects. One of the more serious
of many disagreements between the two men occurred over a sewer project
proposed for Atlanta. Work had begun under the CWA, and the project
was continued by the FERA until 1935, when the city resubmitted it to
the WPA where it was approved. On July 2, 1935, Hopkins and Ickes
reached an agreement that the PWA was to handle applications for
"heavy construction, such as schools, sanitary sewerage systems, sewage
disposal plants." As a result Ickes claimed that the PWA should run this

project, because it involved heavy construction and because Atlanta was well able to raise the 55 percent which was the city's share of the cost. Furthermore, the state had failed to pass a "Sewer Authority Act" that would have provided state funds for municipal sewer projects. Ickes felt that Atlanta was trying to dupe the federal government into building a "practically free sewer project" when the city easily could afford to pay its share of the costs.[14]

Atlanta sources had warned that the residents would never approve a bond issue to cover the city's share of the expenses. Ickes told Hopkins, however, that this should not dictate the president's policies, and Atlanta must understand that it could not get away with providing only 18.5 percent of the project's cost. Hopkins responded to Ickes' letter by noting that the history of the project clearly showed that it was of a nature normally undertaken by the WPA. He conceded that Atlanta might possibly be able to afford the project, but he pointed out that "few agree" with Ickes' assessment. In any case the holding of a bond election would waste valuable time and ultimately "entirely defeat the intention of Congress . . . to supply work on useful projects instead of providing relief which all must recognize fails to conserve our human resources, and by that failure costs even more than work furnished under the present program at security wages." Finally, Hopkins noted that in a July 2, 1935, agreement approved by Roosevelt the WPA was to assume the responsibility for all projects begun under the FERA. The entire problem he suggested, revolved around "the apparent pique of some members of your [Ickes'] staff in Atlanta because of difficulties encountered on your housing program in that city [Techwood and University Homes]." Hopkins concluded by offering a compromise wherein the PWA would construct two waste disposal plants with the WPA handling the rest of the work.[15]

Although Hopkins' position was hardly impregnable, both Miss Shepperson and Mr. Johnston agreed to make it a joint project. Ickes would not accept the compromise. He did agree to let Frank C. Walker, chairman of the NEC's committee on project control, mediate in cases where there were disputes, but when Walker also suggested that the responsibilities be divided, Ickes changed his mind.[16]

All indications pointed to a solution involving joint operations in Atlanta. Roosevelt himself approved of this method, and it did seem likely that a wholly PWA project would not receive support from the city's residents. On the other hand, some groups in the city, notably organized labor, would not favor the program unless at least part of the work was done under contract using nonrelief labor.[17]

Finally Roosevelt prevailed, and Hopkins informed Miss Shepperson of the president's decision to have the WPA undertake the project with the city providing 50 percent of the material. A majority of Atlanta's residents were satisfied and voted the "Million Dollar Bond Issue" in the fall of 1935.

Unfortunately, the matter did not rest there. Soon afterward Miss Shepperson received a wire from Hopkins and Ickes that the PWA would do the job with matching city funds for both material and labor. This action reopened the controversy, especially since the previous bond issue would not cover the city's share under these new provisions. Eventually the misunderstanding was cleared up, with each agency handling part of the work, but not without a great deal of trouble and dissatisfaction.

The case of the Atlanta sewer project served as a good example of how inconsistent national policies could affect work at the state level. Even though both the state PWA and WPA administrators agreed, the Ickes-Hopkins rivalry and the resulting confusion damaged both agencies in the eyes of the public and consequently hurt both Miss Shepperson and Johnston, neither of whom had anything to do with the clash. When these two people were left alone to handle the programs in Georgia without federal interference, both agencies ran rather smoothly, at least in comparison to the trouble which arose over the sewer project.[18]

The wage-scale problem had been solved by the summer of 1935, but the delays in getting projects approved and under way still provoked ill feelings from local residents. The national office continued to move slowly, mainly because of the high cost of the materials per man-year which seemed to characterize applications from the state. Delays also resulted from the PWA's relief work quotas. Officials estimated that approximately 35 percent of those employed on projects in March 1936 were from relief rolls. The NEC director expected the employment load to peak sometime in May or June, but he found that unless contractors were willing to employ a greater number from the relief rolls the peak might not be as high as predicted. Contractors had been pleasantly surprised by the quality of relief workers, but there were few skilled laborers on the rolls. Since much of the PWA's work was of a type that required such employees, little could be done.[19]

On June 22, 1936, the second Emergency Relief Appropriation Act (ERA) was approved, extending the PWA for another year. By the time it was passed, 51 of the 229 projects approved to that point had been completed, 122 were under construction, and 56 were waiting to commence. They were well distributed geographically and by type. By August 29, 1936, 188 projects were completed, and by October 10, all but one project begun under the NIRA and the ERA of 1935 were under construction or finished. Of the 12 projects approved under the ERA of 1936, 6 were already under way. The program of the PWA was at last moving with some efficiency and dispatch.

Only in the last months of 1936 was there any trouble, and this centered around the shifting labor supply. Since increasingly fewer projects were begun in the last six months of 1936, workers on projects initiated in 1935, which were now being completed, had nowhere to go. It was anticipated originally that they would be absorbed by private industry, but a business recession in 1937 precluded any such accommodation.[20]

The Public Works Administration Extension Act, approved on June 29, 1937, lengthened the PWA's life until July 1, 1939. The act required a more substantial contribution on the part of local governments for nonfederal projects and a commitment from them to use more relief labor. Of the approximately 100 applications pending at the time of the act's passage, the sponsors of about 25 indicated that they would be unable to undertake their proposed projects under the new provisions. The NEC director remarked that the new act probably would restrict future projects to larger cities "having both heavy relief loads and strong financial resources."[21]

One further piece of legislation, the Public Works Administration Act approved on June 21, 1938, extended the PWA until June 21, 1941, and amendments to the act lengthened the PWA's existence to June 30, 1942. On July 1, 1939, the newly created Federal Works Agency (FWA) assumed control of all relief and public works organizations including the PWA. The FWA completed liquidation of the PWA on July 1, 1943. During these later years the PWA, along with all other relief and public works agencies, turned its efforts increasingly to defense work. Policies came to be more tightly controlled by Washington, and correspondingly the work of state administrators became more perfunctory. In many instances during the final years these agencies lost their relation to the depression and took on the structure and purpose of a governmental war-preparedness program. Thus, long before they were liquidated, they passed out of the hands of state administrations and also out of the realm of relief and recovery.

Of all the PWA projects the most important in terms of money spent and laborers used was the road program undertaken in cooperation with the Bureau of Public Roads and the state Highway Department. Even so, the project had a rather stormy beginning.

When Governor Talmadge assumed office in 1933, he undertook a purge of all state agencies, among them the state Highway Department. When the state highway director refused to resign, the governor, a great admirer of Mussolini, used martial law to oust him and to control the department. Talmadge also juggled the department's funds. In keeping with a campaign pledge, he had reduced the price of all automobile license tags to a standard $3.00 a tag. Elated Georgians praised his move, little realizing that it was the bus and shipping companies, who otherwise would have carried the lion's share of a graduated tag price scale, that really benefited from the governor's move. Talmadge also diverted highway funds to other departments, counting on federal aid to subsidize the highway department.[22]

In view of these conditions the federal government withheld PWA road funds. Washington finally agreed to give Talmadge the money, providing he would hire a "special supervisory engineer" chosen by Washington to oversee the work. Talmadge refused, saying that he would gladly replace the federal engineers now present with new ones if they were unsatisfactory, but he would not undergo the "humiliation of dictatorship" implied in the government's request. In a private conference with Roosevelt arranged by Atlanta *Constitution* editor Clark Howell, Talmadge persuaded the president to rescind the government's requirement and to release the funds.

Unfortunately, this altercation had prevented any road work from beginning in the state, and on September 28, 1933, Ickes included Georgia in a list of 14 states whose road funds were to be canceled because work had not yet commenced. Eventually Ickes also capitulated to Talmadge and released the money to begin 225 highway and bridge projects in 122 counties.[23]

The road projects finally began, but that was not the end of friction between the state and federal governments. In May 1935 the Federal Roads Bureau refused to approve new construction unless Talmadge "promoted greater efficiency in the highway department." His low salaries had "driven out competent engineers," and the projects were suffering. That June the federal government warned the governor that he would get no part of the road money allotted to Georgia from the new works relief fund unless there was a "complete reorganization of headquarters and engineering" in the state Highway Department. When Talmadge refused, the government decided to set up a separate state agency to handle the money. The controversy evoked considerable publicity in the state, not all of which was directed against the governor. The state NEC director suggested that a quick settlement might be best for all.[24]

With the aid of Senator Walter George the problem finally was resolved. Talmadge agreed to enlarge the engineering and inspection staffs of the state Highway Department. Roosevelt then promised to release all of the funds except for $300,000. This money was to be held in abeyance until some agreement could be reached over the Ball's Ferry bridge project. This project, supported by Congressman Carl Vinson, had become something of a political football in the negotiations during the summer of 1935. Vinson had promised the project to his constituency, and the federal government, enjoying his support, agreed to undertake it. Talmadge, however, felt the project was not worthwhile and opposed it. Since neither side would capitulate, the federal government agreed to release all road money to the state, except enough to cover the cost of the project. All parties seemed satisfied with the arrangement, and as soon as some minor details were resolved, the funds were released.[25]

Perhaps the most innovative and exciting program undertaken by the PWA was in the field of housing. Under the NIRA the PWA was authorized to make grants for the construction of low-cost federal housing. An Atlanta businessman, Charles F. Palmer, initiated negotiations with Ickes for the first such project in the nation, Techwood Homes (later renamed Clark Howell Homes). In 1933 Atlanta's worst downtown slum area stood on Peachtree Street, separating the fashionable northwest section of the city from the downtown stores and businesses. Crime, disease, and fire hazards abounded in this eyesore adjacent to the Georgia Institute of Technology. Palmer and a group of his associates petitioned the PWA for funds to eliminate the slums and to construct low-rent housing in their place.

The PWA approved his proposal on October 13, 1933, and made a loan of $4 million (85 percent of the total cost) to the corporation Palmer had formed. The project originally called for the building of some 600 units employing about 1,000 men for a year. Palmer also petitioned the PWA for another project in the area, University Homes, the only black project in the country.[26]

Unfortunately, friction arose between the corporation and the PWA before the project could be started. Palmer later complained of the "cavalier treatment" he had received from Washington, and he blamed most of the trouble upon "the ineptness of Ickes and his staff." Not all Atlantans were satisfied with the project either. A group of apartment owners, headed by Leopold J. Hass, protested that Atlanta "has no use for 600 new apartment units." He believed that they would "ruin real estate values" in the city.[27]

In January 1934 the United States Comptroller General announced that he was going to review "all projects," halting plans for Techwood. Ickes took this opportunity to replace the local group with the Emergency Housing Corporation. The entire project was to be built at government expense, and it would become government property. Ickes allowed the old corporation to run the local operations for both Techwood and University homes, presumably because of all the time and effort it had spent to that point. Furthermore, he appointed T. Thorne Flagler, one of its members, as manager of the Techwood project to "compensate Mr. Flagler for his efforts." Having completed administrative arrangements Ickes then allowed the project to proceed. The PWA director himself came to Atlanta on September 28, 1934, to detonate the first explosive charge that demolished the old slums.[28]

Unfortunately the local corporation did not represent the entire city of Atlanta in its enthusiasm over the project. While city officials supported the program in theory, they hesitated to provide municipal services for a federal project over which they would have no jurisdiction. City hall told the PWA that the federal government would have to pay a service charge for these facilities, and it threatened to prevent the project from connecting its sewer and water mains to those of the city and to withdraw police and fire protection from the area. Ickes became furious, and his opinions of the municipal government negatively influenced his subsequent dealings with the city, notably in the matter of the Atlanta sewer project.[29]

Despite this altercation and the continuing opposition of certain real estate investors, the projects proceeded with reasonable speed. By the end of the summer of 1935 part of the Techwood project was completed and applications were being taken for occupancy. The PWA restricted clients to those families with incomes over $900 but under $1,800 a year.

By the time Techwood was completed, the PWA had spent nearly $3 million to build 604 family dwelling units with 2,124 rooms. These apartments rented for an average of $6.03 a month. The University Homes project had cost $2.5 million for 675 units of 2,343 rooms, and the apartments rented for an average of $5.87 a month. The PWA had hoped the housing projects would encourage a better standard of living and instill a sense of personal pride in those who resided there. It anticipated that once a family reached the maximum income level allowed, it would move to a private dwelling and take its place in the general community. A 1940 study showed, however, that this was not always the case. "The majority of the ex-residents," for instance, "who were rooming, renting, and living with relatives, moved into and are still living in sub-standard housing." Indeed the project had not reached the core of these families' problems.[30]

This, however, did not detract from the value of the projects, particularly the University Homes (later renamed the John Hope Homes) as landmarks in government housing. Subsequently the program was expanded in both Atlanta and other cities in the state. Two projects were slated for Athens, two for Augusta, two for Columbus, two for Rome, and two for Savannah, equally divided by race. Atlanta itself constructed Grady and Capital homes, and University and Techwood homes were enlarged.[31]

Like the CWA and FERA, the PWA work projects provided many facilities for the state and its cities that otherwise would not have been possible. The agency built schools, waterworks, dormitories at colleges, jails, courthouses, filter plants, disposal plants, hospitals, libraries, auditoriums, swimming pools, sewers, recreational centers, bridges, roads, fire departments, agricultural buildings, and school gyms. The PWA also sponsored a federal art project headed in the southeastern region by J. J. Haverty, president of the High Museum of Art in Atlanta. Most of the artwork was in the form of murals and statuary in public buildings and was of a commemorative nature. At the time the project was closed, Miss Anne Craton, field coordinator for the program, noted that "more

mural work has been done here [Atlanta] than in any other city in the
South. The work is extremely diversified, interesting and well executed."[32]

The types of projects constructed by the PWA did not differ greatly
from those undertaken by the FERA, CWA, and WPA, so the administration of the PWA offered a good comparison of the various assets and
liabilities involved between federally operated and state-operated works
agencies. To be sure, the FERA, CWA, and WPA experienced difficulties
in administration; however, there was never the kind of direct federal-
state animosity that developed under the PWA. Perhaps because the
state was dealing directly with the federal government, politics became
more crucial and PWA controversies involving members of Roosevelt's
immediate administrative family provided the governor and his associates
with more potent ammunition than existed in an argument with the
soft-spoken woman who headed the WPA.

Similar difficulties arose in all state offices of federal agencies in
dealing with the national administration. With forty-eight states funnel-
ing mountains of paperwork through small central offices, every agency
was subject to delays and inadvertent errors. All PWA applications,
however, had to be approved in Washington, while the state administrator of the WPA could handle her applications much more quickly and
efficiently since she made the final decision. The comparison showed
that the more decentralized the agency was, the less this type of trouble
arose, a situation that certainly applied to the PWA, WPA, CWA, and
FERA.

NOTES

1. The agency was not properly titled the Public Works Administration until it came under the Federal Works Agency in the reorganization of 1939. To that time it was referred to as the Federal Emergency Administration of Public Works, but the shorter term, PWA, will be used
here throughout.

2. PWA, Circular No. 1, July 31, 1933, NARG 135, PWA. PWA,
Bulletin No. 2, September 12, 1933, NARG 135.

3. PWA, Circular No. 1, NARG 135.

4. Atlanta *Constitution*, July 23, 27, and 30, August 14 and 18, and
September 15, 1933.

5. "The PWA and Georgia," *Newsweek*, XII, 23 (December 5, 1938),

12. Atlanta *Constitution,* February 25, March 1, and August 11, 1934.
Sarah M. Lemmon, "The Public Career of Eugene Talmadge: 1926-1936"
(unpublished Ph.D. dissertation, University of North Carolina, 1952), p. 186.
Sarah M. Lemmon, "The Ideology of Eugene Talmadge," *Georgia Historical
Quarterly,* XXXVIII, 3 (September 1954), 231.

6. Atlanta *Constitution,* February 25 and October 8, 1934, and
March 20, 1935. Lemmon, "The Public Career of Eugene Talmadge,"
p. 186. Georgia, *Executive Minutes* (1933), pp. 26, 380. "The PWA and
Georgia," p. 12. *Public Welfare,* VI, 4 (November 1933), 1. "Report
of the Proceedings of the Statewide Coordinating Meeting of the National
Emergency Council," April 10, 1936 (Report of J. Houstoun Johnston),
NARG 44, NEC, Corres., Directories, Reports, box 349.

7. "The PWA and Georgia," p. 12.

8. Atlanta *Constitution,* June 19, 1934, and January 7, 1935.
Unsigned report, April 24, 1934, NARG 44, Periodical Reports (1934-38)
box 400. Unsigned report, January 19, 1935, NARG 44, Periodical Reports
(1934-38), box 400.

9. Cochrane to Altmeyer, May 15, 1935 (report), NARG 9, NRA,
Compliance Division, General Corres. with Field Offices, drawer 1098.
Unsigned report, May 8, 1934, NARG 44, Periodical Reports (1934-38),
box 400. Atlanta *Constitution,* August 10, 1934. Unsigned Report,
June 10, 1934, NARG 44, Periodical Reports (1934-38), box 400.

10. "Report of the Proceedings of the Statewide Coordinating Meet-
ing," April 10, 1936 (Report of J. Houstoun Johnston), NARG 44,
Corres., Directories, Repts., box 349. Unsigned report, June 18, 1935,
NARG 44, Digests, box 488. Unsigned report, June 25, 1935, NARG 44,
Digests, box 488.

11. Erle Cocke to Major Noce, August 12, 1935 (memo), NARG 44,
Gen. Corres. with State Directors (1934-35), box 174. Atlanta *Constitution,* May 25, 1935.

12. "Report of the Proceedings of the Statewide Coordinating Meet-
ing," April 10, 1936 (Report of J. Houstoun Johnston), NARG 44,
Corres., Directories, Repts., box 349. Atlanta *Constitution,* June 28 and
August 21 and 27, 1935. Unsigned report, July 9, 1935, NARG 44,
Digests, box 488.

13. Atlanta *Constitution,* August 27, 1935. Unsigned report, July 16,
1935, NARG 44, Digests, box 488.

14. Ickes to Hopkins, August 5, 1935, NARG 69, WPA State Series,
No. 651.106, box 1131. Unsigned report, July 30, 1935, NARG 44,
Digests, box 489. Clark Howell to Hopkins, January 17, 1934, NARG
69, CWA, Administrative Corres. (state), box 11.

15. Hopkins to Ickes, n.d., NARG 69, WPA, State Series, No. 651.106, box 1131.

16. A. H. Martin to Frank C. Walker, August 19, 1935, NARG 44, Division of Applications and Information, Corres. Regarding Projects (1935-36), box 604. Cocke to Lyle Alverson, August 21, 1935 (telegram), NARG 44, Division of Applications, box 604. Ickes to Walker, August 23, 1935, NARG 44, Division of Applications, box 604. Harold L. Ickes, *The Secret Diary of Harold L. Ickes: The First Thousand Days, 1933-36* (New York: Simon and Schuster, 1953), pp. 422, 427.

17. Ickes, *Secret Diary,* p. 427. Marion Smith to Cocke, August 30, 1935, NARG 44, Corres. with State Directors (1934-35), box 174. Aubrey Williams to Shepperson, September 16, 1935 (telephone conversation), NARG 69, WPA, State Series, No. 610, box 1113. Unsigned report, September 24, 1935, NARG 44, Digests, box 492.

18. M. J. Miller to Williams, October 17, 1935, NARG 69, FERA, New Subject File, No. 352, box 147. Senator Russell to Hopkins, September 18, 1935 (telegram), NARG 69, FERA, New Subject File, No. 352, box 147. Unsigned report, October 19, 1935, NARG 44, Digests, box 495.

19. Unsigned report, September 24, 1935, NARG 44, Digests, box 492. Unsigned report, March 14, 1936, NARG 44, Digests, box 502. Unsigned report, February 29, 1936, NARG 44, Digests, box 502.

20. "Report of the Proceedings of the Statewide Coordinating Meeting," April 10, 1936 (Report of J. Houstoun Johnston), NARG 44, Corres., Directories, Repts., box 349. Unsigned report, August 29, 1936, NARG 44, Digests, box 508. Unsigned report, August 4, 1936, NARG 44, Periodical Reports (1934-38), box 400. Unsigned report, November 10, 1936, NARG 44, Digests, box 509. Unsigned report, December 10, 1936, NARG 44, Digests, box 509.

21. Unsigned report, May 14, 1937, NARG 44, Periodical Reports (1934-38), box 399. Unsigned report, May 15, 1937, NARG 44, Digests, box 511.

22. "The PWA Program in Georgia," NARG 44, Division of Field Operations, Statistical Section, Reports on Federal Expenditures in the States (1933-38), box 535. Arthur F. Raper, *Tenants of the Almighty* (New York: Macmillan Co., 1943), pp. 184-5. Lemmon, "The Public Career of Eugene Talmadge," pp. 168-9. Allen Lumpkin Henson, *Red Galluses: A Story of Georgia Politics* (Boston: House of Edinboro Publishers, 1945), p. 115. Interview with Gay Shepperson.

23. Atlanta *Constitution,* August 19, September 7, and October 7, 1933.

24. *Ibid.*, September 29, 1933, and May 23, June 5, 26, and 29, and August 20, 1935. Unsigned report, August 13, 1935, NARG 44, Digests, box 489.

25. Atlanta *Constitution,* August 16 and 28, 1935.

26. PWA, *America Builds.* (Washington: United States Government Printing Office, 1939), p. 207. Franklin M. Garrett, *Atlanta and Its Environs: A Chronicle of Its People and Events* (New York: Lewis Historical Publishing Co., Inc., 1954), II, 908. Atlanta *Constitution,* October 13, 1933.

27. Charles F. Palmer, *Adventures of a Slum Fighter* (Atlanta: Tupper and Love, Inc., 1955), p. 141. Atlanta *Constitution,* October 22, 1933.

28. Garrett, *Atlanta,* II, 908. Atlanta *Constitution,* March 11, May 18, July 21, and September 29, 1934.

29. Ickes to Hopkins, August 5, 1935, NARG 69, WPA, State Series, No. 651.106, box 1131. Ickes to Hopkins, May 1935, NARG 44, Division of Applications (1935-36), box 604.

30. PWA, *America Builds,* p. 283. "Rents Established for PWA Housing," *Monthly Labor Review,* XLVI, 6 (June 1938), 1363. Herman B. Byer and Clarence A. Trump, "Labor and Unit Costs in PWA Low-Rent Housing," *Monthly Labor Review,* XLIX, 3 (September 1939), 585. Elvah Marcia Waters, "The Ex-Residents of University Homes, 1937-1940" (unpublished M. A. thesis, Department of Sociology, Atlanta University, 1941), p. 29.

31. Palmer, *Adventures,* p. 232. William H. Shell, "The Negro and the NYA in Georgia," Georgia NYA Bulletin, No. 13 (January 1939).

32. Office of Government Reports, *Direct and Cooperative Loans and Expenditures of the Federal Government, 1933-1938, by Fiscal Years* (Washington: Office of Government Reports, 1939), p. 5. Georgia, State Department of Education, *Annual Reports* (1934-36), p. 21. Georgia, State Department of Public Health, *Biennial Report* (1933-34), p. 19. Atlanta *Constitution,* December 17 and 23, 1933, and February 22 and 23 and June 15, 1934.

6

"Blue Eagles on Closed Doors"

On June 16, 1933, the president signed the National Industrial Recovery Act establishing the PWA and the National Recovery Administration (NRA). The law provided for the formulation of NRA codes or agreements into which industries and businesses of certain types might enter. By limiting hours, while maintaining production, and boosting wages and prices, the government hoped to reinvigorate business and stimulate the entire economy.

Each industry through a trade or comparable association was to formulate its own code in cooperation with the NRA offices. As the hearings got under way, however, the federal government came to realize how complicated and lengthy the process might be. As an interim measure, the NRA announced the issuance of the President's Reemployment Agreement (PRA) which could be signed by any nonagricultural employer in towns of over 2,500 people. Businesses signing the PRA were entitled to display a Blue Eagle emblem in their establishments and on their products. Unlike the later codes, the PRA did not control trade practices, but dealt primarily with the wages and hours of employees. The agreement was to run to December 31, 1933, but on December 19 it was extended to April 30, 1934.

In the late summer of 1933 the president provided for the nationwide establishment of voluntary boards and councils to administer this "Blue Eagle Drive." He appointed twenty-six District Recovery Boards of seven members each, corresponding to the districts of the Department of Commerce. Each state was to have a State Recovery Board of nine members.

To engage voluntary support the state boards organized State Recovery Councils including, ex-officio, "the presiding officers of any state labor, manufacturing, trade, civil, social service, or welfare association, organization, or club" that applied for membership. The Georgia State Recovery Board divided the state into nine areas, each covering roughly a congressional district. Each state board member supervised a district. In the first months of operation the state board dealt principally with organization and promotion. Its duties were "to organize, recommend and advise as to methods of making the NRA effective." Later it handled complaints and attempted to make adjustments. If it failed to satisfy disputants the matter would be handed over to the district board which in turn would notify Washington if it was unable to conclude a settlement. The state board carried out all instructions from Washington, however. In mid-February 1934 the State and District Recovery Boards combined to form the State Advisory Board, retaining most of the former members of the old boards.[1]

Response to the NRA in Georgia was immediate and favorable. On July 19, 1933, the directors of Georgia Chambers of Commerce established a committee of twenty-two business representatives to conduct a campaign of education and organization. Each local Chamber of Commerce was to form the nucleus for the Blue Eagle drive aided by civic and women's clubs, labor groups, and city and county executives. In small towns the postmaster often was called upon to select a committee. It held meetings with various groups of businessmen to explain what had happened, since the story which emanated from Washington was rather confusing.

Several days before the distribution of the PRA forms, a temporary committee of the Atlanta Chamber of Commerce was formed to coordinate NRA work. It first called a large meeting to generate business enthusiasm. Mayor James L. Key urged cooperation with the president. Those in attendance agreed to form an executive committee to wage a sign-up campaign. The executive committee met subsequently and established certain subcommittees. The operating or steering committee aided the executive committee in formulating plans for the drive. The general committee was composed of heads of cooperating organizations and was formed to mobilize influence and provide materials to inform citizens and to draw volunteer workers. The publicity committee members each were assigned a media to contact to propagandize the drive.

The speakers bureau sent about 125 of its staff to a training school and then used them when called upon by various groups to explain the program. Finally the women's division was set up to handle the second phase of the Blue Eagle campaign, that of mobilizing women to join NRA consumers' clubs. It conducted a block canvass to persuade women to shop only at stores displaying the Blue Eagle.[2]

The sign-up was begun on July 27, 1933, when the Atlanta Chamber of Commerce sent PRA forms to employers. By August 3 the first state figures had arrived at the office of the Department of Commerce, and William L. Mitchell, district NRA manager, disclosed that 10,231 Georgia employers (1,036 in Atlanta alone) had signed. Public support ran high. Henry T. McIntosh, editor of the Albany *Herald,* exclaimed, "Codes, codes, codes! Everybody had a code or is just about to adopt a code or, in case of stubbornness, will eventually have a code thrust upon them. Any day now we expect a new stanza to be added to the Negro spiritual: 'I gotta code, You gotta code, All of God's chillun got codes—.'" By August 13, 15,650 employers with 103,658 workers had signed PRAs.[3]

In late August the Atlanta Junior Chamber of Commerce began a block-to-block canvass to contact those merchants who had not yet signed. The Jaycees campaign lasted five days. By that time 5,076 firms had been visited, of which 3,065 had already signed, 532 signed during the canvass, and 939 refused to sign. PRA signers had added 5,490 employees and increased their payrolls by $418,593.[4]

Mrs. Max E. Land, former member of the state Democratic Executive Committee and head of the women's division, opened the consumers' drive on September 7 with 2,600 women, and a goal of 60,000 consumer club members. At the end of the week-long campaign, the women had failed to reach their goal, garnering 43,689 pledges or about 72.8 percent of the expected total.[5]

Both the imperfect showing of the women's campaign and the high ratio of nonsigners to new signers in the Jaycees' campaign suggested that those who did not cooperate from the beginning did so because of convictions or personal interest, and not because of ignorance or misunderstandings about the program. If the latter had been the case, the Jaycees campaign would have been more successful.

Various other means were used to generate support for the NRA, both before the sign-up period—to encourage participation—and after—to insure compliance. Atlanta, for instance, held a mass rally in support of the NRA at the city auditorium on August 10. The Chamber of Commerce estimated that nearly 3,000 people attended to hear addresses by national and local leaders. The NRA drive stimulated great enthusiasm, receiving support from unexpected sources. The official organ of the Ku Klux Klan, the *Kourier,* displayed a Blue Eagle on the foreleaf of its September issue, although an article within the magazine from Savannah vaguely criticized New Deal politicians for "lining their pockets." In its next issue, however, the *Kourier* labeled the NRA "No Roman Alliance," using the initials of a governmental agency to suit its anti-Catholic bias. The Klan eventually turned away from the NRA and the entire New Deal.[6]

Even Governor Talmadge, later a bitter critic, urged Georgians to give the recovery program a fair trial. He noted in a Labor Day speech at the Atlanta City Auditorium, "Congress and the President acted with the best of motives, trying to help the men who need help." He doubted from the beginning the ability of the NRA to succeed in Georgia, however. Although not yet severely critical, he commented in his personal journal, the *Statesman,* that the government would have to raise farm prices for the NRA to work.[7]

August 31, 1933, was to be the last day of the "old deal," when retail goods would sell at precode prices. This in itself served to give Georgia's economy a boost. Crowds streamed into Atlanta's stores, and the *Constitution* speculated that August 1933 would show an increase of 25 to 30 percent in retail sales over August 1932.[8]

The numerous schemes for enlisting employer and consumer cooperation culminated in mammoth parades throughout the state. The largest march took place in Atlanta on October 4 when an estimated 50,000 people participated. The Atlanta parade was sponsored by the Atlanta *Georgian* with the support of the other two newspapers, the *Journal* and the *Constitution.* One Talmadge supporter claimed that it really was held by the Democratic campaign staff who, reluctant to disband, decided to stage a "monster celebration" under the guise of supporting the NRA. The governor was persuaded to ride in the vanguard, presumably upon a "Georgia mule." Talmadge confided later that he "felt all the time like a damn fool." Whether this was because of his mode of transportation or because he had already soured on the NRA, was not revealed. The months of October and November found other cities around the state holding miniatures of the Atlanta extravaganza. Atlanta kept pace with the festivities by proclaiming Blue Eagle Day, October 17.

Downtown stores displayed Blue Eagle banners and had sales. Although businessmen felt the PRA provisions worked a hardship, in the first months of the NRA Atlanta business, especially retail, reacted favorably to the program.[9]

In order to amass the kind of statistics designed to convince voluntary participants that everyone would jump on the bandwagon, NRA spokesmen, both official and amateur, tended to gloss over many of the initial questions and legitimate objections raised by businessmen. The stock answer to queries at many meetings was to accept the president's agreement now, support him and the drive, and iron out differences later. Unfortunately, there were many objections which could not be satisfied without ignoring the agreement completely.

The signs of failure were present, though not recognized, from the first weeks. When those displaying Blue Eagles did not comply with the PRA, officials blamed it on a lack of knowledge or misunderstanding of the agreement. But the results of the Jaycee canvass should have indicated to them that this was not the case.

The first rumblings of dissatisfaction came from the smaller cities. Initially small businessmen in these towns willingly accepted the PRA. They instituted the eight-hour day, but could (or would) not pay their workers more. Many began to fire marginal employees or to shorten business hours. One scholar decided that the major reason these men accepted the PRA at all was because the first Democratic president since Woodrow Wilson asked them to do so, and, above all, they were loyal Democrats. On the other hand, these men were also "deep South Southerners," wary of regulation and especially averse to being told what wage to pay their employees, particularly the black ones. The exigencies of business and the southern persuasion soon acted to subvert the NRA. One poetically inclined official told Hugh Johnson, national director of the NRA, that the Eagle was becoming a vulture:

> . . . we have listened to the triumphant cry of the Blue Eagle and have sought to spread his wings even wider by one hundred percent cooperation. But we are exclusively an agricultural community and it appears that not only does the recovery act fail to afford any benefit to the farmer but the rapid and continuous decline in the price of cotton is pointing to any early approach of bankruptcy. Is it not possible for you to formulate a plan to better the situation and give

us some hope for the future? B[l] ue eagles on closed doors and
destitute farmers in a bread line is not our conception of a recovery.[10]

Growing antagonism did not remain isolated for very long. By
October, Mitchell noticed that the results of the sign-up campaign were
rather selective. Only a very small percentage of cotton ginners had
signed a PRA, and those that had were now "operating under a tremendous hardship." This hardship was not distinctive by type of business,
however. All marginal business and industry were hard pressed, and there
were many bankruptcies.[11]

Another indication of business reaction could be measured by the
number of applications made to the Complaint Committee of the Blue
Eagle Division for the PRA's "exceptional treatment" clause. By
September there were so many petitions in Washington that the national
office provided for the formation of local compliance boards. The
"literally thousands of cases of violations" going unpunished was proof
to critics that the government's interest was waning and that officials
were "closing their eyes" to chiseling.

Chairmen of the local NRA committees who had conducted the
original Blue Eagle drives were asked to form the new compliance
boards. They were to "convene a nominating committee composed of
individuals representing a cross-section of the economic interest of the
community." This committee would name six members to a compliance
board. There were to be two employee representatives, one from industrial labor and the other from retail or wholesale employees; two employer representatives, chosen along the same lines; one consumer representative, preferably a woman; and one legal representative from among
the practicing legal profession of the community and in good standing
with the state bar. These six people were to select a chairman from among
the retired leaders of the professional or commercial community.[12]

These boards were strictly voluntary. There was no money for salaries
or expenses, although the boards could apply to relief agencies to obtain
relief employees for clerical work. The boards had no final jurisdiction
and no power of enforcement except upon "specific instruction" by the
Recovery Administration. They were concerned only with the PRA, not
the codes. In general their job was to consider applications for exemption,
petitions to operate under union-labor agreements rather than the
wages-hours provision of the PRA, and complaints of noncompliance.

Decisions on the first two considerations needed unanimous agreement.

The original Blue Eagle campaign committees generally had not contained labor representatives, and in many cases the labor contingent of the compliance board turned out to be foremen or superintendents. In some instances the national office approved committees with no labor representative. There was no laborer on the Decatur committee although there was a man "sympathetic to labor." When a local union complained to Mitchell, he suggested that either the man resign or the committee expand to include a union member. The board refused to seat the union's choice, so Mitchell asked that the union submit a list and let the board pick a man. The action was not taken, and Mitchell evaded the problem, claiming that the situation "must be handled diplomatically" since "we are dealing with voluntary workers." If he rocked the boat, there was the possibility he would lose the whole board. Ultimately, as in so many cases, the status quo prevailed.[13]

Even when there was a laborer on the committee, he might not have the approval of organized labor. In Atlanta, for example, labor groups unanimously selected a representative to be the labor member, but the Chamber of Commerce president, Herbert Choate, pre-empted this choice. He seated Ralph Boynton, a man only twenty-three years old and employed for all of thirty days. Lee Ashcraft, chairman of the Atlanta compliance board, stated that he had nothing to do with Boynton's selection, and had agreed to it under pressure, probably from Choate. He said that Boynton seemed to be a good man, however, and the Washington office let the matter drop.[14]

Another complaint about compliance boards, especially in towns under the influence of large cotton textile mills, was that they were controlled by the very interests that were breaking the agreements. One rather naive letter came to Mitchell's desk from the national office concerning a Mr. J. B. Copeland, chairman of the Valdosta compliance board. It "just occurred" to the national office that "Mr. Copeland of the compliance board and Mr. Copeland of Copeland Brothers are one and the same persons. If this is the case, it would apparently seem folly to us to send a complaint to the chairman of the local Board."[15]

In some cases where it was blatantly obvious that an industry "owned" a board, the state board released the offending board, and, rather than replace it, asked another board to serve the city in question. This practice put undue pressure on the remaining board. The problem was exacerbated by an order from the national office that compliance in towns with no board should be handled by nearby towns with boards. The result was that a board would have to cover a large area, and its members might be widely scattered. The same problem later existed with local code authorities covering a zone of ten to twelve counties.

Mitchell noted that the local boards appeared to be "of good quality, but some are not too active and seem to be somewhat uninformed." He later decided that such inactivity, especially in smaller towns, was "fortunate" because of their "hazy idea as to their functions and powers." Local boards in the cities and some of the larger towns, seemed to be doing well by the end of 1933. The only major criticisms were that labor was underrepresented and that occasionally there were misunderstandings. Of the larger cities only Macon seemed to have a board that was both uninformed and showed lack of initiative. Many boards felt they had "no more authority than a hound dog flying up an alley with a tin can tied to its tail, and chased by a gang of boys."[16]

By October 11, 1933, over 35 boards had been established across the state. Thereafter the number fluctuated and stood at 75 in June 1934 when they were dissolved. Their work was then assumed by Compliance Director W. L. Mitchell's office with the assistance of regional adjustment groups in Augusta, Savannah, and Columbus, and later in Macon and Rome. These adjustment boards were composed of three members: an employee named by organized labor, an employer named by local chambers of commerce, and a third person selected by the other two to act as chairman. The old compliance boards were converted into general educational councils.[17]

To protect the consumer, the NRA in cooperation with the Agricultural Adjustment Administration and the National Emergency Council (NEC) set up consumers' councils. These councils were made up of seven members and had to contain at least one manual laborer, one housewife of moderate or less than moderate means, and one member of a consumers' cooperative society or a credit union. The councils considered consumers' complaints against undue price increases and disseminated accurate information concerning the NRA and its effects upon consumers. They were also the agencies through which consumers could articulate their opinions on national recovery. The councils were to aid in the development of more economical and efficient distribution of goods to consumers and to cooperate with the FERA and CWA to speed reemployment by the development of sound civic projects. These high-minded plans never materialized, however.

At the same time the president ordered the establishment of local compliance boards, he announced that the NEC would coordinate its activities. He appointed Andrew McNairn Soule, former president of the College of Agriculture of the University of Georgia at Athens, to be state director of the NEC, with Mitchell as his executive assistant and state compliance officer. At the time Mitchell was also manager for the Department of Commerce in Georgia and compliance director for code industries.

When Soule died on April 16, 1934, Mitchell temporarily assumed control. Banker Robert F. Maddox and publisher Clark Howell were considered for the post, but Hugh Johnson finally decided to let Mitchell continue as acting director until May 2, 1935, when Erle Cocke, formerly with the Reconstruction Finance Corporation, took over. It appeared from the beginning, however, that Mitchell was the one who really ran the NRA.[18]

The NEC was charged with handling complaints from industries or businesses under a permanent code but for which an Industrial Adjustment Agency of local code authority had not yet been formed. Despite Mitchell's frequent complaints to Washington about being hamstrung by an inadequate law and restrictive administrative prerogatives, field examiners praised his work. At one point John Swope, chief of the field branch of the compliance division, claimed that the "Atlanta office was rated as one of the best in the country." Mitchell noted at the same time, that of 1,500 complaints received, the office had adjusted all but 150.[19]

To aid the state compliance officer in his work, the NRA established a state Adjustment Board—a board of review with no powers of administration or enforcement. It considered only those questions put to it by the state director of the NEC. Anything that remained unadjusted after consideration by the compliance officer and the state Adjustment Board was sent to the National Compliance Board for adjudication.

The state board was composed of three members selected by industry and labor. From March 21, 1934, until April 4, 1935, it heard 81 wage cases and gave $5,017 in restitution to employees. The state NEC office followed a policy of referring cases to the Adjustment Board when respondents and complainants had submitted directly conflicting affidavits in regard to the facts of the case. After a few months, however,

the board found that the type of complainant appearing before it "was
generally from a very undesirable class of employees." The Adjustment
Board objected that the "lower" the type of complainants the further they
wished to go in the prosecution of the case.[20]

When asked in March 1935 whether the board should be abolished,
only the labor representative said that it should. Employers "felt their
cases were safer in the hands of the Adjustment Board than before the
Regional Compliance Council." Labor organizations finally decided that
they would not withdraw their member, but would be uncooperative.
Because of this altercation, board meetings were suspended until May 27,
1935. Despite labor's disillusionment only one case presented to the
board was not decided unanimously, and only three of its recommendations
were overruled by the state office.[21]

The Regional Compliance Council came into being late in 1934.
Because it also considered questions of compliance, because of its prolabor tinge, and because its members were salaried, there was always a
certain amount of friction between it and the state Adjustment Board.
Board members threatened to resign en masse when they learned that
council members were to be paid. Mitchell evidently persuaded them to
remain, but they held fewer meetings after this (partly because the
council was considering cases which formerly were handled by the board).[22]

The Regional Compliance Council operated in Region IV (Georgia,
South Carolina, Florida, Alabama, Mississippi, and Louisiana) with
headquarters in Atlanta under Mitchell. All cases formerly sent to the
compliance or litigation divisions in Washington henceforth were sent
to the council, as well as some cases from local compliance offices
which could not be resolved. The council held powers previously resting
only with the national NRA Council.

Labor had felt that the state Adjustment Board was unsympathetic to
the employee. The Georgia Trade Association objected to the regional
council because of the background of industry's representative, Kendall
Weisiger. He had been in a public service corporation (Southern Bell
Telephone), not in an industry, so he was undesirable on those grounds.
It also claimed that labor member A. Steve Nance had taken a position
on the council of "prosecuting attorney" rather than "judge." It
objected to his "labor activities." Mitchell admitted that neither man was
a perfect choice. Weisiger might have been "more aggressive" and, in
fact, gave the distinct impression of affording labor interests a "better

than an even break." Mitchell also said that Weisiger was too easily
influenced by the rest of the council. He was scrupulously honest, however, and this offset his shortcomings. On the subject of Nance, Mitchell
was adamant. He "absolutely opposed" any attempt to unseat Nance
and felt that if he were "too vigorous . . . even his enemies admit that
he is fair and reasonable."[23]

Nance knew that the council was more favorable to labor than were
the code authorities or local compliance boards. In a speech before a
southwide conference of delegates from central bodies and state federa-
tions of labor he advised labor organizations to file complaints with the
state compliance office, apparently in the hope that prolabor compliance
councils would handle them. Even then, he warned that unless labor
pressed for restitution of back pay, the compliance officials would accept
compromises.[24]

Ironically, the council was never as successful as the adjustment board.
L. J. Martin, chief of the Compliance Division, informed Mitchell that
"your Council turns out more sloppy cases than any other one of our
units." Mitchell replied that Martin's criticism was unfair, since the
council had received only "meager instructions." Mitchell did not seem
to take into account that other councils received the same instructions.[25]

Complaints from specific industries were taken out of the state
compliance officer's hands as various code authorities came into being.
Unfortunately the code authorities encountered the same problems which
had confronted the compliance officer. They wanted access to business
records. They felt they were "skimming the surface" by considering only
voluntary complaints. Where compliance was not voluntarily obtained, it
took too long to go through precourt processes. They were "fed up with
red tape, equivocation, and lack of court action." Public relations were
often neglected, and authorities either did not receive or were delayed in
getting code modifications, new interpretations, and policy changes. The
more diversified the code authorities, the weaker they were likely to be.
They were more subject to local control and increasingly susceptible to
financial difficulties. The quality of local authorities varied from city to
city, the larger cities usually having greater success in dealing with a higher
class of employer.[26]

In one instance involving the Retail Drug Code Authority for the Tenth
Congressional District in Augusta, Chairman Dr. W. T. Edmunds, who
was also a member of the state Board of Pharmacy, was allegedly using

his position to "harass the Lane Drug Store" chain. Other complaints charged that officials used the code authority to promote their individual businesses to the detriment of nonmembers. In some instances authority personnel seemed interested only in collecting code assessments, used to finance code authority administration, and not in the other phases of operations. Frequently labor unions claimed that authorities failed to enforce the labor provisions of codes, dealing only with trade practice provisions. Many trade associations and code authorities had the same personnel, and respondents who were not members of the association were discriminated against. NRA official Dillard B. Lasseter felt that in the "first days of their existence" the authorities acted with "too much zeal and their aggressiveness and threats of legal punishment alienated the good will of many industries." What Lasseter did not say was that in many cases these threats also proved to be idle, and authorities quickly lost any respect they might have acquired.[27]

The final insult proved to be that the government itself failed to deal with code industries. Government contracts were distributed according to low bid with only perfunctory insistence that the business comply with the code. This fact became obvious when the government accepted bids that promised prices lower than those under the trade practice agreements. Although various agencies issued warnings, complaints never ceased to arrive at state and national offices.[28]

A particularly injurious situation arose in Atlanta when the NRA scheduled a conference on executive training at the Grady Hotel. Mitchell complained that the Grady was not complying with the hotel code and had gotten the conference over the bid of the Piedmont Hotel which was a code member. The conference finally was changed to the Piedmont, but not before the NRA had lost additional public support.[29]

In evaluating the work of local code authorities after the NRA had been declared unconstitutional, Lasseter concluded, "The Code Authority system of administration and enforcing codes did not, with few exceptions, function successfully in Georgia." The truth lay somewhere between this understatement and the charge that the authorities were "rackets."[30]

Selfish misuse of local compliance boards and code authorities by industry was only one way in which the NRA was flaunted. Patterns of evasion emerged during the peak period of PRA activity and served as guidelines for subsequent effective disregard of codes. Even when there was no direct collusion among compliance boards and businesses, some towns were so small that no organization could escape the implicit pressure of a large textile mill. In one complaint the chairman of a local committee was accused of being a "small town lawyer . . . so steeped in politics that he thinks he cannot afford to make his position known."

When there was no proof of cooperation with industry, employees still were afraid to go to the committee for fear the company would find out. Local complainants were convinced that the national government knew of this situation and did nothing to rectify it. Several asserted that letters written to Roosevelt or Johnson and passed on to the compliance division were not even read. Often those who charged that committees were corrupt or knew of noncompliance and ignored it, were informed that they should "see their local committee." Although this type of bureaucratic injustice occurred in all New Deal agencies, it was particularly prevalent and frustrating within the NRA.[31]

The variety of complaints that employees lodged against employers was limited only by the latter's imagination. Accusations ranged from outright noncompliance with both hours and wages, to shortening hours and not paying scale, or shortening hours and paying scale, but increasing the amount of work required. Any combination of wage-hour finagling was likely to exist. The "stretch-out" system was common, especially in the textile industry. Sometimes employees were paid according to the NRA wage scale, but forced to give a rebate or kickback. A worker might have to sign a receipt for more money than he received. One company deducted a certain amount from its employees' paychecks and paid the balance in vouchers which could be used only at its company store where prices were from 10 to 40 percent higher than anywhere else in town.

In many cases marginal laborers were fired or placed in "managerial" positions not covered under the code. Thus a janitor might be reclassified as "assistant to the office manager." One of the most unjust practices was the fraudulent use of the learner or apprentice category which allowed employers to pay reduced wages to untrained personnel. A company might hire a person for an unskilled job and call him a learner because he was recently hired. When he had been there long enough to have been "trained," he was fired, and another man was hired to take his place at learner's wages.[32]

Until October 14, 1933, compliance was completely voluntary. After that penalties could be imposed. Under the PRA, however, whether there were penalties or not, very few Blue Eagles were actually withdrawn, and those who did lose them did not seem to suffer.[33]

Similar tactics were used under the codes to discriminate against labor, and code authorities and the federal government often helped. The authority might withhold information from laborers so that they did not know what rights were legally theirs. If they complained and were fired, the NRA had no power to force their reinstatement. (This later was changed.) Washington shared in the guilt by generally accepting the decision of the code authority without question. All this served to discourage employees from complaining.

Besides what an employer might do illegally, there was a great deal he could do legally to hurt the laborer. In small towns, by the time the employer had taken all of his exceptions, he was not really complying at all; and, if an employer could not legally take an exemption, the local code authority might come to his aid. In one flagrant case an authority conspired with a local cotton gin by accepting and passing on to Washington a wage rate that both knew would never be allowed. By the time the exemption request had gone through channels and returned disapproved, the ginning season was over, and the company had escaped paying NRA wages for that year.[34]

The federal government played its part by providing for wage differentials. Southern businessmen claimed the differential was aimed at the black, thus gaining the acceptance of local white employees, but often it worked to the disadvantage of the whites as well. In defense of differentials, one scholar noted that in some cases they actually helped increase the hourly earnings of workers lower down on the pay scale. The upshot of such intimidation was that the employee ceased to complain at all, or, in the case of small town business where there were close personal relationships, he "became a party to making the NRA of no effect."[35]

Labor was not completely unrepresented in the administration of the NRA. Besides labor members on general boards, a labor board composed of five labor and five employer representatives was set up in October 1933. Later a state Labor Relations Board sought to adjust labor disputes. The employee also had various labor associations to speak for him, if he was in the right trade. The American Federation of Labor used its regional headquarters in Atlanta under George L. Googe to help in NRA disputes. Organized labor complained that skilled workers did not reap NRA benefits to the same extent as unskilled labor.

Dillard Lasseter agreed that there was a widespread tendency to make the minimum wage the maximum wage. This situation was made worse if one assumed that rising costs of living affected skilled labor first and to a greater degree than unskilled labor.

Lasseter also pointed out, however, that the Georgia Federation of Labor made a net gain of 10,000 members during the NRA period. Furthermore, if they accused employers of interfering with NRA compliance work, they themselves "did not hesitate to use this office as an entering wedge for organizing employees of certain respondents. They developed complaints and pressed charges with the hope that the employer would yield to such pressure and acquiesce to union demands." The efforts of labor organizations and those officials of the NRA who had a genuine interest in seeing the law applied fairly were not entirely foiled by opponents. By the first anniversary of the NRA the state compliance office had restored some $16,000 in back wages and had about $4,000 involved in pending cases.[36]

Compliance in general and popular support, both essentially voluntary, tended to ebb and flow with the tide of the NRA's fortunes. News of NRA triumphs in the courts, reorganization to strengthen administration, and legislation or executive order giving bite to the NRA's bark, led to increased compliance and public support. The NRA's decision in March 1934 to revamp the administration greatly aided officials in "bringing the minority into line," while Johnson's announcement that he intended to do away with local codes for small businesses resulted in increased "chiseling" before any definite decision was made.

Roosevelt proposed new NRA legislation to Congress in March 1935. Coming on the heels of an unfavorable court decision, this announcement tended to ameliorate an adverse trend the decision had caused. When the proposed legislation was held up in Congress, people in Georgia were discouraged. The situation was so bleak, Mitchell reported, "it has not reached the point where we are holding it [compliance] together largely by persuasion. Each week it becomes progressively more difficult to bring about compliance." In May, local newspapers began predicting the passage of legislation to extend the NRA, so public opinion and compliance seemed to rise. When later news became discouraging, compliance work became difficult. Even in minor cases, respondents refused to agree to adjustments without advice of counsel.[37]

The uncertain future of the NRA not only damaged public and

business confidence, but also weakened the morale of the state NRA staff. In his periodical reports Mitchell noted, and was very concerned, that the spirits of his personnel seemed to follow the fortunes of the agency in much the same way as public opinion. NRA officials not only were frustrated as it became more difficult to gain compliance, but also began to fear for their jobs when attacks on the agency increased.[38]

The political fate of the NRA was not the only outside determining factor in compliance. Economic conditions influenced the willingness of business and industry to cooperate. One of the sad ironies of the NRA was that it was criticized no matter what the situation. When it was initiated, businessmen were wary of so much governmental control, but accepted the program because they were desperate. As economic conditions improved, they charged that NRA restrictions were keeping them from making greater profits.

Variations in code standards evoked business and labor displeasure. Lasseter told of a laundry situated next to a pencil factory. The two companies operated under different codes and paid employees in similar positions different wages. The same held true for the Trucking Industry and the Household Moving and Storage Warehouse codes. Lasseter suggested that, of all the codes, the Construction Industry Code providing a minimum wage of $.40 an hour for unskilled labor was the most unpopular. White-collar workers in small towns were often paid less than unskilled laborers on construction jobs.[39]

Whole series of complaints occurred in situations where code requirements proved unworkable and no provision was made for local adjustment. Two such problems appeared under the Master Retail Code. Employers of five or fewer persons in towns of less than 2,500 people claimed that the exemption of the smaller employers would cause "great hardship due to unfair competition," and drugstore owners pleaded for a blanket exemption for delivery boys. Unless such exceptions were made, hundreds of these boys would have to be fired, and often they were essential to the operation of the drugstore.

The Restaurant Code seemed to have been the least understood. Mitchell found restaurant operators in Savannah ignorant or completely misinformed regarding their obligations. "Most of them claimed never to have seen a copy of the code.[40]

One very unusual violation involved the Alcoholic Wholesale Beverage

Industry Code and an Alabama bootlegger, Jack Abraham. He was charged in Georgia and defended himself by saying that Alabama was dry, so he could not get a permit there. Neither could he obtain one from the United States Treasury. Therefore, he contended, he was not subject to the provisions of any code. The charges subsequently were dropped, though officially because of lack of evidence, and not for the reasons he gave.[41]

Of all the codes, however, the construction, the lumber and timber, and the textile codes caused the most trouble. The difficulty encountered with the construction code centered around the minimum wage for unskilled laborers. Kendall Weisiger lamented that this provision had been the most difficult to enforce, since it was "so far out of line with current rates of pay in other lines of work for services of similar character." He might have added that it was above the prevailing wage for services demanding more skill—even white-collar jobs. He felt that if the state could differentiate within the code among various occupational classes, the problem would be solved. But such permission was never forthcoming.[42]

The Timber Code was the first code to be widely violated, and it was only by chance that chickens in New York rather than trees in Georgia spelled judicial doom for the NRA. By 1935 the Timber and Lumber Industry Code had raised wages 380 percent above 1932 levels, and sawmill owners found their meager profits shrinking. From the code's inception the NRA had difficulty in maintaining compliance, and by the end of 1934 the entire industry was in revolt. In October 1934 the Small Mill Pine Association meeting in Columbus repudiated the cost protection provision of the code. Early in 1935 another group of sawmill operators, convening at Augusta, decided to "go off" the code. They claimed that compliance was forcing them into bankruptcy.

The state compliance office hesitated to act because of the pending Belcher Lumber Company case then before the Supreme Court. The United States district judge in Augusta had some Timber Code cases on his docket and was also assuming a watch-and-wait attitude. When the Belcher Case was dismissed by the court, the fate of the Lumber Code was sealed. The larger mill owners who were still complying in April 1935 abandoned the code completely. In the middle of the month Lasseter estimated that only 10 percent of the lumber and timber industry was complying. By May most of these companies had reverted to

the low wages and long hours prevalent prior to the NRA. After the
Schecter decision Lasseter blamed the mass defection of the timber and
lumber industry for leading the way in Georgia to widespread code
violation.[43]

Cotton textiles was, by far, the largest industry in the state. It also
was the best organized and the first industry to present and have its code
accepted by the NRA. Originally the Textile Code boosted wages about
65 percent and distributed the increased payment over a large number of
employees, providing the greatest increases for lower paid laborers. Wage
rates for all classifications of workers increased from July to August 1933.
Those of the lower-paid spooler-tenders, creelers, and frame-spinners
doubled. Male loom-fixers, the highest paid, benefited least, making 54
percent more at the end of the period, while spooler-tenders' wages were
raised over 100 percent. Prior to the NRA, the usual working week had
been 55 hours, 10 hours a day for five days and five hours on Saturday.
Under the NRA, this was shortened to a 40-hour week of five, eight-hour
days. The average wage was $14.00 to $16.50 a week.[44]

Not only did wages in the South increase, but the North-South wage
differential lessened. This trend had begun in 1924, however, and de-
creases from 1924 to July 1933 were greater than those from July 1933
to 1935. An analysis showed that decreased differentials during the NRA
period were due principally to the raising of wages for workers in lower
wage brackets. After 1935 the differential began to increase, as southern
textile mills went off NRA wage standards with a greater vengeance than
in the North.[45]

Originally cotton-mill executives heartily supported the code which
they had helped to draft. In an Atlanta meeting with owners from four
southern states, including Georgia, they "pledged their support to the
textile code" as soon as Roosevelt signed it. Nevertheless, not a month
had passed before George L. Googe, regional head of the American
Federation of Labor, left Atlanta for Washington with reports of about
500 complaints involving around 100 southern mills. Googe said complaints were coming to his office at the rate of "dozens daily." An
example of management's chiseling was the piecework "wage deduction
system" devised by mill owners. Googe said a man was supposed to
earn $12.00 a week minimum. If circumstances beyond his control
allowed him to make only $9.00 worth of piecework in a certain week,
he would still be paid $12.00. If he did $15.00 worth of piecework the

next week, however, he would still get only $12.00 and a slip of paper reminding him of a previous $3.00 "advance" wage payment.[46]

To deal with industrial difficulties which local factory committees were unable to settle, the NRA created a textile board in Washington and state boards. The boards contained three members: one from labor, one from management, and one representing the public. Unfortunately, labor and government failed to bring about harmonious relations. There were more textile strikes in 1933 after the application of the Textile Code than before it, and the code had not been signed by the president until July.[47]

As labor found its voice and assumed that Section 7-A of the NRA was the government's pledge to unionism, a series of strikes occurred from 1933 to 1935. At their peak in the late summer of 1934, as many as 46,000 men from a work force of 60,000 may have been on strike. Well over half the cotton textile mills in the state were closed. The unions used "flying squadrons"—specialized groups of organizers traveling swiftly from town to town initiating strikes. Governor Talmadge, not to be outdone, declared martial law, established his own flying squadrons of national guardsmen, and erected a "barbed-wire enclosure" at Fort McPherson to incarcerate strikers.[48]

In mid-September Mitchell summed up the situation, saying the strike was serious, but not as bad as figures indicated. Although many mills were closed, the strike would not last. Laborers would begin to miss their paychecks, and union threats would not keep them from going back to work. Mitchell felt that "employers generally disregard their obligations under 7-A, and the stretch-out has been employed very extensively." The Cotton Textile Labor Relations Board and the code authority seemed impotent. Mitchell concluded that the central issue, stripped of "wage and hour demands and other similar frills" used for bargaining power, was the right of collective bargaining. He was "convinced that the employers have side-stepped this issue by common consent, and it appears at least that they were aided and abetted by a weak-kneed and employer-dominated Code Authority, and an obscure Administration policy."[49]

Mitchell was correct in assuming that the strike had already peaked. A loss of public sympathy and the use of troops had weakened the strikers' resolve, and unions announced that "strictly regulated picketing by striking workers will be resumed at Georgia mills as soon as necessary rules and regulations can be agreed upon." Labor was about ready to give up.[50]

When more strikes occurred in 1935, Talmadge again called in troops. Through all the disturbances it was evident that the governor sided with the mill owners and used the troops, not to keep the peace, but to end the strikes. One colonel in the Georgia militia remarked, "With the arrest of these strikers we believe that the backbone of the strike is broken."[51]

Sporadic strikes also occurred in other industries during the period, some because of code violations. Unionism in Georgia was never strong, but a series of strikes beginning in 1935 at the Fisher Body and Chevrolet plants in Atlanta led to other strikes, ending in General Motor's recognition of the union in 1937 in an agreement that covered the Atlanta workers. The strikes of the NRA period were not successful, but by making workers aware of what was legally due them and by introducing them to the concepts of union operations, they paved the way for subsequent unionization.[52]

Although one observer after the Schecter decision stated that "there has been no exploitation of labor in the State to any appreciable extent," this was clearly contradicted by other sources. A report to the Robert Committee, investigating the aftermath of the NRA, noted that "the greatest number of departures from the previous hour and wage code provisions are in the states of New York, California, Texas, Massachusetts, Georgia, and Nebraska." Georgia experienced 25 instances of wage cuts, 221 instances of departure from wage-hour provisions, 46 instances of departure from hour provisions, and 11 instances of price cutting during June 1935. Another selective study done in 1937 confirmed these findings.[53]

Ultimately, the NRA failed to achieve its purposes in Georgia because the law was not written to aid a young, growing, but still rather primitive economy. Sufficient capital did not exist in southern industry to allow it to maintain its labor force and raise wages. The accompanying rise in prices could be successful only in an area where most people were employed in industry and therefore could use increased wages to pay the higher prices. Such was not the case in the South.[54]

As far as the administration of the act was concerned, the Georgia staff was quite competent, but it was hamstrung by laws which really did not apply to the economy of the state. The federal administration was unwilling to allow any legal deviation. Local officials consistently acted to subvert whatever good might have come from the NRA. Those industries which existed were decentralized, and all but owned many of the towns where they were located. In such cases the company controlled the local governments, compliance boards, and code authorities. Even where these towns were not under the thumb of industry, they had great difficulty in achieving any kind of success. The state was so large, and businesses were so scattered, that it was hard to acquire the funds to operate. When money was available, it was still difficult for the administration to be efficient because of the distances involved.

Despite any problems state and local offices might have been able to overcome, some crucial faults would still remain. The program was primarily voluntary, and the administration never was given the authority to enforce what laws there were. In an instance which required so much public support and trust, this was the telling blow. When the public and business recognized the impotence of the NRA, all hope for its success evaporated.

NOTES

1. Charles L. Dearing, Paul T. Homan, Lewis L. Lorwin, and Leverett S. Lyon, *The ABC of the NRA* (Washington: Brookings Institution, 1934), p. 65. Atlanta *Constitution*, August 17 and 20, 1933. John Swope to Andrew Soule, March 19, 1934, NARG 9, National Recovery Administration (NRA) Compliance Division, State Director's Reports on Local Compliance Boards, drawer 1235.
2. Franklin M. Garrett, *Atlanta and Environs: A Chronicle of Its People and Events.* (New York: Lewis Historical Publishing Company, Inc., 1954) II, 905-6. W. R. Ulrich to Charles F. Horner, August 8, 1933, NARG 9, Public Relations Division, Chamber of Commerce File, box 7335. "'War Times' at Chamber of Commerce," *Atlanta City Builder*, XVII, 3 (August 10, 1933), 1. William L. Mitchell to E. J. Pace, August 18, 1933, NARG 9, Chamber of Commerce File, box 7336. Atlanta *Constitution*, July 22 and 23 and August 1, 1933. Dearing, *et al., The ABC of the NRA*, p. 65. Charles F. Horner to Postmaster, August 15, 1933, NARG 9, Chamber of Commerce File, box 7335.
3. Atlanta *Constitution*, July 25 and August 4 and 14, 1933. "'War Times' at Chamber of Commerce," p. 13.
4. *Atlanta City Builder*, XVII, 4 (September 10, 1933), 6.
5. *Ibid.,* p. 1. Atlanta *Constitution*, September 7 and 14, 1933.
6. *Atlanta City Builder*, XVII, 4 (September 10, 1933), 1. The

Kourier, IX, 10 (September 1933), 32-4; IX, 11 (October 1933), 25.

7. Atlanta *Constitution,* September 5, 1933. The *Statesman,* II, 32 (August 12, 1933); II, 33 (August 19, 1933).

8. Atlanta *Constitution,* August 29 and September 1, 1933.

9. Garrett, *Atlanta,* II, 907. *Atlanta City Builder,* XVII, 5 (October 10, 1933), 11. Atlanta *Constitution,* October 5, 14, 17, and 18 and November 1, 4, and 8, 1933. Allen L. Henson, *Red Galluses: A Story of Georgia Politics* (Boston: Edinboro Publishers, 1945), pp. 112-113.

10. Arthur F. Raper, *Tenants of the Almighty* (New York: Macmillan Company, 1943), p. 194. Arthur F. Raper, *Preface to Peasantry* (Chapel Hill: University of North Carolina Press, 1936), pp. 238, 242-3. J. O. Barnes to Hugh S. Johnson, August 12, 1933 (telegram), NARG 9, Chamber of Commerce File, box 7335.

11. William L. Mitchell to Leighton H. Peebles, October 2, 1933, NARG 9, St. Director's Reports on Local Compl. Bds., drawer 1235.

12. Mitchell to Peebles, August 16, 1933, NARG 9, Compliance Division, General Correspondence with Field Offices, drawer 1099. Dearing, *et al., The ABC of the NRA,* pp. 69-70. Ulrich to Boaz Long, September 16, 1933, NARG 9, St. Director's Repts. of Local Compl. Bds., drawer 1235. Ulrich to P. G. Finlayson, September 8, 1933, NARG 9, St. Director's Repts. on Local Compl. Bds., drawer 1235.

13. A. Steve Nance to Edward F. McGrady, October 23, 1933, NARG 9, Repts. Relating to Local Compl. Bds., box 1209. Mitchell to Donald Renshaw, November 24, 1933, NARG 9, St. Director's Repts. on Local Compl. Bds., drawer 1235.

14. Atlanta *Constitution,* October 4, 1933. McGrady to E. H. Choate, October 10, 1933, NARG 9, St. Director's Repts. on Local Compl. Bds., drawer 1235. Lee Ashcraft to Swope, October 16, 1933, NARG 9, St. Director's Repts. on Local Compl. Bds., drawer 1235. Swope to Ashcraft, October 25, 1933, NARG 9, St. Director's Repts. on Local Compl. Bds., drawer 1235.

15. Finlayson to Mitchell, January 11, 1934, NARG 9, Gen. Corres. with Field Offices, drawer 1099.

16. Swope to Mitchell, October 11, 1933, NARG 9, St. Director's Repts. on Local Compl. Bds., drawer 1235. William A. Patton to Horner, March 25, 1934, NARG 9, Public Relations Division, General Correspondence, box 7316. Mitchell to Renshaw, November 13, 1933, NARG 9, St. Director's Repts. on Local Compl. Bds., drawer 1234. Mitchell to Renshaw, November 22, 1933, NARG 9, St. Director's Repts. on Local Compl. Bds., drawer 1234. "Survey of Local Compliance Boards," n.d., NARG 9, Compl. Div. Miscellaneous Compl. Bd.

Material, drawer 1237. Mitchell to Renshaw, January 24, 1934, NARG 9, St. Director's Repts. on Local Compl. Bds., drawer 1234.

17. See letters in 1934, NARG 9, Pub. Relns. Div., Gen. Corres., box 7316. Atlanta *Constitution,* June 15, 1934.

18. Atlanta *Constitution,* April 17 and July 6, 1934, and April 17, 1935. General memo, April 17, 1934, NARG 9, Gen. Corres. with Field Offices, drawer 1100. Mitchell to Swope, May 26, 1934, NARG 9, Gen. Corres. with Field Offices, drawer 1100. Atlanta *Journal,* October 24, 1934.

19. Atlanta *Constitution,* July 6, 1934. Mitchell to Peebles, August 19, 1933 (report), NARG 9, Compl. Div., District Manager's Reports. Mitchell to Swope, January 21, 1935, NARG 9, Gen. Corres. with Field Offices, drawer 1099. Mitchell to Swope, December 28, 1934, NARG 9, Gen. Corres. with Field Offices, drawer 1100. J. H. Wooton to Swope, July 23, 1934 (memo), NARG 9, Gen. Corres. with Field Offices, drawer 1100. Dearing, *et al., The ABC of the NRA,* p. 102.

20. "Additional Report of Use of State and Local Adjustment Boards," NARG 9, Compl. Div. Reports, box 1195.

21. *Ibid.*

22. Mitchell to Swope, December 18, 1934 (memo), NARG 9, Gen. Corres. with Field Offices, drawer 1100.

23. Swope to Mitchell, November 21, 1934 (telegram), NARG 9, Gen. Corres. with Field Offices, drawer 1100. Swope to Mitchell, December 5, 1934 (telegram), NARG 9, Gen. Corres. with Field Offices, drawer 1100. Atlanta *Constitution,* November 27, 1934. Ward to Mitchell, April 25, 1935 (memo), NARG 9, Gen. Corres. with Field Offices, drawer 1098. Mitchell to Ward, April 30, 1935, NARG 9, Gen. Corres. with Field Offices, drawer 1098.

24. Dillard B. Lasseter to Swope, February 12, 1935, NARG 9, Gen. Corres. with Field Offices, drawer 1099.

25. L. J. Martin to Mitchell, May 15, 1935, NARG 9, Gen. Corres. with Field Offices, drawer 1098. Mitchell to Martin, May 21, 1935, NARG 9, Gen. Corres. with Field Offices, drawer 1098.

26. Mitchell to Swope, November 13, 1934, NARG 9, Gen. Corres. with Field Offices, drawer 1100.

27. Mitchell to Swope, October 27, 1934, NARG 9, Gen. Corres. with Field Offices, drawer 1100. Lasseter to Regional Director, July 26, 1935, NARG 9, Compl. Div. Repts., box 1195. Lasseter later became head of the National Youth Administration in Georgia.

28. Lasseter to Regional Director, July 26, 1935, NARG 9, Compl. Div. Repts., box 1195. A. Fielder to Harry Hopkins, October 24, 1934,

NARG 69, FERA, State Files, No. 460, box 70. Perry A. Fellows to
Fielder, November 15, 1934, NARG 69, FERA, State Files, No. 460,
box 70. Gay Shepperson to Fielder, December 4, 1934, NARG 69,
FERA, State Files, No. 460, box 70. Ironside to C. Carl Fink, October
31, 1934, NARG 44, NEC, Div. of Field Operations, Gen. Corres. with
State Directors (1934-35), box 174.

29. Mitchell to Swope, September 4, 1934, NARG 9, Gen. Corres.
with Field Offices, drawer 1100. Stanley I. Posner to Mitchell, September
10, 1934, NARG 9, Gen. Corres. with Field Offices, drawer 1100.

30. Lasseter to Regional Director, July 26, 1935, NARG 9, Compl.
Div. Repts., box 1195.

31. Emma Lillian Donoghue to Roosevelt, October 19, 1933, NARG 9,
Compl. Div. PRA Complaints, drawer 908. Martin G. Sembach to Hugh
Johnson, January 20, 1934, NARG 9, Compl. Div. PRA Complaints,
drawer 908. Also see similar letters in this box.

32. Raper, *Preface,* pp. 239-40. Also see complaints in NARG 9, PRA
Complaints, drawer 908. Atlanta *Constitution,* August 4, 1933.

33. Mitchell to Peebles, October 7, 1933, NARG 9, Compl. Div.,
Dist. Manager's Repts. Cochrane to Altmeyer, May 15, 1934, NARG 9,
Gen. Corres. with Field Offices, drawer 1098. Dearing, *et al., The ABC of
the NRA,* p. 76. See forms 1523-1 and 1517-6, October 19, 1934 (?)
NARG 9, Misc, Compl. Bd. material, drawer 1237. J. H. Wooton to Swope,
July 23, 1934, NARG 9, Gen. Corres. with Field Offices, drawer 1100.
Mitchell to Renshaw, January 13, 1934, NARG 9, St. Dir's. Repts. on
Local Compl. Bds., drawer 1234.

34. See letters in NARG 9, PRA Complaints, drawer 908. Raper,
Preface, p. 238. Arthur F. Raper, "Effects of Application of NRA Upon
Negroes," address delivered at the Urban League Conference, Tuskegee
Institute, December 5, 1933, Arthur F. Raper Manuscripts, AFR, 2-B,
1931-33.

35. Roy E. Fossett, "The Impact of the New Deal on Georgia Politics,
1933-1941" (unpublished Ph.D. dissertation, Department of Political
Science, University of Florida, 1960), pp. 110-111. Unsigned report,
December 29, 1934, NARG 44, NEC, Digests, box 487. H. M. Douty,
"Recovery and the Southern Wage Differential," *Southern Economic
Journal,* IV, 3 (January 1938), 321. Raper, *Preface,* pp. 238-9, 240-1.

36. Lasseter to Regional Director, July 26, 1935, NARG 9, Compl.
Div. Repts., box 1195. Atlanta *Constitution,* July 30, August 13,
October 24, 1933, and August 2, 1934.

37. Mitchell to Martin, May 22, 1935 (memo), NARG 9, Gen.
Corres. with Field Offices, drawer 1098. Mitchell to Martin, May 15,

1935 (memo), NARG 9, Gen. Corres. with Field Offices, drawer 1098.
Unsigned report, May 15, 1935, NARG 44, NEC, Digests, box 488.
William L. Handler to Sol Rosenblatt, March 22, 1935, NARG 9,
Gen. Corres. with Field Offices, drawer 1099. Mitchell to Martin,
February 16, 1935, NARG 9, Gen. Corres. with Field Offices, box 1099.
Prentiss M. Terry to Swope, March 28, 1934, NARG 9, Gen. Corres.
with Field Offices, drawer 1100. Cochrane to Altmeyer, May 15, 1934
(report), NARG 9, Gen. Corres. with Field Offices, drawer 1098.
Mitchell to Martin, February 16, 1934 (memo), NARG 9, Gen. Corres.
with Field Offices, box 1099.

    38. Mitchell to Martin, March 2, 1935, NARG 9, Gen. Corres. with
Field Offices, box 1099.

    39. Lasseter to Regional Director, July 26, 1935, NARG 9, Compl.
Div. Repts., box 1195. Unsigned letter, n.d. (1934), NARG 69, FERA,
Old Subject Files, box 74.

    40. Mitchell to National Compliance Director, October 28, 1933,
NARG 9, Gen. Corres. with Field Offices, drawer 1100. Mitchell to
Swope, April 12, 1934, NARG 9, Gen. Corres. with Field Offices,
drawer 1099.

    41. J. Henry Hallam to Compliance Division, May 2, 1935 (memo),
NARG 9, Gen. Corres. with Field Offices, drawer 1098.

    42. Kendall Weisiger to Mitchell, May 16, 1935, NARG 9, Gen.
Corres. with Field Offices, drawer 1098.

    43. W. A. Hartman and H. H. Wooten, "Georgia Land Use Problems,"
Georgia Experiment Station, *Bulletin,* No. 191 (1935), 156. Atlanta
Constitution, October 31, 1934. Bruce Hall to L. J. Martin, February 1,
1935, NARG 9, Gen. Corres. with Field Offices, drawer 1099. Hall to
Martin, April 4, 1934, NARG 9, Gen. Corres. with Field Offices,
drawer 1099. Lasseter to Regional Director, July 26, 1935, NARG 9,
Compl. Div. Repts., box 1195. Mitchell to Martin, May 8, 1935 (memo),
NARG 9, Gen. Corres. with Field Offices, drawer 1098. William L.
Handler to Martin, April 4, 1935 (telegram), NARG 9, Gen. Corres.
with Field Offices, drawer 1099. Lasseter to Martin, April 16, 1935
(telegram), NARG 9, Gen. Corres. with Field Offices, drawer 1098.

    44. WPA, "Employment in the Cotton Textile Industry in Alabama,
Georgia, and South Carolina: Preliminary Report," Research Bulletin
No. J-2 (1936), 5, 10.

    45. N. A. Tolles, "Regional Differences in Cotton-Textile Wages,
1928 to 1937," *Monthly Labor Review,* XLVI, 1 (January 1938), 36, 38.

    46. Atlanta *Constitution,* July 12, 1933.

    47. *Ibid.,* November 28, 1933.

48. *Ibid.*, September 5, 6, 7, 12, and 17, 1934. Arthur Raper and Ira DeA. Reid, *Sharecroppers All.* (Chapel Hill: University of North Carolina Press, 1941), pp. 174-5.

49. Mitchell to Swope, September 14, 1934, NARG 9, Gen. Corres. with Field Offices, drawer 1100.

50. Atlanta *Constitution,* September 20, 1934.

51. *Ibid.*, January 4, March 5, April 30, June 2, and August 16, 1935. Atlanta *Journal,* January 8, 1935.

52. George B. Tindall, *The Emergence of the New South, 1913-1945* (Baton Rouge: Louisiana State University Press, 1967), p. 514. Atlanta *Constitution,* May 3, 1935.

53. "Reports from Field Offices Regarding Changes in Industrial Conditions Subsequent to the Supreme Court Decision of the Schecter Case: Georgia," NARG 9, Compl. Div. Repts., box 1195. Witt Bowden, "Hours and Earnings before and after the NRA," *Monthly Labor Review,* XLVI, 1 (January 1937), 29. Martin to Chairman, Business and Labor Standards Commission, July 9, 1935, NARG 9, Compl. Div., Robert Committee Data, drawer 1257. Unsigned report, November 15, 1937, NARG 44, NEC, Digests, box 512. For a discussion of Georgia's Negroes under the NRA see Michael S. Holmes, "The Blue Eagle as 'Jim Crow Bird': The NRA and Georgia's Black Worker," *Journal of Negro History,* LVII, 3 (July 1972), 276-283.

54. John C. Meadows, *Modern Georgia* (Athens: University of Georgia Press, 1946), pp. 325-6.

7

First Aid
for the Cotton Farmer

Because the agricultural depression preceded the crash of 1929 by
several years, the farm community in Georgia had a longer time to
experiment with home-grown solutions before the federal government
stepped in. The agricultural depression of the 1920s, though extremely
severe, was not generically different from past agricultural depressions.
To some extent, a body of theories and practices existed to which
Georgia's farmers might turn in combating the present problem.

Cotton was the major cash-producing crop in the state, and it was
natural that efforts should be concentrated in attacking the depression
from the point of view of the cotton farmer. Georgians understood that
the one-crop economy had been the root of much of the South's trouble.
As early as 1905 there had been a campaign to restrict the growing of
cotton to fit market conditions. Other attempts were made in 1915,
1921, and 1927, but none had been successful. In the 1920s the federal
government joined with such organizations as the Cotton Growers'
Protective Association, the Southern Cotton Association, the Farmers'
Union, and various farm journals and rural newspapers in the movement
to confront the problem.

Members of Congress periodically advocated McNary-Haugenism, a
plan whereby the federal government would purchase excess cotton
either to hold or dump overseas and pay farmers an "equalization fee"
to compensate for lower world cotton prices. The McNary-Haugen bill
never became law, though its basic principles later were given as an
option to the secretary of agriculture under the Agricultural Adjustment

Act. Other federal legislation, namely the Capper-Volstead Act, exempt-
ing agricultural cooperatives from antitrust restrictions, and the Intermediate Credit Act, providing a series of intermediate credit banks to
offer short-term farm loans and allowing the organization of farmers'
cooperatives, were passed during the early 1920s. Before Roosevelt
became president, therefore, attempts had been made both to restrict
production and to arrange for the absorption of excess cotton.

Two of the basic difficulties involved with crop restriction were the
rather decentralized attack made upon the problem and the long history
of failures when such attempts were made. Although private efforts to
institute restrictions continued into the 1920s, notably in the form of
Louisiana Governor Huey Long's one-year cotton holiday, by the end
of that decade "the South's cotton growers had lost all faith in the
possibility of limiting the crop by voluntary pledges, growers' conven-
tions, courthouse meetings, and exhortation." Southern states "not
only questioned their constitutional power to act but also hesitated to
do so for fear that a limitation by one state might work to the advantage
of other states."

It seemed that, if any controls were to be placed upon the production
of cotton, they would have to be imposed by the federal government.
President Hoover may have recognized this, but the same philosophy
of government which had kept him from going far enough in providing
relief and recovery also deterred him from really confronting the agricultural situation. He did sign the Agricultural Marketing Act of 1929,
which established the Federal Farm Board to promote cooperatives and
make loans to control excess production and the Cotton Stabilization
Corporation to make purchases of this surplus cotton, but because he
was unwilling to interfere directly, he did not supplement this legislation
with a corresponding plan for crop restriction. Farmers, therefore, continued to raise more cotton than could be marketed profitably, and
prices continued to fall. Seeing that no progress was being made, Hoover
ordered the corporation to terminate its activities in 1931, and nothing
more was done by the federal government under his administration.[1]

The handmaiden of cotton-crop restriction was diversification, and
the central difficulty in its implementation was finding suitable substi-
tutes for the cash crop. This problem, in turn, was complicated by two
factors, those of convincing farmers who were "completely dominated
by the [cotton] economy" to turn to other crops and of finding a sub-

stitute which would suit the agricultural conditions of the state and be marketable enough to equal cotton's earning power. Probably the most successful plan involved raising livestock. During the 1920s livestock prices had declined, but not to the extent that cotton prices fell, so that "livestock became relatively more important and produced about 20 percent of the state's gross farm income in that decade." After 1930 the price of cotton continued to fluctuate, but the price of livestock rose steadily. By 1945 profits from livestock represented about 30 percent of Georgia's gross farm income, the most spectacular rise in importance coming in chicken-raising.[2]

Other substitute operations such as peanuts, rabbits, lumbering, milk, and even bootlegging were tried, but all proved unprofitable for various reasons. Farmers who had been induced to switch to these endeavors, quickly found that the agricultural conditions in the state were not favorable or, more often, that there were no suitable markets. The result was that many farmers returned to growing cotton which still reigned as "King" in Georgia.[3]

These failures, however, did not dampen the efforts of those who sought alternate crops. During the 1920s the state, civic clubs, loan associations, the press, and railroads joined with the University of Georgia's College of Agriculture in setting up "Cow, Hog, and Hen" programs. Each time a particular experiment met with success, it was highly publicized and even drew national attention. The most notable instance occurred in Colquitt County where a "five year plan" for crop diversification was instituted in 1923. After seven years the county was able to show gains in peanuts, hogs, watermelons, truck crops, timber, and especially tobacco. The program peaked in 1929, but following the crash of that year, every enterprise except that of beef cattle raising lost money.[4]

Another program designed to aid the distressed farmer arose during the depression, although it met with limited success. If farmers were unable to increase their profits, at least they might be able to reduce their living costs under the "live-at-home" program first begun by the state's 4-H clubs. Farm organizations across Georgia encouraged the growing of vegetables and other crops for home use, so that the farmer would not be burdened with the added expense of having to purchase these commodities. Tenants, however, rarely were able to do this. Landlords required that they plant cotton "right up to their doors," and a traveler looking out across the fields often could see tenant shacks amid a sea of brown and white in the late summer.[5]

Advocates of the program persisted in their crusade. Early in 1930, for example, the Georgia Bankers' Association adopted a resolution supporting such activities and offered its financial support. The resolution called for "the production on each farm of necessary food and feed, . . . the promotion of farm financing methods directing the credit extended to farmers by the banks in such a way as would promote a well-balanced farming program and make crop loans self-liquidating, and the creation of an Agricultural Board in each county under a plan recommended by the Georgia College of Agriculture and by the Agricultural Commission of the American Bankers' Association."

W. S. Elliot, president of the Georgia Bankers' Association, claimed in 1933 that the program had been a success and was largely responsible for cotton reduction during 1930-1932. Despite the optimism of the association, however, the program was not as fruitful as had been hoped. It was a good idea, though, and it subsequently was adopted as one of the programs carried on under the New Deal.[6]

Distressed farmers, like their urban counterparts, were so distraught by 1933 that they would have accepted eagerly any program which held forth the promise of recovery. Textile mill owners and the state commissioner of agriculture, who would later bitterly condemn the Agricultural Adjustment Administration, accepted the new program "as the only practicable way out of their dilemma." Political conservatives finally were willing to embrace a program of federal intervention in matters formerly reserved for the states.[7]

The failure of the National Recovery Administration to aid Georgia was unfortunate, but not of momentous importance, for there was little industry present to begin with. Of far greater significance in affecting the economic recovery of this farm state was the Agricultural Adjustment Administration (AAA), enacted into being on May 12, 1933. The program was based upon well-established, but little-practiced, theories of production control and structured administratively by crop—in this case, most importantly, cotton. The AAA offered growers a cash payment on a per acre basis, varying with the estimated yield per acre, for destroying from 25 to 50 percent of their cotton acreage. If the farmer were willing to gamble that the program would work and the price of cotton would rise, he could substitute for this "cash only" payment a "cash-option" plan, accepting a lower cash payment per acre along with an option at six cents a pound to buy an amount of cotton held by the secretary of agriculture (from the Farm Credit Administration) equal to the estimated amount of cotton he plowed up. Assuming the price of cotton did rise sufficiently, the farmer could then instruct the secretary to sell the "optioned" cotton and return to him the profit, less the six cents a pound he had agreed to pay for the options.

Though seemingly complex, this basic program had been well considered before the spring of 1933 and was readily accepted by most informed agriculturalists. Administration of the AAA, particularly below the national level, however, was not so easily established. Two factors, the great duration and degree of the agricultural depression to that point and the imminency of the current crop season, made the need for an immediately operational administrative structure imperative. To construct a new organization from the local level upwards, as other New Deal agencies were doing, was not feasible here.[8]

It was thus fortunate that just such an organization had existed for about two decades in the form of the Agricultural Extension Service. Farm leaders such as the department's M. L. Wilson and *Progressive Farmer* editor Cully Cobb recognized the possibility of using the extension and suggested this to Secretary of Agriculture Henry A. Wallace and his assistant Rexford Guy Tugwell. Although Tugwell initially expressed some doubts, Wallace accepted the idea and designated each state extension director, or a person chosen by him, to be responsible for all AAA programs in his state. In Georgia, Extension Director J. Philip Campbell, his assistant, Harry L. Brown, and four district agricultural agents formed the administrative core of Georgia's AAA with the county agents as the local leaders of the program.[9]

The county agents were the kingpins of the operation; they represented that point at which the federal program interacted with the farmers. Originally the agents were to handle only the "educational" phases of the AAA, which was essentially what they were doing for the extension. Locally elected county agricultural committees were to supervise the actual work involved. It soon became apparent in Georgia, however, that the entire responsibility for the AAA at the county level was to devolve upon the county agent. The agent became the primary spokesman for the AAA, and as the months passed he assumed control of all the operations with the county committees aiding him in a subordinate role.[10]

The extension service and county agent system had come to maturity with the Smith-Lever Act of 1914. This act marked the end of the "successful-farmer" type of official by replacing him with college-trained agents. The extension service financially and administratively became linked to the Department of Agriculture, the state agricultural college, and the county. After 1914, however, the lines of authority extended more from the county to the state agricultural college, so that by 1933 it was largely a state organization in terms of administration.[11]

In the spring of 1933 the Georgia Extension Service was very weak, and the county agents were in a tenuous position. Through the 1920s and early 1930s, Georgia's county agents had lost favor. Their educational programs had not aided farmers who had been in serious trouble even before 1920. Additional difficulties brought on by the Great Depression had sharply reduced county revenues. Under these circumstances many counties now refused to contribute their part in supporting an agent, believing him to be an unnecessary expense. The result was that by 1933 about a third of the state's 159 counties had no agent at all.

Cotton, Georgia's most important crop, received immediate attention. By the time the AAA was established, Georgia's cotton crop was already in the fields, and, since the harvest normally began in the middle to late summer, Extension Director Campbell asked county agents to forgo elections and appoint county cotton committees. Operating under the assumption that committeemen should be those best able to persuade farmers to sign acreage reduction contracts, virtually all of the agents turned to the "best known" and most successful farmers, merchants, and bankers to fill the posts.[12]

To a great extent, the make-up of the county and local committees determined the "local philosophy" followed and passed on to farmers. The committeemen were usually large landholders and reflected ideas appropriate to their position. Because of this the extension service received criticism that blacks and poor white farmers were discriminated against. Like the members of local relief committees, the actions and ideas of agricultural committeemen were bounded by local customs and shibboleths. They were tied more to the past than to the New Deal. In some cases the county agent shared this attitude, even though he might be better educated. Certainly there existed a tension between past practices and a loyalty to the Democratic Party, Roosevelt, and a farm recovery program. The resolution of these tensions, together with the general effectiveness of the extension set-up in administering the AAA, became evident in the working out of the program.

The new county committeemen attended one of four district meetings to learn about the program, returning home to hold countywide educational meetings with the county agents. It was at the county meetings that local committees, based on communities or militia districts, were formed. The local committees, in turn, held meetings with the farmers. These were usually staggered so that the county agent could attend. Ultimately, the local committees did much of the legwork in the AAA program. The county committee and county agent checked the results of the local committees and handled problems that came up during the course of operations.[13]

To sound out Georgia farmers' reactions to the newly inaugurated program, Assistant Extension Director Harry Brown surveyed nine counties. Of 105 farmers contacted, 101 favored a "feasible plan" of either rentals or options, or both. A month later, a meeting was held of the state board for the cotton program. Originally the board was made up of Governor Talmadge, Extension Director Campbell, Chief Justice Richard B. Russell, and state Commissioner of Agriculture G. C. Adams. This figurehead board formally announced the beginning of the campaign in Georgia. In the following days area meetings were held to disseminate information. The next weekend county and local committees met to organize for the campaign.

After these county and local meetings, committeemen took to the field to secure contracts from farmers who had not already signed. Most of the larger farmers were quite cooperative, although there were many questions and reservations. One farmer asked if he could be paid for reductions made before 1933. He had complied with prior unofficial requests to restrict cotton acreage, and this affected the allotment the county was willing to give him. The administration, of course, could not allow this. In some instances farmers who had thus previously reduced their acreage refused to sign contracts.[14]

Many farmers accepted the program on faith. It was quite complicated, and frequently local AAA officials did not completely understand it themselves. Some farmers distrusted the offer, wondering whether, if after they had destroyed their cotton, the contract actually would be fulfilled. Some did not sign "through ignorance, lack of understanding and prejudice." Others believed that if they did not sign and the plan worked, they would be better off than if they had signed. There were also cases where tenants who wanted to sign could not obtain the permission of their landlords.

A number of smaller farmers refused because of religious reasons. They would not destroy a crop already growing. One committeeman faced with this response asked the farmer if he was "giving the Lord one-tenth of your income." When the man replied that he was not, the committeeman advised that this would probably be enough to send the farmer to hell anyway, so he might as well go ahead and sign the contract. The man agreed.[15]

The hardest group to persuade were those farthest from civilization. Many of these farmers were almost inaccessible. There were no roads, and committeemen could reach them only on foot. These circumstances demanded tremendous efforts and a good deal of time. Often these people were very ignorant. Some did not even know what an "acre" was. If a committeeman was not patient, prepared to spend enough time, or did not understand the program fully himself, he might not be able to convince the backwoods farmer. These agrarians were unbelievably isolated. Their only contact with the federal government was through the delivery of mail, and many did not even have mailboxes. It was difficult for them to grasp the meaning of a program that required an effort by all farmers for each individual farmer to benefit. Even less isolated farmers found it hard to understand how conditions elsewhere predicated demands made of them.[16]

The sign-up campaign threw the county agent's office into a turmoil. One agent reported that he had spent 63 days on AAA work during the year. He organized county and local committees, made 105 visits, held 5 meetings, and had 450 office calls about certain phases of the work. He mailed 125 letters, distributed 450 copies of the circular letter, wrote 5 news articles on the reduction campaign, and secured 313 contracts. The amount of printed material he received from the state and federal offices mounted to a flood, and he was expected to absorb all of this new information to pass on to farmers.[17]

County agents and committeemen were hampered by delays and changes in procedure. D. R. Hungerford, county agent for Coweta County, reported that at the time of the countywide meetings he had not received the forms for crop reduction. This not only delayed the sign-up campaign, but also cost him some enthusiasm on the part of the farmers whom the meetings were supposed to stimulate. Changes in procedure caused extra work. Originally he was instructed to secure two copies of the agreement signed in pencil or ink from the farmer. "That just suited the farmer and committeemen and practically all were signed in that manner." He was then ordered to have all agreements signed in indelible pencil. This required another visit to all farms. No sooner was that accomplished than he received an order requiring three copies of each agreement, and the process had to be repeated.[18]

Besides delays caused by changes in procedure, there were those inherent in the processing of agreements. The agreement passed through many hands on its way to Washington and back. At each stop along the way it was checked, but because it was handled so many times the chance of loss or error was actually increased. Agreements in which mistakes were discovered were returned, rewritten, and then sent back up through the bureaucracy.

Because agreements were signed before committeemen solicited contracts, each farm required at least two visits. Wallace had wanted to be sure of sufficient cooperation before launching the program, so the first question put to the farmer was whether he would cooperate. When the secretary was convinced of enough support, the committeemen had to return to each farm to estimate its yield. After the farmer agreed to the acreage he was to plow up, his contract was returned to Washington to be checked and approved. From there it went back to the farmer again via the committeeman. Thus, each farm required the journey of at least two forms to Washington, and additional trips were necessary each time an error was discovered.

In some counties, newspapers and radio stations helped to inform farmers of the program, and perhaps to reduce errors. The task also might be made easier by good attendance at meetings where knowledgeable county agents could carefully explain the program and answer questions. The agent might avoid confusion by publishing frequent news items in the local paper and by sending out circular letters which notified farmers of modifications. But, on the whole, the cumbersome administrative machinery invited mistakes and delay.[19]

The county agents and their staffs, as they existed before the program, probably could not have handled the work alone. Fortunately they received aid from other sources. Of particular value were the teachers of vocational agriculture who worked closely with the county agents in setting up the program. The College of Agriculture's Department of

Vocational Agriculture organized evening classes concerning the problems involved in the AAA program. During the summer of 1933, 24
teachers received appointments as special inspectors to work outside of
their communities in securing compliances in connection with contracts
signed by farmers. Of 360 requests made for such aid, 358 were filled.
These teachers traveled 20,338 miles in 321 days of special duty that summer. The extension service's home demonstration agents also helped.
Later the AAA provided funds to hire clerks for the county agents'
offices. The Civil Works Administration also contributed some labor,
"though not more than 40 clerks." Harry L. Brown noted that of the
"150" [sic] counties in the state "probably not more than 20 to 25 of
them have any clerical help."[20]

For those counties without an agent the AAA provided funds to hire
special emergency assistants. They were appointed with civil service
status by the Department of Agriculture. Eventually the AAA transferred funds to the extension service for hiring the assistants and for
other office use. There was some complaint that these assistants were
inferior to those selected by the extension service, but this did not seem
to occur in Georgia.[21]

Wallace had said that the program would be implemented, if enough
farmers agreed by July 12. Committeemen were required to send in
daily results of sign-ups to the county agent and to the state extension
office. The state office then forwarded the offers to the secretary of
agriculture, who reviewed and approved them.

By the July 12 deadline, the flood of offers was so great that valida-
tions were slow in coming back to the farmer. The delay created a
problem in the southern part of the state where farmers wanted to
destroy their cotton and plant substitute crops. Finally on July 20
Wallace agreed to accept verbally all contracts drawn prior to July 19.
Campbell distributed emergency permits to plow up in South Georgia
on July 21 and in North Georgia on the next day. On July 24, 1933,
Georgians began to plow up their cotton. These farmers were allowed to
display posters stating, "Cotton Control—This Farm Cooperating with
Uncle Sam," and "We Do Our Part."

The plow-up was scheduled to last until midnight on August 23, but
actually was not completed until September. Counties having a regular
agent seemed to progress on schedule, but in others, notably Clay County,
there were "all kinds of embarrassing situations."[22] Some farmers who

had hesitated in signing contracts approached the plow-up with dread. They lived close to the soil and their crops, and many were loath to destroy them. In Greene County, tenants could not bear to plow up their own cotton and traded fields, destroying each other's crop. From Jonesboro came the report that the mules refused to walk over the cotton rows. One ingenious farmer decided to hitch two mules together and put the plow between them. Thus, the mules would walk between the rows, as they were accustomed, and the plow would travel along the row turning up the plants.[23]

About three weeks after the plow-up began in a county, the local committees again took to the field with steel tapes to inspect the results. Committeemen found that many farmers had underestimated the amount of cotton they needed to turn under. C. B. Gladdin, county agent for Douglass County, noted that 40 to 50 percent of those who signed the contracts had not plowed up enough cotton, and 3.5 percent had destroyed excess acreage. This trend held for the other counties.[24]

Most county agents reported that farmers readily agreed to the demands of the committeemen, however, and there was little trouble in gaining their compliance. Often the committeemen traveled in pairs, reducing the likelihood of fraud and insuring against possible complaints by farmers that their neighbors were not plowing up enough cotton. After the committeemen had approved a farmer's work, they filled out performance and certification sheets to be sent to Washington. There the forms were checked and approved and returned by way of the county agent. This done, the farmers could expect their checks to arrive.

Wallace had permitted the distribution of emergency plow-up permits, allowing farmers to plant substitute crops while there was still time, but some counties could not wait, and county agents advised farmers to interplant their substitute crops between the cotton rows. In many instances it was fortunate that they did this, for the emergency permits had been issued so late that often there was not enough time left to plant and expect to harvest these substitute crops. In some cases these permits arrived only a few days before the regular ones, not saving much time at all.[25]

In signing contracts, farmers had agreed not to use extra fertilizer as a side dressing on the remaining cotton rows. Cobb reminded Campbell of this provision when complaints of such practices reached Washington. Although Campbell replied that he knew "of no such cases in this state," a later report showed that the percentage of acres receiving fertilizer in Georgia had risen from 80 percent in 1932 to 90 percent in 1933. The increase amounted to about 90,000 tons, a gain of 69 pounds of fertilizer per acre.[26]

Farmers were told that checks would begin arriving on August 15, 1933. Some did, but most were delayed and payments still had not arrived in November. Many farmers had anticipated using the money to tide them over until they could sell their remaining cotton. When the checks were not forthcoming as promised, their dissatisfaction grew. Senator Richard B. Russell, Jr., wrote to Wallace inquiring about the situation. Wallace replied that the delay was caused by the large number of checks which had to be processed. He explained that there were over 1,400 people working in three shifts, 24 hours a day, to audit the accounts. After that the accounts had to go to the comptroller's office where they were again inspected before drafts were finally issued.

This explanation may have satisfied Russell, but farmers still demanded prompt issuance of their checks. Delays in various Washington offices throughout the summer of 1933 were the major cause of farmers' dissatisfaction with the program. Unfortunately, much of this animosity was heaped upon the county agent, the AAA representative in that county. Some agents otherwise sympathetic to the program quickly soured and bitterly complained to the extension director in their yearly reports.[27]

Those farmers who had accepted the six-cent cotton options also found themselves waiting impatiently for them. The Atlanta *Constitution* estimated that about 60 percent of all contract signers had taken these options. There was never as much complaint about options as about checks, however. In the first place, those who took options may have had more faith in the program or may have simply been more willing to gamble. Second, most of those who took options were the larger farmers, those more familiar with agricultural economics. Because they were not in such financial straits and realized what was happening in Washington, they were not so apprehensive.[28]

County-agent reaction to the program was mixed. One of the two most often voiced criticisms of the program was that it took too much time and seriously hampered regular extension work. The trouble centered particularly around the county agent's office where a limited staff struggled with mountains of paper work. The agent was forced to do many of the clerical tasks himself. This tremendous pressure was partially reflected in the county agents' yearly reports, which were often statistically inaccurate. Many times the agent simply did not know what figures to record and merely made estimates. For this reason statistical information coming from the counties during this period was not to be trusted. Agents suggested that additional clerical help be provided by the extension. This was done to some extent, but not before the 1933 campaign was completed.[29]

Despite these disadvantages, the AAA was a great boon to the county agent. Before the program began, counties were gradually doing away with county agents. The critical role of the agent in the AAA gave him much more importance and prestige. When the AAA and extension announced late in 1933 that they could no longer afford to provide "free service" in the form of emergency assistants, forty more counties hastened to provide their share of a regular county agent's salary. For political reasons some counties held back, but when they realized that the AAA would indeed remove the emergency assistants, they too fell into line.[30]

The AAA program brought county agents into contact with farmers never before reached. Heretofore, the agent's work had been confined generally to the better farmers (larger) of the county. These men already were active in all agricultural activities and had helped to define agricultural policy in their counties and in the state. AAA work gained the agent renewed respect in the eyes of the large farmer, and new contacts added his backwoods counterpart to the growing circle of the agent's admirers. Future work along extension lines was made easier. While visiting farmers the agent could also discuss extension programs, and some agents commented that there was really no difference between the two — it was all agricultural work.

Farm management services benefited from the AAA. The farmer had to keep accurate farm records to determine acreage and yield. Beginning in 1933, the AAA in cooperation with the extension service distributed record books to farmers and instructed them in their use. Farmers were thus made more aware of the value of farm management practices in general.[31]

Unfortunately, AAA work and extension programs were not always complementary. Diversification and soil-building were in keeping with AAA philosophy, and the existence of idle acres formerly planted in cotton provided the perfect opportunity for experimentation along those lines. However, other extension projects worked at cross purposes to the reduction program. The inability to pursue these programs formed the agents' second major objection to the AAA. Efforts to increase production by planting more on the same amount of land using more fertilizer, for example, were contrary to the purposes of the AAA. Often county agents helped farmers get more production out of acres left to cotton and urged them to take marginal land out of cotton production so that their yields might not be drastically reduced.

In other areas the two agencies did not necessarily work at cross purposes, but the time spent on the AAA limited the agent's actions along other lines. Work in "one variety cotton communities" was at first hampered, though it later flourished, and 4-H projects were restricted. Vocational agriculture teachers and home demonstration agents also found their time limited when they aided the county agent in AAA work. When the emphasis of the government's agricultural program shifted from reduction and control to conservation in 1936, however, the pressure was alleviated.[32]

The state extension service itself was greatly affected by the AAA. Often it had to redirect its specialists to do AAA work, taking them away from their regular activities. On the other hand, the AAA provided additional funds for the enlargement of the extension's staff. As with the county agent, the extension service acquired a new importance in the economic life of the state, and the state extension workers echoed the county agents' sentiments in that they found it hard to separate AAA and extension programs.[33]

Because the extension service relied on state as well as federal funds, it was subject to political pressures from opponents of the AAA. Governor Talmadge previously had opposed the extension service, particularly its director, J. Philip Campbell, because of the support it gave to cooperative marketing. When the extension was designated to administer the AAA, his criticism became increasingly acrimonious, and his attempts to interfere in administration and policy became more frequent.[34]

The AAA made great demands upon the extension and put enormous trust in its administrative ability and capacity to promulgate the program successfully. The Georgia Extension Service fully lived up to this trust. The service benefited materially from new federal funds, and also, more subjectively, from its new position of increased respect and importance to the farmers of the state.

By the end of 1933, it was apparent that the cotton farmers approved of the federal government's efforts. D. L. Floyd, agricultural statistician, reported that the crop season had improved over that of 1932 and was better than any since the beginning of the depression. Although farmers were "not unduly optimistic over the present situation," there was a "marked contrast to the deep pessimism of one year ago." Cotton production was up 30 percent over 1932 on 19 percent less acreage. Only eleven counties ginned less cotton in 1933 than in 1932. The average yield per acre was the highest since 1914 and the third highest in the state's history. By fall of 1933 the price of cotton had risen from six cents to ten cents per pound, where it was pegged by the federal government. Most people felt that the sharp rise in price was due to the cotton reduction program, even though economists later attributed it mainly to Roosevelt's monetary policies.[35]

The improvement in the agricultural scene was reflected in ways other than farmers' praise for the reduction program. A survey of forty-three counties made in November 1933 showed that retail business increased 70 percent as compared to October and November of 1932. The purchasing of mules, still the basic source of farm power, increased 1,000 percent from 1932 to 1933. Atlanta replaced St. Louis as the "mule-trading center of the country." Finally, as noted, counties responded to the success of the program by providing support for permanent county agents.[36]

Georgia farmers' total cotton income under the program was $71,688,945. E. C. Westbrook, extension economist, estimated that this was $28,308,945 more than could have been expected in 1933 without the program. Henry I. Richards of the Brookings Institution arrived at a similar conclusion, although he noted that those not participating in the program gained slightly more from it than those who signed contracts.[37]

Not all Georgians were so pleased with the first year's program, however. In particular, the processing tax, equal to the difference between the current price and the parity price of cotton and applied at the first processing of the cotton, was unpopular with the cotton textile industry and the ginners. The Atlanta *Constitution* attributed a drop in cotton prices in August 1933 in part to the decreased buying by textile mills occasioned by the tax.

In a four-state Cotton Growers Conference at Columbia, South Carolina, representatives agreed that the processing tax "was the cause of the general deterioration of the cotton program." Subsequently Talmadge asked for the removal of the tax. The *Constitution* claimed that the processing tax and increased production costs to mills operating under the NRA's codes had forced the price up. Merchants were buying less because of the lower prices of competing fabrics and imported goods. The resulting build-up of inventory in the mills' warehouses forced the price of cotton down. All this resulted in lower profits for the farmer.[38]

Talmadge did not originally oppose the AAA. When it was first announced, he suggested that farmers go along with the plow-up, although he personally preferred the "cotton holiday" concept he had espoused the year before. His apprehension quickly solidified into virulent criticism, however, although he himself contracted for an acreage reduction on his own farm. He was supported in his attacks by two of his commissioners of agriculture, G. C. Adams and Tom Linder. Political opposition was also forthcoming from Eurith D. Rivers, who later as governor became the New Deal's chief advocate in the state. Despite this, the mass of Georgia farmers spoke compellingly in favor of the 1933 effort by accepting the 1934 program.[39]

In December 1933 and January 1934 county agents and county committees attended district meetings to study the cotton-reduction contracts for 1934-1935. The two-year contracts provided for a reduction of up to 45 percent of the base acreage, and a payment of 3.5 cents a pound on the average cotton yield on the entire farm during the period 1928-1932 up to $18.00 an acre. The contract also included a "parity payment" of 1 cent a pound for 1934 and 1.25 cents a pound for 1935 on farm allotments computed at 40 percent of the base acreage times the average yield thereon during the base period.

The 1933 program had been rushed and handled rather clumsily, but there was much more organization in 1934. Most of the county committees were carried over intact, so that members were familiar with what would be required of them. By January 23, county agents had held some 1,880 program meetings and expected a sign-up of 95 percent. A good part of their optimism had to do with the success of the 1933 program. Although this estimate was high, 81.2 percent did sign cotton contracts, placing Georgia fifth in the United States in percentage of cooperation. County administrations still encountered a vast amount of complicated paper work, but otherwise they were able to operate much more efficiently during the sign-up campaign for 1934.[40]

In order to attack the major problem of the 1933 program, that of delay, the AAA provided for the establishment of state Boards of Review to check contracts. Even with this added help, however, the state extension service was forced to ask for extra time to complete the sign-ups. This was partly because the board was receiving more contracts than it had originally estimated. Nevertheless, the first stage of the 1934 program was completed with relative efficiency and dispatch.[41]

The greatest difficulty in 1934 was that of acreage and yield allotments. Either the carelessness of local committeemen or producers in calculating average production and acreage for the base period, or the inadequate records kept on such phases of farm management, caused generally excessive estimates. L. H. Nelson, county agent of Grady County, found that cotton acreage estimates were 26 percent too high, and average production (in pounds) for the base period was 45 percent too high. Other counties reported similar conditions.[42]

When these counties found that they had gone considerably over the Department of Agriculture allotment figures, they rushed to adjust the contracts. In Grady County the task was so huge that committeemen had no time to investigate each contract and decided to make a flat cut across the board. Those who had purposefully overestimated their acreage and production received an unfair advantage. Honest farmers were so disillusioned by this development that many canceled their contracts.

The situation was particularly bad in Grady County. Even with this adjustment, the acreage was still about 300 acres and the production about 50,000 pounds too high. The county agent felt the farmers would never stand for another reduction, so he decided to make the cuts himself without telling anyone. He then resigned, leaving the new agent, Nelson, to face the farmers' wrath. Nelson finally managed to placate them, but not without considerable difficulty.[43]

The disparity of allotments had the same effect upon the counties as the administrative delays in the 1933 program. Some asked that their county agents be replaced. It was fortunate for the extension service that this demand was not too great, since it was becoming increasingly difficult to secure new agents with sufficient training and experience to carry out the complicated AAA programs. Many of the other new farm agencies were draining the personnel pool in staffing their own organizations.[45]

Many county agents expressed the same dissatisfactions in 1934 as in 1933, although the number of complaints was considerably reduced. AAA duties still encroached heavily on the agent's time, even though extension programs fared better than they had the previous year. One reason for this was that the number of assistants in county AAA offices rose in 1934.

The county agent was also called upon to cooperate with other New Deal agencies. In most cases the agent already served on the various emergency farm loan committees, but in 1934 his work expanded to the local rural relief committees that selected clients for the rural rehabilitation program. The extent of his commitment varied with the county and ranged from supplying records to actually serving on the committee itself.

Once the necessary adjustments had been made on the 1934 cotton contracts, committeemen began to check compliance much as they had in 1933. Some counties hired special supervisors to measure the rented acreage. They were somewhat hampered by a delay in the delivery of measuring chains, but otherwise the work went ahead smoothly. When the measurements were completed, the compliance forms were checked by the county agent and committee and sent to Washington where they were again checked and payments were disbursed. Generally, committeemen found that there was more accuracy than in 1933 in taking the required number of acres out of production. They also noted that the rented acres were being used only for crops allowed under the contract.[46]

As the AAA progressed, one of the main complaints heard from farmers was that some people benefited from the program without complying. So in January 1934, Wallace mailed 3,455 inquiries to Georgia committeemen and crop reporters to ascertain the farmers' feelings about the possibility of a compulsory program. Out of 2,184 tabulated reports, 89.9 percent returned by committeemen and 84.1 percent returned by crop reporters indicated that farmers favored compulsory controls. Of the committeemen and crop reporters themselves, 99.2 percent of the former and 96.1 percent of the latter favored compulsory cotton controls. Wallace used the national results to encourage passage of the Bankhead Cotton Control Bill.[47]

On April 21, 1934, the president signed the Bankhead Act. The AAA had asked for voluntary reduction of cotton; the Bankhead Act put a ginning tax on all cotton raised. The AAA then gave farmers tax exemption certificates to use in lieu of the tax for cotton within what would have been their production control allotment. The tax was prohibitive, set at 50 percent of the average central market price of seven-eighth-inch Middling spot cotton, and not less than five cents per pound. Wallace indicated that the act would be implemented if two-thirds of the cotton farmers of the country approved. Georgia farmers voted 86.4 percent in favor of the program, and the secretary put the plan into motion.[48]

The Bankhead Act, like the AAA, used the county extension office in its administration. Since most county agents were already swamped by their duties in regard to extension and AAA services, they decided to make greater use of the County Cotton Production Control Associations, as the county committees of 1933 came to be named. Their only difference was that in 1934 all members of the committee had to sign a reduction agreement. Later anyone who signed an agreement automatically became a member of the association. The Department of Agriculture provided that Assistant Cotton Adjusters could be hired in any county with over 250 cotton-producing farms as of the 1930 census. Unfortunately, there were so many counties in Georgia which met this qualification that the state allotment for salaries proved to be inadequate. Even though the department promised additional support, Extension Director Brown allowed smaller counties to combine. In this way, one assistant could serve two counties, and the state could operate with the limited funds.[49]

Preparation for implementation of the Bankhead Act proceeded in much the same way as did that for the 1934 reduction program. The extension service held meetings around the state for the county agents and county and local committees. There the act was explained so that these men could return to their counties to hold local meetings for the farmers. Although nonsigners of 1934 cotton-reduction contracts were eligible for tax-exemption certificates, the strong possibility of the passage of a compulsory cotton control bill in early 1934 made it much easier for county agents and committeemen to persuade farmers to sign the voluntary agreements.

When the farmers understood the Bankhead Act, they could make an application for exemption certificates. In cooperation with local committeemen and county agents, they computed their base acreage and average yield. The county committees checked the applications and sent them to a special state Allotment Board. When the board had received the applications from the counties, it computed allotments and issued tax-exemption certificates to the special assistants, who in turn passed them on to the farmers.

Farmers' estimates were almost uniformly too high, and the state Allotment Board reduced most of them. It appeared that the major reason for the high estimates was the inadequacy of farm records for the base period, 1928-1932. Some counties put the blame on the administration's method of collecting data. Although the act specifically stated that allotments would be determined solely by the production of cotton, many county agents suspected that economists had based their results on ginning figures, which were often the only records of production available. When Taylor County received a higher allotment than Macon County, Macon farmers were upset. Taylor County ginned much of Macon's cotton, and Taylor's soil was poorer than the soil in Macon. Catoosa County also ginned from 60 to 75 percent of its cotton outside of its borders. The county agent felt this was the reason Catoosa allotments were out of line with base production. Another reason allotments were less than farmer estimates was that, unlike the reduction contracts which were based on production and acreage, Bankhead allotments were predicated on production alone. This caused some confusion among Georgia's farmers.[50]

As a group, the smaller farmers, especially those whose cotton production was too low to sign reduction agreements, were hit hardest by the distribution of allotments. Even before the bill was passed, farmers who could not sign reduction agreements came to county agents to find out what their allotments would be in order that they might gauge how much to plant. In Catoosa County the agent discussed the matter with the county committee and the state Extension Director, then advised farmers to plant no more than four acres to a mule. In some counties farmers had previously voluntarily cut their acreage, and in others the acreage for the base years had been seriously restricted by the boll weevil. These farmers produced one or two bales of cotton, barely enough to "pay taxes and to furnish some necessities for the farm and home." When the state Allotment Board informed them that they must reduce their production even further, they were affected out of proportion to the larger grower. Regardless of the reason why their acreage was small, the farmers who produced two bales or less were thus uniformly hurt by the act.[51]

Senator Richard B. Russell, Jr., received numerous complaints from these people and passed them on to Wallace. The senator maintained that allotment boards were acting "in direct contravention of paragraph 3, subsection A to Section 7 of the Bankhead Act" which stated that the Secretary of Agriculture should not penalize those farmers who had voluntarily reduced their acreage. Governor Talmadge and Senator Walter George also protested the act's effect on the small farmer. Late in the fall of 1934, Roosevelt reacted by modifying the ginning tax so that it would not apply to farmers cultivating less than five acres or harvesting fewer than two bales of cotton. For the 1935 crop the AAA included a special provision stating that "any farm on which cotton was planted in any year after 1927 and before 1935 and the allotment basis is 956 pounds [two bales] or less, the allotment shall be 100 percent, or if the allotment on any farm planting in this period comes to less than 956 pounds, the allotment shall be 956 pounds."[52]

Another factor which displeased southern farmers was the late passage of the act. Most had planted by the time the act was signed. Those who had not made reduction agreements, but had followed their county agent's advice in restricting their crop, found that they were allotted less than they would produce. Some of those farmers who did sign agreements put cotton on their best lands so that their production allotments also were less than what they actually produced. Even the farmers who were very careful and considered production rather than acreage in deciding how much cotton to sow, as some county agents had suggested, discovered that, when allotments were cut by the state board, they had to either destroy or store their excess crop.[53]

As in 1933 there were complaints of inaccuracies by farmers and of favoritism by committeemen and county agents. In some counties agents made subsequent allotment cuts across the board without consulting the county committee or the farmers. This policy worked to the disadvantage of those who had made conservative estimates of their production.[54]

Farmers also accused county committees of favoritism in distributing allotments. A Duluth, Georgia, farmer wrote that in his county some farmers were producing about 20 percent more than their allotments. The total production for the county would not be 20 percent over the county allotment, however, because many farmers had received allotments "considerably over their yields." The farmer blamed the county committee for this inequitable situation. The AAA's response to charges such as these was to tell the farmer to complain to the county committee or county agent — the very people accused of the infraction.[55]

In general, few farmers of any size were entirely happy with their allotments. In some counties the board had cut estimated allotments over 50 percent. A rural sociologist in Georgia at the time concluded that the Bankhead Act "tended to make permanent the depression of the '20's by fixing the allotment of tax-free bales on the basis of crops in recent years. Idle lands can't be brought back to cultivation." A farmer from Milner, Georgia, wrote to the editor of the Atlanta *Constitution* to say that the boll weevil had cut his crop 50 percent in the five-year base period. When asked to sign up, he checked his records and found that his allotment would come to a reduction of 66 percent for the base period.[56]

When county committees or farmers were dissatisfied with the allotments, they could complain to the state Board of Review. This provision was useless, however, since any revisions would invariably cause production figures to exceed the census statistics. Even when the county was able to provide "indisputable proof of production" and the state Board of Review was satisfied that the allotment was too small, nothing could be done. Since the board could not exceed the state allotment, raising one county's quota would mean cutting that of another county, a move the board was unwilling to make.[57]

The majority of complaints which the state Board of Review received dealt with individual or county allotments. There were few charges of one farmer getting more than another, except in cases where the county agent and county committee might be involved. The universally low allotments brought an avalanche of complaints upon the head of the county agent. In their 1934 annual reports, most agents noted that this was the most serious problem they had encountered. The situation grew so serious in Cobb County, where the individual allotment was only 47.5 percent of the originally accepted base, that the agent suffered a nervous breakdown.[58]

Supposedly, the state Allotment Board could remedy inequitable allotments by use of a 10 percent state reserve. The reserve allotment (10 percent of the total state allotment) was to be used "to take care of new farmers or other farmers who have made drastic reduction in their cotton acreage and are not now cultivating more than 30 percent of their land in cotton." The board could not release the reserve until the regular allotment had been distributed, and this was not completed at the end of August. Senator Russell, who had received many complaints and inquiries, finally called for the immediate release of Georgia's reserve late in September. By October, farmer reaction began to improve.[59]

Once all contracts had been completed and farmers had agreed to the reduced allotments, the state Allotment Board could begin issuing ginning certificates. Because of the late passage of the act and Georgia's early season, the board was not ready at harvest time. Therefore, the AAA allowed it to issue "interim certificates" up to 50 percent of the estimated allotment so the farmer could begin ginning his crop. Still, the lag caused by the early harvest, the late issuance of ginning certificates, and the delay in rental and benefit reduction payments evoked much dissatisfaction, especially in the southern part of the state. Some farmers, moreover, did not realize that the interim certificates represented only a part of their allotment and complained that their quota had been reduced further.[60]

The bulk of the certificates were finally released in late October and November. Farmers who were not satisfied that certificates were arriving fast enough pressured their county agents into going to Athens to get them personally. When most of them had been distributed, some farmers found that they still had raised more than their allotment and would have to pay the high tax, while some had raised less than their allotment and were left with surplus certificates.[61]

Although the certificates originally were not transferable outside a particular county, there was no rule about selling them within the county. In some areas, farmers with more cotton than certificates attempted to "discredit the value of surplus certificates" in order to purchase them cheaply and avoid the tax. This led county agents and committees to cooperate with the AAA in setting the price for surplus certificates at four cents a pound. Over-producing farmers were able to sell extra cotton at a small loss, and farmers whose crops may have been damaged received some compensation. The AAA later set up a national pool so that inter-county and interstate transfers might be made. The county agent acted as intermediary for the pool, arranging transfers and recording them, and Georgia farmers made liberal use of it, since all of their crop was in.[62]

There was never any way to quantify the number of times farmers and ginners violated laws regarding illegal certificates, profiteering, and failure to comply with regulations, but the AAA received enough complaints to send R. C. Stockdale as a field representative to investigate. He reported "a very small number of attempts at sharp practices" in Georgia. Furthermore, 80 percent of the failures to comply with regulations were due to government workers whose bad attitude or misinformation caused illegal sale of certificates. He found "no indications of any effort at profiteering by importing Florida or Alabama certificates," although there was some "cross line ginning by producers using their own certificates." In cases where gins were accused of illegal actions he reported that most of the problems arose out of ignorance and not intent. He noted, "One cannot help feeling like complimenting Georgia on the situation."[63]

Although farmers had signed Bankhead contracts for two years, the secretary of agriculture decided to hold a referendum late in 1934 to sound out farmer sentiment. AAA officials in Georgia were apprehensive about such a referendum's chances for success. There had been a great deal of criticism and dissatisfaction with the act thus far.

In mid-November, district "outlook" meetings took place where extension workers and AAA officials explained the procedures for handling the referendum. An estimated 220,377 Georgia farmers were eligible to vote. As the time for the referendum grew close, AAA officials became more optimistic about a favorable vote. Farmers now had received the 10 percent reserve along with interim or regular ginning certificates. Also the rental and benefit payments from the reduction agreements had begun to arrive.

Some farmers were still not happy, but would vote for continuation anyway. The reduction contracts they had signed would run through 1935, and they wanted to be sure that independent farmers would not benefit from the sacrifices made by agreement signers. Large farmers were "advising" their tenants (including blacks) to vote in favor of the act. Some planters told their tenants that "if the Bankhead plan failed to pass, they would plant no cotton next year." For their part, black owners and cash renters favored the plan anyway, and tenants were inclined to follow the wishes of the landlord. One gray-haired Negro remarked, "We don't vote much, but we likes to."[64]

Governor Talmadge, who opposed all of the government's agricultural programs, advised against voting for the act. When Georgia farmers went against his wishes, it was his "first significant defeat by his 'fellow countrymen.'" Subsequently he remarked, "there was a stream of Negroes voting, who did not own an acre of land, or a plow or an ox."[65]

Georgia farmers endorsed the Bankhead Act by a substantial margin. Out of 146,346 voting, 126,947 or 86.8 percent favored continuation. The national vote was somewhat greater at 89.4 percent in favor, but Georgia farmers had given Wallace the two-thirds majority he sought.[66] To the suggestion that there be compulsory controls on all cotton producers, over 98 percent in all states, including Georgia, agreed. Over 85 percent of the voting Georgia farmers said they would cooperate in such controls. Of those counties which opposed the act, five in the northern part of the state were heavily Republican. Four counties in the north and three on the coast raised almost no cotton and did not vote. Talmadge had been clearly defeated by a margin of six to one, but he did not give up. In a letter to Wallace he claimed that less than two-thirds of the Georgia farmers eligible to vote did so. Wallace replied that the referendum had not been legally required in the first place. Since a large percentage of farmers in the country did vote, however, and over two-thirds of those agreed to compulsory controls, this justified the conclusion that two-thirds of all cotton producers favored continuation. A later study buttressed Wallace's position. In Georgia 66.4 percent of those eligible had voted in the referendum, while only 17.1 percent of those eligible had voted in the last presidential election.[67]

Wallace claimed that the vote represented an endorsement of the program. What he did not say was that certain extenuating circumstances had led farmers to support it. Farmers generally had been able to purchase all of the surplus certificates they desired because a very poor crop in the states of the western cotton region balanced the heavy eastern yields. A drought in the summer of 1934 had seriously reduced western yields, and very few, if any, Georgia farmers had to pay the 50 percent ginning tax on excess production. Arthur Raper sounded an ominous note when he said that "there is something sinister in legislation implemented by droughts!"[68]

Although farmers had supported the program, they were not without suggestions for the AAA. The most common advice concerned allotments. Many farmers still believed that they had received an unfair quota. No one particular solution was offered in preference to others, but all those who protested agreed that there should be a change. County agents suggested that allotments be distributed in February, before the March planting. This plea reflected the continuing timing problem which was especially crucial to the southernmost states.[69]

Criticism continued to be aimed more at the Bankhead Act than at the reduction program in 1935. In both cases farmers seemed happier than they had been in 1934—the result of a greater understanding of the programs by the farmer and smoother procedural arrangements in the county agent's office. Those who opposed the programs on principle did not relent in their attacks, however. Governor Talmadge, their most noted Georgia critic, asked the United States District Court in October 1935 to enjoin the United States district attorney from prosecuting farmers for failure to pay the ginning tax. When federal Justice Gascom Deaner ruled against him, the governor instructed the state attorney general to file a petition with the Supreme Court on the grounds that cotton grown on 160 acres of state prison farmland could not be marketed since the state was not a contractor. The Supreme Court accepted the suit, but before it could be heard the Court ruled the AAA and Bankhead Act unconstitutional in the Butler Case.[70]

Because the bulk of Georgia farmers who wished to accept the two-year reduction program had done so in 1934 and the Bankhead program also ran for two years, the county agent's work was somewhat reduced in 1935. Even so, agents still found little time for extension duties. By this time most had become rather stoical about the situation, however, and began to think in terms of what the AAA might do for the extension program rather than vice versa. There were now more county agents than ever before, and they were receiving much more help in terms of personnel and office machinery.

AAA work always occupied the bulk of the agent's time. District Agent J. A. Johnson noted that the transition had come about so quickly that no way to measure its success had been devised. With the flood of forms coming into the office filled with statistics of every conceivable nature, the agent found it difficult to evaluate the year's work. The district agents themselves, who were supposed to supervise the county agents, could devote little time to them because of their own part in AAA programs. But the mere fact that county and district agents were beginning to stand back and analyze the program, rather than being completely caught up in it, indicated that the pressure was decreasing.[71]

Indirectly, the AAA had caused an increase in the agent's extension work. Farmers whom he had first reached in 1933 for AAA participation were now looking to the agent for extension services. This was a mixed blessing. The agent was glad to have so much interest; it certainly made his position all the more prestigious. One agent noted that he could no longer "walk down the street on a scheduled time for farmers calling us. Fancy this ten years ago!" All this new attention, however, meant increased demands on the agent who was still called upon to aid the

Farm Credit Administration, the Rural Resettlement Division, the Soil Conservation Service, and the Works Progress Administration. Agents in nine northern counties also cooperated in Tennessee Valley Authority farm demonstration work.[72]

If county and district agents were beseiged by all their duties, the state extension office was in no better condition. Its specialists continued to be siphoned off by the AAA. But the extension service managed to continue its programs, and even to expand some of them. Kenneth Traenor, extension economist, successfully used the AAA record books to extend the service's farm management program. He distributed about 100,000 AAA record books early in 1935. Later he cooperated with a WPA project to gather and analyze them. Also by 1935 the extension service's crop diversification program had begun to proliferate on the acres which farmers had rented to the government.[73]

By 1935 the state's agricultural activities were coalescing. The extension service, through its county agents, was ready to approach farmers about a long-term program based on the results of the AAA. It organized Program Planning Group Discussions in the counties. Farmers gathered to consider outlook information, trends in the production of farm commodities, increase and decrease in the number of farms, and the agricultural make-up of the county in order to formulate long-range plans. The discussions were meant to eventually replace the "mechanically worked out" program of the AAA with a "more organic" system.

The county agent's increased optimism was reflected in farmer sentiment. Criticism of the program dropped precipitously in 1935. Higher incomes were partially responsible for this enthusiasm but there was also a growing appreciation for peripheral benefits, such as diversification, which accompanied the AAA. Of course, some were never satisfied. A Fayette County farmer assaulted a member of his County Cotton Control Association, because he was dissatisfied with his rental contract. Fortunately such occurrences were limited.[74]

Despite the obvious pleasure of Georgia farmers, Governor Talmadge continued his assault on the New Deal. Tom Linder, the governor's commissioner of agriculture, carried the attack to the AAA. Following a vicious anti-Roosevelt threat that "if the yoke of Rooseveltism cannot be thrown off any other way, Georgia can secede from the Union," the Atlanta *Constitution* castigated Linder. Linder, in true Talmadge fashion, replied, "If the *Constitution* thinks that a fight to keep the state of

Georgia a white man's state and to keep the Democratic Party a white man's party Quixotic, then I am indeed a Don Quixote. . . . The question of assault on a white woman by negroes and other race questions may not be serious to the *Constitution*. It is of supreme importance to the men and women who live on the farms and in the rural section of Georgia, who work in the fields unprotected to raise food and clothing for those in the cities."[75]

This editorial trading of barbs evoked petitions of support and condemnation from rural counties. Most chose Roosevelt over Talmadge, but the governor was not to be stopped. In speeches around the state and in his newspaper, the *Statesman,* he continued to attack the AAA and Roosevelt.[76]

Talmadge's tactics seemed to evoke only more public support for Roosevelt and the AAA. In May 1935 county meetings were held to select representatives to join a national farmers' delegation which planned to go to Washington and tell Roosevelt personally how much they liked the farm programs. Personnel of the extension service aided in arranging the meetings, but Extension Director Brown made it clear that they were not a part of extension activities. Five hundred Georgia farmers made the trip to Washington to join 2,500 other southern farmers to ask Roosevelt to keep the processing tax and the control program. Of course, not all farmers agreed with this delegation. Talmadge received a number of letters requesting Wallace's resignation as secretary of agriculture and supporting the governor's stand.[77]

Perhaps the ultimate reason for the reduction plan's popularity lay in the benefits to farmers. The extension service state summary report for 1935 showed that Georgia farmers had received $27,555,871 in rentals and benefits on cotton programs through the end of that year. The price of cotton had risen during this period, and the agricultural situation seemed to be improving. With all of his charisma, Talmadge could not fight prosperity. The more he was rebuffed, the wilder his tactics became. At one point he stored 500 bushels of wheat at the executive mansion in Atlanta saying that if he milled it, he would have to pay the processing tax.[78]

As his forays increased, so did popular support of the New Deal farm programs. When the Supreme Court decided that the AAA was unconstitutional in January 1936, Talmadge rejoiced, but the extension service was already looking for ways to continue the cotton program, and the farmers were asking for more, rather than fewer, compulsory controls.

NOTES

1. Willard Range, *A Century of Georgia Agriculture, 1850-1950* (Athens: University of Georgia Press, 1954), pp. 175-77. Everette E. Edwards, "Memorandum Concerning the Campaigns in 1905, 1915, 1921, and 1927 to Decrease the Cotton Acreage" (Washington, USDA, Bureau of Agricultural Economics, 1930). Rupert B. Vance, *Human Factors in Cotton Culture* (Chapel Hill: University of North Carolina Press, 1929), p. 188. Gilbert C. Fite, "Voluntary Attempts to Reduce Cotton Acreage in the South, 1914-1933," *Journal of Southern History*, XIV, 4 (November 1948), 499. Arthur F. Raper, *Tenants of the Almighty* (New York: The Macmillan Co., 1943), p. 193.

2. Range, *Century*, pp. 185, 197. Arthur F. Raper, *Preface to Peasantry* (Chapel Hill: University of North Carolina Press, 1936), p. 246. Georgia Crop Reporting Service, *Agricultural Facts, 1900-1956*, Bulletin No. 511 (July 1957), 9.

3. Raper, *Tenants*, pp. 166-75. Range, *Century*, pp. 185-92.

4. Harold Tyler, "Every Farmer Prosperous," *The Saturday Evening Post*, CCIV, 11 (September 12, 1931), 51, 152-54. Range, *Century*, p. 183. Also see annual narrative reports of county agents, 1933, NARG 33, Federal Extension Service, microfilm reel 58.

5. Sarah B. G. Temple, *The First Hundred Years: A Short History of Cobb County, in Georgia* (Atlanta: Walter W. Brown Publishing Company, 1935), p. 492.

6. W. S. Elliot, "Georgia Banker-Farmer Cooperation," *Manufacturers Record*, CII, 5 (May 1933), 42.

7. Range, *Century*, p. 177. *The New York Times*, November 23, 1933.

8. E. G. Nourse, J. S. Davis, and J. D. Blank, *Three Years of the AAA*, Brookings Institution, Institute of Economics, Publication No. 73 (1937), 95.

9. Cully Cobb to C. B. Smith, October 7, 1937, NARG 33, Correspondence, box 553.

10. John T. Wheeler, *Two Hundred Years of Agricultural Education in Georgia*. (Danville, Illinois: The Interstate Printers and Publishers, 1948), p. 254. Gladys Baker, *The County Agent* (Chiago: University of Chicago Press, 1939), pp. 70, 74, 75.

11. Baker, *County Agent*, pp. 25, 32, 40, 45.

12. Interview with Ralph Fulghum (former Director of Information for the Georgia Extension Service), August 6, 1968. Baker, *County Agent*, pp. 75-6. Annual poultry report of R. J. Richardson, 1933. NARG 33, microfilm reel 58. See county agents' reports, 1933, NARG 33, microfilm reel 57.

13. Baker, *County Agent*, pp. 75-6. Interview with Ralph Fulghum.

Bonita Golda Harrison, "Racial Factors Attending the Function of the New Deal in the South" (unpublished M. A. thesis, Department of Sociology, Atlanta University, 1936), p. 87. See county agents' reports, 1933, NARG 33, microfilm reels 57, 61.

14. Harry Brown, "Attitude of Georgia Cotton Farmers Toward Possible Provisions of Recently Enacted Farm Relief Legislation," May 29, 1933, NARG 145, Agricultural Stabilization and Conservation Service, AAA, Production Control Program, box 31. Atlanta *Constitution*, June 22, 23, 28, and 30 and July 3, 1933. George N. Peek to Walter P. Hines, August 8, 1933, NARG 145, General Correspondence, Richard B. Russell, Jr. (1933-35).

15. Interview with W. A. Minor, Jr. (former Georgia State Extension Service official), September 12, 1968. See county agents' reports, 1933, NARG 33, microfilm reel 59. Annual narrative county agent's report for Early County, Georgia, 1933, NARG 33, microfilm reel 60. Annual narrative report of W. V. Chafin, county agent for Pierce County, Georgia, 1933, NARG 33, microfilm reel 62. Annual report of M.W.H. Collins, county agent for Bartow County, 1933, NARG 33, microfilm reel 58. Annual report of Louis C. Walker, county agent for Appling County, 1933, NARG 33, microfilm reel 58.

16. Annual report of M.W.H. Collins, emergency agricultural assistant for Gordon County, 1933, NARG 33, microfilm reel 60. Interview with Arthur F. Raper, September 13, 1968.

17. Annual report of N. D. McRainey, county agent for Baker County, 1933, NARG 33, microfilm reel 58.

18. Annual report of D. F. Hungerford, county agent for Coweta County, 1933, NARG 33, microfilm reel 59.

19. See county agents' reports, 1933, NARG 33, microfilm reel 60.

20. Annual report of George H. Firor on Project 10-Horticulture, 1933, NARG 33, microfilm reel 57. Annual report of M. W. Lowry on the Soils Extension Project, 1933, NARG 33, microfilm reel 57. Harry Brown to C. W. Warburton, February 1, 1934, NARG 33, Corres. (1934), box 235. Wheeler, *Two Hundred Years,* p. 254.

21. Baker, *County Agent,* p. 79. Warburton to J. P. Campbell, July 7, 1933, NARG 33, Corres. (1933), drawer 215.

22. Atlanta *Constitution,* July 14, 23, and 25 and August 24, 1933. "Instructions to County Agents," 1933, NARG 33, microfilm reel 57. Annual report of J. P. Baker, county agent for Chatooga County, 1933, NARG 33, microfilm reel 59. Byron Dyer to Reuben Brigham, August 7, 1933, NARG 33, Corres. (1934), box 235. C. H. Alvord to R. F. Croom, August 29, 1933, NARG 145, Alphabetical Correspondence, drawer 267.

23. Interview with Arthur Raper. Atlanta *Constitution,* July 25, 1933.

24. Annual report of J. P. Baker, county agent for Chatooga County, 1933, NARG 33, microfilm reel 59. Annual report of C. B. Gladdin, county agent for Douglass County, 1933, NARG 33, microfilm reel 60.

25. Annual report of M. W. Lowry on the Soils Extension Project, 1933, NARG 33, microfilm reel 57. Annual report of C. B. Gladdin, 1933, NARG 33, microfilm reel 60. Annual report of A. J. Nitzschke, county agent for Lamar County, 1933, NARG 33, microfilm reel 61. Annual report of D. F. Hungerford, county agent for Coweta County, 1933, NARG 33, microfilm reel 59. See county agents' reports, 1933, microfilm reels 60-61.

26. "Acreage Adjustment Program: Commercial Fertilizer Used on Cotton," June 4, 1945, NARG 145, Prod. Contr. Prog., box 41. Cobb. to Campbell, August 24, 1933, NARG 145, Alpha. Corres. Campbell to Cobb, August 28, 1933, NARG 145, Alpha. Corres. (1933-35), drawer 79.

27. Annual report of L. S. Watson, county agent for Clarke County, 1933, NARG 33, microfilm reel 59. Report of G. V. Cunningham, 1933, NARG 33, microfilm reel 62. Henry A. Wallace to Senator Richard B. Russell, Jr., September 19, 1933, NARG 145, Gen. Corres., Russell (1933-35).

28. Atlanta *Constitution,* September 23, 1933. Annual report of T. L. Asbury, district agent of district No. 1, 1933, NARG 33, microfilm reel 58.

29. Annual report of A. J. Nitzschke, county agent for Lamar County, 1933, NARG 33, microfilm reel 61. Annual report of L. C. Walker, county agent for Appling County, 1933, NARG 33, microfilm reel 58. Baker, *County Agent,* pp. 117-118. Annual report of L. I. Skinner, district agent of district No. 4, 1933, NARG 33, microfilm reel 58. See county agents' reports, 1933, NARG 33, microfilm reel 60.

30. Walter S. Brown to J. A. Evans, November 3, 1933, NARG 33, Corres. (1934), box 235. Interview with Ralph Fulghum. *The Georgia Extension News,* I, 1 (June 1934), 1.

31. *The Georgia Extension News,* I, 1 (June 1934), 1. Annual report of W. T. Bennett, county agent for Wilcox County, 1933, microfilm reel 63.

32. Annual report for Oglethorpe and other counties, 1933, NARG 33, microfilm reels 57, 60.

33. Interview with Ralph Fulghum.

34. Unsigned report, 1933, NARG 145, Prod. Contr. Prog., box 96. J. A. Evans to Campbell, January 25, 1934, NARG 33, Corres. (1934), box 235.

35. D. L. Floyd to Genung, December 19, 1933 (report), Federal

Records Center, East Point, Georgia, RG 136, U.S.D.A., Agricultural Estimates Division, box 92356. Atlanta *Constitution,* February 1, 1934. Roy E. Fossett, "The Impact of the New Deal on Georgia Politics, 1933-1941" (unpublished Ph.D. dissertation, Department of Political Science, University of Florida, 1960), pp. 85-6. Calvin B. Hoover and Bryce U. Ratchford, *Economic Resources and Policies of the South* (New York: Macmillan, 1951), p. 54. John L. Fulmer, "The Effect of Domestic Policy on the Southern Agricultural Problems," *Southern Economic Journal,* XVIII, 1 (July 1951), 13.

36. "Cotton Production Adjustment," December 15, 1933, NARG 145, Prod. Contr. Prog. (1934-35), box 39. Fossett, "Impact of the New Deal," pp. 85-6.

37. Annual report of E. C. Westbrook, extension officer, 1933, NARG 33, microfilm reel 58. Henry I. Richards, *Cotton and the AAA* (Washington: The Brookings Institution, 1936), pp. 36, 37, 39, 40, 41, 45, 47.

38. Atlanta *Constitution,* August 15 and 23, 1933. Fossett, "The Impact of the New Deal," pp. 84-5.

39. *Statesman,* II, 26 (July 1, 1933); II, 37 (September 18, 1933). Sarah M. Lemmon, "The Public Career of Eugene Talmadge: 1926-36" (unpublished Ph.D. dissertation, Department of History, University of North Carolina, 1952), p. 189. *The New York Times,* July 2, 1933. Atlanta *Constitution,* June 6 and 17, September 24, and November 3, 1933.

40. Nourse, *et al., Three Years of the AAA,* p. 95. "Cotton Production Adjustment," January 23, 1934, NARG 145, Prod. Contr. Prog. (1934-35), box 39, Annual report for Banks County, 1934, NARG 33, microfilm reel 64. U.S.D.A., AAA, *Participation under AAA programs, 1933-1935* (Washington: United States Government Printing Office, 1938), p. 14.

41. Cobb to Harry Brown, January 17, 1934, NARG 145, Alpha. Corres. (1933-35), drawer 68. J. A. Evans to C. L. Chambers, January 31, 1934, NARG 33, Corres. (1934), box 235.

42. Annual report of L. S. Watson, county agent for Clarke County, 1934, NARG 33, microfilm reel 65. Annual report of W. R. Carswell, county agent for Early County, 1934, NARG 33, microfilm reel 66. Annual report of L. H. Nelson, county agent for Grady County, 1934, NARG 33, microfilm reel 66.

43. Annual report of L. H. Nelson, 1934, NARG 33, microfilm reel 66.

44. Annual report of L. I. Skinner, district agent of district No. 4, 1934, NARG 33, microfilm reel 64.

45. J. I. Langdale to Warburton, October 19, 1934, NARG 33, Corres., box 317. Warburton to Langdale, October 24, 1934, NARG 33, Corres., box 317.

46. Annual report of J. A. Johnson, district agent of district No. 3,

1934, NARG 33, microfilm reel 64. Raper, *Preface*, p. 246. Atlanta
Constitution, April 12, 1934.
   47. "Cotton Production Adjustment," April 24, 1934, NARG 145,
Prod. Contr. Prog. (1934-35), box 39.
   48. Fossett, "Impact of the New Deal," p. 87. AAA, *Annual Report*
(1934), pp. 351-8. AAA, *Report* (1933-35), p. 128.
   49. Annual report of L. V. Cawley, county agent for Effingham
County, 1934, NARG 33, microfilm reel 66. Cobb to H. Brown, June 13,
1934, NARG 145, Alpha. Corres. (1933-35), drawer 68. H. Brown to
C. H. Alvord, August 16, 1934, NARG 145, Alpha Corres. (1933-35),
drawer 68. Alvord to Brown, August 22, 1934, NARG 145, Alpha. Corres.
(1933-35), drawer 68. Cobb to W. S. Brown, April 20, 1934, NARG
145, Alpha. Corres. (1933-35), drawer 27. Annual county agents' reports,
1934, NARG 33, microfilm reel 64.
   50. Atlanta *Constitution*, June 23, 1934. Annual county agents' reports,
1934, NARG 33, microfilm reel 67. Wallace to A. E. Wilson, March 16,
1934, NARG 145, Gen. Corres., Russell (1933-35). Also see other letters
to Russell in same file. Cunningham to Wallace, October 16, 1935,
NARG 145, Alpha. Corres. (1933-35), Ga. St. Bd. of Rev., drawer
75. Annual report of J. P. Nicholson, county agent for Catoosa County,
1934, NARG 33, microfilm reel 65.
   51. Annual report of J. P. Nicholson, 1934, NARG 33, microfilm
reel 65. Annual report of L. V. Cawley, county agent for Effingham
County, 1934, NARG 33, microfilm reel 66. Raper, *Preface*, p. 349.
Annual report of L. S. Watson, county agent for Clarke County, 1934,
NARG 33, microfilm reel 65.
   52. Atlanta *Constitution*, September 20, 1934. Wallace to Russell,
April 19, 1935, NARG 145, Gen. Corres., Russell (1933-35). Russell to
Wallace, August 30, 1934 (telegram), NARG 145, Gen. Corres., Russell
(1933-35).
   53. Annual report of J. P. Nicholson, county agent for Catoosa County,
1934, NARG 33, microfilm reel 65. Annual report for Ben Hill County,
1935, NARG 33, microfilm reel 71. Atlanta *Constitution*, June 23, 1934.
   54. See letters to Senator Russell, NARG 145, Gen. Corres., Russell
(1933-35). Annual report of B. M. Drake, county agent for Cobb County,
1934, NARG 33, microfilm reel 65. Annual county agents' reports,
1934, NARG 33, microfilm reel 67.
   55. D. W. Wilson to Russell, October 27, 1934, NARG 145, Gen.
Corres., Russell (1933-35).
   56. Atlanta *Constitution*, September 21, 1934. Raper, *Preface*,
p. 253. Raper, *Tenants*, p. 216.
   57. Cunningham to Cobb, April 17, 1934, NARG 145, Gen. Corres.,

Russell (1933-35). Cunningham to Cobb, April 19, 1935, NARG 145, Alpha. Corres. (1933-35), St. Bd. of Rev., drawer 75. J. Ross Bell to Cunningham, April 27, 1935, NARG 145, Alpha. Corres. (1933-35), Ga. St. Bd. of Rev., drawer 75.

58. Annual report of B. M. Drake, county agent for Cobb County, 1934, NARG 33, microfilm reel 65.

59. C. H. Alvord to Cunningham, May 14, 1934, NARG 145, Alpha. Corres. (1933-35), Ga. St. Bd. of Rev., drawer 75. Atlanta *Constitution,* September 25, 1934. Chester C. Davis to Russell, September 28, 1934, NARG 145, Gen. Corres., Russell (1933-35).

60. Cobb to Russell, August 17, 1934, NARG 145, Gen. Corres., Russell (1933-35).

61. J. A. Evans to M. M. Thayer, October 11, 1934, NARG 33, Corres., box 316.

62. Annual report of L. H. Nelson, county agent for Grady County, 1934, NARG 33, microfilm reel 66. M. L. Wilson to Russell, October 4, 1934, NARG 145, Gen. Corres., Russell (1933-35). Wallace to Russell, October 22, 1934, NARG 145, Gen. Corres., Russell (1933-35). Annual report of Earl M. Varner, county agent for Glascock County, 1934, NARG 33, microfilm reel 66. Atlanta *Constitution,* November 24, 1934.

63. Cunningham to E. L. Deal, January 5, 1934, NARG 145, Alpha. Corres. (1933-35), Ga. St. Bd. of Rev., drawer 75. R. C. Stockdale to R. F. Croom, May 5, 1935, NARG 145, Alpha. Corres. (1933-35), drawer 432. Stockdale to Croom, April 19, 1935, NARG 145, Alpha. Corres. (1933-35), drawer 432.

64. Annual report of Donald Leroy Branyon, county agent for Berrien County, 1934, NARG 33, microfilm reel 64. Raper, *Preface,* pp. 249-50. Annual county agents' reports, 1934, NARG 33, microfilm reel 67. Unsigned report, December 15, 1934, NARG 44, NEC, Digests (1935-37), box 487. Fossett, "Impact of the New Deal," pp. 89-90. David E. Conrad, *The Forgotten Farmer.* (Urbana: University of Illinois Press, 1965), p. 63.

65. Lemmon, "The Public Career of Eugene Talmadge," p. 190. Fossett, "Impact of the New Deal," p. 89. Atlanta *Constitution,* December 15, 1934.

66. Raper, *Preface,* pp. 250-1. AAA, *Annual Report* (1934), p. 54.

67. "Cotton Questionnaire," NARG 145, Prod. Contr. Prog., box 44. Eugene Talmadge to Wallace, December 22, 1934, NARG 145, Gen. Corres. (1937-38), drawer 72. Wallace to Talmadge, January 4, 1935, NARG 145, Gen. Corres. (1937-38), drawer 72. "Revised Statement of Voters Eligible to Participate in Bankhead Referendum, with Some Comparisons," February 9, 1935, NARG 145, Prod. Contr. Prog., box 44.

68. Raper, *Preface,* p. 251.

69. M. J. Paulik to Congressman Braswell Dean, January 18, 1935, NARG 145, Gen. Corres., Russell (1933-35). Annual report of L. H. Nelson, 1934, NARG 33, microfilm reel 66.

70. Lemmon, "The Public Career of Eugene Talmadge," p. 224. *The New York Times,* October 27 and November 19, 1935. Atlanta *Constitution,* November 15 and 16, 1935.

71. Annual report of L. I. Skinner, district agent of district No. 4, 1935, NARG 33, microfilm reel 71. Annual report of J. A. Johnson, 1935, NARG 33, microfilm reel 71.

72. Annual report of L. I. Skinner, 1935, NARG 33, microfilm reel 71. Annual report of L. R. Langley, county agent for Baldwin County, 1935, NARG 33, microfilm reel 71.

73. Annual report of Kenneth Traenor, extension economist in farm management, 1935, NARG 33, microfilm reel 70.

74. Annual report of J. A. Johnson, 1935, NARG 33, microfilm reel 71. Annual county agents' reports, 1935, NARG 33, microfilm reel 71. Atlanta *Constitution,* November 12, 1935. Unsigned report, June 4 and 18, 1935, NARG 44, Digests, box 488. Alvord to Cunningham, April 24, 1935, NARG 145, Alpha. Corres. (1933-35), Ga. St. Bd. of Rev., drawer 75.

75. Atlanta *Constitution,* April 25, 27, and 29, 1935.

76. Lemmon, "The Public Career of Eugene Talmadge," p. 223.

77. See issues of the Atlanta *Constitution* during May 1935. Atlanta *Journal,* May 7, 1935. *Georgia Extension News,* II, 11 (May 1935), 1. Atlanta *Constitution,* September 5, 1935.

78. Annual state summary of extension activities, 1935, NARG 33, microfilm reel 70. Lemmon, "The Public Career of Eugene Talmadge," p. 222. AAA, *Report* (1933-35), p. 296. See Appendix, Table 18.

8

The Back Door for Cotton and the Also Rans

AFTER THE FALL

The Supreme Court's decision in *U. S.* v. *Butler* early in 1936 came as a shock, not only to farmers, but to the AAA itself. Agriculture Department leaders had expected a decision against the processing tax and had prepared the necessary legislation to transform it into a levy purely for revenue. When the Court ruled against the entire program, they found themselves without an immediate alternative.[1]

Georgia farmers and extension workers shared these feelings. The extension service adopted a "stand still" attitude, and upon instructions from the AAA, Harry Brown informed county agents to take charge of all Production Control Association forms, records, and property. Farmers were disappointed and apprehensive about farm prices. They feared that without a crop-reduction program they quickly would slip back into a depressed condition.[2]

In a series of January meetings, farmers and extension workers supported a control program and asked Brown to so inform the AAA. In the extension offices, the staff hastily laid plans for a state program should the federal government fail to act. Washington agriculturists were likewise designing a reduction system that would be constitutional.[3]

Actually, the crisis was not as great as it seemed. One group in the Department of Agriculture had long supported the use of soil-conservation practices as a method of achieving crop control. These men had obtained the legal machinery necessary to advance their ideas with the passage

of the Soil Conservation Act in April 1935. This act set up the Soil
Conservation Service (SCS) superseding the Soil Erosion Service. When
the AAA was declared unconstitutional, they suggested their program
as an alternative.

Reaction to the idea in the Department of Agriculture and in the
state extension service was immediate and favorable. The plan appeared
feasible, and some sort of program was desperately needed before the
1936 planting season began. Some extension workers in the northern
states preferred this new plan to the old production control system.
Southerners such as Cully Cobb were not so happy with the conservation
angle, but realizing that it was workable, endorsed it.[4]

When news of the pending legislation reached the state, farmers again
met to discuss it. Wallace asked the Program Planning Committees, first
set up in 1935, to consider the proposal and make suggestions for its
implementation. Georgia farmers gave the idea their support, and the
state's businessmen followed suit.

As drawn up, the Soil Conservation and Domestic Allotment Act
(SCDA) provided for a shift from commodity to regionally oriented
administration. Thus Cully Cobb, who had been head of the Cotton
Division, ran the southern division of the AAA. In making this change
the government sought to build a regional organization similar to that
of the SCS. But because the state extension service still ran the program,
the regional organization was never as strong as it might have been. This
difference between a regionally organized SCS and a state-administered
SCDA was one of the reasons that the two agencies drifted apart soon
after 1936.

The administrative structure for the Domestic Allotment Act retained
most of the state procedures of the reduction program. The only major
difference was that the extension service put more emphasis on a state
Agricultural Conservation and Adjustment Committee, and county agents
did likewise with the county and local committees. The administrative
transfer at the state level was very smooth. Harry Brown simply ordered
that the old state Cotton Allotment Board become the Agricultural
Conservation and Adjustment Committee. Men who had been working
as assistants in cotton adjustment became assistants in conservation or,
if they were not sufficiently qualified, clerks in the county offices.[5]

The county agents gradually moved out of the picture, leaving the
county and community committees in control This was a continuation

of a trend that had begun earlier, although with the new program their
reentry into the administrative system might have been expected. The
committees themselves consolidated, since there were no longer separate
committees for each commodity. Their position in the administrative
hierarchy strengthened until they handled virtually all aspects of the
agricultural program. The county agent returned to his extension duties
where he was able to give more help to the new program than might
have been possible otherwise.[6]

One reason the state extension service was delighted with the Allotment Act was that it provided for the same practices the extension had
been advocating for years. In 1936 it was not enough for farmers to
agree to limit production. They were asked to take positive steps to
improve their lands. For years county agents had complained that similar suggestions had fallen on deaf ears, so that in 1936 many farmers did
not know how to comply with the Allotment Act. It was up to the
county agent and the SCS to show them, and since the SCS operated
primarily through scattered demonstration projects, the task of local
work fell upon the county agent.

The SCDA provided for payments to farmers in two instances: for
soil building and for soil conservation. The soil-building payment was
made for planting soil-building crops on tilled acreage in 1936 and for
"carrying out . . . soil building practices on crop land or pasture in 1935."
The state set the rate of payment and designated the types of crops and
practices. Soil-conserving payments were made for the farm's base
acreage formerly occupied by any soil-depleting crop, which in 1936
was used for the production of any soil-conserving or soil-building crop
or soil-conserving or soil-building practice. The act imposed one restriction: no payment would be made unless the total acreage of soil-
conserving crops and soil-building crops planted in 1936 equaled or
exceeded either 20 percent of the base acreage of all soil-depleting crops
for the farm, or the maximum acreage with respect to which soil-
conserving payment could be obtained pursuant to the above payment
rates. Finally, the Department of Agriculture established lists of soil-
depleting, soil-conserving, and soil-building crops.[7]

Wallace left it to the county committees to recommend a soil-depleting
base acreage for each farm. Most farmers asked that their base be considered in terms of corn or cotton, and, since it was the end of March
before the program actually commenced, most committees used the

1935 Bankhead bases adjusted for 1936 at about a 7 percent loss on the 1935 contract.[8]

The committees and county agents quickly prepared to do their job. They held educational meetings to inform farmers of the program and to generate enthusiasm. Unfortunately, some of the interest these campaigns generated was lost when the new "work sheets" failed to arrive on time, and farmers began to fear a repetition of the AAA's administrative difficulties.[9]

Some farmers did not cooperate because they were "under the impression that all farm programs were off" after the AAA's invalidation. Others wanted to expand their farms after prices had begun to rise, and they refused to make contracts. A small group of farmers had been opposed to federal farm programs since 1933, and they, too, did not sign agreements. In some instances, county agents found it hard to explain the program, particularly the difference between soil building and soil conservation.[10]

Extension workers predicted that in 1936 fewer farmers would cooperate than in 1935. These prophets were mistaken, however. By mid-June about 85 percent of the cultivated land in Georgia was covered by work sheets. Only slightly fewer farmers were involved in the 1936 program than in 1935, and the acreage withheld from production of soil-depleting crops was about the same as was taken out of production in 1935.[11]

By July, both the number of farmers participating and the acreage covered exceeded 1935 figures. In all 978,800 acres were diverted from soil-depleting crops, and Georgia farmers received $4.1 million in performance payments, plus $1.6 million in remaining rental and benefit payments during the calendar year 1936.[12]

By the end of 1936, farmers found that the new program was working well. The lack of compulsory controls had caused a slight rise in the 1936 yield, however. The increase occurred in spite of an early summer drought and late summer windstorms and hail which did an estimated $40 million to $50 million damage to Georgia's crops. Unbridled by bad weather, the yield increased in 1937, causing a severe drop in commodity prices and triggering once more the farmers' cry for compulsory controls.[13]

Only a few administrative changes were made for the 1937 program. The AAA provided for performance supervisors in each county to check farmer compliance. The county agent "kept close check on the supervisor," and, in some cases, state or district supervisors were appointed to spot-check their work.[14]

Another important development was the "democratization" of the county committees. First, the Department of Agriculture and the state ceased paying committee administrative expenses. Instead, the committee's work was financed from the county's benefit payments, as had been the case previously for the central states. The committee could thus formulate its own budget and have more control over local personnel.

By 1937 the election of local committees became pro forma. (Previously they had been selected by county agents.) The chairmen of the local committees comprised the membership of the county committee. In some instances the county agent served as secretary to the county committee, but he no longer controlled it to the extent he had in the past. Nevertheless, his position on the committee and the increased use of long-standing extension practices in the federal agricultural program insured a more harmonious situation. Complaints from county agents regarding the overbearing demands of the federal programs virtually ceased in 1937.[15]

Another alteration which pleased farmers was the extension of the deadline for soil-building practices. In 1936 it was set at October 31, and Georgia farmers failed to qualify for about $500,000 which they could have earned by carrying out additional measures. In 1937 the AAA moved the deadline to December 31. Farmers were able to plant winter cover crops, to construct more terraces, and to carry out other practices normally undertaken during the late fall.[16]

Unfortunately, even with all these changes, farmers fared poorly in the 1937 crop season. Extension workers had warned growers that rising prices in 1936 would result in increased production and falling profits in 1937. Georgia farmers showed that they knew themselves well when they asked for compulsory controls. They and the extension service both realized what would happen after 1936, and they were correct. Georgia's agricultural income fell by about $3.2 million from 1936 to 1937, the first decrease since 1932. Income from cotton alone fell by about $8.3 million although the loss was partially offset by increases in the profits from other crops and the rise in government payments.[17]

Even with this drop in revenue, Georgia farmers still complained about limited allotments. Frank Ward, extension representative on the state board, informed Cully Cobb that the "reduction in Georgia's quota of cotton acreage from the 3,536,205 acres of 1936 to 3,511,682 in 1937 will work a great hardship on our producers and county committeemen." He said that whereas farmers had been more willing to accept reductions prior to 1937, because they could not prove that the 1934 acreages they had submitted were correct, they now were sure about their acreages and would protest vigorously.

Cobb replied that Ward was wrong; the quota for 1937 remained unchanged. He also noted, "There are no states west of Georgia that have a relative higher allotment in 1937 than Georgia." The reduction which Ward had cited was not really a reduction at all but resulted from "the removal of obsolescence" and the inclusion of new cotton producers. There had been greater expansion in Georgia than in any other southern state since 1933, and the state's quota had been raised accordingly. Cobb did admit, however, that the figures compiled on Georgia for 1934, 1935, and 1936 were reduced as accurate information became available.[18]

This controversy over allotments certainly was not new, and neither was the complaint of delay in initiating the programs. In 1937, as in previous years, Georgia learned of the programs and received the necessary forms for compliance rather late in the planting season. County agents recognized that much of the difficulty they had experienced since 1933 was caused by the state's southern location. A program lasting more than one year, such as the Bankhead Act, drew support for this reason. But even in these cases there were always so many changes from year to year that county agents still could not plan for more than one year at a time.

In addition to the usual problems caused by delay, Georgia administrators had trouble in checking compliance. The Department of Agriculture had planned to supply aerial photographs for this purpose in 1937. To the agents' dismay this was not done, so that in the fall, during the rainy season, the agents and committees were forced to take to the field with measuring chains.[19]

Agents continued to have difficulty in explaining the SCDA to farmers. In a survey taken by Kenneth Traenor, farm management expert for the extension service, thirty-nine counties reported that they encountered most of their troubles in the establishment and explanation of a "soil-conserving base." Five counties found it hard to make farmers understand the "how and why" of the two types of payments. Other counties showed concern over provisions of the act dealing with landlord-tenant division of payments, the nonpayment for some soil-building practices, and the definition of the soil-depleting base.

When questioned, however, most county agents agreed that the basic structure of the program should be retained. They did suggest that small grains and truck crops be classified as soil-conserving and that inter-planting a soil-conserving crop with a soil-depleting crop should con-stitute 50 percent soil-conserving. They also felt that the program did not make adequate provision for new producers. Finally, agents said that the program should be altered so that all soil-building practices, rather than those which would not have been carried out otherwise, be accepted for payment.[20]

By the end of 1937, both farmers and administrators realized that the Soil Conservation and Domestic Allotment Act had failed to take the place of the Bankhead Act. When reports in the spring and summer predicted a "record-breaking" crop, prices began to drop. In April, farm prices stood at 130 percent of their prewar level, but by December they had declined to 104 percent. The 1937 crop was the largest on record and, as it moved to market, prices fell even more.[21]

Farm leaders and the Department of Agriculture sought a way to obtain compulsory controls without risking an adverse Supreme Court ruling. By 1938 they had perfected a plan, and on February 2, 1938, the president signed the second Agricultural Adjustment Act. This act used the Soil Conservation and Domestic Allotment Act as a base, which pleased extension workers. The new farm program would still comple-ment extension work while providing compulsory controls similar to those of the Bankhead Act, but based on a system of "marketing quotas" rather than production allotments.

Georgia farmers responded to the act by voting for cotton-marketing quotas in March 1938. Georgia voted 84.2 percent in favor, while the total beltwide vote was 92.1 percent. In December another vote was taken for the 1939 program, with similar results. This procedure was repeated each year until 1942. Georgia farmers approved of the program by 78 to 92 percent during that time, although the number of farmers voting decreased each year, as the referendum increasingly was taken for granted.[22]

The new program returned the county agent to the center of the ad-ministrative structure. But because it was vastly improved over the 1933 plan, agents did not complain as much. They still experienced the usual delays and misunderstandings; however, the program remained relatively unchanged until 1942, and they were able gradually to reduce the number of problems.

The period 1933 to 1938 had been one of experimentation in federal farm programs. The new act provided the basis for a more permanent solution. It was modified through the years and was supplemented by other plans, but its essence—control of crop production—remained at the core of the government's farm policy through the 1960s.

During the first five years many difficulties arose. Extension service personnel and farmers did not hesitate to inform the Department of Agriculture when they occurred, and many of the subsequent changes were based on their criticism.

A great number of the troubles were related to the newness of the program. In the area of acreage and production allotment, conditions improved as more complete data allowed allotment boards to insure equitable distribution of quotas. County agents and committees also were able to operate more efficiently as they began to understand the complex procedures. To some extent, however, the newness never wore off. In almost every year there was another piece of legislation, and in those years when there was none, there still were new directives handed down from the AAA.

Some problems never were solved. Farmers always complained of the delay in getting each year's program started. They also never quite understood the programs fully. Provisions were very complicated, and this resulted in distressingly involved procedures, especially in the various forms and work sheets farmers were required to fill out. In some instances county agents and county committeemen themselves did not comprehend the programs completely, and the whole county suffered. It was for these reasons that the extension service held so many district meetings and tried to maintain good communications with the county agents. The 1938 act did not eradicate these problems, but by stabilizing the farm program it helped administrators to deal with them in terms of long-range solutions.

The agricultural program was the largest federal program in the state, both in terms of the number of persons it affected and in the amount of money it spent. Much of the credit for its success belonged to the state extension service, and it was perhaps fitting that the sacrifice involved

in the temporary abandonment of its own programs resulted in the ultimate strengthening of its position in the state.

To some, the indirect gains of the AAA outweighed any of its overt
accomplishments. In an agricultural state such as Georgia, farm recovery
had to precede business recovery. As the farm situation brightened, it
was clearly reflected in restored business confidence. Retail and wholesale activity increased and farm credit eased. In the long run the AAA
perhaps was not so important for the crops it withdrew from the market
as for the fallow fields it provided for new crops. It was only by forcing
Georgia farmers to give up cotton that other marketable farm products
might be raised. Both the cattle and poultry industries, for example,
owed their rise to the compulsory limiting of cotton acreage.

Finally, the program from 1936 to 1938, while not so successful in
controlling production, was of tremendous value in educating Georgia
farmers. Conservation practices which county agents had pleaded for in
the past became widespread. This led not only to the preservation of
Georgia's soil, but also to a better informed and enlightened farm population and to more efficient farming methods in general.

THE TENANT'S SHARE

The Agricultural Adjustment Act was intended by those who conceived it in the Department of Agriculture and those who passed it in
the Congress as essentially a recovery measure, not designed to give relief
or to rehabilitate destitute farmers. It operated in much the same way
and existed for the same reasons as the National Recovery Administration. The government sought to put money into the hands of the
best producers who would reinvest their profits in their farms just as
manufacturers would use their profits to increase their own productive
power. This process was expected to regenerate the farm economy. Of
course, poor farmers would also receive AAA payments, but they would
tend to spend the money in ways which would have less effect on the
total farm economy. They would not be using money to make money,
but to satisfy immediate personal needs.

Intentionally or not, the AAA operated principally for the benefit
of the commercial farmer, and those on the bottom of the agricultural
scale succinctly referred to it as the "landlord's code." It was not so

much that the AAA sought explicitly to deny small farmers, tenants, and sharecroppers their fair share; it was simply that they wrote the law in such a way as to leave these people at the mercy of those at the local level. For example, the 1933 AAA contained no specific provision regarding the distribution of benefits between landlord and tenant. Such clauses were included in the later acts, but even then some local administrators turned their backs while the landlord withheld the tenant's share. In either instance, given the proposition that the Department of Agriculture was concerned only with the "top third of the farmers," a position Henry Wallace admitted holding, and given that provisions in the laws to protect the tenant were weak, the tenant's treatment in any state or county depended on the good faith of the landowners and the willingness and ability of state and county administrators to see that he was included.[23]

Owners were in a manifestly superior position. They were more aware of all farm programs and markets and of agricultural economics in general, which allowed them to take full advantage of the laws. They had always been more closely associated with those whose job it was to carry out the programs, and they sat on relevant committees that eventually were to control operations on the local level.

Certainly, opportunity existed for injustices to occur in Georgia. Tenancy was more prevalent in the South than in any other part of the country, and tenancy in Georgia was the second highest in the South in 1930 and 1935. Furthermore, the history of the tenant had not been bright. Each time agricultural depressions had squeezed owners in the past, their first reaction had been to pass on as much of the economic loss as possible to the tenant. When this tradition and the high proportion of tenancy met in a state such as Georgia during a very severe depression, the result might well have been completely disastrous for those on the bottom rung. It came as no surprise, therefore, that tenants failed to share equally in the benefits of the farm programs.[24]

The treatment of the tenant was not as harsh in some states as others. The worst conditions came to exist in an area comprised of the "boot heel" of Missouri, northern Arkansas, and western Tennessee. Conditions there spawned the Southern Tenant Farmers Union, an organization of the disaffected that fought a long, futile battle against a well entrenched owner class. The situation was also bad in Alabama where white and black tenants joined to form the Sharecroppers' Union.[25]

In Georgia, where circumstances seemed riper, no such reaction occurred. Although one observer attributed this to the interracial nature of tenant organizations and the strong opposition of Georgia planters, there was evidence to show that Georgia tenants were treated as well as, if not better than, those elsewhere in the South. Discrimination did exist in Georgia. Tenants, administrators, and observers reported many inequities in the laws and in their administration. But given the inevitable disparities caused by the legislation itself, the tendency in Georgia was not to compound them in the administration of the AAA.[26]

The 1933 act had no specific provision for the distribution of benefits between landlords and tenants. The criterion for contracts was based upon legal ownership of the crop. Since by state law only the highest class of tenant, the managing share tenant, could claim any legal ownership, the bulk of the tenants and croppers were left out. But tenants and croppers did have a stake in the 1933 harvest. They had tilled the soil and planted the cotton; therefore, they had an equity in the destroyed crops. The AAA left arrangements for the tenants' portion up to the landlord, and although no specific studies were undertaken that year, observers claimed that the tenant received almost nothing. Even where the owner made "equitable" arrangements with the tenant, the latter still got very little.[27]

In Greene County, for example, a planter signed up to destroy 25 acres in the summer of 1933. For this he was to receive about $10.00 an acre figured on an estimated per acre yield at six cents per pound. The owner agreed to pay the cropper half of the benefits, but "most of it already belonged to the planter who, under the law, had first claims upon the cropper's income to safeguard the amount furnished by him to the cropper in the production of the crop." The owner also took all of the option money, since he alone had signed for it. The cotton that was harvested brought in ten cents a pound, half of which went to the cropper. In the end the cropper got five cents for each pound of cotton harvested (as did the owner). The cropper got three cents on each pound of cotton destroyed or half of the six cents per pound paid by the AAA. The planter got seven cents per pound for his share of the destroyed cotton— three cents in benefits and four cents in options. The cropper thus lost, at the very least, two cents per pound. The tenant probably received less than this, for the owner certainly would claim that the tenant had some unsettled debts. Even when the tenant qualified for benefits, he might never see the money. Since it was up to the planter to handle the tenant's share, he often "credited the [latter's] account" when the check arrived.[28]

In some instances the landowner might choose to plow up land normally not tilled by his tenants, thus avoiding the necessity of sharing payments with them. Even after the administration made it clear that tenants were to receive their portion of the benefits, the money still came directly to the farmer in a single check. In the case of parity payments, it was not until 1937 that separate checks were issued, and then only to managing share tenants.[29]

The black press was especially concerned about the new farm program's effect upon blacks, since in both 1930 and 1935 they comprised over 85 percent of the tenants and over 52 percent of the croppers in the state. The Savannah *Tribune* was not so concerned about blacks receiving a fair share of the benefits, as it was about blacks being allowed to remain on the land. The paper felt that it was better not to control the production of cotton at all, if it meant the expulsion of tenants. Its sharp criticism of the AAA was somewhat allayed, however, by the administration's announcement late in 1933 that 1934 contract signers would have to promise to keep the same number of tenants they had the previous year.[30]

There has been no agreement as to what extent the ouster of tenants really took place. Lincoln McConnell, the state's Reemployment Director for the United States Employment Service, estimated that 75,000 of the 250,000 Georgians unemployed at the beginning of 1934 were farmers who had been forced off the land for various reasons including the acreage reduction program. Another study in the 1950's corroborated his opinion.[31]

On the other hand, A. H. Ward, Field Representative of the AAA, reported that the administration was aware of the situation and was moving to correct it. Conferring with state relief officials in Georgia and Florida and local relief officials in twenty-five counties of those states, he could discover no complaints that had previously been unreported to the Cotton Production Section of the AAA. Tenants alleged, however, that such efforts did no good. The Cotton Production Section reviewed the complaints and then sent them to the director of extension, who gave them to the county agents. The agents passed them along to the landlord, an action which jeopardized the tenant's security. Landlords accused of unfair treatment of their tenants were hardly those who should have been called upon to see that the practice was altered, especially in those instances where the "county agent was lacking in zealousness" in the protection of his county's tenants. If the complaint of the black tenant reached the black county agent, little could be done. The black agent's position was too precarious for him to interfere.[32]

In 1934 the AAA moved to rectify these injustices to tenants. Paragraph seven of the 1934-1935 cotton reduction contract was inserted to protect them. It stated that the signer agreed to keep the same number of tenants on his farm that he had in 1933. He was to include them in the benefit payments, distributing acreage reduction among them. He was also to allow them use of rented acres for growing food and feed crops for home consumption. Unfortunately, the wording of the section was not particularly strong, and planters found it easy to circumvent the provisions. Only cash tenants and managing share tenants received rentals; other tenants and croppers got half of the parity payments, which amounted to very little. Thus the cropper could expect at best only half of 60 percent of the crop and an eighth of the benefit payments on the other 40 percent. If there was no contract, the cropper got a straight 50 percent of the total crop. Under the program a tenant's profit might increase by 22.4 percent, if the landlord's rose 65.5 percent over what they would have received on the halves basis had not the program been in effect. Both tenants and landowners on farms not under contract in 1934 did better than those who signed. Finally, since only the very highest group of tenants received benefits, planters could increase their personal gain by reducing the status of their tenants and croppers.[33]

The number of those on the farm with whom the benefits had to be shared became of increased importance after the passage of the Bankhead Act. Since tenants who had an interest in the crop received ginning certificates, the number of bales which a planter might market tax-free could be reduced seriously, if he had to share them with his tenants. The situation was alleviated somewhat by the institution of the two-bale provision. Under this order the landowner did not lose any of his allotment by allowing small producers on his land to receive certificates. Still, landlords in Georgia were not satisfied and demanded the payment of standing rent by tenants in the form of tax-free bales. They wanted to make sure that they did not have to use their own certificates to market cotton produced by tenants. In some cases tenants were unaware

of the Bankhead Act, and in signing the many agreements connected
with the various cotton programs they unknowingly gave planters their
certificates.[34]

When the stream of tenant complaints from the southern states did
not lessen in 1934, the AAA arranged for a series of surveys to determine
the extent of these injustices. E. C. Westbrook was assigned to Georgia.
He sent workers into Bartow, Jackson, Spalding, Telfair, Terrell, and
Washington counties to investigate contract violations. His study covered
8,542 relief cases, 1,704 of which were "farm cases." Of these latter
instances, 681 involved tenants, and 347 of them had come from farms
on which the owner had signed a reduction agreement for cotton. His
staff interviewed these 347 tenants, 87 percent of whom were white.

In his report to the Production Control Section, Westbrook noted
that only 14 of the tenants were on relief because of the decrease in the
number of tenants or the lowering of tenancy status on farms where
landlords had signed contracts. He found that the number of contracts
involved represented 0.2 percent of the 5,641 active contracts involved
and that the 14 tenants who came from these farms comprised 2.1
percent of all the tenants on the relief rolls.

After further investigation, Westbrook concluded that in 12 of the
14 cases there were no actual violations. He discovered that from 1932
to 1935 there was little change in the total number of tenant families
on farms found in apparent violation of contracts, some decrease in the
number of cash and share tenants, and some increase in the number of
wage hands.[35]

From October to December 1934, Westbrook was assigned the task
of making adjustments where complaints had been filed. He reported
that landlords were generally cooperative and that most of them had
erred through a "lack of knowledge of the rules and regulations governing the program." There were only a few instances of willful violations.[36]

Westbrook's work was substantiated by that of A. H. Ward, who surveyed Georgia on a broader scale. Ward experienced "the fullest kind of
cooperation from extension directors, district agents, and county agents,"
the county agents being "especially pleased about the investigations."
Furthermore, in the some 200 inquiries he made, not one farmer
resented his presence, and he found fewer than six who "willfully and
maliciously were trying to deprive their tenants of any part of the
government benefits." He discovered more landowners in Georgia and

Florida were giving tenants more than their share of the benefits, than there were landowners trying to deprive tenants of their payments.

Ward concluded that landlords felt a responsibility toward their tenants. They always had taken care of them, and they would continue to do so. Since AAA administrators were not concerned with paternalism, but only with seeing that the tenants received their benefits, this situation did not bother them.

Complaints were usually of four types: (1) Tenants claimed that they were really managing share tenants, but were not included in the contracts. (2) Tenants claimed they were displaced. (3) Tenants claimed they were not allowed to use a portion of the rented acres. (4) Tenants claimed that landlords were withholding benefit payments. About 80 percent of the complaints were of the first type, mostly because the contract and administrative rulings did not clearly define "managing share tenants." In about 95 percent of these cases the complaints were "unjustifiable and without basis." This was due to a lack of information or an improper interpretation of the contract by the tenants or "to the work of some individual who wanted to cause discontent and dissatisfaction among tenants." In the few instances where complaints were valid, either the committeemen had misunderstood the regulations and misinformed landowners or the planters had misrepresented the facts in order to secure all of the benefits for themselves. Ward said that he had little trouble in correcting any of these complaints.

Ward found only ten complaints of tenant displacement, all unjustified. He concluded that there was less shifting of tenants in Georgia and Florida in 1934 than in the previous year, due to the new conditions of the contract. About 10 to 15 percent of the complaints were for denial of the use of rented acres by tenants. Some were authentic, but upon explanation the landowner was usually cooperative. There was some trouble where the landlord owned the tools and livestock, but Ward was able to make adjustments. Finally, he experienced no difficulty in settling questions concerning withheld payments.

Concluding his report, Ward noted that he had found no landlord who criticized the program and only one managing share tenant who was dissatisfied. Most sharecroppers and share tenants felt that the program had increased prices, although some said that they were not getting their share of the benefits.[37] The AAA found that over half of the complaints lodged by Georgia tenants were unjustified, and most of those that were,

had been adjusted by either the county committees or the field representatives. Only six contracts were recommended for rejection from June
through December 1934, and only one from then through June 1935.[38]

The work of the Landlord-Tenant Adjustment Committee, which had
sponsored Ward's investigations, came under severe attack on the national
level for the attitudes of its field adjusters. Doubt was cast upon the
worth of the report. A later statistical study of 126 Georgia counties
from 1930 to 1940, using a cross-sectional regression model, also challenged these results. It showed that acreage reduction had accelerated
the out-migration of farm labor.[39]

Still another report indicated that in 23 cotton counties with
17,655 tenants in 1930 the number increased about 12 percent to 19,111
in 1935. These same counties showed a decrease of 26 percent from
32,484 sharecroppers in 1930 to 24,028 in 1935. The number of white
tenants rose, while the number of black tenants fell. The number of both
white and black croppers declined. Furthermore, the number of wage
hands decreased greatly, indicating that while croppers might have been
displaced, they were not lowered in status. This study tended to confirm
Ward's findings for the period he studied, and the preponderance of
evidence supported the conclusion that most Georgia landlords had dealt
fairly with their tenants and croppers. That tenants were unable to
improve their lot very much was the fault of the tenancy system, and,
possibly the laws themselves, rather than their administration.[40]

Tenancy came into existence in the years following the Civil War.
Large landowners after 1865 devised it to replace the slave system.
They were aided in this by the federal government, which refused to give
confiscated land to the freedmen. Blacks had no wealth with which to
purchase their own land and thus were forced to accept tenant status.
Some of the poorer whites also moved into this class. Because many of
the old southern plantations were broken up after the war, tenancy grew
rather slowly at first. But after 1880 "the better lands of the South have
been progressively concentrated into large plantations under central
management."[41]

With this movement came a change in the type of ownership. More
plantations fell into the hands of absentee landlords and creditor institutions. Depression in the 1930s accelerated this trend. At its height, for
instance, the John Hancock Life Insurance Company owned most of the
better farmland in Greene County.

At the time the AAA came into being, tenancy was on the increase. Much of the criticism leveled at the AAA for tenant problems was actually the result of the system and not caused by the New Deal's farm program. Tenancy had generated its own set of laws, so that one contemporary observer excused the federal government saying, "The economic relationship and the resulting social attitudes had made a situation in which it was difficult, if not impossible, for the government to deal directly with the cropper."[42]

Georgia planters were in an ambiguous position with respect to their tenants and the AAA. On one hand, the planter wanted to "encourage the most dependent form of sharecropping as a source of largest profits." He also wanted to have tenants of the highest possible efficiency. The landlord wished to keep them on the land and dependent upon him.[43]

The tenancy system in Georgia also had kept alive the tradition of paternalism, and many planters felt a sense of responsibility toward their tenants (no matter how warped that sense of responsibility appeared). It was for these reasons that the investigations of the Landlord-Tenant Section revealed little abuse of the tenants under the AAA. The landlord was perfectly willing to squeeze his tenants to a point, but not so anxious to force them off the land. Furthermore, he was pleased that the federal government wanted to take over some of the responsibility for "furnishing" the tenants, and he was willing for the AAA to pay tenants for work that would benefit him.

In 1935 as in 1934 the landlord-tenant investigations showed little discrimination in Georgia. The extension service made sure that landowners understood paragraph seven of the contract and obeyed it. When the Landlord-Tenant Section again sent E. C. Westbrook into the field with six county supervisors, it found the results of his study most heartening. Although there were some complaints that his reports did not include statements by tenants, they did show that there was an average of only one inquiry or complaint for each sixty-nine contracts in the state, and most of these were "occasioned by misinformation or lack of information by the individual writing the letter."[44]

In 1936, the administration's focus shifted somewhat. It was still interested in landlord-tenant relations, but now it was concerned also about the tenants' performance of soil-building practices. The Georgia Experiment Station of the state extension service made two surveys that year, one in Terrell County and one in Newton County. In Newton

County the experiment station found very little difference between owners and tenants in the use of cropland in 1936. In Terrell County, the experiment station noted that tenants "compared favorably with owners" in respect to soil-depleting practices and not so well in regard to soil-conserving practices, although the disparity was not very great. The investigation showed that soil-depleting practices stemmed from the identical farming methods which both groups used. Thus there was little difference in the amount of soil-depleting practices among them. In respect to soil-conserving practices, the report laid the blame for differences directly upon the "unstable tenure conditions" of those lower down on the scale.[45]

Subsequent observers interpreted this condition as an accolade for the tenants. Many of the "crimes charged to tenancy were committed by owners as well as by tenants," proving that these people did not succumb to the demoralizing pressures of their status. In fact "many tenants and sharecroppers had higher incomes than some of their neighbors who owned their own small farms."[46]

In the area of landlord-tenant relations the Landlord-Tenant Section handled 617 cases in 1936 of which only 61 remained unsettled at the end of the year. In 1937, the section received 169 more, making a total of 230 cases to be adjusted that year. Of these, 63 were in reference to cotton adjustment contracts, 27 in reference to cotton price adjustment payments, and 82 in reference to the 1936 agricultural conservation program. Miscellaneous complaints accounted for 58. The cases regarding the 1936 program dealt mostly with instances where the landlord was alleged to have improperly "shown the interests of tenants who were entitled to a portion of the payment." The complaints which involved the price adjustment payments were concerned with "the improper distribution of the cotton price adjustment payments and the failure of the producer to return to the County Agent's office properly executed the form containing the signatures of all persons entitled to a portion of the payment."

Of all the complaints, 129 were settled by the state and county, and 53 were handled through correspondence by the Landlord-Tenant Section with the aid of the state and county. Only 37 cases had to be resolved by investigation. These were "aggravated complaints which could not be settled by local authorities." By the end of 1937, there were 11 cases pending, most of which were under field investigation. The Landlord-

Tenant Section reported that no one county was more guilty of contract violations than another. Georgia's record looked very good indeed.[47]

The tenant's circumstances probably were worse than any of these surveys indicated. Many tenants either did not understand the AAA's programs and did not know what was due them, or they simply did not have enough faith in the intentions of the federal government to appeal for help. In addition, there was much to be said for the charges made against the Landlord-Tenant Section. Even if officials were not actively trying to injure the tenant, it was true that all of them, from Secretary Wallace down to local committeemen, were administering a law which favored the landlord — a situation which existed, in part, because that was the way they wanted it.

In the final analysis, the federal farm program was a mixed blessing for the tenant and cropper. Despite the reports of the Landlord-Tenant Section, some tenants were displaced, and farm laborers suffered a great deal in this respect. Georgia's record was comparatively good in relation to the other southern states.

The AAA also provided an opportunity for landlords to use the program in order to squeeze more out of the tenants. Since the laws took no consideration of "labor's previous interest in the crop," the landowner could get free labor from his tenants without abusing the written agreement. The laws themselves, based on cotton rather than need, did not provide for existing income differentials in the relative amounts paid to tenants and landlords. Finally, supporting programs such as parity payments, price stabilization loans, debt adjustment, and production credit were of greater advantage to landlords than tenants.

It was an easy matter for a planter to secure a production credit loan for 4.5 to 6.5 percent interest and then extend credit to his tenants at 20 percent. Although the debt adjustment program helped many poorer farmers, it never attempted to "scale down owner-tenant debts." Parity payments and price stabilization loans also helped the planter more than the tenant, because the landowner's resources were in capital, machinery, and land rather than in labor, as were those of the tenant. The planter still retained, and even increased his capital under the early AAA. He could make other investments. If fields were allowed to lie fallow, the tenant lost his ability to capitalize on his labor.

The tenant, however, stood to gain more by the soil-conserving and soil-building payments. These required primarily an investment in labor

rather than in capital. If a planter took land out of cotton production,
he had to make a further investment for seed, implements, and perhaps
even labor to turn the fields to other crops. The tenant only had to give
labor, which usually was fixed in any case by the size of his family.[48]

Though the tenants and croppers stood to suffer greatly in the mis-
administration of the AAA and in the discrimination of landowners,
this was not generally the case in Georgia. Of far greater significance to
tenants, and even to small independent farmers, was the existence of a
series of laws which were written and often administered with the commercial farmer in mind. The injustice herein was that it forced them to
lose profits by lowering their production while not providing benefits
sufficient to make up for this loss. The tenant and the cropper often
needed relief. Recovery might come afterward, but nothing could be
done until certain basic conditions endemic to their status were altered.

NOTES

1. Interview with W. A. Minor, Jr., September 12, 1968.

2. George E. Farrell, Director, Division of Grains, to Harry L. Brown,
January 8, 1936, NARG 145, Agricultural Stabilization and Conservation
Service (ASCS), AAA, General Correspondence (1937-38), drawer 543.
Unsigned Report, January 4, 1936, NARG 44, NEC, Office of Govern-
ment Reports, Digests of state directors' reports, box 500.

3. Unsigned report, February 29, 1936, NARG 44, Digests, box 502.
Brown to Cully Cobb, January 31, 1936, NARG 145, Gen. Corres.
(1937-38), drawer 543.

4. Interview with W. A. Minor, Jr.

5. *Ibid.* Cobb to Brown, April 8, 1936, NARG 145, Gen. Corres.
(1937-38), drawer 543. Unsigned report, February 1, 1936, NARG 44,
Digests, box 500. Brown to Warburton, December 24, 1935, NARG 33,
Federal Extension Service, Correspondence, box 339. Brown to Cobb,
April 16, 1936, NARG 145, Gen. Corres. (1937-38), drawer 543.

6. Interview with W. A. Minor, Jr. Annual narrative county agents'
reports of Georgia, 1936, NARG 33, microfilm reel 78. There were 158
of these county associations by the end of 1936.

7. United States Department of Agriculture (USDA), AAA, *Report*
(1936), pp. 175-76, 179.

8. *Ibid.,* p. 177. Cobb to Brown, May 28, 1936, NARG 145, Gen.

Corres. (1937-38), drawer 543. Annual reports, 1936, NARG 33, microfilm reel 79.

9. Unsigned report, April 25, 1936, NARG 44, Digests, box 504. Annual narrative report of Donald Leroy Branyon, county agent for Berrien County, Georgia, 1936, NARG 33, microfilm reel 79.

10. Annual report of Donald Branyon, 1936.

11. Annual narrative report of N. D. McRainey, county agent for Baker County, 1936, NARG 33, microfilm reel 79. Unsigned report, June 23, 1936, NARG 44, Division of Field Operations, Reports Section, Periodical Reports of State Directors (1934-38), box 400. Unsigned report, July 7, 1936, NARG 44, Periodical Reports (1934-38), box 400.

12. USDA, AAA, *Report* (1936), pp. 143-144, 193, 195.

13. Willard Range, *A Century of Georgia Agriculture, 1850-1950* (Athens: University of Georgia Press, 1954), p. 179. Unsigned report, June 6, 1936, NARG 44, Digests, box 505. See also: Periodical Reports, May-July, 1936, box 400.

14. Cobb to Frank Ward, July 31, 1937, NARG 145, Alphabetical Correspondence, drawer 1670.

15. Gladys Baker, *The County Agent.* (Chicago: University of Chicago Press, 1939), p. 78. Annual narrative reports, 1937, NARG 33, microfilm reel 88.

16. J. B. Hutson, Assistant Administrator, AAA, to Senator Richard B. Russell, Jr., December 30, 1937, NARG 145, Gen. Corres., drawer 1234.

17. Georgia Crop Reporting Service, *Georgia Agricultural Facts, 1900-1956,* Bulletin No. 511 (July 1957), 47, 49. Annual narrative report of Herman Nessmith, county agent for Bacon County, 1937, NARG 33, microfilm reel 88.

18. Ward to Cobb, April 10, 1937, NARG 145, Alpha. Corres., drawer 1670. Cobb to Ward, April 13 and 19, 1936, NARG 145, Alpha. Corres., drawer 1670.

19. Annual reports, 1937, NARG 33, microfilm reel 88.

20. Annual report of Kenneth Traenor, extension specialist in farm management, 1937, NARG 33, microfilm reel 87.

21. *Ibid.* State Summary, Georgia, No. 4, June 1938, NARG 145, Production Control Program (1933-38), box 107.

22. AAA, *Report* (1937-38), pp. 111, 112; (1939-40), pp. 43, 48. Range, *Century,* p. 179. For a discussion of other crops covered by the AAA see Michael S. Holmes, "The New Deal in Georgia: An Administrative History" (unpublished Ph.D. dissertation, Department of History, University of Wisconsin-Madison, 1969), pp. 518-543.

23. Charles S. Johnson, Edwin R. Embree, and Will W. Alexander, *The*

Collapse of Cotton Tenancy (Chapel Hill: University of North Carolina Press, 1935), p. 55. Fred C. Frey and Lynn T. Smith, "The Influence of the AAA Cotton Program Upon the Tenant, Cropper, and Laborer," *Rural Sociology,* I, 4 (December 1936), 489. W. L. Blackstone, "Minority Report," *Farm Tenancy.* (Washington: United States Government Printing Office, 1937), p. 21. Unless so stipulated the word "tenant" is used throughout to include all types of tenants and sharecroppers.

24. *Farm Tenancy,* p. 89.

25. Edward Aaron Gaston, Jr., "A History of the Negro Wage Earner in Georgia, 1890-1940" (unpublished Ph.D. dissertation, Department of History, Emory University, 1957), p. 420.

26. *Ibid.,* p. 421.

27. P. W. Burton, "Cotton Acreage Reduction and the Tenant Farmer," *Law and Contemporary Problems,* I, 3 (June 1934), 284. Arthur F. Raper, *Preface to Peasantry.* (Chapel Hill: University of North Carlina Press, 1936), p. 245. Johnson, *et al., Cotton Tenancy,* p. 50.

28. Arthur Raper, "Cotton Plow-Up and Cotton Option: Greene County, Georgia," Raper Manuscripts, AFR 3/A, 1934-35. Johnson, *et al., Cotton Tenancy,* p. 52.

29. Baker, *County Agent,* p. 76.

30. *Farm Tenancy,* p. 98. Savannah *Tribune,* November 2, 30, 1933.

31. Roy E. Fossett, "The Impact of the New Deal on Georgia Politics, 1933-1941" (unpublished Ph.D. dissertation, Department of Political Science, University of Florida, 1960), p. 88. Range, *A Century of Georgia Agriculture,* p. 274.

32. Miscellaneous report, January 9, 1934, NARG 145, Production Control Program (1933-38), box 118. Johnson, *et al., Cotton Tenancy,* p. 56. Baker, *County Agent,* p. 76.

33. David E. Conrad, *The Forgotton Farmers* (Urbana: University of Illinois Press, 1965), pp. 58-61. Johnson, *et al., Cotton Tenancy,* pp. 59-60. Wallace to L. A. Brookord (Summer County), March 8, 1934, NARG 145, General Correspondence, Russell (1933-35). Wallace to Russell, March 14, 1934, NARG 145, Gen. Corres., Russell (1933-35).

34. Raper, *Preface,* p. 252. Cobb to Cunningham, October 3, 1934 (telegram), NARG 145, Alphabetical Correspondence (1933-35), State Board of Review, drawer 75. J. F. Hart, county agent for Laurens County, to Cunningham, December 12, 1935, NARG 33, Correspondence, box 400. Johnson, *et al., Cotton Tenancy,* p. 56.

35. W. J. Green, "A Report on a Survey to Determine What Relationship, If Any Existed Between the Cotton Acreage Reduction Program and the Number of Tenants Enrolled as Emergency Relief Clients in the

Period, January 1, 1934, to March 15, 1935," September 1, 1935, NARG 145, Prod. Contr. Prog., box 119.

36. Annual narrative report of E. C. Westbrook, extension cotton–tobacco specialist, 1934, NARG 33, microfilm reel 63.

37. A. H. Ward, "Report of the Adjustment Committee on the Investigation of Landlord–Tenant Complaints under the Cotton and Tobacco Adjustment Contracts," September 1, 1934, NARG 145, Prod. Contr. Prog., box 118.

38. "Summary of Reports Received to Date by Adjustment Committees from Field Representatives Investigating and Adjusting Landlord-Tenant Complaints, Cotton and Tobacco," NARG 145, Prod. Contr. Prog., box 118.

39. Conrad, *Forgotten Farmers*, pp. 130-131. Roger L. Burford, "The Federal Cotton Programs and Farm Labor Force Adjustments," *Southern Economic Journal*, XXXIII, 2 (October 1966), 236.

40. Frey, *et al.*, "The Influence of the AAA," pp. 298-299.

41. Johnson, *et al.*, *Cotton Tenancy*, p. 32.

42. Harold Hoffsomer, "The AAA and the Cropper," *Journal of Social Forces*, XIII (May 1935), 494-502.

43. Johnson, *et al.*, *Cotton Tenancy*, p. 31.

44. W. J. Green, field representative, adjustment committee, to Harry Brown, April 2, 1935, NARG 145, Alpha. Corres. (1933-35), drawer 79. R. F. Croom to J. G. Oliver, state leader, community work, September 7, 1935, NARG 145, Alpha. Corres., drawer 750. Croom to Brown, November 27, 1935, NARG 145, Alpha. Corres. (1933-35), drawer 79.

45. W. E. Hendrix, J. C. Elrod, and W. T. Fullilove, "Some Aspects of the Farm Tenure Situation in Newton County, Georgia," Georgia Experiment Station, *Bulletin*, No. 237 (January 1945), 40. W. T. Fullilove, J. C. Elrod, and W. E. Hendrix, "A Study of Farming by Tenure of Farms in Terrell County, Georgia," Georgia Experiment Station, *Bulletin*, No. 234 (June 1944), 35.

46. Range, *Century*, p. 277.

47. "Report of the Activities of the Landlord-Tenant Relationship Section–Southern Division, AAA, for the Year Ending November 1, 1937," NARG 145, Prod. Contr. Prog., box 119.

48. John Leonard Fulmer, "The Effect of Domestic Policy on the Southern Agricultural Problem," *Southern Economic Journal*, XVIII, 1 (July 1951), 19. Frey, *et al.*, Influence of the AAA," p. 502. Arthur F. Raper, *Tenants of the Almighty* (New York: Macmillan Company, 1943), p. 216. Johnson, *et al.*, *Cotton Tenancy*, p. 50.

9

More Aid for
Georgia's Farmers

When the first series of New Deal agencies was organized in the summer
of 1933, the Roosevelt administration made no specific arrangements
for rural relief. The AAA was a recovery measure designed to help the
commercial farmer, and although the FERA provided both direct and
work relief for rural citizens, there was no program of on-the-farm aid.
The FERA's Rural Problem Surveys of Morgan, Tift, and Meriwether
counties in Georgia indicated that effective relief for the destitute farm
population would have to conform to special rural needs. The FERA
work program actually was bad for the farmers. It took them off their
land, thus circumventing rather than confronting rural problems. The
surveys concluded that "a principle of any rehabilitation program must
have as its purpose the rebuilding of the fundamental land resources."
This concept of attacking the cause of rural poverty through a program
which also provided relief formed the basis for all subsequent rural relief
agencies. Under subsequent agencies, farmers were given two forms of
aid: direct or subsistence relief and relief aimed at rehabilitating
farmlands.[1]

The FERA developed three interrelated programs for dealing with
rural destitution: rehabilitation loans, resettlement, and submarginal
land purchase. For those farmers who were poor, but living on good
soil, the FERA offered rehabilitation loans through its Rural Rehabilitation Division. These were known as "in place" loans, which provided
for the practice of certain farming and home-improvement methods as
part of the farmer's agreement. If farmers were tilling submarginal soil,

the FERA could resettle them, either individually or in communities, purchasing their exhausted acreage as part of a land-improvement program.

In its reorganization in the spring of 1934, the FERA set up the Rural Rehabilitation Division, but left each state to formulate its own specific projects for rehabilitation. By late April plans had been submitted to Gay Shepperson, and the GERA stood ready to implement the program. Announcing that a Rural Rehabilitation Division would be established in the GERA, Miss Shepperson named Robert S. Vansant, former county agent for Cobb County, as its head.

Miss Shepperson separated the state into six divisions, each embracing ten districts of one to four counties. The divisions were placed under an agricultural supervisor aided by a home economics supervisor and a social work supervisor. The districts were to be managed by a farm supervisor, and there was one aide placed in each county. The counties also had advisory boards consisting of the county agent, the home demonstration agent, the vocational teacher, the county relief administrator, and one citizen named by the rest of the board. The initial work of selecting farmers to receive rural rehabilitation loans was conducted by these boards.

On May 1, 1934, the loan program was launched in Georgia. By May 23, fifty families had borrowed money, and this number had risen to 1,000 by July 21. Unfortunately, delays caused by reexamination of rural relief clients by the county committees and the late start of the program limited its effectiveness in the first year. Farmers were unable to use the loans to improve their 1934 crops, because by the time the money was forthcoming the planting season was over. This led some to advise that the Rural Rehabilitation Division be removed from the GERA to act as an independent agency in cooperation with the extension service. The state NEC director suggested that the GERA continue to investigate rural relief cases, but that the actual operations be handled by those who were "trained in practical supervision of rural and agricultural programs."[2]

One of the primary problems unmet in the early months was that of the displaced farmer or of the farmer living on submarginal soil. The "in place" loans might give these people relief, but their soil was so poor that it was impossible to "rehabilitate" them. Another factor limited tenant participation — his contract which had been signed prior to the planting season. This contract restricted the tenant's use of the land, so that he might not be able to employ the loan to improve his condition. The heavy indebtedness of many tenants also complicated the situation.

To combat these problems Miss Shepperson inaugurated a resettlement program. This would take tenants from the landlords' control, or small farmers off submarginal acres, and move them to better land which the GERA secured. Since the GERA could not purchase land itself, Miss Shepperson set up an independent company, the Georgia Rural Rehabilitation Corporation of Fulton County, with state relief and farm officials as stockholders.

Having established a loan program and erected an organization to rent or purchase land, the GERA set about in 1934 to transfer all "able-bodied farm families" on relief to the Rural Rehabilitation Division. The county boards reevaluated all rural relief cases, and, where possible, made private arrangements with landlords so that tenants might use the standard rehabilitation loans. The rest of the destitute farmers were divided into two classes: those with sufficient farming experience to enable them to prosper and those with limited knowledge.

This new program called for a much more complex evaluation of farmers' needs and abilities. Since farmers were now to be placed on new land, the division was forced to become more involved in farm planning, opening up a whole new area of activity. The division first had to make sure that the lands it purchased were not submarginal. Then it moved the farmer to the land, assured him a house, and provided the farm with livestock and implements. Each farmer signed a contract allowing him to remain on the land as long as he followed the plans worked out with the division. In the case of the inexperienced farmer, the signee was required to raise subsistence crops. All farmers were asked to cooperate with county extension workers in the various programs of home economics and farm management. After ten years the farmer would receive clear title to the land and house. These resettled farmers also were given rehabilitation loans. The loans were distributed on a three-year amortization plan, each loan being secured by a bill of sale covering livestock, capital equipment, household goods, and crops. In addition to the loan, the division provided a certain amount of money in the form of work relief and grants to supplement farmers' needs. This new program caused a rapid increase in the number of farmers who received funds during the last months of 1934.

To administer the increased load, the division hired additional county workers. These employees were all "trained agriculturalists, home economists, and social workers" who supplied the professional control which the early program had lacked. Each worker supervised from 50 to 100 clients, and as a group they offered the farmer a source of aid for almost any farm problem. The division kept the rural rehabilitation boards in the counties to advise the workers.[3]

By the end of 1934 the GERA had placed 5,354 families on new farms at an average cost of $126.50 per family. The Rehabilitation Corporation had purchased 36,812 acres and rented 528,727 acres from landowners to resettle destitute farmers. In all, over 10,000 families had benefited in one way or another from rural rehabilitation.[4]

The program continued into 1935 with minor changes to implement the division's policies. The staff aided in the marketing of its clients' crops by forming a cooperative marketing section under the GERA. Also, the Federal Land Bank in Columbia, South Carolina sent an appraiser to Atlanta to assist in refinancing farms owned by distressed farmers.

Most of the early resettlement took place on individual farms, but the GERA did initiate four rural farm communities, and the Board of Regents of the University of Georgia established a fifth one. The community idea began in 1933 with an agreement between the Board of Regents and the Subsistence Homesteads Division of the Department of the Interior. The board was to construct 500 homes in Jasper County with a federal allotment of $1 million. The project, originally called Chancellorsville Homestead Community, was to be controlled by a "local directing corporation" formed by the board. The board soon found, however, that the federal government planned to direct the project itself. The government feared that "with the University System involved too much attention will be paid to academics and theory." In June 1934 the board withdrew its support, leaving the community to the Division of Subsistence Homesteads, its name changing at this time to Piedmont Homesteads.

As the board's interest waned so did that of the public, and when the Division of Subsistence Homesteads reduced the planned number of houses from 500 to 50, Georgians suspected that the idea would be dropped entirely. By the spring of 1935 only $334,000 had been allotted to the project, and its future seemed bleak. With the establishment of the Resettlement Administration (RA) in July 1935, however, came new funds and better management, so that Piedmont Homesteads survived.[5]

The four GERA-initiated projects were Wolf Creek, Irwinville, Briar Patch, and Pine Mountain Valley. In May 1934 the Grady County farm supervisor for Rural Rehabilitation requested and obtained approval from the state office to purchase 250 acres in that county to settle five families selected from among relief clients. The community was to be called Wolf Creek Farms. The supervisor proposed that these farmers work together to clear the land, build houses, and construct fences. Then each family would settle individual farms of about 50 acres each, signing rehabilitation loan contracts in the usual manner.

Later that year Vansant authorized the supervisor to secure options on an additional 2,100 acres adjacent to the original tract for the placement of another 45 families. The Rural Rehabilitation Corporation bought the land, work stock, and all equipment; and the program commenced. The first year the land was not divided, but worked as a communal farm. Those men not cultivating the soil labored elsewhere to develop the community. Each man was given credit for his efforts to be subtracted from his loan, and at the end of the year the proceeds from crop sales were divided, half going to the clients and half to the corporation. In the second year the corporation divided the land, livestock, and equipment among the clients, and each man farmed his own acreage.

Unfortunately, much dissatisfaction arose among the clients. By the summer of 1935 only five houses were under construction, and these had to be altered when architects from the state office modified the plans. There also was no clear line of authority present on the project, causing "considerable confusion and cross purpose." A local merchant-farmer remarked that there was "too much investigation research and experimentation by inexperienced novices in many cases, with too little positive and definite action.

The project director was extremely capable, but found his actions hampered by the state office. Being a man of some determination, he ignored many of the directives handed down by the "Atlanta social work authorities" and proceeded on his own. When delays occurred in the state office with respect to housing, he hired his own architect to design inexpensive, but decent dwellings. For this he incurred the displeasure of those in the state administration. Ultimately he was vindicated, and when the RA took over the resettlement projects, it established definite lines of authority to assure that all officials were qualified agriculturalists as well as good social workers.[6]

The Irwinville Farms in Irwin and surrounding counties had a social worker as director, and did not fare as well as Wolf Creek Farms. The Irwinville director was a "rather heavy routineer" who evidently did not have sufficient grasp of the agricultural situation.[7] Both Briar Patch and Pine Mountain Valley were begun as rural-industrial communities. Briar Patch, located in Putnam County, was initiated in 1935 by the Rural Rehabilitation Corporation. When it was transferred to the RA, however, it became a subsistence farming community. The Rural Rehabilitation Division had planned to establish an industrial community in conjunction with Briar Patch, but none was ever forthcoming.

Of all the resettlement communities in the nation, Pine Mountain Valley was perhaps the most publicized because of its proximity to Roosevelt's "little White House." It was also "one of the most idealistically planned colonies of the FERA." This was unfortunate for the public image of the resettlement program, for Pine Mountain Valley was never as successful as its proponents had hoped.[8]

In February 1935 Hopkins approved the Pine Mountain Valley plans, which had been drawn up by the Georgia Rural Rehabilitation Corporation; Lawrence Westbrook, assistant administrator of the FERA; and David R. Williams, chief of planning for the FERA's Rural Rehabilitation Division. Unlike the other resettlement communities in the state, Pine Mountain Valley was designed to draw its settlers from white "economically stranded families" or displaced farmers living in Georgia's urban areas.

From its inception Pine Mountain Valley was plagued by difficulties. One of its basic flaws involved the idealistic conception of a rural-industrial community. It became evident early in the program that the project's relation to private industry would be a problem. The nature of the project did not allow for long-term planning that would lead to successful economic competition. The alternative of having residents work for local companies, however, might result in the exploitation of the community by business owners. In a letter to Aubrey Williams, an investigator noted that "this was borne out in a conversation . . . with Calloway, President of the Calloway Mills." Cason Callaway wanted to develop a community in which outside activities would allow clients to "practically support themselves" while laboring in the mills. The exasperated investigator exclaimed, "He is the worst type of paternalistic capitalist that I have yet to meet."

Another problem was one of leadership. During its early stages Pine Mountain Valley had no strong head. Westbrook and Williams were in Washington. The state supervisor of the community projects, O'Neill Ford, was too idealistic and rather ineffectual. Those people from the GERA office concerned with the project were social workers and not agriculturalists or engineers. No one at Pine Mountain Valley "embodied the form and pressure of the experiment." Vansant and Philip Weltner, who had planned the community, were unable to agree on a project manager. They were dissatisfied with Dr. M. F. Haygood, former director of a Georgia sanitarium, whom Miss Shepperson had picked originally to run the project, but they were unable to select a substitute.

Fortunately, there were those at Pine Mountain Valley who were qualified, so that some progress was made in the first stages of development. The man in charge of construction was quite competent, as was the resident architect, and although the more idealistic designers constantly were changing the plans for houses, the construction team was able to start building fifty-two dwellings by July 1935. Once the engineer was permitted to build without modifications, he used the services of enthusiastic settlers to complete a poultry farm and plant and a canning factory by September 1935. About fifteen public buildings and a number of homes were under construction at the end of the summer, and twenty-five homes had been finished.

Dr. Haygood was blamed for much of the community's troubles, and his presence at Pine Mountain Valley represented a weakness which existed at many of the other GERA communities. Social workers or unqualified agricultural personnel were placed in positions where they were called upon to make decisions involving situations about which they knew nothing. When Haygood finally resigned in 1936, William T. (Tap) Bennett, former Spalding County agent, took his place. Bennett, a practical agriculturalist, provided the knowledge and leadership heretofore lacking.

The Georgia Rural Rehabilitation Corporation controlled Pine Mountain Valley until March 1936, when it was taken over by the Georgia Pine Mountain Valley Rural Community Corporation. The new corporation set up a five-man board to run the community along with a project manager of the board's choice. The manager acted as resident director and sat as secretary to the board.

The WPA handled all construction from March 1936 until 1939.

Although the RA, which had assumed responsibility for all the other communities in 1936, had no direct control, it still exercised influence over Pine Mountain Valley, especially at the local level, and as the old planners dropped out of the picture, the lines of communication and control between the community and Miss Shepperson grew tenuous. She complained to Hopkins, "These people are nice, they are pleased that they have this project; but it is all in their hands now they think, and they won't listen to me except what I wheedle out of them." Hopkins insisted that Miss Shepperson retain command as WPA administrator until the project was completed, but it appeared that there was constant friction.

The combination of a somewhat utopian overview in competition with the immediate practical necessities spawned many of the difficulties in leadership and direction. The entire matter was exacerbated by the tremendous amount of publicity the project received. Problems of leadership and development which existed at all of the resettlement communities were magnified under public scrutiny, and the resulting criticism and constant pressure from the administration did not help to smooth them over.

Sensitive officials in Washington had hoped that Bennett's accession to the directorship would solve all the community's problems. This was not the case. The GERA had erred on the side of laxity and uninformed administration. Bennett reversed this situation, governing the community with a firm hand, but in doing so, he soon incurred the animosity of some residents. By August 1936 the situation was so tense that Bennett sought to evict a number of the families. Although Bennett won his battle, the spirit generated during the early idealistic days was broken. Hereafter, there was a growing turnover of residents.

Pine Mountain Valley also suffered from the same troubles which befell the other resettlement communities. Often the GERA had chosen ill-qualified clients. Since the community was designed for stranded families, many of those selected came from urban areas, increasing the chances for failure. On the other hand, being from cities, these people were more likely to be familiar with the possibilities of collective action. When their debts mounted at Pine Mountain Valley and the organization became less democratic, they were more inclined to take positive action than their counterparts in other communities.

On Bennett's behalf, it must be said that he saved the community from financial disaster. By the end of 1938 the project had expended all of its surplus funds and was relying solely upon the income it could generate for survival. Bennett could not hope to bring the community's assets up to a point where they equaled the government's investment. The project had been too costly for that. It had incurred $1,447,995.36 in losses since its inception, but in 1943 its estimated value was $1,001,000. Holding the net loss to only $446,995 probably was remarkable, given the conditions under which the community was planned and operated, especially in its early days.

Liquidation of Pine Mountain Valley began in 1937, as provided for in the conception of all resettlement communities. Residents were given the opportunity to purchase the land so that they might become independent farmers. They had built up such great debts, however, that the process proved to be a discouraging experience.

On November 6, 1939, the stockholders and board of directors of the Pine Mountain Valley Rural Community Corporation met and transferred their stock and jurisdiction to the Farm Security Administration (FSA). The directors served afterwards to help with administration, but the policies by which they were guided were those of the FSA. The FSA continued the liquidation of the project until 1947. The final dismemberment of Pine Mountain Valley and the other resettlement communities had nothing to do with their economic status, although many were not financially successful. Pine Mountain Valley was doing rather well in 1944, when congressional pressures forced the FSA to close all resettlement projects.

Pine Mountain Valley was the best known resettlement community in Georgia. It was also one of the most idealistic projects undertaken. It was administered in an unusual manner, not following the development of other such settlements. All these factors made the community atypical, and yet, because of the publicity surrounding it, Pine Mountain Valley exemplified the entire resettlement program. Perhaps it was not entirely misleading for this to be so; for historian Paul Conkin's assessment of Pine Mountain Valley—that it was beneficial if not practical— stood as a fair description of the entire resettlement program.[9]

The FERA's submarginal land purchase program began rather late in Georgia and was soon taken over by the RA. In the spring of 1935 the GERA announced that it would purchase about 100,000 acres in Baldwin, Wilkinson, Hancock, Jones, Twiggs, and Greene counties.

Earlier, the GERA had bought land in Jones, Putnam, and Jasper counties. With this second acquisition, the GERA established a formal headquarters for the program at Eatonton in Putnam County to administer the Submarginal Land Division. It was unfortunate that the program began so late in Georgia, for the state had a large amount of depleted land. The extension service estimated that about two-thirds of the state's agricultural area generally was unfit for prosperous farming. On this submarginal land over 37,000 farms covering 3.5 million acres were operating in 1935, or 15.9 percent of all land in farms and about 15 percent of all the farms in the state. The extension service also noted that nowhere else in the nation had the "depletion of soil resources taken place so rapidly." Under the National Industrial Recovery Act, $236,425 had been appropriated for submarginal land purchase in Georgia, but as of March 1, 1935, none had been disbursed. Once the program was initiated, the GERA acted quickly. By April 10, 1935, the division had spent $46,841 to purchase submarginal lands.[10]

One other program came under the partial aegis of the GERA. Part of the problem in making rehabilitation loans to tenants was their heavy indebtedness. In order to lighten this debt load, the Farm Credit Administration (FCA) and the FERA combined to offer landlords and tenants a system of farm debt adjustment. Originally, the GERA supplied the funds and the FCA administered the program, but in 1935 the RA took over the entire enterprise. Under the farm debt adjustment program, Governor Talmadge was permitted to select a state Farm Debt Adjustment Committee (Commission), and the GERA appointed five supervisors to work with it. The program also provided for the establishment of local committees in farm-debt adjustment. By the summer of 1935, when the RA took over the program, the administration had released nearly $1.2 million in frozen loans.[11]

The decision to create the RA revolved around national policies, but for Georgia it meant the consolidation and professionalization of the farm programs that were under the RA's control. Although the RA retained Vansant as head of the program in Georgia, it placed much more emphasis on a regional structure. Plans under way in June 1935 called for the appointment of Philip Weltner as regional director and Vansant as state director. The RA provided two assistants for Vansant and five state specialists. It also gave the extension service a larger role in the farm programs. Both Harry Brown and Gay Shepperson were pleased with an arrangement reached with the RA on June 10, 1935. Miss Shepperson told Brown that she hated "to give up the rural rehabilitation work but . . . it is going where it really belongs."

This agreement had a great impact upon the program in Georgia. Many of the administrative complaints leveled at the Rural Rehabilitation Division had concerned the use of social workers in cases where agriculturalists should have been employed. Now the county resettlement officer and the county agent worked more closely, often sharing the same office. The extension service, through its county workers, took from the GERA the task of appraising the resources of families proposed for rehabilitation or resettlement. It developed and supervised rehabilitation plans for clients. The RA itself assumed "the responsibility for adjusting debts, making loans, purchasing and leasing lands, constructing and repairing buildings, supplying human subsistence, feed, seed, fertilizers, tools, machinery, equipment, farm animals and other rehabilitation goods, as well as negotiating all legal and business transactions incident thereto." As a final gesture of cooperation with the extension service, Weltner moved the state RA office from Atlanta to Athens. There he completed his plans for organization and proceeded to implement the various policies of the RA.[12]

Unfortunately, the speed with which Weltner was required to set up the programs in Georgia and the complexity involved in the consolidation of so many enterprises into one new agency combined to cause serious delays and confusion. Added to these was the problem of continuing programs already under way, but heretofore devised and prosecuted by an agency with a different philosophy, different aims, and different organization.

One of the first issues which the RA faced was the payment of debts incurred by the GERA. The GERA's office had been lax in its financial dealings with private concerns, and the RA inherited bills for goods and services rendered as far back as April 1935. This fact caused many businesses to hesitate before dealing with the RA.[13]

The RA itself experienced some auditing difficulties. Payroll checks had to be cleared through both Washington and the state treasury office. The state NEC director reported as early as January 18, 1936, that paychecks were being delayed, and the establishment of a separate payroll office in Atlanta the next month did not solve the problem. By June 1936 the administration had fallen several months behind in its payment of salaries and expenses due personnel and bills owed to private concerns.[14]

The transfer of farm programs to the RA created other administrative problems. The public was confused by the swift consolidation of so many operations, and the staff which made the switch had to adjust to new policies. As a result, the RA had difficulty in making progress initially.

Harry Brown blamed the delay on the "serious handicap" of insufficient "latitude" given to state workers by the regional office. The state NEC director noted that the new procedures were "too detailed and arbitrary . . . leading to dissatisfaction in some areas." He suggested that more power be given to county workers to take some of the pressure off the state office. Most of these problems eventually were overcome, but some of the programs never managed to achieve real success.[15]

The rural rehabilitation program changed very little under the RA, although its policies and procedures were modified considerably. One of Weltner's first changes involved reducing the number of districts and workers. He lowered the number of district farm and home supervisors from six to five and cut the number of their county counterparts from 155 to about 120. The reduction amounted to about 30 to 35 percent in personnel, payrolls, and number of offices. The remaining workers were extremely competent, and the simplified organization increased the efficiency of district and local offices. An investigator for the RA noted that the "efficiency and attitude" of rehabilitation workers were excellent probably because the state and regional offices seemed to have been able to avoid political appointments. The investigator felt, however, that the administration was in danger of losing some of its better staff members because salaries were so low. Another 20 percent reduction in administrative funds the next year made it even more difficult to keep qualified employees.[16]

Another problem confronting the new rural rehabilitation agency was that of undesirable clients. Many people in the state opposed making loans to the lower classes of farmers. These critics never expected rehabilitation clients to pay back the money. The RA found that the GERA had indeed been very careless in its selection of borrowers, so in 1936 it made a 10 percent cut, eliminating about 1,300 persons who were "misfits, uncooperative, or unrehabilable." At the same time, the agency added some new clients, lending nearly $2.9 million to 11,511 people. The next year the RA further reduced the number of loans to 10,500. By insisting on more careful selection, the agency was able to regain public support.

Local financing institutions found that many farmers who had repaid their rehabilitation loans in 1936 were now borrowing from them. Before the summer of 1937, resentment to rehabilitation loans had been overcome; for by the end of 1936, 1,500 of the 11,511 families receiving loans that year had repaid them in full.[17]

The rehabilitation loan program continued without much modification under the Farm Security Administration when it superseded the RA in 1937. In its annual report for 1941, the FSA estimated that 11,941 families had received loans only; 16,832, grants only; and 24,933, loans and grants from 1934 to June 1941. Through 1940 the various rehabilitation agencies had advanced Georgia farmers over $20.3 million and granted them $2.1 million. The FSA noted that 88.8 percent of the maturities on these loans had been collected. Georgians subsequently decided that the rehabilitation project was the most successful of the farm-relief programs once the stigma of the indolent farmer had been overcome.[18]

In the summer of 1935 the GERA handed the RA a resettlement program besieged with problems. The federal government had allotted Georgia funds for the purchase of 39,537 acres on which 1,241 families could be settled in communities or by "infiltration." About 25 to 30 percent of those already on new lands were considered unqualified farmers. Some had been moved so rapidly that "proper consideration was not given to the ability of their land to support the family with a sufficient margin for the reduction of their loan."

The GERA had also leased or purchased much land that was, at best, only marginal, and this too was bequeathed to the RA. Also some of the unpaid debts incurred before July 1935 were for resettlement projects, and the personnel of the new RA rural resettlement section faced the same recalcitrant businessmen that the rehabilitation division was forced to deal with.[19]

The RA immediately set about to remedy the complications left by the GERA. Clients who showed "lack of interest and effort" were dropped in 1936, and extra care was taken in the selection of new applicants. The RA provided more capable leadership in the resettlement communities replacing social workers with agriculturalists.[20]

Other problems, however, were not so easily solved. Two complaints were often present in the state NEC director's reports: the cost of the individual units was excessive, and the agency took a long time in paying for land under option. These two difficulties were never resolved. The construction of most communities, moreover, was slow because of frequent changes in administrative procedure, especially in regard to relief laborers. Under the FSA's rules, farmers were not allowed to do certain types of construction, and securing relief workers from the WPA was often difficult.[21]

The rural resettlement project at Irwinville ultimately proved to be the best in Georgia. Irwinville was of particular historical interest to Georgians, and the state office did not want to give it up. This town had been the county seat of Irwin County and the location of the old J. B. Clements estate. The GERA had begun the project with a 10,769-acre purchase from the estate on the advice of William P. Bryan, master farmer of Tifton.

Upon assuming control of the project, the RA immediately replaced the social worker in charge with a "practical farmer." Because the planners had taken over a deserted town for the rural community, the overhead was minimal, and the additional buildings were well constructed, though not according to plans handed down from the Washington office. When Washington suggested that its plans be used, the project officials balked at the specifications, saying that the houses would be too expensive to build. Irwinville also managed to select settlers of "merit," so that it escaped some of the criticism leveled at other communities. Perhaps most important, the community was situated on good soil which promised adequate harvests for the residents.

Originally, the RA considered using the old town to house all of the farmers. This would give the project more of the atmosphere of a true town. The administration discarded this idea, however, in favor of the more conventional arrangement of unit farms. The jail was left standing because of its historical interest, and the courthouse also remained to be used as a meeting place for the project's residents. All of the other original buildings were demolished.

The GERA had begun work on seven houses, fifteen barns, and miscellaneous dwelling repairs before it turned the project over to the RA. The RA completed these structures, built nineteen additional houses, and made repairs on twenty-two existing buildings. It also constructed outbuildings and dug wells for residents. By the time the RA was dissolved there were forty-eight units on the project. Then the FSA took over and erected another thirty-four units, bringing the total to eighty-three.

Although the resident staff was not particularly creative, conditions were so favorable that the community prospered. In 1937, 900 acres were added to the original 9,720-acre tract. By 1939, residents had completed eighty-five farm units and four town units on 6,621 acres, and there were eighty-three families living there. Will W. Alexander, head of the FSA, visited Irwinville in 1939 and decided that the project had gone far enough to start "a number of the best families toward ownership." This signaled its gradual liquidation.

Under the FSA and RA, the community expanded its efforts. A canning plant was built, a health service and school were begun, a social life was established, and all sorts of related farm services were initiated. In March 1939 the project had proved so successful that W. T. Anderson, editor of the Macon *Telegraph,* ran a feature story on Irwinville beginning, "Believe it or not, I have found something in the New Deal which I can approve."[22]

Briar Patch Farms originated as a proposed rural-industrial community. The industrial complex did not materialize, however, and when the RA assumed control, it decided to forgo the industrial experiment and convert the project to subsistence farming. In 1936, the land was resubdivided into twenty-two "economical farm units" embracing the thirty-five original tracts of 10,582 acres. By 1938 families were living on all but one of these units, and the project was being liquidated through a transfer of ownership from the RA to the residents.[23]

Wolf Creek Farms, begun as a cooperative farming community, also experienced a change of direction under the RA. The most serious problems which had arisen on the project under the GERA resulted from a confused and powerless local administration. The resident manager had selected only eight of the forty-six families living on the project at the time the RA assumed control, and some of these were "of very low character and ambition."

By the summer of 1935 very little progress had been made. Some lumber had been cut, temporary buildings had been erected, and materials had been purchased for twenty five-room houses. The GERA, however, had gone no further than to lay the foundation for the community. Once the RA assumed control, the program moved ahead swiftly. By the end of the year twenty-four houses on fifty-acre farm units had been constructed. These units were no longer communal, and each family was responsible for its own farm. The families themselves

also seemed to be more successful. Their early resentment to cooperative farming had disappeared, and most were making greater progress
towards private ownership.

The project was to remain fairly small, however. Although thirty
units were planned, only the original twenty-four were settled by 1939.
Instead of expanding their numbers, the project manager opted to
increase the size of the existing farms, feeling that this would be more
helpful in assuring the success of those already in residence.[24]

In the long run, Briar Patch, Irwinville, Wolf Creek, and Piedmont
farms were only moderately successful. They remained small and aided
only a few farmers in gaining private ownership of arable land. Their
cost was very high in relation to the number of people they helped. As
experiments in cooperative or subsistence farming, they were complete
failures, and the RA abandoned such attempts very early in its history.
Perhaps the farms were most successful as unofficial demonstration areas
for farm management and farm practices. Families residing on resettlement farms were required by their contracts to follow certain guidelines,
and these were of great help in the residents' struggles to attain financial
independence. Other farmers in the area were certain to be impressed by
such success and inclined to adopt these productive farming practices.[25]

One settlement begun under the hegemony of the RA was of
particular importance as an all-black project. The Piedmont Homesteads
project originally called for ten black families from urban centers to be
included in the subsistence farming program, and some blacks were
helped through the RA's infiltration projects. Beyond this token effort
little had been done to help destitute black farmers under the FERA.

In September 1935, Gay Shepperson asked permission to organize a
black community in Georgia along the lines of the Pine Mountain Valley
experiment. Lawrence Westbrook, Hopkins' assistant, replied to her
inquiry that, while he approved of such a project, it could not be undertaken by the FERA. He suggested that Miss Shepperson contact the RA.
The RA was receptive to the idea and began to search for an appropriate
location.

By March 1936 a desirable site in Peach County had been chosen and
plans initiated for the Fort Valley Farms. The RA selected this place for
obvious reasons. Peach County was over 50 percent black, was centrally
located in the state, and was the home of the Fort Valley Normal School
for Negroes. Walter E. Packard, acting director of the Rural Resettlement

Division, and J. H. Wood, acting regional chief in charge of rural resettlement, both agreed to the project. Packard said, "The whole set-up is exceptional and the program should be pushed vigorously."[26]

The residents of Peach County were not so receptive to the idea. By August enough opposition had developed to force the RA to halt work on the project. The regional office reported to Resettlement Administrator Rexford G. Tugwell that only a few people in the county seriously objected to Fort Valley Farms, but their criticism was so vocal that the administration was "unable to get very strong favorable expressions from the others." Those who resented the project evidently were prominent in the county's ruling hierarchy, and their opposition was enough to stifle all support. In the summer of 1936, therefore, the regional office began searching for a new location. While officially maintaining the Fort Valley plan the RA sent appraisers and option takers to other counties and decided that, if pressure became too great in Peach County, they would move the project to Macon County.

When it became apparent that no progress could be made at Fort Valley, the RA officially closed it and announced the opening of Flint River Farms in Macon County. The 228 acres in Peach County were turned over to the state Board of Education to be used by the National Youth Administration for a black recreational project. In Macon County the RA once more encountered opposition from local residents. The Macon County *Citizen* and Montezuma *Georgian* spoke out against the project, and a prominent citizen, Benjamin F. Neal, circulated a petition among residents to stop its construction.

Neal did not control all opinion in the county, however, and other important people supported the idea. When the local Kiwanis Club of Montezuma voted in favor of Flint River Farms, many signers of the critical petition came forward saying that they had "signed under misconception." The regional RA director reported that upon investigation of the unfavorable letters received he found "the opposition is in the main confined to persons who have some selfish reason for opposing the project." The forces at work in Macon County resembled those the RA had encountered in Peach County, but because the people were not solidly against the project, the director believed that once the RA announced the purchase of land, opposition would die out. The director also sounded out the congressional representative from the third district, Stephen Pace. Pace told him that he was in favor of the idea, but thought that the county should be allowed to decide. He believed that most people wanted the project, but he was unwilling to "be responsible for deciding in favor of it."[27]

Ultimately, the RA prevailed over local opposition, and construction began early in 1937. Seventy-seven of the black families accepted as clients were taken from among the tenants already on the land, and only twenty-nine came from other areas. This tended to reduce any remaining dissatisfaction. By June 1937 the project was well under way. The RA provided 107 units averaging ninety-three acres each and made loans to fifty-six families for the construction of homes and barns and other improvements. In the spring of 1938 the RA made seventeen more loans and approved a budget for thirty-four additional units. At this time the project contained eleven tracts of 10,653 acres. A total of seventy-seven families resided there. Those who moved to the farms were in severe financial difficulty. Their average net worth was only about $78 per family. But with the guidance of the federal government, they prospered. Within one year the net worth of the first families had increased to about $300.

The administration instituted farm-related programs such as food preservation and canning, subsistence gardens, crop diversification, and farm-home management. It constructed a community center, began a health service, built and staffed an excellent school, initiated a cooperative marketing association, and instituted a "training school" for young farmers. The success of this project far outdistanced any of the other resettlement communities. Because it was initiated under the RA, Flint River Farms escaped much of the trouble caused elsewhere by the GERA, and the local manager was able to make rapid progress from the very beginning. RA officials were particularly impressed with its progress, since they were dealing with a group of farmers who "accepted and followed a program different from anything they had known in the past."

This success, however, failed to excite some people, and they withheld their support. Even those who might overtly praise the community found that their attitudes toward blacks had not changed enough to allow them to help it. For instance, Miss Katherine F. Deitz, regional education and community activities adviser for the RA, reported that the county superintendent of education and his board were "not in sympathy with the school [on the project] as they are fundamentally opposed to doing anything for negroes." Miss Deitz also wrote that the County Medical

Association was uncooperative. Twice it had refused to supply supervision in running a health association for the project.

Still, these obstacles could not destroy the ultimate accomplishment
of the farms. Above all, blacks had shown whites that they were capable
farmers and that their former positions as tenants and croppers were
not a result of some innate inferiority, but the product of the state's
economy and certain definite attitudes about their color. It was unlikely
that this point ever was accepted by local residents, but the facts remained for later generations to consider.[28]

Apart from the community-type resettlement program, the RA
assumed responsibility for individual "infiltration" resettlement projects.
These it lumped together under the heading of Georgia Scattered Farms.
In most cases the GERA had purchased a tract of land and resettled a
small number of families on it. Although, for example, all of the 86
families living on the project in Laurens County were considered part of
Wheeler Farms, each client was dealt with separately.

Originally, the RA planned to continue the GERA's eight scattered
farm projects accommodating 543 families at a cost of $48,000. All of
the farms were run from the state headquarters in Athens. Because they
were not concentrated in large communities, these clients were more
exposed to other farmers in the area, who often regarded them with some
scorn. Such farmers in Greene County were referred to as "government
farmers or Rehabs" and sometimes as "A-rabs." By 1941 there were
seven family units planned or completed on an area of 1,069 acres. The
entire capital investment was $24,473.[29]

In 1936 most of the infiltration projects were transferred to the RA's
new Georgia Farm Tenant Security Program. When a bill providing for
tenant purchase loans died in committee that year, the RA decided to
experiment with 1,000 tenant farmers in the South (112 in Georgia),
"giving them a chance to own land under conditions similar to those
proposed in the bill." The work was handled through the regional office
in cooperation with the state office. Vansant asked for $297,000 for 100
families in 25 counties and the use of up to 270 men in constructing
farm buildings on the projects. He then drew up the state's plans, and they
were accepted by the RA. By April 1936 he had selected 50 families to
be placed in 22 counties, and by 1937 all tracts had been secured, providing 116 units.

The Farm Tenant Security Program proved to be of greater value than

the community projects. Each client was considered separately, so that
more attention was paid to his individual needs. Furthermore, the infiltration projects did not draw the scrutiny attracted to the communities. There
was little of the utopian nature about them.

By April 1939, 106 units in 35 different counties had been completed,
and all but seven families had improved their conditions during the
previous year. The clients, however, were experiencing some difficulty
in acquiring supplemental income. The state office attempted to change
the situation in 1939. In North Georgia the supervisors aided farmers in
developing small hog and large cattle pastures. They also stimulated the
production of pimiento peppers where advisable. In South Georgia more
possibilities existed. Farmers fenced large areas for combined hog and
cattle pastures. In suitable sections, supervisors helped farmers build
tobacco barns and aided them in securing AAA contracts. They also encouraged the production of pecans and poultry.

When the FSA superseded the RA, it transferred the management of
infiltration resettlement from the Resettlement Division to the Rural
Rehabilitation Division. This obviated the necessity for having two
officials in counties where infiltration units existed. Under the new organization the county rural rehabilitation supervisor assumed the responsibility for the infiltration clients.[30]

Much of the land on which resettlement farmers had lived was taken
over by the Division of Land Utilization of the RA. In fact, the decision
as to which families in the state were to be resettled often depended upon
the plans of land utilization officials. When the RA replaced the GERA,
there were six submarginal land projects in the state. The area under the
Submarginal Land Division of the GERA had been put to use in a number
of ways. The earliest tracts were turned into game preserves. They were
followed by acreage added to state parks and to resettlement communities
as demonstration areas.

The RA continued along the lines set up by the GERA with moderate
success. In an early reevaluation of the problem, the Georgia State Land
Planning Consultants reported that 3,517,000 acres of submarginal land
in Georgia should be retired. The RA was given $1,426,522 for this pur-
pose, but it was only enough to purchase 204,116 acres. The administration was able to add another project at Alexander Stephens Memorial
Park to make a total of seven projects in 1936. One project on the
Savannah River was authorized but not being developed, so by the end

of the year there were six projects under way at an approved cost of $433,944. When the RA was dissolved in 1937, the land utilization program was taken over directly by the Department of Agriculture.

The Land Utilization Division was almost immediately confronted with the problem of securing labor. The RA had been allowed to use residents as well as WPA labor on the projects in 1935. The land utilization projects were not included in the state WPA allotment, but Hopkins informed Miss Shepperson that they could take priority when the government cut the resident labor supply. WPA laborers, however, were subject to the rule that at least 90 percent of the workers on any project had to be taken from relief rolls. All rural projects were hard pressed by this order, and the RA's program suffered accordingly. In January 1936, therefore, the WPA exempted the RA from the rule in an attempt to alleviate the difficulties. Unfortunately, the administration reversed its position on both matters in the late summer of 1936, and the RA found itself back where it had been a year earlier. Only as the number of projects was reduced did the problem lessen.

The Land Utilization Division also was plagued by a lack of funds. No sooner had the program commenced, than the division's budget for acquisition was cut from $108 million to $44 million. It was not until the three projects adjacent to park areas had been turned over to the National Park Service that conditions improved. There were some complaints that the division took too long to pay for land it optioned, though most vendors were satisfied when the RA informed them of the status of their transactions.

By 1937 it had become evident to the state NEC director that the land utilization projects were of little value. The agricultural demonstration areas suffered from the same limitations as those of the Soil Conservation Service. They were too isolated to be of use to those farmers who stood to benefit most from their presence. The division had really offered "very little assistance" to those on demonstration land. Some farmers also complained that blacks were employed on utilization projects in areas where they were needed on private farms, although the assistant regional director stated, "we have absolutely no intention of working anyone on our projects at security wages or on any other wage basis who can obtain employment elsewhere."

What support the utilization programs enjoyed came mostly from civic organizations and white-collar workers in their immediate vicinity.

Land purchases were "extremely beneficial to local tax situations," and the recreational projects were popular with those close enough to make use of them. The projects also added their part in taking up surplus labor. They were of little educational, demonstrational, or recreational use, however, outside the immediate area. They were also rather expensive undertakings and, ultimately, probably not worth the investment.[31]

Another program taken over by the RA and pursued as part of its total farm program was that of farm debt adjustment. Its administration was much the same as that of the rural rehabilitation section. The regional office provided the services of two specialists who aided a state staff composed of a director, executive secretary, and five divisional supervisors. In addition, the RA set up a voluntary State Farm Debt Adjustment Committee and county committees. The state committee was appointed by the governor, and it recommended local committees to him.

The state committee was composed of ten men, and the county committees contained three or more members. The local committees had existed while farm debt adjustment was under the control of the GERA and the FCA. When the transfer took place, they became disorganized and their interest slackened, so that few adjustments were made in the first months under the RA. From September to December 1935, most of the section's work was devoted to reorganizing the committees to insure efficiency under the new program.[32]

From September 1, 1935, to March 31, 1936, only 459 cases were adjusted, lowering the debts of these people by $125,731. By November 1936, however, the section had received 2,250 applications and had adjusted 1,117 of these by $306,062. By June 30, 1940, 4,820 cases had been adjusted involving reduction in debts of $997,537 or 15.6 percent of the indebtedness.

The RA experienced an overall cut in funds in 1937, and Regional Director Rufus W. Hudgens decided to reduce adjustment work. He planned to give the supervision of debt adjustment to the rehabilitation supervisors, since so much of the adjustment work involved families receiving these loans. When news of this move became public, he received a number of complaints. Besides not wanting the program reduced, some observers felt that rehabilitation supervisors were not equipped to handle the adjustment program. Subsequently Hudgens relented to their demands and only reduced the number of Farm Debt Adjustment supervisors.[33]

On July 22, 1937, the president approved the Bankhead-Jones Farm

Tenant Act, and on September 1 Wallace established the Farm Security Administration as a division of the Department of Agriculture. The FSA assumed all of the responsibilities formerly held by the RA (which was dissolved) except for the land utilization program, which was moved directly to the Department of Agriculture. In addition to regular resettlement, rehabilitation, and debt adjustment activities, the FSA also undertook administration of the Tenant Purchase Program provided for by the Bankhead-Jones Act. The FSA expanded some of the regular programs and sought generally to integrate all of its activities in working toward the single goal of uplifting America's farm population. The ultimate achievement of this trend was exemplified in Georgia by the creation of a Unified Farm Program in Greene County after 1938.

The Bankhead-Jones Act provided loans for tenants, sharecroppers, and farm laborers, to be repaid in forty years at 3 percent interest. This was a step up from the standard rehabilitation loan and as such drew more support from Georgians. Furthermore, by allowing local committees to select recipients, the FSA could be assured of some interest in the counties.[34]

Before the act was passed, Georgia's farmers had expressed a desire for such a program. In a 1936 Gallup Poll appearing in the Birmingham *News,* Georgia and Alabama samples gave 90 percent approval to such a plan. At the time the act was passed few farmers realized what it meant, but FSA officials in the state applauded the move. They noted that about 65 percent of all farms in the state were operated by tenants and sharecroppers, and they estimated that 16,000 farmers would be eligible for assistance under the act's provisions.[35]

By the end of 1937 the FSA had begun to construct its administrative organization for the disbursal of loans and to allocate funds to the various states on the basis of farm population and tenancy. Of the $10 million which Congress appropriated, Georgia received $635,003. The secretary of agriculture then appointed a state Farm Security Advisory Committee to select the counties which would receive the money. Fifteen prominent farmers and agricultural leaders were nominated and approved in Washington, and then the state FSA office selected nine of them to sit on the committee.[36]

The state committee began meeting early in 1938 to select the eligible counties, and drew up a list of thirty-five chosen on the basis of farm population and tenancy. The regional director promptly approved the list, and the state committee and state FSA officials set about organizing the local staffs and committees.

By March 16, 1938, forty-two options had been taken at an average cost per farm of $2,347. In assessing the first months of operation, Vansant noted that interest was steadily growing as all loan dockets neared completion. He felt, however, that many tenants did not apply because they believed with the small number of loans (five in each county) "their chance for getting one was too limited to justify the effort." Vansant also stated that the number of applications would have been twice as large if the sign-up period had been in late summer or early fall, before tenants had made arrangements with their landlords for the next year.[37]

Still, enthusiasm ran high. Although the deadline for applications had been January 15, tenants were still applying in February. Tenants from nondesignated counties asked for loans, and 10,000 to 20,000 farmers inquired about the program.

As of October 21, 1938, there were 164,331 tenants in Georgia, 106,091 of whom resided in the designated counties. Of these, 13,132 whites and 3,984 blacks filed applications for tenant purchase loans. This figure represented 16.13 percent of those eligible, and the percentage was second only to Florida, which had the least number of tenants in the region.[38]

During 1938 the state committee was asked to select counties to receive loans during fiscal 1938-1939. The committee chose 75 counties. The next year the number was raised to 99. Most of the counties originally selected continued to receive the loans. Of the 99 counties included in the 1939-1940 list, 40 were carried over from the previous fiscal year, and 59 had received loans for all three years.[39]

The farm tenant purchase program was a tremendous success for those who obtained the loans. The basic problem lay in the limited funds appropriated. So many were eligible and needy and so little money was available that only 185 out of 5,000 applicants were awarded loans in 1937-1938. As the program became more popular, the situation grew worse. In 1938-1939 only 400 farmers out of 17,000 who applied received loans.[40]

The tenant purchase program represented the culmination of the government's shifting loan policy. Its two shortcomings were that it did not aid the most depressed farmers and the program was never adequately funded. Poorer farmers invariably were filtered out by the local selecting committees. For them there remained only the rehabilitation loans. Only a very small percentage of those eligible to receive the tenant purchase loans ever obtained them. On the positive side, the tenant purchase plan was the most sophisticated and successful of the loan programs. Although there were no figures, observers believed that a greater number of these people achieved private ownership and a certain amount of economic independence than the recipients of any other type of farm loan.

All of the FSA's efforts culminated in the unified farm program experiment in Greene County. In 1928 Arthur F. Raper, then a student at the University of North Carolina at Chapel Hill, wrote a doctoral dissertation on Greene and Macon counties. In 1934 the Rosenwald Fund awarded him a fellowship to continue his studies which resulted in a book, *Preface to Peasantry*. Dr. Will W. Alexander, director of the fund, was impressed by Raper's work, and the book played an important role in influencing his selection of Greene County for the new program when he became director of the FSA in 1937.

Early in 1938, planning began to establish a program whereby all of the agricultural agencies would cooperate to uplift this depressed county. Originally the state extension service and the Bureau of Agricultural Economics developed a blueprint of operations, but they were not able to secure the necessary funds until the next year. When residents of the county learned of the plans, however, they became "quite excited about it."

County officials and civic organizations seemed to think that the federal government was going to undertake "some wholesale spending campaign" and the FSA had to explain that such was not the case. The project called for extensive planning and cooperation aimed at "long-time period improvements." This misunderstanding and the delay involved in starting the program, nevertheless, did not dampen the county's enthusiasm.

While the farm agencies awaited funds in 1938, they set about to formulate specific plans and were well prepared to begin operations in 1939. The task of organization fell to a county Program Planning Committee of twenty-one citizens advised by field representatives of each farm agency and the state Land-Use Planning Committee. This Program Planning Committee first surveyed the county and made detailed reports of its findings. The results were published by the county Land-Use Planning Committee in 1939.

Various farm organizations each pursued a special task. To those in the area, the program appeared a great success, serving as a model for other such experiments. It proved to be only a stopgap measure, however. Greene County was steeped in a poverty which sprang from poor soil and limited resources, a condition that the unified farm program could not reverse. The most it could ever hope to accomplish was to hold the line against complete destitution. Even World War II, which brought prosperity to so many urban and rural areas, failed to help this county, and it remained a depressed area into the 1960s.[41]

This evaluation of Greene County's experience pointed to a flaw in all of the agricultural relief programs, for all shared in the battle. Ultimately, there were certain areas which could not be reached, certain conditions which could not be improved. The only solution to such massive problems was evacuation of the destitute farm population, and for those whose families had lived in a county for generations, this was no answer at all, only a surrender.

The programs of the FSA and RA were not complete failures. In many parts of the state conditions were such that rehabilitation of the farm population was possible. In these areas the FSA and RA made great progress, rescuing those whose poverty stemmed from a purely economic situation. Many tenants were helped to purchase their own farms, and those who abandoned cotton established the foundation for successful operations in poultry, cattle, and substitute crops.

None of the farm programs, however, was able to eradicate the one-crop economy and its handmaiden, tenancy. They were able to reverse cotton's deleterious effect upon the land and the people to some extent, but not to erase it completely. This did not imply a condemnation of the programs in Georgia, for the deficiencies were shared by all states to some extent. The New Deal, in general, did not solve the farm problem; it only helped some to escape it and others to survive within it.

Although these farm agencies did not defeat the agricultural depression, they made certain inroads. Furthermore, they became increasingly more effective. From the FERA to the FSA stretched a road littered with inadequate planning, uninformed social workers, and unrealistic utopian communities as the programs moved from the FERA's rather ineffective administration of farm projects to the FSA's sophisticated and knowledgeable integrated attack on the problems. As was so often the case in this period, the idealists found their castles were merely clapboard tenant

shacks, and the social workers discovered that without specific knowledge
and skills they could not hope to combat conditions which they did
not understand.

NOTES

1. FERA, Research Section, "The Cotton Growing Area of the Old
South: Meriwether County, Georgia," Rural Problem Areas Survey Report
No. 29 (E-29) (1934), pp. 1-2. (Also, Survey Report No. 28 on Morgan
County and Survey Report No. 30 on Tift County.)

2. Atlanta *Constitution,* April 26, May 19 and 23, and July 21, 1934.
FERA, "Monthly Report" (May 1934), p. 8. Unsigned report, July 3, 1934,
NARG 44, NEC, Office of Government Reports, Periodical Reports
(1934-38), box 400. Leggett to Bruce McClure, quoted in unsigned report,
July 6, 1934, NARG 44, Gen. Corres. with State Directors (1934-35),
box 174. See Appendix, Table 20.

3. Atlanta *Constitution,* October 3, 1934. "Report on Rural Re-
habilitation Activities for Directors of the Georgia Rural Rehabilitation
Corporation Meeting in Session, February 12, 1935," NARG 69, FERA,
State Files, box 64. "Reorganization of Rural Relief," n.d., NARG 69,
FERA, Old Subject Files, box 59.

4. Atlanta *Constitution,* January 1 and February 21, 1935.

5. *Ibid.,* January 6, February 16, and August 7, 1934 and June 4
and 11, 1935. Report of Gilbert Parks, July 18, 1935, NARG 96,
Farmers Home Administration, Farm Security Administration, Piedmont
Homesteads, box 80. Unsigned report, March 28, 1934, NARG 44,
Periodical Reports (1934-38), box 400. F. O. Clark to Dr. Carl Taylor,
September 3, 1935 (memo), NARG 96, Piedmont Homesteads, RH-GA-2.

6. Jule G. Liddell to Dr. C. C. Taylor, August 13, 1935, NARG 96,
Wolf Creek Farms, 85-GA-17, box 8. "Wolf Creek Farms," NARG 96,
Rural Resettlement Division, Project Correspondence, January 26,
1936, box 83. "Wolf Creek Farms," March 1939, NARG 96, Division
of Information, Wolf Creek Farms, box 79. Judge Charles N. Feidelson
to Col. Lawrence Westbrook, April 11, 1935 (memo), NARG 96,
Corres. (1935-38), box 69.

7. "Irwinville Farms," 1939 (?), NARG 96, Division of Information,
Irwinville Farms, box 79. Feidelson to Westbrook, April 11, 1935
(memo), NARG 96, Corres. (1935-38), box 60.

8. For a detailed history of the Pine Mountain Valley experiment

see: Paul K. Conkin, "It All Happened at Pine Mountain Valley," *Georgia Historical Quarterly*, LXVII, 1 (March 1963), 1-42.

9. Atlanta *Constitution*, February 4 and July 2, 1935. "Pine Mountain Valley," January 17, 1940, NARG 96, Pine Mountain Valley, 85-10-61-163-01, box 107. Genung to Williams, March 20, 1935, NARG 69, FERA, State Files, box 64. Paul K. Conkin, *Tomorrow a New World: The New Deal Community Program* (Ithaca: Cornell University Press, 1959), pp. 138-140. Feidelson to Westbrook, April 11, 1935 (memo), NARG 96, Corres. (1935-38), box 60. Ralph W. Langley to Perry A. Fellows, October 19, 1935, NARG 69, Region III, No. 132.3, box 185. Shepperson to Hopkins, July 10, 1935 (telephone conversation), NARG 69, State Series, No. 651, box 1129. C. Arild Olsen to R. W. Hudgens, July 22, 1944, NARG 96, Cooperative Associations, Georgia, box 24. Shepperson to Corrington Gill, November 10, 1939, NARG 69, State Series, No. 651, box 1129. All material not contained in the above citations may be found in the article, "Pine Mountain Valley," by Paul K. Conkin.

10. Atlanta *Constitution*, April 9, 1935. Georgia Experiment Station, *Bulletin*, No. 191 (1935), pp. 1, 16. U.S. Congress, Senate, Document No. 40, 74th Cong., 1st Sess., 1935, p. 199. U.S. Congress, Senate, Document No. 56, 74th Cong., 1st Sess., 1935, p. 592.

11. "Report of the Proceedings of the Statewide Coordinating Meeting of the National Emergency Council," April 10, 1936 (Report of H. A. Cliett), NARG 44, Corres., Directories, Reports, box 349. "Report on Rural Rehabilitation Activities for the Directors of the Georgia Rural Rehabilitation Corporation Meeting in Session, February 12, 1935," NARG 69, State Files, box 64. Atlanta *Constitution*, June 7, 1934, and April 2, 1935.

12. For a discussion of the national politics involved see: Sidney Baldwin, *Poverty and Politics* (Chapel Hill: University of North Carolina Press, 1968), pp. 85-125. Atlanta *Constitution*, June 29 and July 4, 1935. Ada M. Barker, "A Report of the Social Security Survey in Georgia," Georgia State Department of Public Welfare and the WPA (1937), p. 12. Unsigned report, July 30, 1935, NARG 44, Digests, box 489. H. L. Brown to C. W. Warburton, June 22, 1935, NARG 96, Corres. (1935-42), box 317. *Georgia Extension News*, III, 1 (July 1935), 1. Annual report of L. I. Skinner, district agent for Northwest Georgia, 1935, NARG 33, Agricultural Extension Service, microfilm reel 71.

13. Unsigned report, August 13, 1935, NARG 44, Digests, box 489. R. D. Smith, "Personnel Report, Georgia, Division No. 1," August 17, 1935, NARG 96, Corres. (1935-42), box 104. Unsigned report, July 2, 1935, NARG 44, Digests, box 488.

14. Unsigned reports, January 18 and February 1, 1936, NARG 44, Digests, box 400. Unsigned report, December 21, 1935, NARG 44, Digests, box 498.

15. Unsigned report, September 24, 1935, NARG 44, Digests, box 492. Unsigned report, December 7, 1935, NARG 44, Digests, box 497. Brown to Warburton, November 14, 1935, NARG 33, Corres., box 399.

16. R. D. Smith, "Personnel Reports," August 3, 1935, NARG 96, Corres. (1935-42), box 104. "Rural Rehabilitation General Personnel Reports, Resettlement Administration," miscellaneous reports beginning on July 27, 1935, by P. S. Fisher, R. S. Ryan, and R. D. Smith, NARG 96, Corres. (1935-42), box 104. R. D. Smith to A. C. Jewett, August 6, 1935, NARG 96, Corres. (1935-42), box 104. Unsigned report, June 6, 1935, NARG 44, Digests, box 505.

17. Report of R. D. Smith, July 27, 1935, NARG 96, Corres. (1935-42), box 104. Unsigned report, December 10, 1936, NARG 44, Digests, box 509. R. L. Vansant, "Annual Report of Activities of the Rehabilitation Division of the Resettlement Administration in Georgia for 1936," NARG 16, Secretary of Agriculture. Unsigned report, January 10, 1937, NARG 44, Digests, box 510.

18. Office of Government Reports, "Direct and Cooperative Loans and Expenditures of the Federal Government, 1933-1938, by Fiscal Years" (Washington: Office of Government Reports, 1939), p. 3. Farm Security Administration, *Annual Report* (1941), pp. 28-30. See Appendix, Table 21.

19. Tugwell to Frank C. Walker, September 9, 1935, NARG 96, Corres. (1935-42), box 313. "Reports," n.d., NARG 96, Corres. (1935-42), box 104.

20. Unsigned report, November 23, 1935, NARG 44, Digests, box 496. Walter E. Packard, January 5, 1937 (memo), NARG 96, Corres. (1935-42), box 159.

21. Unsigned report, January 1, 1937, NARG 44, Periodical Reports (1934-38), box 399. Unsigned report, December 12, 1935, NARG 44, Digests, box 497. Unsigned report, February 15, 1935, NARG 44, Digests, box 501.

22. Farm Security Administration, "Irwinville Farms," Miscellaneous publication (mimeograph), 1941. "Irwinville Farms," 1939 (?), NARG 96, Division of Information, Irwinville Farms, box 79. Packard to Tugwell, March 26, 1936, NARG 96, Corres. (1935-38), box 5. Morris R. Mitchell to Miss Agnes King Inglis, n.d., NARG 96, Corres. (1935-42), box 336.

23. "Briar Patch Farms," March 15, 1939, NARG 96, Division of Information, Briar Patch Farms, box 79.

24. Walter E. Packard to Tugwell, March 26, 1936, NARG 96, Corres. (1935-38), box 5. "Wolf Creek Farms," March 1939, NARG 96, Division of Information, Wolf Creek Farms, box 79. Unsigned memo, January 26, 1936, NARG 96. Rural Resettlement Division, Project Corres., box 83.

25. Kendall Weisiger to W. W. Alexander, November 18, 1935, NARG 96, Corres. (1935-42), box 159.

26. Farm Security Administration, "Flint River Farms," Miscellaneous publication (mimeograph), 1941. Richard M. Sterner, *The Negro's Share* (New York: Harper and Brothers, 1943), p. 423. Lawrence Westbrook to Shepperson, September 30, 1935, NARG 69, State Series, No. 651, box 1129. Report of J. H. Wood, March 17, 1936, NARG 96, Fort Valley Farms, FF-GA-27, box 86. Packard to Tugwell, March 26, 1936, NARG 96, Corres. (1935-38), box 5.

27. H. B. Evans to Alexander, August 5, 1936, NARG 96, Corres. (1935-42), box 159. Hudgens to Tugwell, October 28, 1936, NARG 96, Fort Valley, box 86. Macon County *Citizen*, March 18, 1937. Montezuma *Georgian*, March 18, 1937. Hudgens to Alexander, May 4, 1937, NARG 96, Fort Valley, box 86. Hudgens to Alexander, April 1, 1937, NARG 96, Fort Valley, box 86.

28. "Flint River Farms," March 1939, NARG 96, Division of Information, Flint River Farms, box 79. FSA, "Flint River Farms," Misc. publ. (mimeo), 1941. Unsigned report, March 1939, NARG 96, Flint River Farms, 85-10-163-01, box 8. "Report of Flint River Farms Project, RR-GA-27," NARG 96, Fort Valley Farms, RR-GA-27, box 86. Progress report of Katherine F. Deitz, June 1941, NARG 96. Corres. (1935-42), box 330. Progress report of Miss Deitz, September 1938, NARG 96, Corres. (1935-42), box 336. Progress report of Miss Deitz, January 1939, NARG 96, Corres. (1935-42), box 336.

29. "Report of the Proceedings of the Statewide Coordinating Meeting," April 10, 1936 (Report of R. L. Vansant), NARG 44, Corres., Directories, Repts., box 349. U. S. Congress, Senate, Document No. 213, 47th Cong., 2nd Sess., 1936, p. 43. Arthur F. Raper, *Tenants of the Almighty* (New York: Macmillan Company, 1943), p. 197. FSA, *Annual Report* (1941), p. 36.

30. W. W. Alexander to Congressman Carl Vinson, May 21, 1937, NARG 96, Miscellaneous Resettlement Material, Proj. Corres., Farm Tenant Security Project, RP-GA-26, box 84. Senate Document No. 213, p. 41. "Report of the Proceedings of the Statewide Coordinating Meeting," April 10, 1936 (Report of R. L. Vansant), NARG 44, Corres., Directories, Repts., box 349. A. J. C. Fox to Alexander, April 17, 1939, NARG 96, Misc. Reset. Mat., Proj. Corres., Farm Tenant Security

Project, RP-GA-26, box 84. Baldwin, *Poverty and Politics,* pp. 93-4. See Appendix, Tables 21-23.

31. Resettlement Administration, Finance and Control Division, Special Reports Section, "The Program of the Resettlement Administration," NARG 96, Corres. (1935-42), box 159. Hopkins to Shepperson, n.d., (telegram), NARG 69, State Series, No. 651, box 1129. Unsigned report, January 4, 1936, NARG 44, Digests, box 499. "Report of the Proceedings of the Statewide Coordinating Meeting," April 10, 1936 (Report of Dr. W. A. Hartman), NARG 44, Corres., Directories, Repts., box 349. "Special Report: Submarginal Land Purchase and Development Program, February 23, 1939," NARG 44, Gen. Corres. With State Directors (1939), box 320. W. J. Morton to Congressman Carl Vinson, March 21, 1936, NARG 96, Corres. (1935-36), box 19. William A. Hartman to Vinson, March 26, 1936, NARG 96, Corres. (1935-36), box 19. Unsigned report, April 10, 1936, NARG 44, Digests, box 503. Unsigned report, August 1, 1936, NARG 44, Digests, box 507. Unsigned report, September 12, 1936, NARG 44, Digests, box 509. Unsigned report, October 10, 1936, NARG 44, Digests, box 509. Unsigned report, March 3, 1937, NARG 44, Digests, box 510. See Appendix, Table 24.

32. Atlanta *Constitution,* June 7, 1934, and April 2, 1935. "Report on the Proceedings of the Statewide Coordinating Meeting," April 10, 1936 (Report of H. A. Cliett), NARG 44, Corres., Directories, Repts., box 349. Philip Weltner to Tugwell, December 20, 1935, NARG 96, Corres. (1935-42), box 104.

33. Senate Document No. 213, p. 58. R. L. Vansant, "Annual Report of the Activities of the Rehabilitation Division of the Resettlement Administration in Georgia for 1936," NARG 16, Secretary of Agriculture. Congressman Stephen Pace to Hudgens, July 24, 1937, NARG 96, Corres. (1935-42), box 78. FSA, *Annual Report* (1941), p. 42. (Reduction for the entire country was 24.1 percent.)

34. Willard Range, *A Century of Georgia Agriculture, 1850-1950* (Athens: University of Georgia Press, 1954), p. 276. Interview with Arthur Raper.

35. George B. Tindall, *The Emergence of the New South: 1913-1943* (Baton Rouge: Louisiana State University Press, 1967), p. 424. Unsigned report, September 15, 1937, NARG 44, Digests, box 512.

36. "Farm Tenancy—Progress Report of Rural Rehabilitation (?), Region V." NARG 96, Corres. (1935-38), box 60. C. B. Baldwin (?) to Alexander, October 30, 1937 (memo), NARG 96, Corres. (1935-42), box 290.

37. "Farm Tenancy," NARG 96, Corres. (1935-38), box 60. Vansant

to State Committee, February 2, 1938, NARG 96, Corres. (1935-42), box 294. Hudgens to Alexander, March 16, 1938, NARG 96, Corres. (1935-42), box 263. Hudgens to Alexander, February 1938, NARG 96, Corres. (1935-42), box 263.

38. Hudgens to Alexander, February 1938, NARG 96, Corres. (1935-42), box 263. Hudgens to Alexander, October 22, 1938, NARG 96, Corres. (1935-42), box 310.

39. "State Summary of County Supervisors' Weekly Reports— Tenant Purchase," NARG 96, Corres. (1935-42), box 263. Harry Brown to Congressman W. Ben Gibbs, October 24, 1939, NARG 96, Corres. (1935-42), box 15.

40. "Activities of the Farm Security Administration in Georgia," February 18, 1939, NARG 96, Corres. (1935-42), box 160. See Appendix, Table 25.

41. "Greene County Georgia: The Story of One Southern County," October 1, 1940, NARG 96, Corres. (1935-42), box 61. FSA, "Greene County, Georgia," Misc. Publ. (mimeo), 1940. Hudgens to Alexander, February 8, 1938, NARG 96, Corres. (1935-42), box 177. D. Young to Mrs. Anthony, February 10, 1938 (memo), NARG 96, Corres. (1935-42), box 177. Alexander to Hudgens, April 20, 1938, NARG 96, Corres. (1935-42), box 177. Vansant to Julian Brown, March 30, 1939, NARG 96, Montgomery, Projects (1935-40), 85-060-85-073, box 1916. (The County Planning Committee was made up of the county agent, assistant county agent, home demonstration agent, FSA district farm supervisor, five FSA farm supervisors, five FSA home supervisors, two vocational agriculture teachers, a CCC junior soil conservationist and a SCS junior soil conservationist. The state Land-Use Committee was made up of the extension director, the state FSA Director, the administrative Officer in charge of the state AAA Office, the state SCS coordinator, and the state Bureau of Agricultural Economics representative.)

10

"The New Deal?"
"It's Done Been By Here"

It should be apparent that the question of the New Deal's success or failure, even in a single state, is extremely difficult, if not impossible, to answer. A simple yes or no would require enough qualifiers to make the reader suspect the author of saying one thing and meaning another. Nevertheless, it is to be hoped that the student of this complicated era can now ask the right questions and perhaps begin to form some partial answers.

In the first place, to inquire merely whether the New Deal was a success is not going to be productive. Any answer will be too broad and too superficial, because the New Deal was too complex in its administration and too diverse in its goals. Part of the problem in, for example, the area of recovery would be to distinguish between economic upswing caused by the government's programs and that brought about by other factors, including the non-recovery portions of the New Deal. Furthermore, the goals of the agencies were so varied in scope and intent that saying the New Deal was successful refers to only the most nebulous kind of accomplishment. If not, it would mean that bookmobiles and cotton subsidies or archaeological digs and wage and price controls all achieved their own specific purposes, no matter how unrelated. Even our presently incomplete comprehension of the New Deal indicates that is not so.

This does not suggest that an attempt to understand the New Deal is fruitless, only that to start by questioning its overall impact is unrewarding. One must instead proceed by discovering other ways that will ultimately lead to the overview, ways that will also provide an insight, not just to what extent but also why the New Deal succeeded. The author's hypothesis has been that this can be achieved by studying each major agency, as an entity, in the context within which it actually operated, that is, the state. To do so provides the scholar an opportunity to consider organizations whose goals and administration can be isolated and studied in relation to the various internal and external factors operating upon them. There was, of course, some overlapping of agencies with respect to both goals and administration, and there was variation from program to program within individual agencies, but using the agency approach at least allows the student to examine the New Deal in manageable portions.

An immediate criticism of this tactic might be that, in its own way, it is just as useless as beginning with the overview. If taking the latter course leads to answers which are too superficial, then following the former may result in a whole series of individual answers that are difficult to relate to one another in some sort of overall synthesis. Therefore, it has been the object of this study not only to trace the history of each agency, thus gaining an understanding of its operations, but also to do so within parameters that will finally allow the historian to compare the different agencies. These parameters are not, however, assumed; rather they emerge in the course of careful consideration of each agency's history in relation to the others.

If taking the overview provides too little specific information about the workings of the New Deal, studying each agency is likely to produce too much. The records of the agencies are Pandora's boxes of material, and this is perhaps why those who have written histories of the agencies thus far have not chosen to examine them from top to bottom—from the central offices in Washington to the individuals they were supposed to help. Since the premise is, however, that the whole might be known by its parts, there is a solution. Using as background the many studies of New Deal agencies that primarily are concerned with the "Washington" point of view, the historian may proceed to a discussion of them on the state level, choosing a single state—in this case, Georgia.

Of course, the same "forest for the trees" objection occurs here, but it can be answered as above. One may examine an agency in a particular state and be assured that basically it operated the same way in the other states. Such differences that might exist would be caused largely by local conditions which varied from state to state. If the parameters within

which an agency is considered are carefully selected so as not to be
parochial, the agency may be compared, not only to other agencies in
the same state, but to the same agency in other states.

To that end the purpose and method of this study have been intertwined. The hope has been that tracing the histories of the major agencies
in Georgia will provide an understanding of how each worked, whether
or not each was successful, and what sort of conditions were prominently
involved in determining the agencies' fate. If the conditions prove to be
similar in the case of each agency (which they are), and if they are not
so parochial as to be applicable only to Georgia (which is yet to be proven),
then the historian has a sort of lattice structure or grid which he can
figuratively place upon any agency in any state showing him how that
agency related to different agencies in that state and similar agencies in
other states. As more states or agencies are studied in this manner, there
should then emerge a deeper understanding of the New Deal and perhaps
even a meaningful yes or no to the original question of the New Deal's
success or failure.

The parameters by which one might judge an agency were listed in
the introduction, and presumably their efficacy has been shown in the
text. These parameters cover three areas and the relations among them:
the national offices of an agency, the state and local offices of an agency,
and the state itself. To begin with, the agencies were all created by laws
that applied equally to every state. If an agency was poorly conceived
at this level, there could be little chance for success anywhere. It was not
simply a question of strength in terms of national enforcement. The
problem of applicability was also important. The goals and procedures of
each agency might be the same in each state, but all states were not the
same. Some agencies were well-suited to one kind of state while being
ill-suited or even injurious to others. Few programs proved entirely
unworkable in many areas. With one law, however, applied in forty-eight
states, each with varying conditions, it was common for certain procedures to come into conflict with circumstances requiring different
solutions. When this happened, federal officials could make modifications, if the law allowed. Whether they took this opportunity usually
depended upon its probable effect upon the rest of the program.

For an agency to succeed at the national level, therefore, it had to be
appropriately devised. Its programs needed to provide the necessary
solutions to national problems. It could not take too narrow a focus;

rather it had to take into account different conditions throughout the country. It had to be capable of enforcement. Finally, it had to allow flexibility for the national administrator to make local modifications.

Regarding this last point, what was true for national officials also held for those at the state level. At times state administrators asked the national office to make exceptions to the rules. The federal administrator either could do this himself on a case-to-case basis, or could grant state administrators the prerogative to make certain kinds of adjustments.

The goals and structures of some agencies required that the national office have almost total control. In others this was the choice of the agency head. Most agencies, however, delegated some policy-making powers to the state offices. The greater such powers were, the easier it was for state administrators to modify programs so they operated in harmony with local conditions.

As this balance of power shifted to the state office, however, the quality of that organization, and particularly of its leader, became critical. In such agencies the national office depended heavily upon strong, honest, and capable state administrators. The administrator, in turn, needed to select a good staff, especially if he or she followed the national office's example by delegating authority to area or local offices.

The same held true for organization. State administrators had to establish clear lines of control and communication both ways. It did no good to acquire able personnel, if the administrative structure was poor. Some agencies escaped the structural problem by using state or federal agencies already in existence. But this was the exception rather than the rule. The quality of staff and structure, therefore, was relative to that of the administrator, when he or she had control over the state organization. Agencies which limited administrators' prerogatives generally tended to have inferior state operations.

It was always possible, of course, that there might be a state administration with great power that had a weak administrator. This never occurred in Georgia, but there were incidents of it in other states. What was more likely was incompetence in the state and local staffs. Professional training in critical fields might be sparse, making the acquisition of adequate personnel difficult, if not impossible.

Even if the agency's state staff and structure were first rate—even if the programs it carried out were enforceable and applicable to the state's overall condition—success still was not assured. The nature of the political, economic, and social climate in each state could cause the same agency with able organizations throughout the country to emerge with a spotty record. In the political area, the governor was usually the key figure. As popular leader of his state, the governor might possess great powers of persuasion and use these powers either to rally his state to the New Deal or to undermine support generated by the national administration. As political leader of his state, the governor could introduce and support state legislation designed to supplement New Deal programs. On the other hand, an antagonistic governor might refuse to send enabling bills to his legislature or might veto such bills should they be passed without his aid. Such a man, furthermore, might actively impede agencies that needed his cooperation. He could delay or refuse to perform his duties. He might even attempt to sabotage agencies that he disliked or could not control.

Many agencies required the assistance of cooperating state departments, usually within the executive branch. When this occurred, governors favorably disposed to the New Deal were influential in facilitating good relations. Opponents of the programs applied considerable pressure, either directly or through party loyalty, to insure that state departments reflected their views. The responsiveness of the departments, of course, also depended upon the attitudes of their administrators who might oppose the governors' efforts. Such situations bred uncertainty in the agencies and often resulted in tensions that might not otherwise have occurred. Opposition to the governor in Georgia, moreover, always was extremely difficult because of the state's one-party system. There was no other organization through which dissidents might channel their discontent. At the same time, the one-party system greatly expanded the governor's political range and power. Every politically active person in the state had to belong to the same party, thereby being directly subject to pressures from the governor. Divisions within the party, furthermore, tended to be informal, while the governor held control of the only official machinery. Finally, the one-party system encouraged personality cults, so that even out of office a former governor might wield significant political power.

Not all political opposition to the New Deal existed because of the governor's efforts. Some local officeholders had their own personal political reasons for objecting to it. In their case, opposition stemmed not so much from principle as from their desire to retain political control of their bailiwicks. Domination of Georgia's counties, that under the county unit system were the basis of political power on the state level, was maintained by the complete dependency of county residents upon their leaders for the fruits of government. The New Deal was especially dangerous to local leaders when it broke this chain, showing the populace that it need not depend entirely upon the county's ruling class. To the local politician this meant that ultimately he might not be able to deliver the solid county vote for whichever candidate his political faction supported. If this occurred, he would be of no further use to the faction and would cease to receive the patronage that the successful faction could distribute. Eventually, he would have to be replaced, and that, of course, is what he feared.

Political opposition to the New Deal was not the most serious obstacle to its success, because political considerations motivated only a small portion of the state's population. Far more important were the economic and social forces involved. It was the area of recovery that was affected most by economic conditions, and if recovery failed, relief as a temporary measure to tide people over until they could be re-employed by the private sector of the economy was bound to fail also. The three recovery agencies sought to lift the nation out of the depression by stimulation and control of the primary productive areas. The depths to which the economy had plummeted in a state naturally would determine the distance needed to be traveled to recovery. Not every portion of the economy suffered equally in any state, so that the problems encountered within a state might vary from agency to agency. More significant than this, however, was the nature of the distress in each area. All of the recovery programs were based on solutions that presupposed specific nationwide problems. If that were not so, if the reasons for the economic ills of industry or agriculture, for example, varied from state to state, then the solutions would not be applicable everywhere. They might, indeed, even be harmful in certain circumstances.

This, in turn, would affect the relief programs. The deeper the economic troubles of a state, the longer it would take to reach prosperity. Such states presumably would need more relief for a greater length of time. The relief program in any state, therefore, depended heavily on the recovery program, and both were affected by the severity and causes of the depression in each sphere of economic activity.

The final set of conditions impinging upon agencies in the states

centered around social attitudes. Provincialism in general interfered with citizens' acceptance of federal intervention in state affairs. In states with particularly rigid class or caste hierarchies, structured around political, social, economic, or racial factors, the populace fought agencies that threatened to subvert or destroy "time-honored traditions." Religious attitudes toward poverty and social views on labor often determined stands taken on relief. Any of these social conditions, and many more less tangible ones, might influence the state's relations with various New Deal agencies. In some instances social considerations were of greater importance than economic circumstances, and whole groups of people rejected the financial benefits of the New Deal to maintain social status.

These, then, are the factors to be considered in judging the New Deal in an organized fashion. In some respects specific pieces of evidence might not have applied to all states, or at least not in the same way or proportion as in Georgia. Racism, for example, did not play such an overt role in the North, but there were still social forces which did. Examining New Deal agencies in other states would probably reveal that none of the conditions found in Georgia existed elsewhere to the same degree or in the same relationship. They varied in importance from agency to agency within Georgia, too. All of the major factors, however, were operative throughout the nation. Given, therefore, the laws which applied to a greater or lesser degree across the nation, it was the quality of the state administrative structure and personnel, the latitude they were given by the laws or by the federal administrations in adapting the programs to meet local conditions, and the political, economic, and social environment facing them in the states which determined their achievements.

An examination of the relief program, particularly in comparison with other agencies, provides a good example of the insights obtainable within this framework. To ask whether relief was successful is not just fruitless, it is ironic. Many of the relief program's greatest accomplishments came about precisely because other New Deal agencies (the AAA, NRA, and PWA) failed to promote recovery. The federal government's assumption that recovery would be swift, and relief, therefore, short-lived, determined the nature of the laws which established the FERA, CWA, and WPA. The acts creating and extending these agencies did so only on a year-to-year basis. This seriously affected both planning and funding. State administrators could not promise sponsors the completion

of multi-year projects, so the type of project undertaken was usually
very restricted or designed so that it could be completed in parts. Then,
if funds were cut off at the end of a particular year, the value of the
project would not be lost entirely. Yearly planning also made construction
more expensive. Only enough material for a year's worth of work could
be obtained, and bulk purchases that would have reduced unit prices were
prohibited. In the area of funding, changes in the percentage of sponsors'
contributions often increased the cost to local governments. This caused
great dissatisfaction, especially if the sponsor lacked enough funds. The
sight of a school building left unfinished for this reason stood as a
monument to local citizens of a promise unfulfilled.

The relief acts also determined the amounts and distribution of payments to destitute families. Under the FERA this amount was based on
the needs of the state as a whole and individual families as units. Georgia
was a poor state to begin with, and by 1933 many of its citizens were
destitute. Those who then received relief were undoubtedly glad of it and
in some cases probably survived only because of it. On the other hand,
Georgia did not get relief funds in proportion to its percentage of poor
people relative to other states. Even those who were given money did not
receive as much per capita as in most states outside of the South.

The FERA distributed aid to families on the basis of need. Although
wages on work projects were fixed, the hours a laborer was employed
depended upon how much his family needed to maintain an acceptable
standard of living. Under the WPA, however, this changed. The "security
wage" was based on current rates for comparable jobs in private enterprise, thus limiting the agency's effectiveness as a source of relief.

Not all revisions of national policy were detrimental to these agencies.
Relief administration and structure later were adapted to cope with long-term
poverty. While procedures were still restricted, the types of programs
undertaken were greatly expanded, particularly in nonmanual areas.
By 1940 relief projects employed those engaged in almost every human
endeavor, and the New Deal had become truly ubiquitous.

As this occurred, the relief agencies seemed to acquire a Midas touch.
Everywhere the WPA was effective, standards were improved, efficient
planning was initiated, and higher goals were set. Health programs, for
example, not only provided more and better nursing service in Georgia,
but also coordinated this service with sanitation projects in a total
effort to treat and prevent disease. So persuasive were the results that

the state had no choice but to continue this effort when the WPA was abolished.

This, of course, did not happen in every program. The more esoteric projects, such as music and theater, were essentially unworkable in a primarily rural state whose cities lacked cultural sophistication. These isolated failures, however, appear minimal when compared to the overall unsuitability in Georgia of the NRA, an agency designed totally for industrial areas of the country. Furthermore, Harry Hopkins, an enlightened federal administrator, did not often insist upon the promulgation of the more marginal programs. The NRA state head had no such prerogatives, and, in fact, labored under a law which could not even be enforced. Even in the AAA, where Henry Wallace could make adjustments, such was the case only in regard to crops like wheat that held little importance in the agricultural economy of Georgia. When farmers petitioned the AAA for modifications in the cotton program, Wallace refused.

Hopkins did not confine his flexibility to specific exceptions, for he recognized that with an agency of such diverse programs a certain leniency would have to be continued. It was for this reason that he placed much of the decision-making power in the hands of the state administrator to an extent unique among New Deal agencies. In some states this led to chaos or corruption, but Georgia was fortunate in having Gay Shepperson at the helm. She was one of the most capable state FERA, CWA, and WPA administrators in the nation. Her ability was manifest throughout the state as it expressed itself in the attention she paid to staffing and programming. She realized, furthermore, the great responsibility placed upon her by the power she held, and she was always wary of those areas, such as local selection committees or the federal projects, over which she had limited authority.

Miss Shepperson did have some administrative problems. She was forced to comply with frequent reorganizations of her operations when the national office decided to make the changes. She also had trouble finding enough personnel to fill positions requiring certain specializations. Her greatest difficulty was that she was a woman holding a position unheard of in southern society. Nevertheless, she avoided the potentially serious consequences by using extreme care and foresight and by employing her basic strength, ability, and honesty. From an administrative standpoint, then, Georgia's relief effort appeared to be assured of

success, especially when compared to the PWA, which had no formal
state organization, or the NRA, whose state administrator was given
very little power by the national office.

It was in the final area, that of state conditions and relations, where
trouble arose for the relief agencies. The primary and overall circumstance
was that Georgia was so large and had such a small population, most of
which was widely scattered. This made it difficult, in terms of administration and program development, to reach the people who needed help.
The state had 159 counties, each containing very few people, but still
requiring a county relief office. This presented massive problems of
organization, staffing, and control.

Most counties were poor and could afford to sponsor only the most
inexpensive projects. Labor in these counties was dispersed and generally
not skilled. Projects had to be suited to low density population areas.
Farm-to-market roads, for example, might be acceptable. Skilled labor
requirements were minimal, outside funding was available, and the needs
of a rural populace would be served. Any sort of public utility or building
would be of limited value, however, considering the absence of population
concentrations. Such a project also would require a certain amount of
skilled labor and a substantial amount of internal financing. Very few of the
nonmanual projects could be initiated outside of Georgia's cities. The only
ones that enjoyed any sort of success were statewide, sending personnel
out into rural areas, rather than requiring citizens to congregate in one place.

Every New Deal agency faced one or more of these general problems.
The NRA found a large number of businesses, particularly textile mills,
outside of the cities. Much of Georgia's industry was engaged in
"first processing" and tended to be close to the sources of supply. This
caused the NRA's administrative structure to be almost as widely dispersed as that of the FERA or WPA. The PWA faced the same problem
as the WPA in finding suitable locations for its construction projects.
That is why most of the PWA's funds were used to build highways. Even
the AAA, which presumably was of greatest importance in an agricultural
state, had difficulties because of the number of counties. Having a
small population scattered over a large area made it hard for any agency
to maintain constant contact and firm control in each locality.

Beyond this general condition were the three specific areas: political, economic, and social. Political problems constantly plagued the
relief administration. At the state level there was a governor committed

to destroying the New Deal. Eugene Talmadge had been a very popular state secretary of agriculture, and, as governor, completely controlling the state's one-party system, he used this popularity to turn the populace against the relief agencies, rendering them ineffective. Fortunately for the agencies, however, it was the governor who suffered most, for as Georgians began to receive the assistance and benefits afforded by the New Deal, they repudiated Talmadge at the polls.

In his official role, Talmadge tried to destroy the FERA. He refused to allow state contributions for relief. He questioned the relief rolls, asking why so many people needed so much money. He attacked choices for staff, alleging that they were "carpetbaggers," and he would not sign checks for the release of federal relief funds that came through his office. When it became apparent that none of his actions was going to eliminate the agency, he decided to use it for his own purposes. Attempting to reward political allies, he proposed their names as candidates for procurement officers.

The governor's efforts were not limited to situations where he himself was in a position to do damage. He always sought to make sure his views were echoed by the entire state government. Sometimes, as in the case of the state highway department, he did this by exercising particularly stringent personal control. In other cases he used party loyalty to impose his will on others. In any event, whenever state cooperation was needed in a relief program, the administrator feared it would be withheld. Actually this occurred to varying degrees, usually depending upon how politically critical a state department might be. Any highway or education project could expect difficulty, because the departments involved were important in Georgia's political milieu. Library or health programs were not similarly affected and, indeed, owed much of their rather impressive success to the active interest and support of cooperating state units.

Outside of the executive branch, Talmadge used his position as state Democratic Party leader to control politicians. His power in this area was enhanced by the one-party system of the South, for there could be no organized opposition from those who disagreed. The extent to which the governor was able to influence state legislators, for example, was occasionally frightening. Even Eurith D. Rivers, who later as governor presided over Georgia's little New Deal, began by joining with his fellow solons in systematically refusing to pass any enabling legislation for New Deal programs.

Talmadge's opposition to the New Deal was not completely irrational or unwarranted. He understood the threat to the social, economic, and political structure of the state that the agencies posed. He recognized the futility of the NRA operating in a state that was primarily agricultural. Ultimately, he accepted many of the New Deal's benefits, not because he endorsed the principles involved, but because he realized that Georgians would still have to pay the tax dollars from which these benefits came.

It was Talmadge's attack on the FERA that prompted Hopkins to federalize the agency in January 1934. Although the FERA encountered fewer problems from the governor afterward, there was no doubt that he had caused Georgia to "miss the tide of enthusiasm" which firmly entrenched the popularity of the New Deal in states with more sympathetic governors.[1] Furthermore, his rejection by the people of Georgia for election to the Senate in 1936 and 1938 did not indicate that political opposition to the New Deal had ceased. It took over two years for the state legislature to provide enabling legislation for the Social Security Act of 1935. Talmadge, despite personal defeat, still wielded some political clout, and, if he did not, there were others of importance to take his place who also disliked the New Deal. One of the ironies of Talmadge's political life, in fact, was that he was defeated for the Senate in 1936 because he opposed the New Deal while Senator Richard Russell supported it, and lost his 1938 bid because his opponent, Senator Walter George, was being attacked by Roosevelt for fighting against New Deal programs.

It was impossible to say exactly why Talmadge detested the New Deal. His actions, while not completely irrational, were certainly inconsistent with his stated motives. But it was fairly clear that he operated from some notion of principle. County leaders also were moved by principles, but political considerations were extremely important to them. Under the county unit system, power derived from their ability to deliver a majority vote. Local politicians used the rigid paternalistic caste and class system as a conduit through which flowed all governmental blessings to the people, one way, in return for votes which flowed the other. In between were the political leaders who appeared as the "sole provider" of the fruits of government. To them a grateful citizenry gave its votes which were then traded to the state faction offering the most patronage.

When relief officers came into these areas, spending more money than anyone had ever seen before and bypassing traditional routes, local leaders feared for their power. Some of these men were able to co-opt the relief programs by convincing residents that the aid still came through them. Miss Shepperson, aware of the situation, did not object as long as they made no attempt to subvert her objectives. But when such sub-version was practiced or when opposition was immediate and overt, political battles erupted in which local leaders were determined either to control relief or to destroy it by withholding necessary support or persuading their constituents that it was harmful. Potentially this problem existed for all agencies operating at the county level. The AAA avoided confrontation by selecting local leaders to sit on county and militia district committees. The NRA did likewise for compliance committees and refused to make adjustments when conflicts of interest arose.

At the county level, as in the executive branch, opposition was not total, and even its presence did not necessarily result in the obstruction of New Deal agencies. The most striking example was Talmadge himself, whose bluster was out of proportion to his destructiveness. It did mean, however, that New Deal programs achieved varying success. When support was present, when antagonism was absent or ineffective, or when political adversaries could be circumvented (for example, by federalizing the FERA), then programs succeeded, assuming there were no other prob-lems. If the reverse were true, agencies could expect difficulties at best, and often failure.

Intertwined with political conditions were economic and social factors. The economic situation was much more important with regard to the recovery programs, but it did have some effect on relief. The salient fact was that the depression in Georgia was not temporary and did not spring from conditions emanating in the 1920s. These forces only made a bad situation worse. Georgia's problems were deeply rooted in her economic makeup. It was an agricultural state in a primarily industrial national economy, and it was dependent on a single cash crop. The country's economic system had long caused agricultural areas to generate less profit than industrialized states. The dominance of agriculture in Georgia also dictated a seasonal economy, and this situation was worsened by the one-crop system. If that crop should fail, as it did with the invasion of the boll weevil, or if prices should plummet abroad (since a good portion of the crop was exported), there was no other crop that could take its place to buoy up the economy. But even if the boll weevil

had not descended upon the South or even if the world market for
cotton had not collapsed, Georgia would still have been in trouble. By
1929 the broad plains of Texas and Oklahoma were planted in cotton,
thus increasing the supply greatly. Cotton, moreover, was produced
more cheaply there than in Georgia because machinery could be used
on the flat plains.

The result of all these conditions was predictable. As prices fell,
landowners economized, and great numbers of tenants and croppers
were thrown off the land. And there was no place for them to go. Again,
as in most rural states, little business or industry existed, and that which
did was too small or weak to absorb the surplus labor force.

This, then, was the economic situation. Agriculture was chronically
ill, industry was weak or nonexistent, and the result was a large unemployed labor pool. The New Deal was not equipped to handle such a
situation—nor was it ever meant to do so. The NRA might aid large
industries, but there were few of these in Georgia. The AAA did help
commercial farmers survive, but it did not attack the basic causes of
the agricultural depression. What was needed was reform of the economic
system, but reform was not what the recovery program sought.

Some efforts at reform through the rehabilitation loans, resettlement
projects, and land use programs were initiated by the FERA, RA, and
FSA, but these never received enough attention and support from the
federal and state governments. They tended to be expensive and only of
long-term value. They also were often the least popular and as such were
sacrificed in favor of other programs. None of the resettlement communities, for instance, was ever financially successful. None of the rehabilitation loans allowed tenants to become commercial farmers quickly. None
of the land use projects was of immediate value, not even the farm demonstration areas. Only the TVA was exceptional in this respect, and its influence in Georgia was restricted to a small corner in the northwest part
of the state.

This, of course, did not mean that all three recovery agencies "failed
equally." The NRA was certainly the least successful, because in conception it was so totally unsuited to Georgia's economic conditions.
The AAA did enable commercial farmers, at whom it was directed, to
remain financially afloat, and, although it did not eradicate the disease,
it did treat the symptoms effectively enough to endure into the 1960s.
The PWA aided Georgia's construction industry when it was active. It

erected useful public projects, gave business to failing contractors, and employed skilled and unskilled labor. The PWA's problem was not that it was unsuited to Georgia's economy, but rather that its federal administrator, Harold Ickes, was unwilling to move fast or far enough. Too few projects were initiated too slowly, so there was relatively little impact from its programs.

The effect of recovery's general failure was to put increased pressure on the relief agencies. This was true throughout the nation, but one possible reason why Georgia's relief population received less per capita than other states was that recovery was less effective in this agricultural state than in industrialized areas of the country. The state's long-term, pervasive poverty meant that a great deal of money was needed to have much impact. Poor economic conditions also strengthened local politicos' control of their constituents, because the favors they were able to grant were worth so very much. Finally, the impotency of recovery, in the face of an economic malaise it was never intended to cure, meant that relief needed to be rendered as an extended service, not as the stop-gap measure it was originally designed to be. This was principally what caused most of the problems of funding and administration encountered by the state office.

Social conditions also affected all New Deal agencies. Almost everyone in state politics, as well as many others, were suspicious of federal interference in the state. It was only the severe economic distress and the state's inability to cope with it that prompted Georgians to accept federal intervention in the first place. State leaders did this with great reluctance, however, and thereafter maintained a critical scrutiny of all the agencies. To be sure, personal political aspirations and possible alliances with the Talmadge faction prompted much of the intense criticism, but even those who appreciated the agencies' aid were often beset with a gnawing fear of federal intervention and control.

The relief program had a further effect upon local social conditions. The social stability of the paternalistic southern rural class and caste structure was part of what the county hierarchy sought to maintain. Social as well as political relations were disrupted by the relief programs. Pervasive religious notions of a Protestant work ethic kept many people, even those in need, from accepting the idea of the dole and, often, of work relief. As with most Americans, Georgians believed that financial success was somehow linked with grace, while poverty indicated sin.

If this were so, then the "sinner" had better look to his soul and not to
the WPA. Furthermore, what man would want to publicize his shame by
being a "reliefer"? To give relief would, in fact, keep men from "honest"
work and thus insure damnation. It would encourage evil, it would reward
those who were already sinful and too lazy to work, and it would even
place those lower down on the economic scale above righteous people
who were out of a job but too proud to accept a handout. Relief was
the devil's invention, created to lead men into a life of leaf-raking, which
was idleness, which was sure damnation.

Such attitudes were not disingenuous, even though those at the top
often used them to keep those at the bottom "in their place." Nor did
these feelings result entirely from some sort of mystical concept. It was
true, for example, that by 1935 those who had clung to their jobs
tenaciously during the early years of the New Deal, only to lose them,
were in worse condition than those who had accepted relief immediately.
The relief rolls were filled, and there was no room for these people. Moreover, it was the skilled worker who most often had held on, so that in
1935 labor's elite was unemployed while the "dregs of society" at least
got relief work. Skilled union members were thus doubly incensed at
the WPA. Not only were they unemployed while the less deserving had
jobs, but unskilled laborers were working at the jobs for which they
were untrained.

Much of this disenchantment sprang from economic causes, but
some was socially motivated, since the relief system threatened labor's
hierarchy. The same was true for farmers who disliked relief agencies
that offered higher wages and drew tenants and croppers off the land
during planting, chopping, and harvesting seasons. In one respect their
complaints stemmed from the higher wages they would have to pay to
keep their workers, but they were also upset because the agencies
were destroying the paternalistic social pattern in rural Georgia that
had allowed them to maintain a certain exploitative relationship with
the tenants and croppers.

Precisely the same situation existed in the business community, and
everyone from the president on down was made aware that relief was
forcing wages in private enterprise to increase beyond reason. The
Roosevelt administration responded either by reducing wages or by
establishing regional wage differentials. This was done in the PWA as
well as the FERA. When pressure continued, the federal government

responded by establishing the "security wage" system for the WPA. This placed relief wages slightly below those for comparable work in private enterprise, and essentially abandoned the FERA's primary emphasis on relief rather than "works." Throughout the New Deal period, state relief administrators had to reassure farmers and businessmen that the agencies were not aiding those who could be employed elsewhere. This extreme sensitivity in Georgia resulted in a degree of caution with respect to the size of relief rolls that often denied aid to those who needed it, even though the state office knew well what fate awaited them in the labor market.

Similar attitudes were encountered by administrators in the reform programs, not only from the upper class, but from those who stood to gain by these reforms. Here, also, economic and political facts were intertwined with social forces, so that opposition to Social Security sprang from convictions about relief as well as fears of losing political and economic control of the populace. Resettlement was alien, and cooperative operation of resettlement communities was downright communistic. Even those living in such places rejected communal sharing and opted instead for private ownership. Anything that threatened the accustomed operation of southern society was viewed by the people of Georgia with a jaundiced eye. As a result, the reform programs normally proved to be the least successful and most controversial.

Of all social forces affecting the administration of New Deal agencies in Georgia, racial considerations were the most notorious. All the laws creating the agencies (with the exception, later, of the Civilian Conservation Corps) contained nondiscrimination clauses that directly challenged deeply ingrained southern racial patterns. Some agencies that were weak or were led by those sympathetic to southern feelings simply acceded to demands for discrimination. Others, such as the National Youth Administration, FERA, CWA, and WPA, resisted. Even so, when a local government threatened to halt its support of all New Deal programs if racial discrimination was not allowed, state administrators often capitulated. They may have been proponents of civil rights, but they were more committed to the success of their agencies and were willing to sacrifice the rights of a minority for what they considered to be the welfare of the majority.[2]

Many wealthy white southerners had long used racism to control all poor people. Citing the need to "keep the Negro in his place," they were able to maintain a low wage scale for all workers. These same southerners used the economic equality ploy in their fight against the relief agencies by convincing poor whites that equal relief benefits meant social equality as well. The ironies of this situation were manifold. The lower class whites were persuaded to abandon economic status (higher wages) for social status (caste differentials), but the upper class, which used this tool so callously, fell victim to it in a more subtle manner. They upheld the caste system to avoid class conflict, but in so doing they inhibited the South's ability to progress. The federal government's agreement to regional wage differentials in the WPA and PWA insured that this practice would continue. Since one of the New Deal's goals was to increase the purchasing power of all laborers, the federal government was actually defeating its own purpose in allowing discrimination in general and wage differentials in particular.

These, then, were the conditions which affected the relief administration. The same overall circumstances determined the fate of recovery and reform as well, although the impact of some individual factors differed, depending on the specific program. Because of this situation, it is therefore most difficult to say whether or not a small portion of the New Deal was successful, even when just one state is considered. It is much easier to make some general statements, however, once having examined the detailed evidence—not that the conclusions are proven; more that they are suggested.

There were some limited achievements, but on the whole the New Deal did not extract Georgia from its depressed condition. It did not do this, because it failed to confront and change the conditions that had caused the depression in the first place. On the other hand, it did provide a way, after World War II, for Georgians to live with these conditions. If the agricultural programs did not eradicate the one-crop system, at least they introduced other crops to the state, crops that were later to be of commercial value, and they also guaranteed to those who continued to grow cotton a minimum income. The methods perfected under the New Deal still represent the government's basic way of dealing with farmers.

The physical accomplishments of the New Deal also still remain and are appreciated. Monuments to the works administration stand in the form of rather unaesthetic sandstone buildings, roads, bridges, swimming pools, schools, and a host of other utilitarian public facilities. These projects are certainly useful, but presumably they would eventually have been constructed anyway as need and available funds dictated.

Many of the social ideas underpinning the relief and reform administrations remain as part of America's welfare structure. The continuation and expansion of Social Security is probably the most important result of this new attitude. Individual programs, such as WPA public health projects, gave impetus to state departments and, in fact, were able to modify permanently the organization of state governments. All these things were "good" in that they have enabled America to hold the line within an economic system which may be less than adequate, but which cannot be easily changed. This, however, was not the purpose of the New Deal.

In one way, nevertheless, the New Deal was successful, not so much at the time, but because it sowed the seeds of later change, a change which involved the people themselves. Some years after the tumultuous days of "relief, recovery, and reform," Arthur Raper returned to Georgia and to the close friends he had made in Greene County. While driving along a country road he came upon a poor black farmer sitting by the way. Raper's own conclusions about the New Deal were now a matter of record, having been published in his study of Greene and Macon counties, but this poor black farmer, and all those whom he represented, had yet to speak. So Raper asked him, "What do you think of the New Deal?"

"The New Deal?" the man queried.

"Yes," Raper replied, "you know—relief, crop control, plow-under-your-crops, and that sort of thing."

"Oh, the New Deal? Yes sir, I know," he said. "It's pretty good I guess, pretty good. It's done been by here."[3]

The farmer did not say that the New Deal was bad, only that it was gone. He had gladly accepted and spent money given him for relief and crop restriction, but in the end he found himself where he had begun, on the bottom of the economic, social, and political ladders. Some thirty years later Raper was to chuckle about this incident, but then becoming serious, he said that the farmer was wrong. In fact the New Deal had changed things for this farmer, or at least for his progeny, though not in the way that Democrats were to claim for a long time afterward. Roads, buildings, screens, privies, and even schools were secondary considerations. A people might obtain all these things if they had political power.

To gain this power required an awareness of the world outside their
severely circumscribed lives.[4]

This is what the New Deal accomplished. It took an isolated farmer,
far back in Georgia's pine barrens, and a worker hidden amid countless
others of his ilk in some small mill town and made them realize that
they were part of something larger than that with which they came into
contact in their daily lives. They were part of a nation, perhaps even of
the world, and this nation and this world offered opportunities, ideas,
and new ways of doing things. The implications of this discovery were
not often immediate, but they were far-ranging and terribly important.
They meant that these so-called common men did not have to rely upon
their traditional wealthy protectors for laws or charity. If they could
vote to insure the implementation of the Bankhead Act, they could vote
to elect their governments. They could demand that their leaders build
schools, roads, or anything else they wanted, and, what is more, their
children could and would some day use this knowledge to tear down
the economic and political boundaries which had barred the way to
power, to equality, and thus presumably to their opportunity for success.

NOTES

1. Roy E. Fossett, "The Impact of the New Deal on Georgia Politics,
1933-1941" (unpublished Ph.D. dissertation, Department of Political
Science, University of Florida, 1960), pp. 2, 28-29.

2. Michael S. Holmes, "The New Deal and Georgia's Black Youth,"
The Journal of Southern History, XXXVIII, 3 (August 1972), 443-460.

3. Arthur F. Raper, *Preface to Peasantry* (Chapel Hill: University of
North Carolina Press, 1936), pp. 6-7, 272. Arthur F. Raper and Ira DeA.
Reid, *Sharecroppers All* (Chapel Hill: University of North Carolina Press,
1941), p. 133. Jonathan Daniels, "Witch Hunt in Georgia," *Nation*, CLII
(August 2, 1941), 94.

4. Interview with Arthur Raper, September 13, 1968.

Appendix

Table 1

FERA: Obligations Incurred for General and Special Emergency
Relief Programs in Georgia, 1933-1937

Period	Federal Funds Amount	Pct.	Local Funds[b] Amount	Pct.
1933				
First quarter	$ 414,575	100.0	—	—
Second quarter	1,038,396	100.0	—	—
Third quarter	1,333,030	95.0	$ 70,051	5.0
Fourth quarter	2,906,731	96.7	100,722	3.3
1934				
First quarter	2,646,465	91.7	238,345	8.3
Second quarter	4,576,858	95.1	234,643	4.9
Third quarter	5,091,108	96.2	203,293	3.8
Fourth quarter	6,547,217	95.8	285,985	4.2
1935				
First quarter	7,613,690	94.7	426,357	5.3
Second quarter	7,328,891	95.3	363,047	4.7
Third quarter	3,794,059	90.8	385,594	9.2
Fourth quarter	1,586,477	77.7	455,022	22.3
1936				
First quarter	369,606	45.1	449,601a	54.9
Second quarter	323,303	50.3	319,412a	49.7
Third quarter	172,660	36.0	307,578	64.0
Fourth quarter	98,822	22.7	335,888	77.3
1937				
First quarter	91,088	24.8	276,267	75.2
Grand total	**$45,932,976**	**91.2**	**$4,451,805a**	**8.8**

aEstimated.

bState contributed no funds.

SOURCE: FERA, *Final Report,* p. 304.

Table 2

FERA: Obligations Incurred for General Relief
and Number of Cases, 1933-1941

Date	Amount	No. of cases
1933		
January	$ 93,229*a*	11,362*a*
February	84,638*a*	9,638*a*
March	171,756*a*	22,893*a*
April	204,711*a*	33,864*a*
May	323,605*a*	53,029*a*
June	376,341*a*	57,349*a*
July	294,277	53,727
August	416,008	50,157
September	491,778	51,698
October	935,776	74,142
November	1,088,743	93,402
December	460,016	39,975
1934		
January	603,268	54,254
February	634,427	61,035
March	752,098	74,561
April	858,759	71,101
May	1,123,004	79,266
June	1,129,021	81,992
July	1,008,700	80,239
August	1,065,790	85,560
September	1,191,982	101,586
October	1,281,259	97,793
November	1,447,653	98,152
December	1,178,137	90,132
1935		
January	1,261,146	86,274
February	1,250,264	86,003
March	1,398,532	84,567
April	1,363,845	83,943
May	1,329,916	80,712
June	1,040,778	62,432
July	996,587	61,655
August	1,093,370	59,714
September	672,272	44,924
October	760,472	39,759
November	309,782	34,291
December	102,115	8,484

FERA: Obligations Incurred for General Relief
and Number of Cases, 1933-1941 (cont.)

Date	Amount	No. of cases
1936		
January	$ 139,000[a]	21,100[a]
February	177,000[a]	20,200[a]
March	130,000[a]	19,300[a]
April	126,000[a]	20,500[a]
May	125,000[a]	19,100[a]
June	125,660	17,092
July	120,370	17,523
August	99,002	16,535
September	87,160	15,561
October	91,765	16,019
November	95,310	15,834
December	95,814	16,976
1937		
January	87,029	15,736
February	74,682	15,567
March	69,143	14,826
April	79,935	15,311
May	77,854	15,013
June	76,690	14,929
July	70,142	11,973
August	53,021	9,507
September	45,886	8,019
October	47,100	7,237
November	48,158	7,143
December	56,403	8,030
1938		
January	55,048	8,359
February	51,395	8,202
March	50,338	7,916
April	45,224	7,495
May	43,915	7,364
June	43,291	7,283
July	43,816	7,146
August	43,989	6,991
September	43,566	6,959
October	44,919	6,832
November	43,654	6,941
December	48,118	7,331

FERA: Obligations Incurred for General Relief
and Number of Cases, 1933-1941 (cont.)

Date	Amount	No. of cases
1939		
January	$ 46,335	7,328
February	43,405	7,081
March	42,132	6,893
April	39,538	6,451
May	36,135	6,273
June	32,710	5,933
July	29,008	6,036
August	30,314	6,257
September	30,414	6,125
October	31,012	6,176
November	32,560	6,358
December	32,872	6,551
1940		
January	37,419	7,493
February	41,558	8,629
March	37,444	7,080
April	42,303	6,979
May	42,523	6,885
June	42,063	6,780
July	42,946	6,880
August	42,679	6,839
September	44,555	6,617
October	41,665	6,567
November	40,546	6,295
December	42,056	6,334
1941		
January	44,686	6,873
February	42,220	6,473
March	41,138	6,298
April	39,475	5,979
May	38,367	5,962
June	$ 38,342	5,880

aEstimated.
SOURCE: FERA, *Final Report,* pp. 128, 136, 145, 387, 393.

Table 3

**FERA: Average Relief Benefits in Georgia for Selected
Months, July 1933 Through October 1935**

Date	Amount per case
1933	
July	$ 5.48
October	12.62
1934	
January	11.12
April	12.08
July	12.57
October	13.10
1935	
January	14.62
April	16.25
July	16.16
October	$19.13

SOURCE: WPA, "Average Relief Benefits," p. 18.

Table 4

FERA: Obligations Incurred and Number of Cases Receiving Work Relief Under General Relief Program, 1933-1935

Date	Amount	No. of cases
1933		
July	$190,723*a*	37,543*a*
August	309,515	35,206
September	368,042	38,429
October	688,257	56,603
November	713,023	66,004
December		
1934		
January		
February		
March		
April	281,517	12,386
May	401,369	15,403
June	454,806	23,175
July	459,658	27,685
August	576,843	33,847
September	533,035	35,552
October	643,349	42,510
November	897,295	52,542
December	764,670	60,366
1935		
January	881,638	62,884
February	934,689	62,871
March	973,633	59,714
April	964,178	57,906
May	944,343	55,919
June	918,667	52,859
July	853,754	52,413
August	916,881	50,075
September	515,268	32,032
October	574,287	28,257
November	77,425	6,460
December	$ 248	9

*a*Estimated.
SOURCE: FERA, *Final Report,* pp. 154, 160.

Table 5
FERA: Emergency Education Program, 1933-1935

Date	U.S.	Georgia
1933-34		
No. teachers employed	100,825	9,239
Total obligations incurred	$14,869,333	$1,599,057
No. schools kept open	45,220	4,619
No. pupils attending	3,627,176	572,818
1934-35		
No. teachers employed	52,703	a
Total obligations incurred	$7,116,547	
No. schools kept open	16,750	
No. pupils attending	1,446,882	

aProgram not in operation.
SOURCE: FERA, *Final Report,* p. 112.

Table 6
FERA: Obligations Incurred for Emergency
Education Program, 1933-1935

Date	Amount	
	U.S.	Georgia
1933		
October	$ 182	—
November	2,159	$ 131
December	10,792	400
1934		
January	28,093	810
February	34,109	1,077
March	33,034	1,213
April	26,163	1,182
May	17,486	816
June	9,209	409
July	9,166	307
August	9,663	43
September	14,177	1,826
October	24,472	1,083
November	31,281	1,207
December	34,631	1,289
1935		
January	39,848	1,480
February	42,424	1,629
March	44,118	1,748
April	43,588	1,743
May	40,876	1,724
June	32,239	1,595
July	28,285	683
August	31,579	115
September	25,259	658
October	19,397	977
November	16,595	1,114
December	$ 7,867	$ 200

SOURCE: FERA, *Final Report,* pp. 228-30.

Table 7
FERA: Students Employed Under College Aid Program, 1933-1934

Date	Number	
	U.S.	Georgia
1933		
December	130	—
1934		
January	1,114	—
February	31,185	685
March	60,955	1,291
April	65,532	1,341
May	64,210	1,324
June	33,923	418
July	—	—
August	—	—
September	68,943	1,445
October	96,375	2,021
November	99,734	2,064
December	100,095	2,064
1935		
January	102,296	2,148
February	103,254	2,136
March	104,740	2,158
April	104,445	2,146
May	100,013	2,250
June	52,191	1,282

SOURCE: FERA, *Final Report,* pp. 231-2.

Table 8
Summary of CWA Federal, State, and Local Funds

	U.S.	Georgia
Federal funds	$844,066,788	$14,092,128.00
State funds	87,036,273[a]	57.60
Local funds		1,314,025.80

[a]State and local.
SOURCE: WPA, "Survey of Relief and Security," pp. 93-4; and "Analysis of Civil Works Program Statistics," p. 30.

Table 9
CWA Projects

Projects	No.	No. hours	Amount labor	Amount material approved	Amount material fur. locally
City streets	369	12,590,180	$ 1,798,898.21	$ 117,886.67	$ 327,133.19
Roads	955	7,744,148	2,601,081.16	128,406.79	992,794.75
Malaria control (drainage)	1,370	12,664,372	5,038,282.87	49,370.87	129,121.67
Public buildings and equipment	140	1,598,577	976,430.65	276,798.73	385,359.67
Parks and playgrounds	124	1,548,012	686,528.25	23,637.24	77,901.10
School grounds	545	2,000,053	870,858.07	16,564.60	62,047.21
School additions	275	2 373,817	604,236.41	70,084.19	138,630.40
School repairs	498	2,019,408	1,346,984.91	363,054.79	166,789.87
School buildings	115	582,036	330,747.20	72,270.93	147,911.29
Utilities (power lines, gas mains, etc.)	5	16,296	13,950.00	3,864.50	2,684.00
Waterways	12	687,203	280,531.00		2,091.20
Water supply (water main)	45	483,956	242,154.98	26,487.26	91,269.08
Sewers	31	2,189,895	1,016,895.94	408,752.79	208.425.40
Sanitation (pit privies)	137	525,924	242,610.01	1,420.25	87,679.60
Federal projects	1,007	4,344,451	1,969,217.58	209,391.44	86,212.51
Airports	29	1,213,100	511,710.00	58,310.31	65,776.50
Rodent control (state)	62	133,957	53,883.43	10,206.25	356.00
Phony peach (state)	11	61,740	23,454.54		
C.W.S. women's work and clerical	684	2,510,492	1,182,061.41	40,127.45	74,486.18
Miscellaneous	126	566,185	289,046.71	85,417.37	19,141.52
Total	6,540	44,522,702	$20,079,563.33	$1,962,052.43	$3,736,176.14

SOURCE: "The CWA in Georgia," p. 186.

Table 10

Georgia CWA Payrolls, November 17, 1933, Through March 29, 1934

Week ending	Number of employees	Hours worked	Amount of payroll	Weekly hours per employee	Weekly earnings per employee
November 23, 1933	17,897	282,270	$ 107,048.67	15.77	$ 5.98
November 30, 1933	64,171	1,632,090	622,513.27	25.43	9.70
December 7, 1933	64,706	1,754,318	682,428.35	27.11	10.55
December 14, 1933	65,997	1,801,172	720,896.85	27.29	10.92
December 21, 1933	71,876	1,942,367	798,893.67	27.02	11.11
December 28, 1933	72,502	1,833,438	77,544.63	25.29	10.72
January 4, 1934	74,685	1,967,974	851,706.25	26.35	11.40
January 11, 1934	76,339	2,029,324	885,073.61	26.58	11.59
January 18, 1934	77,189	2,098,007	934,294.99	27.18	12.10
January 25, 1934	76,577	1,356,820	645,584.62	17.72	8.43
February 1, 1934	74,346	1,237,969	602,980.86	16.65	8.11
February 8, 1934	74,995	1,374,639	665,519.13	18.32	8.87
February 15, 1934	73,028	1,293,024	635,158.64	17.70	8.69
February 22, 1934	70,147	1,227,328	619,587.57	17.49	8.83
March 1, 1934	52,153	924,965	498,232.89	17.73	9.55
March 8, 1934	42,144	828,758	419,411.85	19.66	9.95
March 15, 1934	36,213	723,099	366,275.86	19.96	10.11
March 22, 1934	31,599	615,523	332,916.60	19.47	10.53
March 29, 1934	25,930	532,017	299,853.36	20.51	11.56
Total		25,455,102	$11,465,921.67		
Average-weekly	**60,131**	1,339,742	603,470.01	22.28	$10.03

SOURCE: "The CWA in Georgia," p. 181.

Table 11

WPA Expenditures in Georgia in Comparison With Total U.S. Expenditures Through June 30, 1942

Project type	Expenditures			
	U.S.[a]	% of total	Georgia	% of total
Division of Operations				
Total	$9,738,835,157		$136,816,435	
Airports and airways	376,457,549	3.0	5,639,022	3.1
Buildings	1,329,850,874	10.6	19,291,468	10.5
Conservation	448,343,326	3.6	930,907	0.5
Engineering surveys	52,049,374	0.4	998,855	0.5
Highways, roads, and streets	4,812,348,988	38.2	77,656,952	42.1
Recreational facilities (excluding buildings)	982,106,566	7.8	4,246,659	2.3
Sanitation	233,077,180	1.8	7,479,462	4.1
Water, sewer, and other facilities	1,277,110,209	10.1	16,954,196	9.2
Other	277,561,101	1.8	3,618,914	2.0
Service Division				
Total	2,780,779,857		46,747,814	
Public activities	905,772,205	7.2	11,116,032	6.0
Research and records	511,367,577	4.1	7,737,131	6.0
Welfare (including sewing)	1,363,640,095	10.8	27,894,651	15.1
Division of Training and Reemployment	62,988,251	0.5	1,012,437	0.5
Public Work Reserve	943,463	c	36,742	c
Miscellaneous[b]	7,611,225	0.1	-211,998	-0.1
Grand total	**$12,591,157,953**		**$184,401,430**	

[a]Including territories.

[b]Includes adjustments for excess of deposits in the supply fund over payments out of the supply fund and for items in transit to control accounts and sponsors' expenditures for land, land leases, easements, and right of way.

[c]Less than 0.05 percent.

SOURCE: WPA, *Report on Progress* (1942), pp. 73-5.

Table 12

WPA: Average Number of Persons Employed on Projects, Semi-Annually, December 1935 Through June 30, 1942

Date	U.S.[a]	Georgia
1935		
December	2,667,190	53,724
1936		
June	2,285,622	34,469
December	2,247,461	33,602
1937		
June	1,878,008	25,447
December	1,596,676	24,272
1938		
June	2,743,025	47,187
December[b]	3,161,080	67,203
1939		
June	2,578,041	57,367
December	2,123,431	47,707
1940		
June	1,755,532	35,388
December	1,859,594	41,995
1941		
June	1,410,930	30,061
December	1,053,095	24,430
1942		
June	697,701	16,376

[a]Including territories.

[b]Includes persons employed on projects (WPA) operated by other federal agencies (in this and all following months).

SOURCE: WPA, *Report on Progress* (1942), p. 62.

Table 13

WPA: Monthly Earnings of Persons Employed on Projects During the Winters (December, January, and February) of 1936, 1938, 1940, and 1942

| Year | Average wage | | Georgia's rank from bottom |
	U.S.	Georgia	
1936	$45.92	$26.06	10th
1938	52.38	32.16	9th[a]
1940	50.81	38.92	7th
1942	62.46	53.33	10th

[a]Tied with Virginia.
SOURCE: Howard, *The WPA and Its Program,* p. 182.

Table 14

WPA Accomplishments in Georgia in Comparison With Total U.S. Accomplishments Through June 30, 1942

Project	U.S.	Georgia
Construction programs		
Highways, roads, and streets, etc.		
Miles of road (new and improved)	643,977	8,939
No. of bridges and viaducts (")	122,758	2,713
No. of culverts (")	1,161,381	35,379
No. of public buildings		
Schools		
New construction and additions	7,797	346
Reconstruction or improvement	31,092	544
All other		
New construction and additions	30,851	498
Reconstruction or improvement	52,078	1,499
Outdoor recreational facilities		
No. of parks (new and improved)	7,937	131
No. of playgrounds and athletic fields (")	17,984	390
No. of swimming and wading pools (")	2,045	25
Public utilities and sanitation		
No. of utility plants (new and improved)	3,820	58
Miles of water mains and lines (new)	15,758	328
Miles of storm and sanitation sewers (new construction)	23,708	483
No. of sanitary privies (")	2,287,070	55,577
Airport facilities		
No. of landing fields		
New construction and additions	393	20
Reconstruction or improvement	415	4

Table 14

WPA Accomplishments in Georgia in Comparison
With Total U.S. Accomplishments Through June 30, 1942 (Cont.)

Project	U.S.	Georgia
Airport facilities (cont.)		
Linear feet of runways		
New construction	4,090,864	123,580
Reconstruction or improvement[a]	1,023,771	24,300
No. of airport buildings		
New construction and additions	1,310	25
Reconstrucion or improvement	2,776	1
Selected service programs		
Work in sewing rooms[b]		
No. of garments produced	374,917,435	11,283,824
No. of other articles produced	111,654,901	1,288,116
No. of school lunches served[b]	1,093,203,103	51,975,551
Food preserving		
No. of quarts canned	73,033,902	837,525
No. of pounds dried	9,176,171	65,916
No. of visits made by housekeeping aides[b]	31,028,430	967,230
Enrollment in adult education activities[c]		
Naturalization and literacy	98,646	6,130
Other	308,376	5,571
Enrollment in nursery schools[c]	35,229	1,061
Attendance at music performances[c]	2,423,217	5,931
No. of health institutes and agencies assisted or operated[c]	1,210	6

[a]Includes surfacing.
[b]Cumulative through June 30, 1942.
[c]During January 1942.
SOURCE: WPA, *Report on Progress* (1942), pp. 82-4.

Table 15
WPA: Service Projects (Partial List)

I. Sewing.

II. Library.
  A. Service
    1. librarians
    2. library extension
      a. high school libraries
      b. demonstration libraries
      c. branch libraries
      d. hospitals
      e. bookmobiles
      f. rural libraries
    3. special services
      a. children
      b. pamphlet collections
      c. iconographic collections

  B. Book repair
    1. general
    2. school textbook

III. Feeding.
  A. Surplus commodity distribution
    1. food
    2. clothing
    3. small household articles

  B. School lunch

  C. Housekeeping aide

  D. Food production and preservation
    1. garden projects
    2. home preservation
    3. community canning

IV. Health.
  A. Nursing
    1. child hygiene
    2. tuberculosis
    3. communicable diseases
    4. training project
    5. dietary
    6. midwife and prenatal
    7. health classes
    8. home visitation

  B. Training
    1. nonprofessional support
    2. social service
    3. dietary
    4. outpatient

V. Indexing and Surveys.
  A. Indexing
    1. deed and mortgage
    2. birth and death records
    3. state records
    4. marriage records
    5. superior court dockets
    6. county police records
    7. city ordinance codification
    8. numerical real property

  B. Surveys
    1. public administration
      a. rural real property identification
      b. land use and zoning
      c. cartographic
      d. air-raid warden mapping
    2. socio-economic (for each city)
    3. traffic and transportation
    4. truck and bus inventory
    5. mineral resources
    6. public utilities
    7. social security
    8. trends in population mobility
    9. dairy farms and cost of milk production
    10. Atlanta milk shed
    11. criminal court procedures
    12. crippled children
    13. tax
    14. historic buildings
    15. historical records
    16. archaeological
    17. financial statistics of local governments
    18. ports
    19. commercial fisheries
    20. parks
    21. parkways
    22. semi-public recreational areas and facilities

Table 15

WPA: Service Projects (Partial List) (Cont.)

23. recreation and conservation areas
24. forest planning

VI. Recreation.
  A. Playground and sports supervision
  B. Arts and crafts
  C. Community drama
  D. Music
  E. Weekly radio programs (13 stations)
  F. Community centers
  G. Training

VII. Education.
  A. Nursery schools

  B. Elementary schools
  C. General adult (mainly literacy projects)
  D. Workers
    1. school for workers
    2. unemployed women's camps
  E. Vocational
  F. Rehabilitation

VIII. Federal Art.

IX. Federal Music.

X. Federal Writers.

XI. Federal Theater.

Table 16

WPA: Publications of Reports, Research, Statistical, and Survey-Type Projects as of January 1, 1939

Title	Date of publication
"A Report of the Social Security Survey in Georgia"	1937
"A Survey of Crippled Children in Georgia"	1937
"Georgia's Blind"	1938
"Father-Son Occupations Among Negroes in Atlanta"	1937
"Occupational Characteristics of White Collar and Skilled Negro Workers of Atlanta"	1937
"Local Job Descriptions for the Garment Industry"	1937
"Local Job Descriptions for the Slaughtering and Meat Packing Industry"	1936
"Permanent Census Tract—Greater Atlanta"	1936
"Permanent Census Tract—Greater Macon"	1937
"Permanent Census Tract—Greater Savannah"	1937
"Survey of Criminal Court Procedure in Georgia"	1937
"Rural, Rural-Urban, and Urban Georgia in Relation to Criminal Court Procedure"	1937
"The Time Element in Criminal Cases Before the Georgia Courts"	1938
"Financial Statistics of Local Governments in Georgia"	1938
"Commercial Fisheries of Georgia"	1937
"Park, Parkway, and Recreational Area Study"	1938
"Port Study"	1938

SOURCE: Georgia State Archives RG 24, Child and Family Service (Department of Public Welfare), General Administration, Division of Institutions (Central Files), WPA, General Correspondence, Carton 38.

Table 17

Publications of the Federal Writers' Project of Georgia as of August 28, 1941

Title	Progress
"Atlanta, A City of the Modern South"	Final dummy complete
"Augusta Scrapbook"	Ten articles approved
"Augusta in Business"	Research complete; manuscript being written
"Augusta Trading History"	Research about 90 percent complete
"Chatham County Map Portfolio"	Almost completed
"Chatham County Plantation Series"	Eleven monographs published
"Georgia Historic Sites Survey"	Unit of five workers doing this work transferred August 9, 1941, to historical records survey
"Georgia Picture Book"	Dummy complete
"Keys to Augusta"	Approved manuscript received; ready for publication
"Men at Work"	Last writer in charge gone; to be voided
"Metropolitan Opera Performances in Atlanta"	Three articles published; others in various stages
"Pan American Articles"	Several chapters in draft form in hands of prospective publishers
"Progress of Education in Wilkes County"	About half complete; suspended
"Story of Your City"	Pamphlet in draft form
"Story of Your State"	Pamphlet in draft form
"Streams on Georgia's Fall Line"	Two articles published; others in various stages
"This is America"	—
"U.S. Travel Atlas (Georgia Portion)"	Dummy forwarded to Washington

SOURCE: S.Y. Tupper to J.D. Newsom, August 28, 1941, NARG 69, State Series, No. 651.317, box 1139.

Table 18
Cotton Production Reduction Campaigns in Georgia, 1933-1935

	No. farms under contract	No. contracts	No. acres taken out of production	Rental and benefit payments
1933	105,108	97,296	692,780	$7,904,830.27
1934	135,949	105,358	1,103,360	8,181,026.24
1935	140,569	a	1,106,407	5,506,027.85[b]

[a]Not given.
[b]As of October 1, 1935.
SOURCE: State director of extension and AAA annual reports, 1933-1935.

Table 19
Farm Income from Government Payments in Georgia

Year	Amount (millions of dollars)
1933	$ 7,932
1934	14,209
1935	12,615
1936	6,787
1937	10,030
1938	20,218
1939	25,794
1940	24,419

SOURCE: *Georgia Agricultural Facts*, p. 49.

Table 20

Advances Under the FERA's Rural Rehabilitation Program, 1934-1935

	Number of cases receiving advances	
Date	U.S.	Georgia
1934		
April	325	—
May	32,393	67
June	41,573	671
July	41,868	1,380
August	39,906	1,470
September	40,166	1,553
October	46,131	1,758
November	52,466	2,833
December	68,625	3,832
1935		
January	72,238	5,001
February	87,275	6,978
March	172,862	10,017
April	209,830	12,276
May	205,330	12,574
June	203,570	12,581

SOURCE: FERA's *Final Report,* pp. 233-4.

Table 21

Expenditures of the RA and FSA in Georgia, 1936-1942

Year	Rural rehabilitation loans	Farm tenant purchase loans	Grants	Rural Settlement projects
1936	$2,336,466	—	$ 89,136	$243,179
1937	2,971,062	—	360,908	739,166
1938	2,213,096	—	191,376	850,923
1939	6,493,047	$1,528,944	340,463	98,530
1940	4,012,308	1,674,889	1,115,310	88,464
1941	5,409,950	3,557,570	743,902	115,259
1942	6,560,483	2,975,749	1 076,771	37,738

SOURCE: Wheeler's *Two Hundred Years,* p. 390.

Table 22

Resettlement Administration's Resettlement Program, 1936

City	County	Project	Type
Monticello	Jasper	Piedmont Homesteads	Former subsistence homstead (being developed)
Eatonton	Putnam, Jones, Jasper	Plantation Homesteads	Agricultural (being developed)
Cornelia	Habersham, Banks, Stephens	Northeast Georgia Upland Game Conservation	" " "
Waycross	Brantley, Ware	Georgia Coastal Flatwoods Upland Game	" " "
Madison	Morgan	Hard Labor Creek Park	Park (being developed)
Crawfordville	Taliaferro	Alexander Stephens Memorial Park	" " "
Chipley	Harris	Pine Mountain Park	" " "
New Holland	Chatham	Savannah River Migratory Waterfowl Refuge	(active)
Irwinville	Irwin	Irwinville	Former FERA (being developed)
Eatonton	Putnam	Briar Patch	" " " "
Cairo	Grady	Wolf Creek	" " "
	Wheeler, Laurens	Wheeler Farms	Resettlement-active
	Houston	Houston Farms	" "
	Gwinnett	Gwinnett Farms	" "
	Henry	McDonough Farms	" "
	Lee, Sumter, Terrell	Dawson Farms	" "
	Lowndes, Brooks	Lowndes Farms	" "
	Worth	Worth Farms	" "
	Bartow, Cherokee	Etowah Farms	" "
	Bartow, Cherokee	Georgia Tenant Purchase	" "
Fort Valley	Houston, Peach	Fort Valley Farms	" "

SOURCE: "Report on the Objectives, Accomplishments, and Effects of the Resettlement Administration Program," p. 63.

Table 23

Progress of Resettlement Projects Under the FSA, as of June 30, 1941

	Units planned or completed	Area (acres)	Cost	Total capital investment
Communities				
Irwinville	105	12,749.54	$166,726.31	$919,387.27
Briar Patch	22	7,456.00	58,539.45	297,198.08
Flint River	146	12,634.34	260,128.20	718,268.08
Wolf Creek	24	2,249.36	26,435.97	255,036.49
Subsistence				
Piedmont	50	15,268.88	89,493.66	652,701.68
Scattered Farms				
Farm Tenant Security	106	11,003.00	222,250.31	666,108.27
Scattered farms	7	1,069.00	17,717.76	24,473.21
Greene County	125	19,493.00	$195,215.00	$316,319.26

SOURCE: FSA's *Annual Report* (1941), p. 33.

Table 24

Resettlement Administration's Land Use Program, 1936

	Plantation Piedmont	N.E.Ga. Game Conservation	Coastal Flatwoods	Hard Labor Creek	Alex. Stephens Mem. Park	Pine Mt. Park	Savannah River
No. of families to be resettled	15	1	6	15	5	1	23
Cost	$769,761	$340,388	$157,866	$60,430	$17,230	$29,300	$51,547
No. of acres to be purchased	118,703	44,451	32,600	4,464	900	3,453	5,916
Total funds available	$216,875	$194,669	$132,500	$66,000	$58,000	$74,200	
Total allotment as of March 31	$106,875	$ 96,369	$ 82,500	$36,000	$20,100	$49,200	
Percent allotment encumbered as of March 31	87.4	73.1	75.7	67.0	90.5	81.9	
No. men on project Apr. 3 May 1	963 701	1,096 700	512a 510	463a 144	307a 430	427 740	
Percent completion as of April 15	15.0	10.0	16.0	20.0	35.0	40.0	

aIncludes CCC men.

SOURCE: U.S. Senate, 74th Cong., 2nd Sess., 1936, Document No. 213, pp. 28, 34.

Table 25
FSA Tenant Purchase Loans, 1937-1941

Fiscal year	No. of counties	No. of loans	Amount loaned
1937-38	35	185	$ 633,983*a*
1938-39	75	389	1,597,051
1939-40	99	613	2,465,100
1940-41	129	910	$3,329,204

*a*These figures vary with those compiled by Wheeler—see Table 21.

Bibliographical Essay

PRIMARY SOURCES

The principal difficulty in researching the administration of any New Deal agency in Georgia is a lack of state office records. Neither the federal nor the state governments have made any attempt to preserve these files. There are some state office records of the CWA on microfilm at the National Archives which were produced under the WPA, but these are very sparse. One must therefore depend almost entirely upon the national records of the agencies to find out what occurred in the state. Letters and reports from Georgia appear there, but correspondence within the state that would give a more complete picture of local administrative processes is missing. The nature of the problems encountered can be determined from the national records, because many problems were referred to Washington, but the extent to which these difficulties were present remains a matter for conjecture.

In the National Archives the records of the federal agencies vary considerably in volume, completeness, and value. Probably the most comprehensive in terms of state material is record group 69, which contains material from the FERA, CWA, and WPA. These records are divided into three major parts, one of which is a state series. In the other two parts there are also state classifications, although they are a little harder to locate. Record group 69 contains more state material than any other similar group.

The files of the Federal Extension Service, record group 33, are the

next most valuable source of information. In this record group the microfilmed annual reports of county agents give a good personal view of what
was happening in the counties with respect to the farm programs. Of
course, the information reflects the county agent's own bias, but since
there were a great number of these agents in Georgia, a wide spectrum of
attitudes is represented. The manuscripts in record group 33 are of some
value too, but they are not as complete as the microfilmed reports. Unfortunately, the Georgia State Extension Service has not seen fit to
maintain its state files from the period. At one time there was an order
from the AAA for these files to be sent to Washington, but there is no
indication that they ever arrived.

The records of the Farmers Home Administration (record group 96)
contain files from the Resettlement Administration and the Farm
Security Administration. The main body of material is in the National
Archives. It is arranged by code number and is difficult to use. There are
also FHA records at the Federal Records Center in Suitland, Maryland.
These are the resettlement project files, which are voluminous. They
have not, as yet, been removed from the large storage boxes, and are
thus cumbersome. The major deficiency of all the records in this group
is the lack of state office material.

Anyone studying the New Deal in the states should make a special
trip across the Potomac River to the Federal Records Center at Suitland.
There he will find the reports of the state directors of the National
Emergency Council. Although these reports (record group 44) do not
cover the entire New Deal period, they are intensive from 1935 through
1938 and present a viewpoint from within the state, yet apart from the
state government and the other federal agencies. They are also excellent
sources for immediate public reaction to the various programs.

The two least helpful record groups contain the files of the PWA
(record group 135) and the Agricultural Stabilization and Conservation
Service, which includes the AAA (record group 145). The former record
group is so limited that it is virtually of no use at all. Most of the PWA's
files were destroyed inadvertently before they reached the National
Archives. The AAA records contain primarily central office files, and not
those of the officials in charge of the programs. During those years the
federal government allowed these officers to retain their own files; thus
they are not present in the collection. The arrangement of the record
group also makes it difficult to use the documents. Most of it is filed
by title or subject and then by year, but very little is classified by state.

Even when these obstacles are overcome, the researcher may find himself frustrated by a lack of information. There are boxes upon boxes with personal files of AAA officials.

The records of the NRA (record group 9) have more subsections than any other. Fortunately, however, most of these have state headings. For some periods there are state directors' records, but these are scattered. The collection suffers generally from incompleteness and a lack of intrastate material.

Despite their faults, the manuscripts in the National Archives were the most valuable primary source for this study. The Federal Records Center at East Point, Georgia, has virtually nothing to interest a scholar pursuing this topic. The Georgia State Archives is interested in collecting twentieth-century material, but has obtained little as yet, and the "Georgia Collection" of the University of Georgia at Athens has even less. Georgians seem to have confined most of their collecting efforts to the antebellum period. Appropriations are small, and since most of the demand upon them centers in the earlier periods, those have been the only areas of concentrated collecting. Although state agencies are required by law to submit all of their records to the State Archives, this has not been done, and the records of the Department of Public Welfare, for example, are simply nonexistent both in the Archives and the Department offices. The State Library, on the other hand, has a fairly good collection of material printed by the state. Complete sets of reports and serial publications exist for most state agencies. The State Archives contains some administrative material from the Talmadge and Rivers years, but this consists primarily of routine reports and correspondence. Very little private or interoffice material is present.

A third possibility for manuscript material is personal collections, of which there are very few. With one exception none of Georgia's political leaders of the period have given their papers to research institutions, and besides Miss Shepperson, who has some material in her possession, none of the New Deal agency heads have contributed their papers. Senator Richard B. Russell has bequeathed a large body of material to the University of Georgia at Athens, but this is not yet open to scholars. The only substantial collection of any real value is that of Arthur Raper. This well-organized material is in his possession. The Franklin D. Roosevelt Library at Hyde Park offers another possibility for research, but most of its holdings concern national rather than state affairs. In the case of Georgia, almost all of the pertinent material was duplicated in the holdings of the National Archives. The papers of national officials at Hyde Park contain some state material which is within easy grasp of the scholar because of excellent indexes, but this also is limited to occasional reports or offhand references.

There were, of course, a respectable number of newspapers in Georgia representing most points of view. The Atlanta *Constitution* and the Atlanta *Journal* were the state's two major publications, and they contained good coverage of local news outside of Atlanta. The Atlanta *Georgian* presented the opinions of the opposition, and the Atlanta *World* and Savannah *Tribune* represented black thought for the period. If the researcher so desires, there are other newspapers covering the state which may be consulted. These are valuable mainly for their editorial positions, since most of the news items can be found in one of the Atlanta papers.

Newspapers and periodicals outside the state provide another source of information, although it is primarily of a political nature. The commotion created by Governor Talmadge usually found its way to the pages of national news media. Some of the more specialized journals such as the *Monthly Labor Review* and *School and Society* also contain material pertinent to Georgia.

The final major source of primary material is the government publication. At the state level the annual reports of departments cooperating with New Deal agencies are valuable, especially when supplemented by special publications concerning specific areas of joint effort. Regular federal publications, such as the *Census,* are important as are the reports of the various New Deal Agencies—particularly the AAA, FERA, and WPA. Studies undertaken by the FERA and WPA encompassed a broad field of topics, and many provide excellent source material for Georgia. The federal government's monthly guide to publications presents a good starting point for entering this mass of material. In general, federal publications, particularly annual agency reports, offer the best source for state statistics and the most complete and condensed explanation of agency operations.

SECONDARY SOURCES

None of the major monographs concerning the New Deal address themselves to the administration of the agencies in the state. Those which purport to investigate the New Deal in a state inevitably concentrate on the effect of that phenomenon upon state politics, rather than vice versa. This is likewise the case with James T. Patterson's *The New Deal and the States: Federalism in Transition* (Princeton: Princeton University Press, 1969). Some books, such as Josephine Brown's *Public Relief, 1929-1939* (New York: Henry Holt and Company, 1940), Donald S. Howard's *The WPA and Federal Relief Policy* (New York: Russell Sage Foundation, 1943), Gladys Baker's *The County Agent* (Chicago: University of Chicago Press, 1939), or the Brookings Institution studies of the AAA and NRA, are valuable as general sources dealing with aspects of the New Deal which applied to all states. There are also a number of monographs covering the various agencies. Ellis W. Hawley's *The New Deal and the Problem of Monopoly: A Study in Economic Ambivalence* (Princeton: Princeton University Press, 1966) analyzes the NRA, while the New Deal's involvement in the arts is treated by Jane De Hart Matthews in *The Federal Theater 1935-1939: Plays, Relief, and Politics* (Princeton, Princeton University Press, 1967) and by Jerre Mangione in *The Dream and the Deal: The Federal Writers' Project 1935-1943* (Boston: Little, Brown, 1972). The FERA, CWA, and WPA are dealt with by Charles F. Searle in *Minister of Relief: Harry Hopkins and the Depression* (Syracuse: Syracuse University Press, 1963), and the PWA is described by Harold Ickes in *The Secret Diary of Harold L. Ickes: The First Thousand Days, 1933-1936* (New York: Simon and Schuster, 1953). Sidney Baldwin's book, *Poverty and Politics: The Rise and Decline of the Farm Security Administration* (Chapel Hill: University of North Carolina Press, 1968), and David Conrad's *The Forgotten Farmers: The Story of Sharecroppers and the New Deal* (Urbana: University of Illinois Press, 1965) are more recent studies of the farm relief agencies. Paul K. Conkin's *Tomorrow a New World: The New Deal Community Program* (Ithaca: Cornell University Press, 1959) concentrates on the resettlement communities. The principal problem with studies of the various agencies is that they very rarely penetrate beyond the national level. It is unusual to find one that discusses the operations of the agency at the state level, and even more, to discover one that analyzes relations between the agency and the state governments.

There are some monographs which do concentrate specifically upon Georgia. Of particular value among these are the works of Arthur F.

Raper. His *Preface to Peasantry: A Tale of Two Black Belt Counties* (Chapel Hill: University of North Carolina Press, 1936), *Tenants of the Almighty* (New York: Macmillan Company, 1943), and *Sharecroppers All* (Chapel Hill: University of North Carolina Press, 1941), the last done with Ira DeA. Reid, present a moving story of rural conditions during the depression.

There are a few county histories for Georgia, some of which include sections covering the New Deal. Most, however, do not extend beyond World War I. John C. Meadows' *Modern Georgia* (Athens: University of Georgia Press, 1946) is presently the only state study which devotes more than a couple of paragraphs on the New Deal, but it is fairly general in its coverage. Another study of this period in Georgia's history is now being undertaken by William Holmes. It will presumably offer a much more complete overview. Willard Range's *A Century of Georgia Agriculture, 1850-1950* (Athens: University of Georgia Press, 1954) devotes a number of pages to the effect of New Deal agricultural policies upon the state, but it does not concern itself with the administration of the agricultural agencies in Georgia.

A number of regional studies exist which also proved to be of value. These appeared in periodicals such as the *Southern Economic Journal,* but the most interesting emanated from the new regional school of sociology founded by Howard Odum at the University of North Carolina. Odum's *Southern Regions of the United States* (Chapel Hill: University of North Carolina Press, 1936), along with a multitude of his other writings, formed a massive study of the South during this period, and his work was embellished by that of some of his students, such as Arthur Raper and Rupert B. Vance.

A few unpublished secondary sources are useful. Roy E. Fossett's "The Impact of the New Deal on Georgia Politics, 1933-1941" (Ph.D. dissertation, Department of Political Science, University of Florida, 1960) and Sarah M. Lemmon's "The Public Career of Eugene Talmadge: 1926-1936" (Ph.D. dissertation, Department of History, University of North Carolina, 1952) provide some insight into the relationship of the New Deal to the state government, but they are both hampered by the absence of Talmadge and Rivers manuscripts. Neither is concerned with the administration of the New Deal agencies in Georgia.

Only under the general heading of Negroes and the New Deal in Georgia are there many interesting studies. Edward Aaron Gaston, Jr.'s "A History of the Negro Wage Earner in Georgia, 1890-1940" (Ph.D. dissertation, Department of History, Emory University, 1957) goes into great detail describing the treatment of the Negro by New Deal agencies in Georgia. Allen Francis Kifer's "The Negro under the New Deal, 1933-1941" (Ph.D. dissertation, Department of History, University of Wisconsin, 1961) also sheds light on this subject and can be used in comparison to Gaston's work. Richard M. Sterner's *The Negro's Share: A Study of Income, Consumption, Housing, and Public Assistance* (New York: Harper and Brothers, 1943) and Raymond Wolters' *Negroes and the Great Depression: The Problem of Economic Recovery* (Westport, Connecticut: Greenwood Press, 1970) are also helpful on a more general level. There are a number of more specific, but less ambitious studies, in the form of master's theses completed at Atlanta University. Bonita Golda Harrison's "Racial Factors Attending the Functioning of the New Deal in the South" (M.A. thesis, Department of Sociology, Atlanta University, 1936) is perhaps the best.

Fortunately, some of those who worked for New Deal agencies in Georgia are still living, and interviews with them proved helpful. Meetings with Ms. Gay B. Shepperson, Ms. Hilda Smith, Mr. and Ms. Kenneth Douty, and Ms. Amber Warburton provided information concerning relief activities in Georgia. Ms. Shepperson was particularly generous with her time, and her memories of the period and its personalities are still quite sharp. Mr. W. A. Minor and Mr. Ralph Fulghum were helpful in illuminating agricultural activities in the state. An interview with Arthur Raper, however, was the most valuable. His deep personal involvement and wide interests, combined with his professional involvement, provided the basis for a more philosophical and interpretive analysis than would have otherwise been possible.

Index

Abercrombie, Dr. Thomas F., 49, 72

Abraham, Jack, 199

Adams, George C., 65, 215, 224

Agricultural Adjustment Act (1933), 212, 253; and tenant farmers, 254-55, 269

Agricultural Adjustment Act (1938), 251-52

Agricultural Adjustment Administration (AAA), 7, 9, 190, 209-64, 309-10, 313-14; and assistant cotton adjusters, 227; and the cotton textile industry, 223-24; and county committees, 214-15, 224-25, 227, 229-31, 235, 245-49, 252, 259-60; and financial benefits, 223-24, 236, 248; and local committees, 214-16, 218-19, 226-27, 229, 246-49, 252, 259, 262; and the plow-up campaign of 1933, 212-24; and the production control program, 226-36; and tenant farmers, 214-16, 219, 232, 253-64

AAA Conservation and Adjustment Committee, 246

AAA Cotton Production Control Associations. *See* AAA and county committees

AAA Cotton Production Section, 256, 288

AAA Landlord-Tenant Adjustment Committee (Section), 260-63

AAA Program Planning Group Discussions, 235, 246

AAA State Allotment Board, 227-31, 246, 252

AAA State Board of Review, 225, 230

Agricultural Extension Service, 51-52, 144; and the AAA, 213-14, 217-18, 221-23, 225-27, 234-36, 245-49, 252-53; and rural rehabilitation, 278-79, 293; and tenant farmers, 256, 261, 271

Agricultural Extension Service county agents: and the AAA, 213-22, 224-27, 229-31, 233-35, 246-53; and rural relief, 52,

ABOUT THE AUTHOR

Michael S. Holmes received his B.A. from Rice University and his M.A. and Ph.D. from the University of Wisconsin at Madison. He is assistant professor of history at the University of Wisconsin at Parkside. Professor Holmes has published articles on the NRA and Georgia's black workers, and on the New Deal and Georgia's black youth.